Mahua Sarkar

VISIBLE HISTORIES, DISAPPEARING WOMEN

Producing Muslim Womanhood in Late Colonial Bengal

zubaan

Visible Histories, Disappearing Women
by Mahua Sarkar
Published (2008) in South Asia by

ZUBAAN
an imprint of Kali for Women
K-92, 1st Floor
Hauz Khas Enclave
NEW DELHI- 110 016
Email: zubaanwbooks@vsnl.net and zubaan@gmail.com
Website: www.zubaanbooks.com

and in the rest of the world by
Duke University Press
Durham and London

ISBN 978 81 89884 43 7 (HB)

Printed at Raj Press, R-3 Inderpuri, New Delhi 110012

for my parents

and to the memory of

Pishi (Labanya Prabha Acharya)

Contents

Acknowledgments

I have incurred many debts in the long process of writing this book, and it seems quite impossible today to adequately acknowledge everyone who has contributed in so many ways to its fruition.

The book is based in part on my dissertation research. I want to thank Antoinette Burton, David Scott, and Beverly Silver for their early guidance, thoughtful and generous criticisms, and continued support over the years. In a less direct way, Partha Chatterjee and Giovanni Arrighi have been sources of both inspiration and encouragement from the very inception of this project. I thank them, too. Mrinalini Sinha and Gail Minault read a chapter early on. Their enthusiasm and generous comments were sources of much needed courage at the time, and since. Ananda Chanda, Ethel Hazard, Michael Dorsey, Morten Hansen, Amitabh Chowdhry, and, especially, Sarah Khokhar played important roles, directly or indirectly, in the conception of this book during my years at Hopkins.

The Program in Comparative International Development, Department of

Sociology, Johns Hopkins University, provided two travel grants that made possible a large part of the archival research presented in this book. I thank the staffs at the Bangiya Sahitya Parishad, Kolkata; the Bangladesh Mission Library, Kolkata; the National Library, Kolkata; the Asiatic Society, Kolkata; the Office of the Director of Census Operations, Kolkata; the British Library, London; the Bangla Academy, Dhaka; and the Bangladesh Bureau of Statistics, Dhaka, for their patience and help. Special thanks go to Kaliprosad Bose at the Centre for Studies in Social Sciences, Calcutta, for his support.

My debt to the women I interviewed for generously sharing their experiences with me is surely immeasurable. Premangshu Banerjee and Rama Banerjee provided useful advice early on regarding archives, while Hossainur Rahman and the late Gauri Ayub were instrumental in putting me in touch with members of the Muslim middle class in Kolkata. Many of my contacts in Bangladesh, in turn, came through the personal networks of the women I interviewed in Kolkata. I am particularly indebted to Zeenat Ameen, Selina Hossein, Akbar Hossein, Reza Ali, Nayeema Ali, Meena Sarkar, and Nripen Sarkar for opening their homes to me in Dhaka. My friend Susan Lee and her family were my refuge. I am also grateful to Maleka Begum, Professor Anisuzzaman, and the late Sufia Kamal for their invaluable advice.

At Binghamton University, insightful conversations with my colleagues over the years, especially with Kelvin Santiago-Valles, Gladys Jiménez-Muñoz, Lisa Yun, and Lubna Nazir-Chowdhry, have greatly augmented my critical thinking. Nayan Shah continued to be a great source of support and critical appreciation even after his move across the continent. I thank the Coloniality of Power Collective, and especially Vandana Swami, Preeti Sampat, and Israel Silva-Merced, for commenting on early versions of some chapters. Thanks also go to the dean's office at Harpur College, Binghamton University, for a research grant in 2001 which allowed me to do further fieldwork.

Parts of the manuscript were presented in conferences. I am grateful for the comments I received from the participants. Special thanks go to Anjali Arondekar, Dipesh Chakrabarty, Indrani Chatterjee, Malathi de Alwis, and especially Kamala Visweswaran for their encouragements over the years. The anonymous readers at Duke University Press and Palgrave offered many suggestions that helped make the manuscript stronger. Thanks also go to my editor at Duke, Miriam Angress, and to Urvashi Butalia at Zubaan, for their enthusiasm and patience.

Other debts are harder to describe. Mita Datta has been a source of constant support and love for many years. The intellectual camaraderie and friendship of Melegh Attila and Susan Zimmermann in Budapest have been increasingly important over the last few years. Friends in India and in the United States have been a consistent source of encouragement. I want to thank especially Nipa Ghosh, Avik Dey, Mita Dey, Archishman Chakraborty, Nandini Ghatak, Joyjit Ghosh, Suranjita Sinha, Sudeshna Basuroy, and Ratna Sen.

My parents, Bhabani Bhusan and Lily Sarkar, will always be my anchors. Their contribution to this book is immeasurable. Bhaskar Sarkar and Bishnupriya Ghosh continue to be indispensable sources of love and intellectual enrichment. It would be quite impossible to acknowledge all the members of my vast family in and around Kolkata who helped me in myriad ways to keep my spirits up over the years, but I do want to thank Tapan Chaki (Dadaji) especially for a lifetime of unconditional love. Mihir Sinha, Anil Bhattacharya, Binoy Mukherjee, and Kanti Sengupta each enriched this project with their advice and experience. I wish they were here today for its completion. Others, including Anil Sarkar, Ruchira Chakraborty, Satyesh Chakraborty, Kishwar Jahan Quadir, Fazle Quadir, Maya Gupta, Krishna Mukherjee, Vanumathy Vasudevan, Smita Sinha, and Subha Sengupta, to name only a few, have been lasting sources of affection and confidence. I do not have the words to thank them enough.

As for Bilgin Ayata, Prasad Kuduvalli, Patricia Landolt, Indira Ravindran, Smita Sampath, and Dharnija Vasudevan, over the past fifteen-odd years they have sustained me in ways that belie acknowledgment or calibration. Much of what I write here has taken shape through conversations with them. This book surely belongs to them as well.

Finally, I thank József for his critical insights and his formidable patience, and because he is.

INTRODUCTION

Writing Difference

This book studies the production of Muslim women as invisible and oppressed/backward in the written history of late colonial Bengal. Unlike in projects of recuperation, the intent here is not to correct the problem of invisibility/silence of Muslim women by recovering them as visible/vocal subjects within the familiar terms of conventional history—a history that denied them such presence in the first place. Instead, my focus is on understanding the discursive and material contexts that have historically produced Muslim women as victimized, invisible, and/or mute. What I seek to make visible in this project, in other words, is not so much Muslim women but rather the contexts of their specific (dis)appearances in writing and the ways in which they have been marginalized and/or made to (dis)appear within both the conventional (colonial and nationalist) and critical historiography of colonial Bengal.

Feminist scholars have amply documented the phallocentric tendencies of normative historiographies that typically ignore women as historical subjects.[1] Recently, feminists in India have engaged in further reflection about the implicit Hindu majoritarian biases of not just nationalist/normative histories but even feminist scholarship.[2] These recent intellectual developments provide important points of departure for my research. However, I do not read the relative absence of Muslim women within the history of colonial Bengal simply as an effect of the (unintentional) phallocentrism and majoritarian preoccupations of extant histories. Instead, I locate their invisibility or erasure in writing at the intersection of two discourses of modernity: nationalism, which treats nations as the rightful subject of modern history, and liberal feminism, which privileges certain notions of agency while discounting others as the proper markers of feminist/modern subjecthood.[3] As I will argue later in this chapter and hope to show throughout the book, the nation-centeredness of history as a discipline and the intellectual politics of liberal feminism have together produced Muslim women as the oppressed, mute, backward, and eventually invisible "other" of the normative modern (read conscious and/or rights bearing, Hindu/liberal, citizen/feminist) subject within the written history of colonial Bengal, even when they (Muslim women) exercised all kinds of agency—whether as subjects who should have been easily recuperable within the terms of nationalist or feminist accounts or as subjects who refused the lures of a modernity that exceeded the limits of their comfort or perceived abilities.

The book, thus, investigates silence itself as constitutive, and not simply an oversight, of dominant—conventional and critical—historical accounts. History appears in this study not as an "incomplete record of the past" in need of correction but an active participant in the "production of knowledge that [legitimizes] the exclusion and subordination"[4] of subaltern groups—such as Muslim women—designated as nonmodern in an ongoing process of producing and reaffirming a normative modernity.[5] For progress, as Walter Benjamin's insights into the "temporal paradox of modernity" teach us, can only be mapped through the systematic invention of images of the archaic, of what is superseded, perhaps even destroyed.[6] An important underlying concern of this study, therefore, is to explore the very possibility, and hence the difficulties, of writing a feminist history that reads difference not as "lack" or "lag," but as indicative of the "complex genealogy of the modern."[7] To this end, I also interrogate the somewhat uncritical uses of the notion of "agency" and "subjecthood" as they figure, at times, in feminist scholarship, especially in the small but growing body of work on Muslim women in colonial India. And, finally, while the widely acknowledged importance of the past for understanding the present certainly informs it, this study is also an ongoing reflection on the myriad ways in which the present influences how we read or approach the past.

I begin in this introductory chapter with a critical engagement with recent significant feminist and postcolonial scholarship to map out "when and where" Muslim women "enter" into the written history of colonial Bengal.[8] In four interrelated chapters, the substantive core of the book then traces Muslim women as they appear or disappear in colonial, Hindu nationalist, and liberal Muslim writings in late colonial Bengal, as well as in the private memories of pre-partition Bengal of both Muslim and Hindu women today. The concluding chapter of the book ends with some reflections on the linkages between the "epistemic violence"[9] of past representations and the very real corporeal violence against Muslim women in contemporary India.

BEGINNINGS

The project began with the following observation: while recent decades have seen an extraordinary explosion of scholarship on women in colonial India, much of this literature is preoccupied with Hindu (typically upper caste or middle class) women.[10] When Muslim women do appear—more often in studies of postindependence India—they are often portrayed as oppressed and lagging behind.[11]

A common assumption underlying the silence about Muslim women in the literature on colonial Bengal is that very few among them wrote or did anything that merits attention.[12] Indeed, a survey of mainstream periodicals, popular magazines, and newspapers—which together made up a nascent public domain based in crucial colonial cities such as Calcutta and Dhaka in the mid-nineteenth century—would seem to confirm this impression. The dominant issues, such as *sati*, widow remarriage, or even the Sanskritization of Bengali, being debated at that time on the pages of these periodicals were all concerns of a new, predominantly Hindu middle class. The fortunes of this Hindu gentry, now known as the *bhadralok* in Bengal, was intimately tied to the fate of the colonial economy, and especially the prominence—both economic and cultural—of Calcutta as the main seat of colonial rule in nineteenth-century

India.[13] By all accounts, Muslims in Bengal were marginal to this early process of middle-class formation.[14] Nor were they part of the cultural "renaissance" spearheaded by a mainly Calcutta-based, middle-class, Brahmo and Hindu intelligentsia in response, at least in part, to British criticism of the putatively inherent inferiority of colonized subjects.[15]

However, recent research has revealed that by the third quarter of the nineteenth century a small but growing body of middle-class Bengali Muslims had themselves taken to the print media, and were even cultivating Bengali as a language, in the teeth of concerted opposition from the Muslim orthodoxy. Faced with both colonial attempts to classify them as largely fanatical and "low-caste Hindu converts" and Hindu representations of them as dissolute, alien, and inferior, Muslims began systematically questioning, developing, and honing their identity as a community. In Bengal, this attempt resulted in the publication of a slew of Muslim-edited periodicals and popular magazines, which began to appear sporadically, mostly out of Calcutta, by the end of the nineteenth century. These publications together provided an important discursive space in which Muslim intellectuals could express themselves and contest the dominant constructions—both colonial and Hindu—of community and class identities in late-nineteenth-century and early-twentieth-century Bengal. Some of these journals further problematized Muslim-ness by encouraging Muslim women to publicly call into question their specific gender oppressions. Consequently, we find that by the first decade of the twentieth century many Muslim women in Bengal *were* writing, some quite prolifically, in the Muslim and Hindu journals spawned by the vibrant material and cultural economies of urban centers such as Calcutta and Dhaka. Records of similar efforts by Muslim women outside of Bengal, in cities such as Lahore and Bombay, are also not uncommon.[16] Their contributions in the form of articles, short stories, poems, autobiographies, and travel accounts—all of which helped to change women's roles within the home and outside—have been considerable. Yet it is not easy to find mentions of Muslim women or their contributions in Indian nationalist or even postcolonial history.[17] The recorded history of women in pre-partition Bengal, for instance, continues to be overwhelmingly a narrative of the reformist experiments of a small minority of Hindu/Brahmo women, who actively participated in the modernizing projects of the new "liberal" elite.[18] Needless to say, the intellectual and reform efforts of many accomplished Muslim women in other parts of colonial India have gone similarly unnoticed.[19] Until recently, even much of feminist scholarship has failed to highlight the work of Muslim women, presumably because, as Meredith Borthwick puts it, it "deserves a separate study" or because "the Muslim gender system differed significantly from the Hindu," as Dagmar Engels would have it.[20] The assumption, it would seem, is that Hindus and Muslims in the subcontinent have separate histories that can be, indeed, need to be, recorded as discrete, largely self-referential accounts.

In the course of the last decade, more nuanced and/or revisionist efforts have attempted to redress this lacuna, but such attempts have rarely gone beyond the inclusion of Rokeya Sakhawat Hossain's (1880–1932) work,[21] ignoring in the process other Muslim woman writers who made significant literary and critical contributions in pre-partition Bengal.[22] How *does* one explain this continued occlusion of Muslim women in much of the written history of colonial Bengal produced in postcolonial India?

VISIBLE SYMBOLS

The connection between "woman" and "nation" has been the focus of much feminist inquiry.[23] While "hegemonic theorizations" of nations and nationalisms—and, I would add, even the more critical readings by such scholars as Benedict Anderson and Etienne Balibar that recognize the nation form as modern, imagined, and constitutive of identities—typically pay little attention to the workings of gender, feminist theorists insist that the nation is in fact a *gendered* construct that accords unequal access to power and resources to men and women.[24] What is more, as feminist writers—such as Carole Pateman, Carol Delaney and Deniz Kandiyoti, to name only a few—contend, the gendered inequity in modern society is not accidental but rather constitutive of the very definition of the nation and the modern (nation-)state.[25] Women are often constructed within nationalist discourse as "inherently atavistic—the conservative repository of the national archaic,"[26] and as such they are considered fundamentally undeserving of membership in the national political community except as the dependents of men and under the latter's moral supervision.[27] Consequently, as feminists point out, the twentieth century may have brought impressive gains in terms of formal political rights for women, with their "promise of justice and equality," but women's substantive positions as citizen-subjects in the public realm are still undercut by their very "real subordination" within the private/familial domain,[28] or what Rajeswari

Sunder Rajan has recently called the "masculinity of nationalist ideolog[ies]" and the "fictions of citizenship."[29]

Meanwhile, this continued marginalization of women stands in stark contrast to the almost compulsory foregrounding, even valorization, of women as emblematic of nations and communities.[30] To quote Kandiyoti, the centrality of women to the nation is "reaffirmed consciously in nationalist rhetoric where the nation itself is represented as a woman to be protected" or manifested "less consciously in terms of an inordinate degree of attention on women's appropriate sexual conduct."[31] In their influential work, Nira Yuval-Davis and Floya Anthias also highlight this "intense preoccupation" with controlling women and their sexuality in processes of national and ethnic identity production, which understand the principal role of women to be bearing sons for the nation.[32] That haloed place, strategically accorded within nationalist discourses to the idealized construct "woman," has meant that any attempt to raise the issue of women's positions or rights, both in the colonial and post colonial era, are invariably enmeshed in larger debates over "women's appropriate place and conduct" that are widely considered to be crucial "boundary markers" of the "cultural authenticity and integrity" of communities/nations as they embark on various modernizing projects.[33] As feminist scholars argue, analyses of the position of women in any society must therefore be grounded in an examination of the historical processes of nation and state formation and the specific ways in which women were incorporated into these projects.

Feminist theories regarding the importance of gender in the process of imagining nations and the selective inclusion of women in nationalist discourses are in fact useful in understanding the rise of cultural nationalism in colonial India. However, these arguments do not adequately explain why Muslim women in India, irrespective of their classes or ethnic locations, are subject to yet another degree of inequality or occlusion: they are denied even the limited visibility that women supposedly enjoy within nationalist discourses as symbols of the nation. In India, the relationship between the "redescription" or "re-casting" of women, as Kumkum Sangari and Sudesh Vaid put it,[34] and the formation or redefinition of community and national identities have been the stuff of much feminist scholarship. They have also been the focus of inquiry—albeit to a much lesser extent—of the Subaltern Studies collective in India, especially in the writings of Partha Chatterjee and Gayatri Spivak, as well as other, more recent collaborations with feminists on the unholy nexus among gender, community, and violence.[35] If the discursive centrality of the "woman question" in the colonial era—in both British justifications of their presence on the subcontinent and the cultural nationalist responses—has constituted one privileged topic of inquiry for these scholars,[36] the other has been the uses of women, especially women's bodies, which are both valorized and violated, as symbols of religious communities in the more recent history of the postcolonial state.[37]

While this body of work has been widely acclaimed for its insistence on the salience of gender in the workings of colonial and nationalist discourse and practice—especially its analysis of how "new ideas" about modern womanhood brought not only "emancipation" but also new forms of control to women's lives—it has also been criticized for its inadequate attention to women's agency, especially its portrayal of women as the "ground," to echo Lata Mani's formulation, on which the encounter between a colonial state and a subjected people might take place.[38] The anxiety seems to be that by focusing exclusively on male discourses that privilege the status of tradition and culture as the real concerns, these studies present women "primarily as [passive] objects of reform and manipulation," foreclosing, in the process, the possibility of seeing them as historical actors.[39]

Perhaps a more serious charge against this scholarship is that it (implicitly) accepts the "explicit privileging of the politics of anti-imperialism over that of gender" in nationalist rhetoric,[40] thereby becoming complicit, so to speak, in the nationalist project of silencing/erasing any trace of women's subjectivity, even if only in writing.[41] The problem, in other words, is not that these studies fail to record women's agency—which was not their objective in the first place—but rather that they miss or underplay an important way in which such agency was and is contained within the logic of nationalist discourse. As Kamala Visweswaran has argued, the domestication of women ought not to be read as a mere by-product of a nationalist "strategy for contesting colonial hegemony," as some scholars have contended, but also as an explicit ploy to curb the agency of women and file it down to dimensions that suited the needs of men and their nations.[42]

This latter line of critique is particularly helpful in framing the preoccupations of the current project—that is, the invisibility, or, rather, disappearance, of Muslim women in the Hindu-dominated nationalist discourse in colonial India and its historiography. The problem, as I see it, is not just that the existing scholarship privileges Hindu women and ignores Muslim women as its object of inquiry but rather that it typically *fails to as much as register* Muslim women's invisibility as something that might need explaining. Indeed, by routinely conflating the terms *Hindu upper caste/middle class* with *Indian* or, worse yet, *Bengali*, some of these studies directly contribute to the occlusion of Muslim women from even the middle class—a class that historically has been the protagonist in the nation story—in the subsequent written history of colonial Bengal.[43]

This is not to suggest that individual authors are unaware of the broader implications of the Hindu cultural nationalist casting of the upper-caste/middle-class Hindu woman as the "ideal Indian woman" for women of other communities and/or classes.[44] There have even been studies that relate the overwhelming visibility of the elite Hindu woman as the symbol of the emerging nation in the nineteenth century to the disappearance of lower-caste/working/poor women from nationalist history.[45] But overall this literature does not seem to offer any particular insight into the mechanisms through which the specific marginalization of Muslim women was secured within nationalist discourse or, more important, what such invisibility/silencing might have "signified"—to invoke the question raised by Visweswaran in the context of women of subaltern classes—"for the deployment of [the nineteenth-century, Hindu-dominated] nationalist ideology and its (counter-) historiography."[46]

In short, in much of the extant feminist and postcolonial scholarship on colonial India Muslim women's discursive absence is not interrogated at all; it is simply assumed, ignored, or sometimes entered into the discussion as epiphenomenal, something that can be read off from the logic of nationalist resolutions of all kinds of complicating questions concerning community, gender, sexuality, class, or caste. The typical appearance of Muslim women in studies on "women in colonial Bengal," for instance, is in the preface or introduction of a text where they are often cited as examples of who or what will be left out, underscoring the idea of both their supposed difference (or is it deviance?) from the norm (Hindu upper-caste/middle-class women) and their apparent irrelevance to an understanding of the history of the "woman question" in Bengal and, by extension, the process of nation formation in colonial India.[47]

As we shall see in chapter 2, Muslim women were in fact invoked often as the "backward/oppressed" other of the new woman (Hindu) of nationalist imagination in late-nineteenth-century and early-twentieth-century (Hindu) nationalist discourse in Bengal. Their invisibility within nationalist history, therefore, was far from given; it had to be discursively produced. The task of a critical history ought to be to investigate the specific ways in which that invisibility and silence were secured and to what end.[48] As the following discussion shows, attempts to restore Muslim women to history without interrogating the contexts of their erstwhile neglect or occlusion are similarly fraught with problems.[49]

WOMEN AS AGENTS

If the works discussed above are primarily concerned with the discursive *structures*—colonial and nationalist—that sought to both define "woman" as a category and control women's lives, a second genre of feminist writing on colonial India takes the question of "women's *agency*" as its problematic. Faced with "a past that spoke on public institutions, political activity, social and economic structures, entirely of men and by men,"[50] feminist scholars have turned increasingly to the task of recovering a different history, one that would give the lie to western imperial notions of the "silent" and "victimized" Indian woman, as well as address the largely neglected issue of women's participation in the nationalist movement.[51]

The more nuanced among such works on women in colonial India locate the question of women's agency squarely within a careful interrogation of the specific repressive structures that women had to negotiate in the nineteenth century and the early twentieth century.[52] As these works have demonstrated, some of what women wrote, and not necessarily for public consumption, was in fact very "critical," indicating their considerable independence of "thinking and intellectual autonomy."[53] These writings, thus, provide useful correctives to male-centered accounts of the nineteenth century in which women are overwhelmingly portrayed as passive recipients of male reformist largess.[54]

For a significant proportion of the work within this loosely defined field of women's agency, however, the focus has been trained squarely on the theme of the "emergence" of the "new woman" of the nationalist imagination—typically, though not necessarily, the Bengali *bhadramahila*—as a historical category that enjoyed the privilege of voice and visibility, albeit limited.[55] The main impetus in such scholarship has been to present "women as actors and subjects," to borrow Nita Kumar's words, "with the will, rationality and meaning to re-make the world." typically within the framework of a nation-centered history.[56]

One strand of these "contributory" histories, as Geraldine Forbes has called them, further concentrates on the emergence of "autonomous women's organizations" in the twentieth century, most notably the Women's Indian Association (WIA), the National Council of Women in India (NCWI), the All India Women's Conference (AIWC), and their various provincial chapters.[57] By the 1920s, these associations, increasingly founded by women themselves, were seeking both political rights for women and legislative action in support of their reform efforts in the face of the reluctance of, if not explicit opposition from, men.[58] Such activities—referred to in the literature as women's "political activism," where politics is presumably taken to be the preserve of the extra-familial realms of civil society and the state—are also celebrated in this kind of scholarship as proof of an emergent "conscious feminist movement in India."[59]

However, even this literature, concerned as it is with women's *actions* in the public sphere rather than their symbolic appropriation within colonial and nationalist discourses, overwhelmingly focuses on the activities of Hindu elite women. Subaltern engagements with the nationalist agenda, not to mention accounts of women's involvement in social or political movements "whose founding premises," in V. Geetha's words, "were not . . . definable within the terms of Indian nationalism," are of course simply not visible within these nation-centered and majoritarian narratives of women's emergence into modern political subjecthood.[60]

Muslim women do appear within this literature but only selectively in separate studies that focus on Muslim women exclusively or, more often, only mentioned in passing as women who did not participate in or hindered the various Hindu-led feminist initiatives.[61] A few Muslim women who are present in many standard narratives of the women's movement—such as Jahan Ara Shah Nawaz, Abbas Tyabji, Sharifah Hamid Ali, and Abadi Banu Begum (widely known as Bi Amman)—were typically active in social-reform organizations tied to the larger project of nation building as part of either the Congress Party or the Muslim League and/or were prominent members of the main national women's organizations or their provincial arms.[62] Even such representation can be rather contingent and unstable. Let me give one example. In "All the Women Were Hindu and All the Muslims Were Men," Jana Everett, for instance, discusses the courageous and oppositional stance taken by Begum Shah Nawaz vis-à-vis not only Hindu women leaders but also Muslim men. And yet, in the end, Everett somehow arrives at a baffling conclusion: "The dynamics during the period examined were such that in terms of the gender identity of the *visible political actors* in the arenas of political representation and personal law, *all the women were Hindu and all the Muslims were men*."[63] It would seem, as Siobhan Lambert-Hurley has recently contended, that even the public exercise of agency on the part of Muslim women does not automatically ensure their representation within the bulk of the existing feminist scholarship on women in colonial India.[64] Such activities have to be deemed "significant by . . . [the] standards" of a dominant discourse that reserves two positions for Muslim women:[65] either "in synch," so to speak, with the politics of the national(ist) women's associations mentioned or "separatist."[66] In contrast, Lambert-Hurley points out, an organization such as the short-lived All India Ladies Association (AILA)—founded by the Nawab Sultan Jahan Begam of Bhopal in 1918—which was formed, at least in part, to forge alliances among women across sectarian divides, has received little or no acknowledgment within the majoritarian nationalist logic that continues to underpin much of the writing on colonial India even today. In 1928, in a speech given at the All India Women's Conference by Begum Sultan Jahan, by this time a dowager, seems to have reiterated some of the ideas she had put forth a decade earlier about the importance of "women working for women."[67] As Mrinalini Sinha recently pointed out in her discussion of such efforts, if the "celebration of an inclusive and broad-based identity of women was . . . premature and problematic, . . . the very act of imagining a collective identity for women on the basis of a shared cause that potentially bridged sectional and communal differences" was still an achievement worth noting.[68]

Inattention to the women of nondominant groups is one oversight of the women's agency literature that can be fixed relatively easily by making Muslim women visible within the terms of the existing historiography. There are, however, other problems inherent in the way in which the idea of agency is deployed within much of this scholarship, and I believe they bear some critical rethinking. I take my cue here from Chandra Talpade Mohanty, who insists that her critique of the "analytical strategies" of "Western feminist" discourse, which produce "the West" as the "implicit referent, i.e., the yardstick by which to encode and represent cultural Others," also applies to "third world scholars writing about their own cultures."[69] It seems that, while criticizing the "ethnocentric universality" or "sanctioned ignorances" in the work of scholars from the geographic West has become something of a commonplace in postcolonial scholarship,[70] the strategies used by postcolonial/third world writers in their attempts to rewrite history have remained relatively unscrutinized.

What follows is not an exhaustive review of the existing literature on Muslim women in the Indian subcontinent but a critical engagement with a few key texts as an exercise in thinking through some of the problems of writing histories of difference in and around the cracks of normative teleologies of the modern.[71] Specifically, I reflect on the ways in which a particular notion of feminism, as a metanarrative of emergence and progress toward an apparently known end, operates to inform and shape this historiography and its underlying structure of desires, best exemplified in the recurring metaphors of visibility and voice, in specific, if unintended, ways.[72] Note also that the metaphors of change and the "emancipation of women" are certainly not the sole preserve of the texts cited below. The broader implications of the arguments presented here may well be relevant to other feminist histories written in/on the subcontinent as well as in other contexts.

THE PROBLEM WITH VOICE/VISIBILITY

In recent decades, feminist scholarship in the West has been subjected to much criticism for its continued, if unacknowledged, adherence to its liberal roots, especially its investment in preserving the coherence of "woman" as a category, which, like the liberal "individual," hides its specific ethnoclass composition behind a language of universalism.[73] As critical interventions by black, third-world/postcolonial, and lesbian feminists have rightly pointed out, insistence on a universal category such as "woman," based on a single axis of identification/signification, occludes the simultaneous workings of other axes such as race, community, class, or sexuality (to name a few) that position women differently as subjects.[74] Given the homogenizing tendencies stemming from a liberalism that Ann Snitow describes as "an essential thread" running through "Anglo-American feminism," — albeit increasingly acknowledged — it is perhaps not surprising that feminist scholars interested in writing histories of difference have taken up the task of making experiences of previously marginalized women visible as an important counterstrategy.[75]

The recent burgeoning of historical research on Muslim women in colonial India can be read as part of a similar move to counter both the overwhelming visibility of Hindu middle-class women and the near invisibility of Muslim women or their persistent representation as "backward" within normative historical accounts, perhaps best exemplified in an assertion by Gail Minault:

"These invisible [Muslim] women . . . needed to be rendered visible."[76] However, to the extent that this "writing back" and "making visible" is reactive and moored to a project of recovery, it is often beset by some typical problems.

For one, much of this research simply takes categories of difference, such as "Muslim" or "Hindu," for granted without attempting a relational reading of how such difference, and especially the specific content with which we imbue these categories today, came to be constructed in the first place and to what end. Consequently, the descriptive labels that mark different women also typically end up naturalizing such differences.[77] These, in turn, form the basis of separate, typically additive histories of Muslim women.[78]

At the same time, the overwhelming tendency is to also present these "different" women as somehow similar or comparable. As Joan Scott has argued for women's history in general, the "herstory" mode of rewriting history, which characterizes much of this literature, tries to "fit a new [or previously ignored] subject—[in this case, Muslim] women—into received categories [such as modern, liberal, or feminist], interpreting their actions in terms recognizable" within the dominant historiographic tradition in question.[79] The effect, as I have argued elsewhere, is precisely to flatten the very difference that apparently mandated this "new" history in the first place, and to represent Muslim women as "just like," or rather "almost like," the fabled subject positions "liberal" or "feminist."[80] As a result, what might be a rich and complex history of negotiation and resistance becomes an exercise in the service of producing sameness.[81]

Take, for instance, a recent historical work that undertakes a comparison between two Bengali women from the late nineteenth century and the early twentieth: Sarala Devi Chaudhurani and Rokeya Sakhawat Hossain. As the author, Bharati Ray, puts it, both Sarala and Rokeya "wrote profusely, strove for women's education, advocated advancing the social position of women, and built women's organisations. . . . [But one] of them came from a privileged and relatively 'progressive' background, and the other from one with a more stifling atmosphere; they belonged to two different religious communities, one was a Hindu-Brahmo, the other was a Muslim, and they chose separate philosophies to serve a common cause: the advancement of women."[82]

From the very beginning, then, the reader is invited both to assume differences between the two women and to subsume them under what appears to be a transcendental similarity, that is, "the advancement of women." The differences being highlighted are: in their "early experiences," expressed in terms of a "progressive background" versus a "stifling atmosphere"; their respective belonging to "two different religious communities"; and, finally, their "separate philosophies." And, while the author is careful not to draw explicit causal linkages between the various elements of difference that she lays out to mark the two women off from each other, the homologous presentation of binaries—"progressive" and Hindu/Brahmo on the one hand and "stifling" and Muslim on the other—carries a powerful suggestion, intended or otherwise, that the two religious communities differ significantly in their social ideologies and that such supposed differences produced radically different "experiences" for the two women in question and, therefore, somehow underlay the subsequent divergences in their analyses of the roots of women's oppression. Indeed, as Ray elaborates later:

> [While] Sarala held women primarily responsible for their backwardness, and . . . showed no particular ire against men . . . [for Rokeya] men were the real culprits. . . . The reason for this difference of opinion between Sarala and Rokeya may be attributed partly to the *difference in their early experiences*. Sarala enjoyed greater privileges than were allowed to women of her generation and therefore did not share Rokeya's *bitterness*. Besides, *liberal men in Bengal* stood by her. . . . Sarala wanted to make educated women capable homemakers and ardent *nationalists*, while Rokeya's emphasis was on making women self-respecting *individuals* at home and ideal *Muslims* in society."[83]

There are many ways to address this passage. One could question, for instance, the verity of the assumption that Rokeya had no support from liberal Muslim male intellectuals.[84] One could also challenge the intimated conflation of the category "liberal men in Bengal" and the Hindu/Brahmo bhadralok or disagree with Ray's appraisal of Rokeya's writing as being "laced with bitterness,"[85] an appraisal that, incidentally, was made a hundred years ago.[86] It has since been summarily discredited by a bevy of scholarship produced not only by her contemporaries but also by more recent commentators.[87] One could also comment at length on the significance of Ray's reading of the divergences in Sarala's and Rokeya's visions of educated women; "homemaker" and "nationalist" are clearly geared toward serving the (*Hindu*) *family* and the (*Hindu*) *nation* while both "individual" and "ideal Muslim" may be seen as subject locations (potentially) at odds with the collective interests of the family and the (Indian) *national* community.[88]

What I would like to focus on, however, is the way in which "difference" and "similarity" appear in this analysis as readily interpretable categories with fixed meanings that apparently need no further scrutiny. How can we assume such naturalized notions of difference, especially in the context of late colonial Bengal, where a majority of the Muslims were purportedly converts and the bhadralok, that is, a rentier and/or western-educated middle class, constituted a small proportion of even the Hindu population?[89] And is it possible to treat what appear to be two very different imaginations of "women's advancement"—home-making nationalists versus individualist Muslims, as Ray would have it—as equivalent, or even *similar*?

Ray is far from alone in this impulse to assume the essentiality of certain differences among Hindu and Muslim women and to subsume others. Much of the existing scholarship on Muslim women in colonial India seems to be similarly preoccupied with proving that Muslim women underwent a set of changes—variously described as "enlightenment," awakening," or "modernization" and defined in terms of a familiar infusion of westernized practices in institutions such as education, seclusion, and family.[90] These are widely recognized as stable elements of modernizing projects in the late nineteenth century and the early twentieth in many parts of the world.[91]

In her recent book on the "emergence of feminism" among Indian Muslim women, Azra Asghar Ali, for instance, systematically documents the creation of "various kinds of 'spaces' in which Muslim women were increasingly able to participate in the public sphere, created in large part by changes emanating from the impact of the colonial state."[92] And these new public spaces within which "reassessed gender relations could develop" were, according to Ali, "central to the evolving position of Indian Muslim women from the end of the nineteenth century."[93] Ali also focuses on efforts made by both the emergent middle classes and reform-minded older elites in the nineteenth century. As she rightly points out, these early efforts among Muslims may have been propelled more by a desire to improve the image of the community than by a serious impulse to bring wide-ranging reforms to women's lives, but even these rudimentary changes set the stage for more serious reforms in the late nineteenth century and the early twentieth.[94]

In a similar vein, Sonia Nishat Amin's work on Muslim women in colonial Bengal analyzes the links between the "emergence of the Muslim 'gentlewoman'" and the "broader reform movements of the time emanating from the Brahmo, Hindu and Islamic discourses."[95] Like Ali, Amin is concerned with locating this emergence within what she calls "a larger socio-cultural reorientation of the upper/middling strata of Bengal Muslims" and the "problematic of Bengali Muslim culture."[96] Amin's work is especially rich in terms of the historical information it unearths and distills for us about Bengali Muslim women who, as she rightly points out, have been largely "overlooked" within conventional historical accounts of the subcontinent.[97]

As early feminist scholarship on Muslim women in English that brought the discussion about Muslim women to a wider audience both within the subcontinent and beyond there is, of course, much that is valuable in these and other such works.[98] And yet in the end much of this literature seems to leave us with two overwhelming impressions: *the fact of Muslim women's difference*, which is assumed but not quite explored; and the idea that Muslim experiences of "reform" at the end of the nineteenth century and the beginning of the twentieth were *similar* to those undertaken by Hindus (and, in the case of Bengal, Brahmos) half a century earlier.[99] Questions of how these reform processes among the different groups might be related to each other, and, indeed, how the very *difference* of Hindus and Muslims was constituted through the various reform discourses of the nineteenth century, inhere in these works but remain firmly outside their critical purview. Amin even explicitly discusses the "applicability" of the terms *bhadralok* and *bhadramahila*—coined by the newly emerging Hindu/Brahmo middle class in colonial Bengal to refer to themselves—to Muslims in terms of their objective class status, but she seems to shrink from addressing the politics of exclusion/inclusion underlying the use (or withholding) of such terms.[100] As my analyses of periodical articles from late-nineteenth- and early-twentieth-century Bengal, as well as the oral testimonies of Muslim women today, will show, the Hindu *bhadrasampraday* saw the overwhelming majority of Muslims in Bengal as the antithesis of everything that was *bhadra*—educated, typically upper caste, middle class, and sometimes even liberal—and were not inclined to expand this category to include Muslims.[101]

A second feature of the existing literature on Muslim women seems to be the frequent use of and relationship to the idea of "feminism," where feminism functions as a common denominator that allows comparison between different women but itself remains remarkably underspecified.[102] On closer scrutiny, what emerges is something of a paradox: an automatic invocation, on one hand, of the terms *feminism* and *feminist* in discussions of the life and works of Muslim women in late colonial India; and a simultaneous uncertainty about using them. Consequently, some of the texts seem to be preoccupied with proving that their subjects were adequately feminist.[103] I will use one example from Amin's book in which she considers similarities between British and Bengali women, only to follow swiftly with what reads like an almost apologetic disclaimer:

> [Were] Bengali women experiencing a similar construction of the private and public *and* erosion of its distance, as Victorian/Edwardian women [were]? . . . A *cogent, apparent, and historically concrete ground for comparability* of Victorian/Edwardian and colonial Bengali women was the phenomenon of "First Wave Feminism." . . . It is in the [large, multifaceted] nature and the objective of this feminist movement that the linkages between the British and Bengali—*Brahmo* and Muslim—models are discernible. At the same time it must be pointed out that this is only an analogy . . . valid only from a distance far enough to blur incongruencies.[104]

Now it may well be that the particular women Amin discusses in her book are in fact feminists according to standards established in the West. Or it may be that they do not qualify as such. Given the enormous power of metropolitan intellectual politics and academic institutions on the process of knowledge production and dissemination even within third-world or anti-imperial locations—defined geographically or otherwise—one can certainly appreciate the stakes involved in such attempts to recuperate the experience of women, especially their resistance, as "feminist."[105] But the question that I would like to pose for our consideration is this. Is it possible for us to understand or appreciate Muslim women's work in the teeth of intense opposition in colonial India without entering into a discussion of how well they fared in a race to an already determined feminist finish line? What I wish to unsettle, in other words, is the stranglehold of a particular definition of *feminism* that privileges the social/political experiences of *some women* in the West on the very terms within which we are obliged to pose, indeed evaluate, questions of women's agency or consciousness in *any* context.[106]

It would seem that as feminist scholars writing within or for the Euro-American academy our options are threefold: We write only about those women who easily fit the feminist bill as defined in the West; second, we strain to prove that those erstwhile ignored women whom we would like to "restore to history" do in fact pass the litmus test of adequate feminism/liberalism or whatever kind of normalcy we wish to sanction; or, third, we interpret the so-called difference of all other subjects in terms of "distance" (temporal, as in "lagging behind," and/or substantive, as in "different/deviating") from what we define as the ideal and apparently common end.[107] The result, it would seem, is to force instances of difference into a hierarchy rather than considering them laterally, in their full measure of complexity and richness or, as Trinh T. Minh-ha would have it, as "a tool of creativity to question multiple forms of repression and dominance."[108]

A third and related problem in this literature on Muslim women in colonial India seems to be a wholesale acceptance of post-Enlightenment notions of visibility and voice in the public sphere as the only legitimate markers of subjecthood, and the automatic equation of such visibility/voice with a feminist subject position in some of these accounts.[109] As the activities of right-wing Hindu women in contemporary India—marked, most recently, by their enthusiastic participation in the pogroms against Muslims in Gujarat—amply demonstrate, it is not, or at least no longer, possible to celebrate automatically the presence of vocal and visible women in mass political movements.[110] What is more, as Pathak and Sunder Rajan have pointed out, "It is not always the case that 'to speak is to become a subject.'"[111] Such analytical conflations of subjecthood and visibility/voice in the public sphere also foreclose the possibility of appreciating other, sometimes collective forms of agency/resistance that women have historically deployed within the "private," and hence less visible, sphere to cope with gender oppression.[112]

We are all familiar with stories of women braving social ostracism in their fight against seclusion and purdah to emerge as "unified and freely choosing" subjects that constitute a staple of feminist accounts of women in colonial India or anywhere else in the third world for that matter.[113] However, accounts of women's contribution from behind purdah, or resistance and refusal by women who did not wish to pander to their liberal husbands' desire for appropriately "modern" consorts, seem to be routinely glossed over as so much inconvenient detail that unnecessarily complicates the story of modernity as the "normalized telos of a developmental process," even in its embattled feminist version.[114] Such elisions point, I think, to the continued purchase of feminism's foundational liberal moment, with its investments in a specific definition of a normative subjectivity, in the praxis of feminist intellectual politics even if we think we have tackled the beast in theory.

The final problem I want to raise here is that of time. It is not uncommon to find within this literature particular Muslim women being presented as exceptional in the sense of being "ahead of their time," and often even "out of place." This particular formulation is most apparent, of course, in discussions of Rokeya Sakhawat Hossain and the formidable legacy of her work.[115] Scholars are frequently moved to try to locate the roots of her critical thinking in a context other than the *zenana* in late colonial Bengal.[116] Consider Sonita Sarker's article, which attempts to place "this particular Bengali woman's engagement with modernity in a milieu larger than Bengal so as to emphasize that her membership lies also in a greater community of thinkers, namely in the company of women intellectuals in other parts of the world . . . women who address the roles of technology and its rationality in describing the new woman who can own the property of reason."[117]

Later, Sarker comments on Rokeya's now famous *Sultana's Dream*, published in 1905: "In conceiving [the world of Sultana] . . . Hossain should be seen as a contemporary of the feminist writers of utopias . . . such as the North American Charlotte Perkins Gilman (in *Herland*, published in 1915) and the Britisher Virginia Woolf (in *Three Guineas*, published in 1938) who also placed Women in direct relationship to science."[118]

I draw our attention to these quotes to highlight in what terms these and other attempts to establish Rokeya as exceptional construct, consciously or not, the temporal and spatial contexts that she *did* inhabit. For to accept the view of the zenana *only* as "the repository of weakness, ignorance and temptation" is to ignore the courage and grit of a long line of women (and men) who were engaged in the work of cultural and political resistance and reform for over half a century before Rokeya was born.[119] To trace the genealogy of Rokeya's critical consciousness to a community of intellectual women who published ten to forty years after *Sultana's Dream* was published—*in English*—but by all accounts never acknowledged her work is to lend credence to the claim that all that is valuable, in terms of both ideas and material goods, originates in the West and then travels to other places.[120] It is also to condemn to oblivion women and men with remarkable fortitude and resourcefulness who peopled Rokeya's world and shared her struggles.

VISIBLE HISTORIES/DISAPPEARING WOMEN

This book locates its problem area beyond the bodies of scholarship discussed above in a number of important ways. First, it goes beyond the nation-centeredness of both normative and critical histories of colonial India, which, I will argue, produces Muslim women as invisible and silenced. To "go beyond" nation-centeredness, however, does not mean wishing the nation away for, as we shall see in this book, the insistent presence of the nation can hardly be ignored even in the realm of popular writings and private memories. Rather, it signals an effort to foreground other formations, concerns, and modalities of identification that shaped the lives of middle-class Muslim women in late colonial Bengal. In this sense, my work may be seen as a small attempt at "rescuing history from the nation," to borrow Prasenjit Duara's memorable formulation, so that we might begin to pose the question of subjects, whose concerns may not have been defined solely or even mainly by the exigencies of nation formation, even though they, too, participated willy-nilly in modernizing projects, not all of which were tied to the impulse of nation building.

Second, while I share the broadly conceived, critical, postcolonial and feminist interest in interrogating the "sanctioned ignorances" within normative historiography in India, I approach the counterproject of making Muslim women visible as "unified, freely-choosing" subjects within existing historical accounts with some reservations.[121] Two insights from recent critical feminist scholarship on the difficulties of writing histories of difference are useful for my purposes here. The first insists that "the restoration of all that has been denied cannot be accomplished through simple affirmation."[122] The second points out that although projects of recovery record the existence of different groups they do not necessarily further our understanding of *how* or *why* different conceptions of selves or groups are produced in the first place, how and through what mechanisms difference operates, and how it "constitutes subjects."[123] Or, as Joan Scott puts it, "the project of making history visible precludes critical examination of the workings of the ideological system itself, [and] its categories of representation . . . as fixed immutable identities."[124]

Instead, *Visible Histories* is premised on the view that what is needed is a careful examination, perhaps excavation, of the discursive processes, or the "processes of differentiation," as Christina Crosby would put it, that have produced Muslim women as different *in specific ways* (i.e., as inferior to or lagging behind Hindu women or simply as invisible or mute) within the written history of colonial Bengal.[125] Accordingly, the book concentrates on materializing a series of discursive sites or contexts in which Muslim women in colonial Bengal appear and disappear in particular ways: in colonial discourse on "native" women; in Hindu (nationalist) discussions on Muslims; in revivalist and liberal

Muslim writings, including work by Muslim women from late-nineteenth- and early-twentieth-century Bengal; and, finally, in the private memories of Muslim women today. And through this analysis of interlinked discourses, as well as an ongoing parallel discussion of historical and feminist scholarship on the late colonial period, what I seek to recuperate, if anything, is not the excluded figure of the Muslim woman but the contexts of her (dis)appearances in the written history of colonial Bengal.

However, Bengali Muslim women do not appear only as silent and invisible or solely as "objects" of discourses in this book; as intellectuals in their own right beginning in the early twentieth century, and as members of a class with considerable influence on the cultural life of that time, especially among Muslims, as well as narrators of their life stories today, they are certainly present as subjects with both voice and visibility, even if limited, in the public world. As my discussion in chapter 3, which builds on extant feminist and historical research on Muslim women intellectuals in early-twentieth-century Bengal, will argue, these early women writers were not only, or always, echoing what their male counterparts were formulating; at times, they were also framing both their own interventions and those of others.[126] My analysis of the oral histories of Muslim women in chapter 4 will further demonstrate that it is hardly possible to imagine the middle-class narrators in *these* stories only as "native" informers who are "incapable of strategy towards [western scholars]" even if their stories are necessarily mediated through my writing.[127]

At the same time, it is important to note that the impressions of Muslim women's agency, as constituted both through their writing and in their life stories, often disrupt the normative definition of a unified, autonomous subject exerting her will freely toward clearly defined and transparent ends. For the women they write and talk about deploy or want to deploy resistance in ways and sites that are not conventionally associated with the idea of agency within western liberal discourse. Keeping these complexities in mind, *Visible Histories* approaches the question of agency necessarily as a process of negotiation with structures—often subversive rather than frontal or visible, and as likely to involve capitulation—and not simply as a linear, unidirectional story of overcoming and eventual emergence into modern, liberal, and/or "feminist" subjecthood.[128] For, as nationalist movements—indeed, modernizing projects in general—have demonstrated, the moment of nation-state formation may be a crucial moment of mutation for patriarchal systems when they reinvent themselves as "modern" and implement reforms as part of their politics of accommodation, but such reform projects typically build in "controls in the very texture of how [new] possibilities are conceived."[129] Or, as feminists studying the "project of remaking women" have repeatedly pointed out, "modernity" is seldom "what it purports to be" and the control of "the family," especially women, is at the very heart of "the production of discourses about the [modern male] self."[130] Consequently, the end of seclusion or veiling and the emergence of women in the public domain, which are associated with modernizing projects worldwide, have also brought new contractions and demands for respectability in their wake.[131] This has forced women to adopt "new forms of puritanism that could be activated as a symbolic shield" in the public domain, sometimes even resulting in women imposing "new forms of silence [or silencing] on themselves."[132]

As we shall see later in this book, especially in the analyses of Muslim women's writings in chapter 3 and their oral histories in chapter 4, the project of modernizing for Muslim women in late colonial Bengal was similarly marked by contradictions, including self-censuring for some and social opprobrium for others, and the deployment of women's agency, both in the service of modernizing projects and against them, in challenging technologies of control or subverting them by using them to ends unintended (by men).

The issue of complex agency takes on a special poignancy in the analyses of oral histories, which are by definition subjective accounts of the past,[133] recounted within a dialogic context in which the interviewee appears as a dynamic partner even if the relationship between interviewer and the narrator is often marked by asymmetries of power.[134] However, as oral historians and ethnographers often point out, and as I elaborate in my discussion in chapter 4, the relationships between interviewers and narrators are also typically "complex and shifting."[135] The latter often use their considerable power, at least within the interview context, to steer the conversation in particular directions, emphasize certain issues, and obscure others.[136] At times they even refuse or subtly avoid cooperation.[137] Any attempt to write a history of difference, or, rather, to write about the processes of differentiation involving women, has to be sensitive to these myriad forms of agency and not simply to those that can be easily recuperated as "feminist," defined narrowly in historically contingent and particular ways.[138]

Two sets of questions animate this book. First, how are Muslim women produced historically as invisible and silent/silenced subjects? What, if any, is the relationship between the invisibility or victim image of one group of women (Muslim) and the overwhelming visibility of another (Hindu, middle class/upper caste) as the embodiment of "ideal womanhood" in normative accounts of a nation's transition to modernity and self-rule? Second, how does one write a history of difference that goes beyond the impulse simply to recuperate the previously marginalized into the existing categories of normative history? Is it possible to record the erstwhile muted voices of nondominant/subaltern groups such as Muslim women in a Hindu-dominated nation-state? In what intellectual-political context might one attempt such a project of recovery? Can the past—embodied in written history and collective rituals of remembrance—be implicated in the way it serves a specific present?

While the overarching empirical focus of the book is on Muslim women in late colonial Bengal, I begin by exploring some of the central concerns of the book regarding the incorporation and uses of women within dominant historical accounts through an examination of the sexual relationships between British men stationed in the Indian subcontinent and their "native consorts"—concubines, common law wives, and *nautch* girls—in the late eighteenth century and the early nineteenth.[139] Such encounters between the colonizers and a specific subset of the "subject people" are romanticized and at the same time trivialized as frivolous sexual dalliance in much of the extant historical accounts of colonial India. Drawing mainly on secondary literature and a few important primary sources, "The Colonial Cast" (chapter 1) revisits colonial accounts of such relationships, as well as their later representations in the historiography of that era. It argues that relationships between "native" women—Muslims and Hindus in the main—and British men were a crucial element in the reproduction of the East India Company's workforce in the subcontinent. Both the relationships and the women whose sexual and other labor was appropriated through such relationships thus merit more careful attention. The second half of the chapter traces some important changes in the terms of interaction between the British—now increasingly self-assured and arrogant representatives of an empire—and their "subject" populations in the nineteenth century. It argues that while easy mingling with natives, especially interracial relationships, were frowned on in the official colonial discourse of the nineteenth century, native women's sexual and domestic labor continued to provide important services to the colonial enterprise. The chapter ends with a brief discussion of the ways in which the changing representations of "native" women in colonial discourse in turn influenced subsequent reformist and/or nationalist discourses of the indigenous middle classes on the "woman question" in the nineteenth century.

The question of the strategic visibility of women is, of course, an important concern of feminist theories of nation and state that highlight the ways in which women are frequently appropriated as visible symbols of the nation even as their rights as citizens are undercut by the workings of gender ideologies. In "The Politics of (In)visibility" (chapter 2), I take these theories as a point of departure but then draw on critical feminist scholarship—which emphasizes differences among women rather than identity as crucial for theories of gender oppression—to highlight ways in which gender and racially defined communal and class ideologies worked simultaneously to deny even middle-class Muslim women the limited visibility accorded to Hindu upper-caste/middle-class women as embodiments of an "ideal Indian womanhood." Through an examination of periodical and newspaper articles from late-nineteenth- and early-twentieth-century Bengal, I argue that the representation of Muslim women as backward, victimized, silenced, and eventually invisible by contemporary Hindu/Brahmo writers—both men and women—undergirds the construction of other identity categories in colonial Bengal; that in effect it secures upper-caste, middle-class, Hindu/Brahmo women as liberated, modern embodiments of the new ideal Indian woman; that it produces the category "Muslim" as male, inherently dangerous, oppressive, and nonmodern; and, last but not least, that it helps shore up the image of the Hindu middle-class male as the normative citizen-subject of the emergent nation. I further argue that, while the literary productions of women have typically been lauded as signs of "progress" and "enlightenment" among the Bengali bhadrasampraday, their involvement in this process of producing identities in late colonial Bengal, has gone largely unscrutinized.[140] An important aim of the chapter is to foreground the complex ideological functions of Hindu/Brahmo women's literary agency that helped define the gendered and communal underpinnings of Bengali middle-class identity locations within an increasingly communalized nationalist agenda in late colonial Bengal.

Members of the Hindu middle class were, of course, not the only ones casting Muslims in derogatory ways. Indeed, underlying Hindu representations of Muslims in the nineteenth century were British practices of categorization that locked Muslims in the Indian subcontinent into binary formulations such as foreign/indigenous, authentic/convert, aristocratic/low caste, and victimized/dangerous. The profound effect of such representations—both colonial and Hindu—on Bengali Muslims forms the underlying focus of the second half of the book.

"Negotiating Modernity" (chapter 3) surveys mostly articles by middle-class Muslim men and women that addressed a wide range of social and political issues of the day. These discussions, carried on in the pages of a bevy of periodicals that were in circulation in the first half of the twentieth century in Bengal, rarely enter into normative historical accounts of colonial Bengal produced in postindependence India, which privilege the story of the Partition and, hence, implicitly reinforce the popular notions of the Muslim as "separatist" and "conservative." As my analysis shows, a significant number of Muslim intellectuals opposed political separation, even as they insisted on their cultural specificity and criticized the implicit majoritarianism of many Hindus. They were also interested in a wide range of social reforms, including those that would have a significant impact on the lives of women. What is more, women intellectuals and reformers not only took part in but were sometimes at the forefront of such critical public exchanges during the first decades of the twentieth century. However, unlike most of their male counterparts, their understanding of the problems, as well as the solutions, were not necessarily defined by the needs of the nation/community. As I argue in this chapter, the marginalization of Muslim women's work has to be understood in terms of this larger process of obfuscation of the rich and internally fissured discussions carried on by members of the Bengali Muslim middle class and not simply as a by-product of the androcentrism of conventional historiographies.

The last substantive chapter, "Difference in Memory" (chapter 4), turns mainly to the oral histories of five Muslim women who were born or lived in Calcutta and/or Dhaka in the first half of the twentieth century. The interviewees were asked about their childhoods, experiences in school, friends, neighbors, social activities, memories of their mothers and other women of both their own and previous generations, and the relationships between different generations, as well as between men and women in each generation. Within this loosely defined set of concerns, the interviews remained mostly unstructured, with the speakers deciding what they wished to recount. The oral accounts provide a rich source of information about the social fabric of urban Bengal during the final years of colonial rule seen through the eyes of subjects who have rarely appeared in the extant historiography of those times. As Luisa Passerini puts it, they represent "a manifestation of a subjective reality which enables us to write history from a novel dimension unconsidered by traditional historiography."[141]

One striking feature of these accounts is the insistence with which the biography of the nation, the story of Hindu-Muslim animosities, and especially the impetus to address or challenge certain stereotypes about Muslims and their separatism interrupt the most private accounts of Muslim women's lives. Consequently, as I highlight in the chapter, even in their own stories Muslim women sometimes disappear from the narrative as active subjects.

It is tempting to think of private memories as repositories of alternative histories and subaltern truths and, hence, ready-made sites of resistance to normative history, that simply need tapping into. My analysis reveals, however, that in responding to the strong voice of official history private memories sometimes reconsolidate the structures of the very history they seek to resist even if in denial. It thus points to the need to treat memories not as readily "known and knowable" but rather as "problematic sites of query in themselves."[142]

While much of the empirical focus of the book beyond this introductory chapter is on colonial Bengal, the conclusion brings us back once again to the present or more precisely to a consideration of some complex linkages between the constructions of Muslim women in the past and the ways in which they are still represented in academic and popular discourses in India today. The chapter ends with a brief reflection on the possible connections between the dominant representations of Muslim women today and the kind of public violence that has been visited on them in contemporary India.

1

THE COLONIAL CAST

The Merchant, the Soldier, the "Writer" (Clerk), Their Lovers, and the Trouble with "Native Women's" Histories

It is not possible to know today who [or how many women inhabited Sikander's] . . . antahpur [in the first half of the nineteenth century]. . . . [Of the three whose names are known] Ishwari [Khanum] was Muslim . . . [another,] Manu, was . . . Hindu . . . [and] Sofia was Christian . . . possibly Anglo-Indian. . . .

[Sikander is believed to have fathered] eighty two children, but there are no records . . . of his marriage . . . [to any of] his "companions." . . . Ishwari's grave is still there in Hansi, as is Manu's, since she eventually converted to Islam—but who will account for the others?—How will such accounting happen?[1]

In her recent research on "colonial companions"—consorts of British colonial servants—in the eighteenth century, Durba Ghosh has argued that in much of the existing historiography of British colonial rule in the Indian subcontinent the figure of the "native" female companion is "presumed" but "specific information about the women themselves" is missing. Consequently, as Ghosh puts it, none of the existing accounts of "the Anglo-Indian encounter can be extended to describe the quotidian lives of 'native' women and the Europeans with whom they cohabited."[2] I begin my discussion of native women in colonial discourse with Ghosh's work because her observations on the colonial archive touch on issues that are central to the concerns of this book, that is, the appearance/disappearance, visibility/invisibility, and centrality/marginalization of women, especially women of nondominant groups, within written history.

Ghosh herself seems to approach the absence of "colonial companions" from written history mainly as a "problem of sources"—the combined effects of the practices of partial naming and name changing of native subjects in general and the silence of native women in particular in colonial records, which makes it difficult to retrieve "subaltern subjects from the archives."[3] Another recent work, in which the author admits to drawing on sources that conventional historians "normally avoid and consider unworthy of discussion," similarly points to the problem of the disappearing "companion" of Europeans in eighteenth-century India.[4] And yet, as the research of these writers demonstrates, the information on native women in colonial archives is not insignificant in volume even if it is dissatisfying in terms of detail.[5] In other words, the marginalization of colonial companions within the written history of colonial rule in the subcontinent cannot be simply a consequence of lack of information about them. Besides, are we to assume that a more complete or greater presence within the colonial archive, or, indeed, the expansion of the archive itself to incorporate other, perhaps less conventional historical sources, as Sripantha would have it, would have guaranteed more visibility and voice for colonial companions in the official history of colonial India?[6] Or does their absence or insignificance as subjects point to the need for a more complex understanding of the connection between what archives carry and historical accounts foreground beyond the matter of the presence or lack of adequate information or the scope and definition of archives? Indeed, not to beg the question, why should we care about colonial companions at all?

Ghosh is well aware of some of the questions that frame, or ought to frame, any project of recovery. For she also writes, rather provocatively, that "the histories of these women, who lived with, married or were the sexual partners of Europeans is . . . [treated as] tangential [in the existing historiography]."[7] Taking up this latter suggestion, which inheres in her work, and anticipating something of the arguments I make later in the book regarding the problem of the invisibility or victim image of Muslim women in the written history of late colonial Bengal, I would propose that the marginalization, if not disappearance, of colonial companions—many of whom were Muslim and hence of particular interest to the current project—within the existing historiography of colonial India should not be treated as an oversight that simply awaits correction but as symptomatic of a tendency to present sexual relationships as epiphenomenal to (colonial) history, the mere by-products of the physical needs of European men stationed in the colonies without access to the company of European women, that systematically devalues the sexual and domestic labor of native women and the significance of these relationships as constitutive of the social fabric of colonial India.[8]

As the following discussion will show, in the first century of British colonial rule in the subcontinent, relationships between native women and British or other European men were in fact *central to the very reproduction* of the East India Company's workforce in an alien world. While relationships with women from aristocratic families helped forge important political connections for the Company's servants, liaisons with women of lesser status—some of whom may have been "slaves . . . [who received] their freedom on the death of their master"—also provided a host of quotidian services and comforts that were taken for granted but invaluable.[9] Neither the relationships nor the women involved in them should be treated as incidental pleasures of the colonial enterprise, notwithstanding what an uncritical reading of colonial archives—which undercuts the importance of native women and their sexual and domestic labor—might suggest to us.

BRITISH INDIA IN THE LATE EIGHTEENTH CENTURY

Until well into the eighteenth century, the English East India Company (henceforth, the Company), founded in 1600, was merely one of several European companies trading in Asia within a dense competitive network that also involved European free traders and Armenian and other diasporic merchants.[10] By all accounts, the English company was not the most successful among the European joint stock enterprises. Until the 1740s, that distinction belonged to the Dutch East India Company (known as VOC), which had established early control over the lucrative spice trade based in the Malay archipelago.[11] What marked a reversal of fortunes for the English company in the subcontinent was not so much a windfall in trading as a crucial battle that it fought and won against the minor nawab of Bengal, Siraj-ud-daulah, in Palashi (also known as Plassey in British sources), Bengal, in 1757. Indeed, Palashi not only changed the position of the English East India Company in South Asia but ushered in a major change in the geopolitical and economic position of Britain in the world. For the plunder that followed the victory at Palashi, and the subsequent accession of the Company to the *diwani* (stewardship) of Bengal in 1765, initiated a most spectacular transfer of wealth from the subcontinent to Britain, estimated to have totaled between a hundred million and a billion pounds over the next few decades.[12] This infusion of funds allowed Britain, first and foremost, to pay off its national debt (most notably to the Dutch), "leaving her [it] nearly free from overseas indebtedness when it came to face the great wars" with its chief competitor, France, beginning in 1793."[13] Some would even argue that the "gentlemanly capitalism" of the East India Company was more influential than industrialization in shaping Britain's imperialism in the eighteenth century.[14] In time, the continued plunder of Bengal, now increasingly disguised as commercial ventures and tribute, would underwrite a sixfold increase in public expenditures in Britain between 1792 and 1815 and a resultant tremendous boost to British industrial development. What is more, the acquisition of Bengal provided the British with a crucial territorial foothold that facilitated all its subsequent conquests, eventually creating an empire that would, in turn, supply vital demographic and fiscal resources for Britain's overseas adventures and ensure its hegemonic status in the world throughout the nineteenth century.[15]

In the 1770s, however, Britain's dominance of the world was far from a fait accompli. The outbreak of the American Revolution in 1776 and the capture of seven West Indian islands by France signaled a (temporary) loss of Britain's commercial and military hold over the Atlantic.[16] Access to the vast resources of Bengal, and through it to those of large parts of the subcontinent, was thus of critical and increasing importance to Britain in the last quarter of the eighteenth century. Not surprisingly, it was around this time that British attitudes and official policies toward the subcontinent and its peoples and cultures underwent a significant change.

COLONIAL VISIONS, PRACTICES, AND NATIVE WOMEN

Unlike their predecessors, Company employees who came to the subcontinent in the late eighteenth century were sent not just to trade but to lay the foundations of a lasting empire. They were, therefore, required to "think and act like . . . Asians." Indeed, in these early years of Company rule, "going native"—widely understood in Britain to be both pleasurable and profitable even if not quite respectable—was often not so much a matter of choice for Company representatives as one of political necessity.[17] It gave the Company legitimacy in the princely courts and allowed it to successfully secure trading rights and alliances to further its interests.[18] Moreover, as William Dalrymple recently pointed out in his study of eighteenth-century Hyderabad, the continued relationships between women in the household of the Nizam and those in the households of East India Company officers were of seminal importance in this process of building and brokering political relationships.[19]

The intellectual content of this shift in attitude is reflected in the works of early orientalist scholars such as William Jones, Henry T. Colebrooke, William Carey, Nathaniel Halhed, and Charles Wilkins, which are marked by a certain drive to accumulate and organize knowledge about the subcontinent—its languages, culture, and history. Understanding Indian culture was to be the basis for a "sound Indian administration," and mastering local languages was a key element in this process since it would reduce, if not eliminate, British dependence on local informants and translators over time.[20] As Gauri Viswanathan puts it,

> Underlying Orientalism [the official policy of early British rule] was a tacit policy of what one may call reverse acculturation, whose goal was to train British administrators and civil servants to fit into the culture of the ruled and to assimilate them thoroughly into the native way of life. . . . [The] exhaustive research [produced by the orientalists] had ambitious goals ranging from the initiation of the West to the vast literary treasures of the East to the reintroduction of the natives to their own cultural heritage. . . . [But] there is no denying

> that behind Orientalism's . . . immense scholarly achievements . . . lay interests that were far from scholarly.[21]

Thus, while much has been made of both the "benign influence" of orientalist scholars and the "new kind of civil servant" associated particularly with the administration of Warren Hastings, especially their admiration and affinity for Indian languages and cultures, this new appreciation must be located within both an insistent logic of empire building as a means of realizing Britain's ambitions to outwit and dominate its European competitors and perhaps a somewhat uncertain and defensive moment in that larger process.[22]

While orientalist scholars made significant contributions to the fields of philology, archaeology and history, they were curiously silent on the specific forms of inequality that existed in contemporary Indian society. When they did address issues such as sati, they typically privileged the textual position on such practices and the interpretations of the indigenous literati rather than studying the customs as they were actually practiced.[23] The orientalists were, thus, not only "recuperating" knowledge about India's past but also adjudicating which "facts" and what sources were authentic and significant and what ought to count as culture and what as atrocity, setting the course of future debates in the process, especially debates over Hindu culture and women's position within it.[24]

For a vast majority of the new class of civilian officials who arrived in the subcontinent in the last three decades of the eighteenth century, however, the colonies still represented an opportunity to indulge in the kind of opulent lifestyle that they could not possibly have afforded in Britain. By all accounts, the East India Company representatives in the eighteenth century typically amassed great personal fortunes, lived lavishly, emulated the lifestyles of the local aristocracy, and even called themselves nabobs.[25] As the following doggerel popular at that time suggests, a key element in going native was the company of native women, who thus acquired a new importance in contemporary British discourse.

> We are sure to find something blissful and dear
> And that we are far from the lips we love
> We make love to lips that are near.[26]

Travelogues and memoirs written around this time routinely invoked images of untold riches and an "erotic East," dotted with seraglios teeming with languid, dark-skinned "syrens" and seductive *nautch* girls, where "prostitution was a perfectly respectable profession" and women understood "in perfection all the arts and wiles of love, . . . [were] capable of gratifying any tastes, and in face and figure . . . [were] unsurpassed by any women in the world."[27] Other stories conjured up pictures of helpless women imprisoned in harems, widows sacrificed as sati, and women acting as *devdasis* who were forced to "sell sex in order to earn revenues for the upkeep of the holy places."[28] As a result, eighteenth-century English attitudes toward Indian women often revealed "a curious mix of erotic fascination and a missionary zeal to rescue them from their societal prison."[29] In the process, the English secured for themselves a self-proclaimed image as saviors and civilizers.[30]

Records show that many Company servants and officers took native mistresses, some had bibis (or "common-law" wives), and some maintained harems or zenanas inhabited by multiple women.[31] According to one eighteenth-century observer of Calcutta society, even ordinary "writers" (clerks) maintained seraglios, although their incomes could hardly have supported such an expenses.[32] While the policy of active encouragement of cohabitation with native women—in vogue in the early years of the Company's presence in the subcontinent—was on the wane by the end of the eighteenth century, even as late as 1814 we find an anonymous British commentator who visited Bengal writing about "exquisitely formed . . . *hindoostanee* women"—a term he used to refer to "both Hindoos and Moslems"—who were like a "cluster of delights." He surmised that "three parts of . . . [the unmarried British officials retained] concubines."[33] Indeed, the practice seems to have been common enough even in the early nineteenth century to warrant a whole section of advice in a contemporary guidebook for Company servants on "how to keep a native woman" written by a certain Capt. Thomas Williamson who had spent a considerable length of time in Bengal.[34] Williamson's account reveals something of the quotidian practicalities involved in these interracial relationships, albeit from the British male point of view: Native companions were supposedly faithful; they had clean personal habits; they were not very likely to steal; they cooked, cleaned, and procured provisions; and, most important, they provided "invaluable" attention during times of sickness.[35] However, Williamson also warns his readers that, despite all their positive qualities, native women could be violent, unpredictable, given to opulence, and prone to peculiar habits—signaling that, while interracial cohabitation was thought to be practical, even inevitable, under the circumstances, by the beginning of the nineteenth century native women were increasingly considered less than ideal companions in the dominant British discourse on colonial domesticity.[36]

A second context in which the British encountered and interacted with native women at that time was that of the nautches.[37] According to an account written in 1754 by one Mrs. Kindersley, the *nautch* was one of the most popular forms of entertainment in British circles in eighteenth-century India. She wrote, "When a black man has a mind to compliment a European, he treats him to a *nautch*. . . . It is . . . [the dancers'] languishing glances, wanton smiles, and attitudes not quite consistent with decency, which are so much admired."[38] Indeed, while the upper-class officials of the East India Company sometimes entered into long-term relationships with local women in eighteenth-century India, the junior clerks — or "writers" as they were called — as well as lower-ranking soldiers with much fewer financial means mostly depended on the company of *nautch* girls and the commercially organized prostitution involving them. As Sumanta Banerjee has pointed out, among the nautch girls Muslim *baijis* — the commonly used name for courtesans associated with the North Indian courts — held a special position: "The *baijis* were the darlings of [the] late 18th–early 19th century . . . [among both the Bengali elites and their British patrons because they] evoked the ambiance and charm of the feudal aristocracy of the Moghul era."[39]

Banerjee mentions the names of several legendary baijis, including Nikki, Ushoorun, Begum Jan, Hingool, Nanni-jan, and Supun-jan, "who used to grace the '*nautch*' parties in early 19th century Calcutta and its suburbs" as professional singers and dancers.[40] In a similar vein, Ratnabali Chatterjee notes that well into the nineteenth century "a *nautch* was seen as an aristocratic gathering of 'natives' [by Europeans] and definitely to be distinguished from the revelries of the vulgar."[41] The courtesans or baijis — many Muslim women among them — were generally seen as highly accomplished musicians who had wealthy patrons, including the king in some cases, and were sometimes incorporated into aristocratic households through contract marriages.[42] As the autobiographical novel *Nashtar*, written in 1790 by Hasan Shah, a *munshi* (clerk) in the retinue of a British military officer of the East India Company, records or as the story of Begum Samru, a Muslim nautch girl by the name of Farzana who became the companion of a professional soldier in the service of the English East India Company, testifies, by the late eighteenth century such patrons also included European officers.[43]

Contemporary paintings record striking changes in the ways women were represented during the period of rapid transition from Mughal to British dominance in the eighteenth century.[44] Suddenly, the power of representation was no longer in the hands of the erstwhile court painters; now it was the European "artists" who produced arresting images of both the newly conquered land and its women. The "noble beauty" of the *nayika*, or ideal woman, in the paintings of the Mughal and later nawabi courts were replaced by images of bejeweled mistresses, nautch girls, and women as victims of "native customs"—typically those of devdasis and satis.[45] In the words of Ratnabali Chattopadhyay and Tapati Guha Thakurta, native women figured "as an important ingredient of the India imagined and invoked by the British [in colonial paintings]. Like the landscapes, images of 'native' women, in the exoticism of their costumes and jewellery, exuded the same sense of untapped mysteries and primeval nature. . . . For visiting British painters, eager to probe the 'essence' of India, women were seen to be the carriers of the ageless traditions of native civilizations."[46]

According to Mildred Archer, who has compiled many of these early paintings of courtesans, nautch girls, and the common-law wives of British officers, the European artists' access to the zenanas of the Indian aristocracy—Muslim and Hindu—was necessarily restricted.[47] However, as recent research has shown, relationships between women at the court and Company representatives were not uncommon and afforded the latter vital connections to the princely zenanas, which were "important spaces" not only for "exchanging information" but also for "conducting negotiations."[48]

In sum for Company servants in the eighteenth century, the foreignness of India was not something to be avoided; in fact, it was precisely the mysteries of this strange land and the great wealth it promised that lured them to it. And native women—Muslims, Hindus, and even some Christian Eurasians—were at the very heart of this foreign, alluring, and perhaps dangerous attraction. The images that colonial paintings, novels, travel accounts, and other sundry writings from the late eighteenth century and the early nineteenth served up—of the seductive nautch girls; the coy, bejeweled bibis, isolated and yet content within the intimacy of the homes of Company servants; the desperate, if mysterious, sati in need of rescuing, like "India" itself, from the cruelty of native men or the jealous, unpredictable, "less than ideal" companion—all presented native women, and, by extension, the subcontinent, as utterly accessible to and desirous of the colonizing male subject.[49]

At the same time, it is important to note that British men rarely envisioned taking their bibis back to England with them.[50] Consider, for instance, the following song published in 1800.

> 'Tis thy will and I must leave thee
> O thou best belov'd farewell,
> I forbear lest should grieve thee,
> Half my heart felt pangs to tell.
> Soon a British fair will charm thee,
> Thou alas her smiles must woo,
> But tho' she to rapture warm thee
> Don't forget thy poor Hindoo.[51]

In other words, the native companion may have been the object of desire, affection, and even nostalgia, but above all she was *necessary*. Nonetheless, for all her usefulness and allure, in the end she was a mere possession unfit for metropolitan living and therefore, unlike the noble *nayika* of Indian male fantasy, entirely dispensable. In sharp contrast to the mobile, enabled self of the British male subject, she is portrayed as inert and stationary, something to be used and then forgotten. Note also the remarkable arrogance of appropriating the native female voice as the conduit for enunciating the very ideology that discounts her worth as a person/woman, asserting thereby the normalcy, if not the naturalness, of her specific exploitation.

It is possible, I think, to read the song quoted above and the meanings embodied in it as an allegory for Britain's evolving relationship with, and attitude toward, the Indian subcontinent from the beginning of the nineteenth century: a very obvious and growing dependence on the resources of this rich colony and a simultaneous attempt to both deny that need or dependence and represent the plunder that followed as reasonable, even natural.[52] And, while Britain is portrayed as progressing (industrializing, developing, and modernizing), its colonies are seen as stagnating and waiting, their exploitation taken for granted, sanctioned apparently by their desire for British colonial penetration and hence entirely reasonable.[53]

Indeed, if eighteenth-century paintings, memoirs, and travel literature describe native companions as alluring, records also suggest that, notwithstanding the euphemistic references to them as "bibis," "housekeepers," "companions," or "female friends," many such women "under the protection" of European men were little more than "slave-concubines" who were bought, often were transferred between households and men (especially in the cantonments), and were typically not free to leave unless their masters so decided. It was not uncommon for slave-concubines to be given to beneficiaries in the wills of deceased European masters and mistresses, or to be advertised as part of the houses that their European companions/masters were seeking to sell before leaving the subcontinent.[54] In Indrani Chatterjee's words, "Historians of India [have] romanticized . . . [the] presence [of the concubines] either in terms of nostalgia (the epitome of racial harmony), or in terms of female agency ('consensual cohabitation'), and tended to brush aside the political and economic contexts of these transactions and transfers, as well as the consequences for . . . the making of colonialism in India."[55]

As we shall see, even such ambiguous representations of colonial dependence and exploitation in terms of fleeting "consensual" cohabitation with natives disappeared in the nineteenth century. The need for the resources of the land and the labor of native populations, including the caretaking and sexual labor of native women, however, continued to be of central importance to the running of the growing empire.[56] What changed, and quite drastically, in the nineteenth century were the terms in which such needs and the attempts to meet them were recast and the kind of discourse on the natives that was invented to justify it.

BRITISH ATTITUDES AND DISCOURSE IN THE NINETEENTH CENTURY

If the Peace of Vienna of 1815 inaugurated the era of Pax Britannica—a hitherto unimaginable hundred years of peace in Europe brokered by Britain, the most powerful European state of that time—it also marked the beginning of a century of constant warfare in, and a deepening exploitation of, the overseas colonies of Europe facilitated precisely by the unprecedented peace on the home front.[57]

By the middle of the nineteenth century, it was clear that Britain was dependent on India's export surplus to offset its deficits elsewhere.[58] And yet the colonial regime was constantly straining to invent noneconomic reasons to justify its presence in the subcontinent. If the eighteenth century was marked by a certain fluidity of social and cultural contact between the servants of an as yet uncertain nascent empire and local populations, and even an early orientalist fascination with India's Vedic past, the nineteenth century—influenced by European race theories that interpreted phenotypic differences of the non-European other as signs of inherent and unalterable inferiority, as well as by Britain's increasing arrogance as the most powerful nation of the world—was a time to drive home the "separate and superior nature" of the British as the master race and Indians as their "subject" people.[59]

While signs of contempt toward native culture and apprehension of "corrupting influences from native society" had already manifested themselves during the rule of Cornwallis (1786–93), the early deliberations of the British Parliament at the beginning of the nineteenth century were ironically more focused on the issue of the "depravities" of Company administrators and merchants and a perceived need to "educate the natives." Under the continued influence of orientalists, the official policy at this time was still to establish institutions for the teaching of "oriental languages and literature." During the first half of the nineteenth century, a later generation of orientalist scholars, especially Max Muller, Mrs. Speier, and Clarissa Bader, slowly transformed the "Hindu golden age," which had been "discovered" by Jones and Colebrook at the end of the eighteenth century, into an "Aryan golden age"—the word *Aryan* suggesting "vigour, race and a conquering group"[60]—whose culture and learning traditions were worth preserving and could presumably "act as bulwark against the forces of violent change unleashed by the British presence."[61]

By the third decade of the century, however, as Britain's position both in India and vis-à-vis its European rivals became more secure, the administration became more receptive to missionary arguments about the innate immorality of the natives, the worthlessness of native traditions, literatures, and contemporary social practices, and the urgent need for their moral improvement. In the words of Uma Chakravarti, "In seeking a psychological advantage over their subjects colonial ideology felt compelled to assert the moral superiority of the rulers in many subtle and not so subtle ways. . . . Throughout the first half of the nineteenth century, and even before, writers like Mill, Orme, Dubois, Macaulay and Bentinck were labouring to certify the 'natives' as a frail, cowardly, and soft-bodied little people."[62]

In sharp contrast to orientalist views, the missionaries and Anglicists mounted a veritable campaign of denigration around issues of the abysmal material and moral position of native (especially Hindu) women and the degeneration of Indian (Hindu) civilization, which allowed both the degrading treatment of women and the immorality and indecency of the popular indigenous cultural forms that kept the native mind debased.[63] To quote Geraldine Forbes, "The formula was simple: 'Among rude people, the women are generally degraded; among civilized people they are exalted.' . . . Having learned about Hindu society through reading . . . a translation of the Code of Manu, some religious works, and accounts written by travelers and missionaries, Mill concluded: 'nothing can exceed the habitual contempt which the Hindus entertain for their women.'"[64] Or, as Partha Chatterjee has observed, "By assuming a position of sympathy with the unfree and oppressed womanhood of India, the colonial mind was able to transform this figure of the Indian woman into a sign of the inherently oppressive and unfree nature of the entire cultural tradition of a country."[65] In this infinitely harsher view, improvement of the essential "Indian character" was deemed possible only through its introduction to "useful," that is, Western, learning and not through the "promotion of native culture" as the orientalists had argued.[66] Amid the changing political climate of the mid–nineteenth century, British discourse and practice in the subcontinent thus took yet another sharp turn: domination of India by a racially and culturally superior Britain was now seen as both "natural and inevitable."[67]

While recent research by historians has suggested that the "building blocks" of colonial imperial ideology were already being developed, even deployed, in the late eighteenth century, some contemporary popular perceptions seem to echo the idea of a fairly drastic change in British attitudes toward Indians in the course of the nineteenth century.[68] As late as 1790, in *Nashtar*, Hasan Shah was describing his employer, Ming Saheb (possibly Manning), as

> a generous, noble, kindly Englishman . . . [who] treated me with respect and courtesy, and also gave me valuable presents. . . . He belonged to a breed of large-hearted, bold, and adventurous Englishmen. He made me sole in-charge of his business and trusted me implicitly.[69]

A hundred years later, in 1893, Shah's description must have struck an odd note, for Kasmandavi, who translated *Nashtar* into Urdu, felt compelled to add the following comment qualifying Shah's warm tribute to Ming:

> This was an Englishman of those times. Today they call us native, black man, barbarian. They misbehave with us and crush our rights as much as they can, although we have become much more educated now. . . . But a century ago the

> English who came here were gentlemen, and we were also a decent people. Now both they and us have [be]come equally bad.[70]

It seems Kasmandavi was not wrong in his assessment. As the following excerpt from a letter written by Elgin in 1895 shows, at the end of the nineteenth century scientific notions of intrinsic racial hierarchy, which placed white Europeans at the top, had indeed changed Hasan Shah's and Ming's world of relative mutual trust and respect:

> We could only govern by maintaining the fact that we are the dominant race . . . [and] we must reserve the control to ourselves, if we are to remain at all.[71]

Such notions of European superiority were bolstered, in turn, through frequent rehearsals of a by then well-entrenched set of ideas about the specific inferiorities of the "native mind." To quote from one contemporary essay by Mary Pinhey published in the *Indian Magazine Review* in 1891:

> The astute Oriental mind rather delights in crooked ways. . . . There is a certain lumpiness about the Oriental character, a want of pluck and backbone, and general ignorance of what is expressed by the word 'honour', which can only be got rid of, if at all, by a thorough immersion in the spirit of English life.[72]

As Antoinette Burton pointed out in her analysis of this and other such articles that appeared in the *Indian Magazine* toward the end of the nineteenth century, what was "at stake" was the "preservation of imperial rule," as well as the "social-cultural hierarchies of colonialism in everyday life," both in India and "at home" in Britain.[73]

E. C. P. Hull's *The European in India or Anglo-Indian's Vade-Mecum* (1878), which included extensive sections on housekeeping in the colonies and "native servants," is another useful source that demonstrates the low opinion of natives held by the British in general, and the poor treatment of native employees in the colony in particular.[74] Consider, for instance, the following account of colonial living recorded by an Englishwoman and quoted in *The European in India*: "One of the most disagreeable feelings in India is that of constant suspicion induced by the native character; the mistress of a house is compelled to look after the most trifling details, or peculation will surely creep in . . . and life becomes a wearisome struggle against small encroachments."[75] Hull also records two memorable anecdotes that illustrate "the utmost contempt" with which British "masters" often treated their "native" servants—one involving a butler who was kicked down the stairs "for some trifling fault" by his employer and the other about an officer who would routinely administer much higher doses of medication than was warranted to his native servants, ignoring the possible adverse effects, perhaps even untimely deaths, that could result from such overdosing.[76] What is even more telling, perhaps, is the "tone" of jocularity and nonchalance with which such incidents were presented to the English reading public. As Hull quite effectively sums it up:

> The young Anglo-Indian arrives in . . . [India], as a rule, burdened with prejudices and misconception regarding native character. One person has told him, that the natives of India are "great liars"; another, that they are "dreadful thieves"; and altogether, he has unconsciously drawn for himself a picture of the "mild Hindoo," in which the worst horrors of the mutiny, human sacrifice, suttee, infanticide, thuggism—to say nothing of sensualism and mendacity—are the prevailing colours.[77]

Hull himself appears to have been considerably more "kindly" disposed toward the natives, although he admits that native servants "are indeed at times stupid, lazy, and careless . . . and by no means regardful of the truth. . . . [They also seem to lack] the spirit as is . . . often shown in England [by the housemaids, for instance]."[78] But, as he puts it, "they also possess characteristics, which in servants "cover a multitude of sins," being as a general rule respectful . . . and anxious to please their employers."[79] He also seems to be truly appreciative of the "fertility of resource of the native servant" and especially their patience with "Anglo-Indian querulousness" (produced apparently by the climate!). In short, as Hull sees it, Indians make good servants. As the following rather approving reference to the comments of another writer on the subject of native servants suggests, for all his appreciation he, too, was entirely convinced of the inferior location of the natives on some imaginary evolutionary hierarchy of the human species.

> An experienced observer writes: "I am often told that it is a proof of weakness to show consideration for servants . . . but I cannot divest myself of the idea, that he is, if *a very bad specimen of 'a man and a brother,'* at all events a fellow-creature, and I really cannot persuade myself or others that it does well to treat him like a brute . . . or to prevent his having his meals or sleep in peace." *A very proper view of the subject.*[80]

As Hull's account reveals, most British employers in the colonies clearly fell far short of even such obviously patronizing "considerate treatment" of natives.

If nineteenth-century notions of the essential inferiority of Indians facilitated mistreatment of native employees, it also dovetailed neatly with the colonial administration's preoccupation with making empire "respectable" through the scrupulous establishment of social, spatial, and sexual distance from natives in general.[81] The increased presence of British women in the colonies, especially after the opening of the Suez Canal in the mid-nineteenth century, facilitated the administration's efforts to cultivate practices "befitting the ruling race," set examples of adequate and proper femininity and masculinity, and maintain the "purity of the race."[82] And, of course, such efforts necessarily meant the end of official tolerance of interracial alliances between native women and British men, especially men holding high-ranking posts within the colonial establishment. Hull's *The European in India or Anglo-Indian's Vade-Mecum* (1878) offers an interesting contrast in this regard to the 1810 edition of Captain Williamson's *The East India Vade Mecum*. While the earlier publication devoted considerable attention to "native women," in Hull's account they make very few direct appearances. One exception, of course, is the "ayah,"[83] who, in Hull's idealized presentation, occupied "no unimportant sphere in a household where there . . . [were] ladies or children. . . . [She] quite . . . [identified] herself with her mistress's interests . . . and . . . [was] always ready to report any improper proceedings which may be going on among the other servants."[84]

In other words, even in her much demoted capacity as the mere servant, the native woman—Hindu or Muslim—continued to identify with and look after the interests of the colonizers! Note also the distinction Hull makes between the "Mohammedan" ayahs, who apparently "decline[d] more in the way of work than to 'do' her mistress's hair" and were "fastidious" and "better avoided," and the "Hindoo" ayahs who were "much more useful and obliging."[85] While Hull mentions nothing about concubinage or prostitution in his account, his passing comment on the relative willingness of "Hindoo ayahs" to do their masters' bidding seems to be curiously analogous to the growing popularity of Hindu prostitutes because they reputedly had "more attractive manners" than their Muslim and Christian counterparts.[86] Official accounts from the second half of the nineteenth century point to the growing number of Hindu upper-caste women—mostly widows or wives from *kulin* Brahmin families deprived of the option of remarriage or easy access to their husbands within the oppressive system of *kulin* polygamy—who joined the sex industry.[87] It is not inconceivable that some of these women also took up domestic work, a profession that was widely understood to involve some form of sexual service.[88]

Meanwhile, older forms of open interpersonal relationships between British men and professional dancers—captured in both accounts such as Hasan Shah's *Nashtar* and the paintings of nautch girls by European artists—began to disappear under the twin weight of the injunction against such intimacy and the increasing racial and cultural snobbery that now marked British attitudes toward native art forms. Indeed, British interventions, which gradually put an end to the supremacy of the Mughal and nawabi aristocracy in much of North India, also forced the profession of courtesans to the brink of extinction. By the latter half of the nineteenth century, therefore, courtesans who, as skilled musicians and dancers, had always enjoyed and depended on aristocratic patronage were forced to descend, indeed disappear, into the swelling ranks of conventional sex workers, which stripped the profession of much of its intellectual and artistic content, as well as its social standing.[89]

All this did not mean the end of contact between British men and native women, only now it happened within very different kinds of discursive frameworks and institutional arrangements. While "damsel-errantry"—the practice of British women traveling to the colonies in search of husbands—and the threat of severe social, even official, ostracism successfully "safeguarded" upper- and middle-class British officials from contact with Indian women, the colonial administration still had to worry about the sexual needs—or, as one British official put it, the "animal instincts"—of the large body of soldiers and sailors who arrived throughout the nineteenth century to maintain colonial rule.[90] As Sumanta Banerjee notes, the high incidence of venereal diseases among these soldiers as early as the 1820s eventually inspired the authorities to devise a solution that would fundamentally reorganize the profession of sex work: "an ample supply of 'native' prostitutes" who would be "adequately sanitized" for safe handling by the forces.[91] The result was the invention of a new class of "registered" prostitutes who were allowed to serve only British soldiers, were obliged to reside in specific areas known as Lal Bazaars (literally, "red markets"), and were subjected to periodic scrutiny for signs of venereal diseases.[92] In the 1880s, the total number of such registered prostitutes in Calcutta was about 7,000.[93] Of these, 5,834 were reported to be Hindu, 1,049 Muslim, and a mere 117 "European and other."[94] Thus, once again native women's sexual labor was pressed into the service of the queen's empire but this time within the much more violent discursive and material context of high imperial domination marked by ruthless contempt for, moral distance from, and organized abuse of native women.

The basic cognitive schemes of the interactions between British colonial servants and native women thus underwent a significant change over the course of the nineteenth century: from individually contracted relationships of "protection" and "belonging" to interactions between representatives of a colonizing state and some of the most vulnerable members of a subject population who were reduced to mere "bodies" that were treated as potential sources of disease and contamination, fit only to service the uncontrollable sexual urges of the "lowly Tommies." It is not hard to see how such handling of native women as chattel might have been facilitated by, and in turn reinforced, nineteenth-century European discourse about the discounted humanity of colonized populations.

There was yet another kind of British colonial narrative about the native woman. By the latter part of the nineteenth century, some British women—as missionaries, medical professionals, and reformers—had gained limited access to the zenanas of upper- and middle-class Hindus and Muslims who practiced (i.e., could afford to practice) seclusion of women. It was through the writings of professional and missionary women that the zenana—which until then had resisted penetration—appeared before the "public/colonial gaze" to offer yet another representation of Indian womanhood that could be used as further justification for the civilizing mission of colonial domination.

As Janaki Nair argues, in these writings Indian women seemed to inhabit "the very limits of society, the shadowy margins, now keeping out chaos and disorder, now embodying it."[95] It is also worth noting that, while at the beginning of the nineteenth century the zenana was seen as a site of potential reform and change, by the latter half of the century, in keeping with the new theories of the inherent and unalterable inferiority of non-European peoples, it was increasingly presented as a symbol of backwardness and the past, a site of "resistance to civilization," and even a source of "female power"—always, surely, the very antithesis of enlightenment.[96]

The new knowledge about the invisible "dark zenanas" also heightened existing doubts about the adequate "manliness" of Indian men by commenting on their tendency to "gossip like women,"[97] or do "women's work,"[98] in what appeared to observers as a gross "violation of the codes of nature."[99]

And, of course, it was the white colonizer's burden to rescue native women from the unnatural cruelty of both native men and native traditions. As recent work by feminist scholars has argued, British women who partook enthusiastically in the campaign to uplift—morally and otherwise—colonial subjects, especially women, did so to shore up support for the continuation of Britain's imperial projects abroad, as well as their own claims to a superior location in the ethnoclass-moral-cultural hierarchy that was at the center of imperial ideologies. To quote Antoinette Burton:

> The redemption of colonial peoples was considered to be instrumental to the survival of the nation-in-the-empire, and this may be counted as one reason British feminists adopted Indian women as objects of feminist salvation. . . . Taking responsibility for Indian women was at once a fulfillment of imperial duty and proof of imperial citizenship. . . . As the white woman's—and white feminists'—burden, Indian women represented . . . the colonial subjects in whose name British women's political authority in the imperial nation-state was justified.[100]

These were the various images of native women that circulated in British colonial discourse in the second half of the nineteenth century: backward, morally debased, diseased but useful—if only for the sexual gratification of lesser men or as servants—ready to please, victims of oppressive traditions, and objects of salvation. And behind this abominable state of native women, which the British made full use of both in discourse (to denigrate native peoples and cultures) and in practice (by exploiting the sexual labor of prostitutes, who were often forced into the profession by the growing impoverishment of the land and the destruction of indigenous rural industries under colonial rule) was the real villain of the colonial story: the worthless, oppressive and *unmanly* native man.[101]

CONCLUSION

Colonial discourse on native women in the subcontinent went through a discernible transformation in the course of the nineteenth century: from portrayals in an earlier era of Company rule, when native women often appeared in colonial accounts as housekeepers, servants, and slave-concubines but also as seductive nautch girls, mistresses, companions, and even common-law wives or bibis, to nineteenth-century portrayals of them as overwhelmingly debased and victimized—the ultimate proof of the barbarity and inherent inferiority of "Indian" cultures and men and hence a compelling justification for colonial rule in the subcontinent.[102] And these colonial representations, in turn, seem to have had a profound impact on subsequent discussions among reformists and nationalists—both reformists and traditionalists among them—over the woman question in the nineteenth century.

There is, of course, much debate among scholars over the extent to which Indians were influenced by British criticisms of native culture and traditions and the terms in which various factions among the indigenous literati, emerging middle classes, and even subaltern groups colluded with and/or resisted colonial discourse and praxis aimed at criticizing and "civilizing" natives.[103] Much has been written in this regard, and it would be futile to rehearse all of it here. Suffice it to say that the emerging middle classes among both Hindus and Muslims did in fact undertake reform initiatives in the mid- to late nineteenth century that were in part, though by no means entirely, shaped by British attitudes and practices toward Indian society. It is also true that neither the Hindu nor the Muslim elite in the late nineteenth century spoke in a unified voice; sections of the liberal middle classes among both Muslims and Hindus differed significantly from and sometimes clashed viciously with more orthodox factions, as well as the colonial administration, over the specific content of reforms, and such differences may have been both sharper and more publicly debated among Hindus than Muslims, at least in late-nineteenth-century Bengal if not in other parts of colonial India.[104]

For our present purposes, it is important to note that in the course of the long, drawn-out debates over the woman question in the nineteenth century indigenous elites, when they engaged colonial discourse at all, consistently privileged those colonial representations of native women that pertained to women as symbols of the glory (in orientalist interpretations) or denigration (in Anglicist and missionary views) of indigenous cultures and men.[105] Earlier colonial discourses on the seductive allure of native women, or even a critical appreciation of the appropriation of women's sexual and caretaking labor by the colonizers were, by contrast, conspicuously absent from nineteenth-century Hindu or Muslim elite deliberations over the appropriate place, conduct, education, and morality of women from the upper and middle classes and upper castes.[106] Indeed, it would not be far-fetched to read the specific absence from these discourses of "native companions"—who apparently "chose," or at least tolerated, European male company, thereby adding substance to nineteenth-century British mockery of the inadequate manliness of native men as a consequence of the reformist/nationalist impulse to suppress all female agency—even fictive accounts of them—that did not further the middle-class project of community and nation building.[107]

Finally, it is worth noting that this elite discourse of the nineteenth century and its many internal conflicts and contradictory concerns continue to preoccupy much of the historical scholarship on this era, making it difficult even to pose the question of native women companions within the terms of this historiography. In the preceding pages, I have argued that, whatever their legal status, sexual liaisons between native women and British men played a crucial role in the reproduction of the colonial workforce and were therefore a centrally significant social institution, even if colonial archives systematically undercut their specific importance and later historical accounts often presented these relationships as incidental, or even contrary, to the logic of high imperial domination, which demanded social distance between the rulers and the ruled. If the lack or suppression of specific information about or the undermining of the importance of interracial relationships in colonial accounts has to be understood as a desire on the part of the colonizers to clean up the image of the empire, then their absence from subsequent inquiries, within both nationalist discourse and its historiography, should also be read as a move, conscious or not, to make the nation and national history "respectable."[108] For the disappearance or specific appearance of native women—indeed, all subaltern subjects—from and in written histories is surely also a problem of the questions one brings to the (colonial) archive and the terms in which they are posed and not simply an unintended consequence of incomplete records.

2

THE POLITICS OF (IN)VISIBILITY

Muslim Women in (Hindu) Nationalist Discourse

The absence of Muslim women from the written history of nineteenth-century Bengal is typically explained in terms of their apparent "traditionalism/backwardness." As the conventional story of the Bengal Renaissance would have it, Muslim women in Bengal, unlike many Brahmo/Hindu upper-caste/middle-class women, were largely unable (perhaps even unwilling) to partake in the nineteenth-century reforms initiated by the Brahmo/Hindu bhadralok. And since normative historical accounts of nineteenth-century Bengal, if not India, typically center around the story of the birth of a cultural nationalism that was intrinsically linked to the Bengal Renaissance, Muslim women rarely appear in them except as footnotes, even when such accounts deal explicitly with women.[1] Indeed, from a survey of the extant historiography, one might get the impression that, as far as the public life of late colonial Bengal was concerned, Muslim women almost did not exist.

A closer look at the many periodicals in circulation in late-nineteenth-century and early-twentieth-century Bengal, however, yields a considerably more complex picture. As we shall see, it was in fact not uncommon to find references—both explicit and oblique—to Muslim men and women in the public discussions carried on by the Hindu/Brahmo bhadralok *and* bhadramahila. What is more, by the end of the nineteenth century, members of a slowly emerging Muslim middle class—a number of women among them—were also writing both in Brahmo- and Hindu-run periodicals and in others started by Bengali Muslim intellectuals themselves. Why, then, are Muslim women so often occluded in dominant historical accounts of late colonial Bengal, at least those that are produced in independent India when they were obviously present in contemporary public discourse both as objects of attention and increasingly as active participants in the early twentieth century?[2] And what, if any, is the relationship between the terms within which they were made visible in the popular Hindu/Brahmo discourse of colonial Bengal and their absence in much of the historiography of that era?

In the following pages, I investigate the ways in which gender and communal ideologies—inflected by British discourses of racial hierarchies—worked simultaneously to deny Muslim women even the circumscribed and sometimes dubious attention granted to Hindu/Brahmo women within a Hindu/Brahmo-dominated nationalist discourse, and to produce them either as invisible or as silent victims even when they wrote and spoke publicly.[3] I will argue that representations of Muslim women as "backward" and "victimized" have to be understood in relation to the production of the category "modern, ideal, Indian woman" as Hindu, upper caste, and middle class, and the simultaneous normalization of the category "Muslim" as predominantly male, violent, hypersexual, dissolute, and medieval, within bhadralok nationalist discourse in late-nineteenth-century and early-twentieth-century Bengal.[4] These images of the "backward/violent" Muslim man and the "modern/liberated" Hindu woman, in turn, underpinned the self-(re)presentations of the bhadralok—marked increasingly as the "effeminate *babu*" by the British—as civilized, modern, and liberal and hence deserving to lead the emergent nation. Finally, I will examine the role played by early Brahmo/Hindu women writers in producing Muslim women as the backward other and hence in bolstering their own image as liberated and modern.[5] While the literary productions of middle-class Brahmo/Hindu women in the late nineteenth century and early twentieth have been celebrated often enough as signs of "progress" and "enlightenment" among the Bengali *bhadrasampraday*, their complex ideological functions within nationalist discourse have remained relatively unscrutinized.[6] Recent critical work has gained some distance in highlighting the "tensions" immanent in the writings of the bhadramahila resulting from the "mismatch" between the limited concessions that the nationalist male elite were prepared to make and the desires, demands, and experiences of elite women themselves.[7] In light of this infinitely more nuanced appreciation of Brahmo/Hindu women's agency—not all of which was identified in an uncomplicated way in male nationalist projects—it becomes all the more necessary, I believe, to analyze the specific contributions of Brahmo/Hindu women in securing the negative images of Muslim women and/or their invisibility within nationalist discourse in late colonial Bengal.

Representations should, of course, not be confused with "material realities." To borrow Chandra T. Mohanty's words, the "connection between women as historical subjects and the re-presentation of Woman produced by hegemonic discourses is not a relation of direct identity, or a relation of correspondence or simple implication."[8] As mentioned above, notwithstanding the dominant discourses about the "progressive" Hindus and the "lagging behind" of Muslims in nineteenth-century Bengal—discourses that have been largely reinforced by the overwhelming focus on Hindu/Brahmo women in the subsequent historiography of that period—not all Muslim women were backward or victimized any more than all Hindu women were enlightened and emancipated, that is, according to the discourses of "progress" and "modernity" subscribed to by the liberal reformist/nationalist elite in Bengal.[9] Indeed, if the preponderance of Hindu women—many upper caste widows and kulin wives fleeing the myriad forms of oppression of the Brahminical Hindu patriarchal order among them—amid the twelve thousand or so prostitutes in mid-nineteenth-century Calcutta is any indication, Hindu women, especially from the upper castes and classes, were no less, and perhaps more, victimized than their Muslim counterparts.[10] And, of course, there was little to differentiate Hindu and Muslim women among the poor and lower castes—at least in terms of their experiences of both the material and discursive aspects of the processes of modernization and progress.[11]

My aim here is not so much to *correct* the problem of victim image and invisibility of Muslim women, or the overwhelming visibility of Brahmo/Hindu women in nationalist discourse and its historiography, as it is to understand the discursive practices that produced that invisibility/visibility, and locate the material contexts in which such discourses were embedded.[12] In the following two chapters, I investigate middle-class Bengali Muslim women's efforts to negotiate, and in the process "give the lie to," dominant representations of Muslim-ness prevalent at the end of the nineteenth and throughout much of the twentieth century.[13] Here I merely concentrate on untangling some of the links between the invisibility and victim image of Muslim women and the specific visibilities of both Muslim men and Brahmo/Hindu women within a Hindu-dominated nationalist discourse in late colonial Bengal and in the process attempt to rethink the silence around Muslim women in the written history of colonial Bengal as constitutive of normative historiography and not its unintended oversight. As I see it, such rethinking is urgently needed if we are to move beyond the tendency to read the absence or erasure of subaltern/non-dominant populations in and from historical accounts as either a "mistake" or, worse, indicative of some "lack" in such populations (e.g., "they did not participate" in the myriad rituals of modernity such as attending schools outside the home or participating in public political meetings and so on) toward a more critical understanding of how dominant and subaltern identities are constructed, in what terms the difference between them is established and normalized, the role of historiography—witting or unwitting—in that process, and, indeed, what counts as history.

The empirical focus is on representations of Muslim women within nationalist discourses in colonial Bengal; however, the problem of marginalization and negative images it addresses was certainly not unique to a single geographical or sociopolitical context or to Muslim women.[14] The chapter takes feminist theories of state and nation as its point of departure. It then brings some critical theoretical insights of black and third world feminist scholarship to bear on the problem of the occlusion of Muslim women from historical accounts of Bengal in the late nineteenth century and early twentieth produced by intersecting discourses of gender, community (religious in this case), and nationalism. In the second part of the chapter, I draw on articles from Bengali periodicals to show the ways in which Muslims in general, and Muslim women in particular, were constructed in the Brahmo/Hindu/ nationalist imaginary. I also reflect on the relationship between this economy of representations and the social, economic, and political formations that produced it.

FAMILY-NATION-WOMAN

Feminist scholarship in recent decades has repeatedly pointed out that women's integration into the modern nation-state system has historically followed a path fundamentally different from that of men.[15] According to feminist readings of social contract theory, men's original political rights in the public sphere derive not from their rights as "freeborn" sons but from masculine rule or the *husband's unquestioned sexual access to his wife's body* in the private sphere. And it is this "God-given" sexual right exercised over women within the family that defines men as individuals or citizens and women as their other, the fundamentally dependent subjects.[16]

The feminist argument about the connection between women's subordination within the private sphere and men's claim to political power can be profitably applied to the study of anticolonial nationalisms. One could argue, for instance, that in a colonial context, which by definition violates the "natural freedom" of colonized men, gaining legitimacy within the private or inner/spiritual realm of the family/nation takes on a certain poignancy for anticolonial nationalist men. In the context of nineteenth-century Bengal, for instance, this impetus to control women found powerful expression in the discourses of both the liberal and more conservative factions of the bhadralok. It seems that both liberal reformers and the Hindu revivalists in the nineteenth century saw the "Hindu way of life," especially as it related to the home and family (i.e., women), as the appropriate and only autonomous space in which they could launch their emancipatory project of creating a unique national culture.[17] But the two factions differed considerably in their respective approach to the "woman question." While the Hindu revivalists rejected the idea of "internal reform" and glorified Hindu domestic practices, especially the inhuman sacrifices demanded of women—best exemplified in the trauma of the child bride and the austere self-denial of the widow—as sacred, the liberal reformers, echoing orientalist interpretations, saw them as "distortions of an earlier purity" and a "symptom of present decay."[18] For the latter, forging a national culture involved the reforming of key institutions such as language and education but, most important, the family and women's position within it. The "ideal Indian women" of the liberal reformist imagination were expected to "modernize" themselves in order to become appropriate consorts of the modernizing bhadralok and, eventually, fitting emblems of the emergent nation.[19] And, as the household manuals of the late nineteenth century reveal, there were, perhaps for the first time, "unprecedented possibilities in the conditions of women's existence."[20]

It is important to remember, however, that while the liberal reforms initiated by the bhadralok brought important changes in the lives of many Hindu upper-caste and middle-class women in the course of the nineteenth century, in the final analysis, women's roles—even in their new incarnations—were scripted to meet the twin exigencies of vindicating Hindu men and culture. For all their differences, both the reformers and the Hindu revivalists, much like the British, were invoking the woman question as a means first of establishing their adequate manliness—defined, presumably, by the degree to which they could control or co-opt women within the family—and then of asserting and justifying their respective claims to or desire for political power. As Tanika Sarkar puts it, "Virtues accumulated through proper expertise in conjugality could equip the man to a share of power in the world; equally, proof of the absence of moral leadership here would disqualify him and explain his subjection."[21] Consequently, even in the liberal reformist nationalist imagination, the creativity of the new ideal woman was to be confined strictly to the realm of the family. Any agency shown by women that fell outside the limits of acceptable codes of behavior was liable to be denounced, ridiculed, and ultimately given short shrift within nationalist discourse at the end of the nineteenth century.[22] To quote Ghulam Murshid:

> The modernized women's unorthodox behaviour, particularly their reluctance, even refusal, to obey the custom of female seclusion, their acceptance of jobs and the gradual development in them of personal liberty in defiance of society antagonized the attitude of these men. . . . [T]he so-called reformers were prepared to allow women only "limited" freedom, the kind of freedom that would not substantially minimize men's authority over women.[23]

Or, as Malini Bhattacharya points out:

> The nationalists wished to perceive their women as mothers and sisters (maybe even lovers, as it turned out in Rabindranath Tagore's *Ghare Baire*), who must use their pristine power primarily to inspire them to be true "males" dedicated to the service of the motherland.[24]

Second, note that the said reforms—concerned with issues such as sati, widow remarriage, child marriage, kulin polygamy, and female education—

were aimed at changing the lives of upper-caste and middle-class Hindu women. The "myth of the golden age of Indian womanhood" popularized by the orientalist scholars, which provided much of the impetus behind these reform efforts, did not accord the same position of pride to *all* women. In the words of Uma Chakravarti, "This image foregrounded the Aryan woman (the progenitor of the upper-caste women) as the only object of historical concern. [Meanwhile] the Vedic dasi (the woman in servitude), captured, subjugated, and enslaved by the conquering Aryans, but who also represents one aspect of Indian womanhood, disappeared without leaving any trace of herself in nineteenth century history. . . . [The] Aryan woman came to occupy the centre of the stage in the recounting of the wonder that was India."[25] Women's participation in activities outside the domestic sphere in performance, religious preaching, or the labor force would mark them as deviants and prostitutes.[26] Thus, in colonial Bengal poor women who had to seek work outside the domestic sphere, indeed, whose labor enabled the *bhadramahila* to attain and maintain the high standards of refinement and chastity required of them, found themselves first ostracized by the bhadralok's vigorous campaign to distance their women and the *andar mahal* (inner quarters) from "the contaminating culture of the lower orders," and eventually simply written out of the new nation's normative history.[27]

Class and caste were not the only mechanisms of exclusion. In late colonial Bengal, yet another set of inequities—and one that remains mostly unexamined—existed between the discursive representations of Hindu and Muslim women even within the middle classes. It is true, as Ratnabali Chatterjee reminds us, that Muslims were generally "excluded" from deliberations over the substance of Hindu nationalist reforms in the nineteenth century.[28] However, as we shall see, such exclusion was neither automatic nor incidental; it had to be argued into place. What is more, Hindu/Brahmo women had an important role to play in this process of securing the negative representations and eventual invisibility of Muslim women in the dominant imaginations of the national modern.

Gender inequality is widely defined as a problem of men dominating women. Without in any way minimizing that particular equation, in the following section I would like to turn my attention to the problem of inequality among women in terms of their different appropriation and positioning within the dominant nationalist discourse in colonial Bengal and much of its subsequent historiography.

AMONG WOMEN

Feminist scholars have rightly taken the universalist pretensions of nationalist discourses to task by making exclusions (or inclusions) based on gender visible as constitutive elements in the process of imagining the nation and the definition of citizenship. However, as in their efforts to foreground gendered exclusions, mainstream feminists in the West have often glossed over, and even homogenized, the diverse experiences of different groups of women. In the famous words of the late Audre Lorde, "To imply . . . that all women suffer the same oppression simply because we are women is to lose sight of the many varied tools of patriarchy. . . . The oppression of women knows no ethnic nor racial boundaries, true, but that does not mean it is identical within those differences.[29]

Three insights from the internally differentiated but still loosely identifiable body of black/third-world/postcolonial/lesbian feminist scholarship, which repositions itself around the issue of difference (racial/sexual/class/community), are relevant for my purposes here.[30] First, the consciousness of being a woman is not only a product of gender ideologies, but also "the intersections of the various systemic networks of class, race, (hetero)sexuality, and nation . . . [which] position us as 'women.'"[31] Second, black/third-world/postcolonial feminists insist that gender, racial, or class oppressions—and privileges, for that matter—do not just coexist, but are *mutually constitutive*.[32] Treating these oppressions as parallel obscures the compound exclusions faced by poor, lesbian, and nonwhite women.[33] Third, and perhaps most important, these theorists argue that gender, racial, and class oppressions and privileges are *relational* in nature.[34] So, for instance, as Leila Ahmed has pointed out, when feminists in the West today assume that the only path to women's emancipation anywhere is through the blind adoption of western models, they, too, are implicated in a continued project of undermining "local" cultures that formed a core element of colonial politics in the past.[35] Or, as Kamala Visweswaran argues in her discussion of subalternity in India: "The gendered relation of subalternity means that with regard to the nominal subject of nationalist ideology, the figure of woman is subaltern; with regard to subaltern women, the recuperated middle-class woman as nationalist subject certainly is not."[36]

In other words, women become "women" not just in relation to men but also in relation to other women. According to such understandings of identity formation and assertion, therefore, the construction of the self is inextricably linked to the definition of an other. Indeed, as William E. Connolly put it: "Identity is established in relation to a series of differences that have become socially recognized. These differences are essential to its being. . . . Identity requires difference in order to be, and it converts difference into otherness in order to secure its own self-certainty."[37]

Unfortunately, the relational and contingent nature of identity is mostly ignored in studies of women in India. It is quite common, for instance, to treat the "problems" of different classes/communities (religious or otherwise) of women as distinct objects of inquiry; comparisons of the "status" of one group of women to that of another are also common. But it is hard to find attempts to systematically relate the "exclusions/exploitation" experienced by one group of women to the selective "inclusions/privileges" of another. Black/third-world/postcolonial feminist scholars would contend that it is not possible to understand representations of black women and their sexuality in the Americas without considering the corresponding constructions of white women as chaste.[38] As I see it, it is similarly impossible to fully appreciate the disappearing figures of the poor, low-caste, and Muslim women—irrespective of their class positions—in nationalist discourse and its historiography without considering the simultaneous foregrounding, indeed celebration, of Hindu middle-class/upper-caste women as the *adarsha bhartiya nari* (ideal Indian woman). This dominant nationalist discourse also produced the category "Mussalman" as violent and predominantly male even as it occluded the presence and work of Muslim women in colonial Bengal. In other words, it simultaneously gendered Muslim-ness and rendered the category "ideal Indian woman" Hindu.[39] But first a few words about the socioeconomic and political contexts that both gave rise to and were shaped by these discourses of representation are in order.

HINDU CONSTRUCTIONS OF MUSLIMS

At the end of the eighteenth century, the British East India Company introduced a set of land reforms in Bengal known as the Permanent Settlement of Land Revenues (1793), which ushered in, for the first time in the history of rural Bengal, the institution of private landholding in place of the system of overseer rights that existed under the Mughals. The Company's motivation behind this new measure was twofold: to stabilize a source of revenue for itself by fixing in perpetuity the revenue demands of the state on zamindars; and to create a comprador rentier class that would be loyal to British rule in the subcontinent. While the initial revenue assessment rates of the company administration were considered extremely high, forcing some members of the older aristocracy to lose their estates, in the long run the new arrangements left the zamindars virtually free to extort any amount of rent and cesses from their tenants and even evict them at will.[40]

Landownership thus emerged as a secure form of investment at the end of the eighteenth century, exempt as it was from further revenue assessments or government intervention. The result was a "radical transformation" in the organization of rural class relations in Bengal. On the one hand, the settlement undermined the social and economic control of the older, mostly Muslim, aristocracy and brought the peasantry—caught between the arbitrary rent and cess demands, and the threat of eviction—to the brink of ruin; on the other, it produced a new middle class of property owners with varying degrees of investment in landownership whose social and economic viability was tied to the rise and fall of the colonial economy.[41] In 1837, when Persian was replaced by English as the official language of administration, this new middle class, which was comprised mostly of upper-caste Hindus eager to learn English and, by some accounts, even to imitate the new rulers, further consolidated its socioeconomic position by monopolizing most of the jobs open to non-Europeans within the government bureaucracy.[42] Records suggest that some Bengali entrepreneurs even had enough surplus income to invest in shipping, mining, and insurance, both in collaboration with European capital, albeit limited, and in independent commercial ventures.[43]

The nineteenth-century "intellectual revolution" in Bengal, and the social reforms that came with it, are also widely understood to be the achievements of a particularly "enlightened" section of this new English-educated Hindu/Brahmo middle class. By all accounts, Muslims had little to do with this so-called renaissance in the first half of the nineteenth century.[44] Public debates over reforms in Bengal—as reflected in the pages of a slew of Bengali periodicals and newspapers, which appeared from the second decade of the nineteenth century onward—were also mostly preoccupied with issues pertaining to Hindus.[45] Muslims were not part of these debates on sati, widow remarriage, child marriage, kulin polygamy, or the systematization or, rather, Sanskritization, of Bengali as the appropriate medium of instruction; they seem to have taken to the print media much later.[46] Yet, interestingly enough, by the end of the nineteenth century we find these periodicals run by Hindus replete with disparaging representations of Muslim men and women. While the modernist and even secular among the Hindus/Brahmos earlier in the century had also "operated with a conception of 'Muslim tyranny' or [a] 'medieval' dark age . . . from which British rule . . . had been a deliverance," this sudden interest among the Hindu/Brahmo bhadralok in openly and insistently defining Muslims as the inferior other in the public discourse of this historical juncture needs some explanation.[47]

It is true that the nineteenth century began well for the newly emerging Hindu middle class. Indeed, up to the mid-nineteenth century, and even beyond, the bhadralok seem to have been secure enough for the more socially conscious among them to indulge in a degree of self-criticism over the issue of the rampant exploitation of peasants under the existing system of elastic rent and cess collections backed by British common law with its strict protection of private property. There is even evidence of some attempts at agrarian improvements on the part of enterprising zamindars interested in transforming landownership into a profitable enterprise beyond parasitic dependence on rent extraction alone. But the flush of confidence that accompanied the limited entrepreneurial success for some among the bhadralok in the early decades of the century began to wane as the financial boom fizzled by the 1840s. While foreign trade was always dominated by the British, in the second half of the century Bengali entrepreneurs increasingly lost control of local trade to enterprising Marwari merchants.[48] Bengali capital was gradually pushed out of all significant business ventures—widely understood to be not only the source of prosperity but the very condition of self-respect at that time.[49] The result was an increased dependence on landholding—sometimes only "petty intermediate tenure-holding"—as the only "safe form of investment."[50] Employment in foreign administrative and commercial establishments of course continued to be the other source of reasonable income for the bhadralok. But here also the most lucrative jobs in all sectors were typically reserved for Europeans. Consequently, as Sumit Sarkar reminds us, while "English education [may have] brought reasonable success in professions and services for some [among the bhadralok,] . . . [for] many more, it came to connote only humble clerical jobs (*chakri*) in government or mercantile offices, once again usually British-controlled."[51] Needless to say, such employment was both insecure and burdened with daily tribulations and ignominy in the context of a racialized colonial society. In the second half of the nineteenth century, Bengali middle-class existence was thus hardly an example of undifferentiated, seamless material prosperity, and establishing its claim to moral or intellectual leadership in any sphere—"inner/spiritual/of the nation" or "outer/material/of the state," to borrow Partha Chatterjee's formulations—was no mean task for the bhadralok.

The colonial administration, meanwhile, was experiencing its own changes. As we saw in chapter 1, throughout the nineteenth century, and especially in the wake of the 1857 revolt, the British were moving away from their earlier practice of relatively easy mingling with the "natives" toward an official policy of establishing greater social distance between themselves—the "ruling race"—and their Indian subjects. One consequence of this shift was an increased interest in categorizing peoples into "supposedly primordial communities of ascription . . . constituted by castes, tribes, races, and religious groups," which, as Mrinalini Sinha has recently pointed out, were in fact "newly homogenized modern constructs . . . [that] became the preferred avenues for class mobility as well as for retention of status and class power in India."[52] A second consequence was that the new colonial administration under crown rule began to take a greater interest in actually governing the erstwhile ignored and increasingly restless (mostly rural) masses, albeit to manage and control them in order to safeguard the interests of the British empire.[53] This changing attitude of the administration is reflected in the "Dedication" of W. W. Hunter's 1871 book, *The Indian Mussalmans*. Hunter writes, "The greatest wrong . . . that the English can do to their Asiatic subjects is not to understand them. . . . In these pages I have tried to bring out . . . the past history and present requirements of [a] persistently belligerent class [the Muslim and low-caste peasantry] . . . [which continues to be] a source of permanent danger to the Indian empire."[54] Hunter was referring to the religiously syncretic *atrap* (converts to Islam) and low-caste Hindu peasants of East Bengal who had endured extreme forms of exploitation by the zamindars since the introduction of the Permanent Settlement. Since the 1840s, these *ryots* (peasants) were involved in periodic uprisings around issues of caste and class oppression by zamindars and planters, forcing the colonial government to pay attention to some of the grievances of this "belligerent class," which they both despised as racially inferior and were wary of.[55]

If the rent reforms—undertaken in the wake of violent peasant resistance to the forced cultivation of indigo by European planters and instigated in part by missionary interventions on behalf of the ryots against both zamindars and planters — were among the first policy manifestations of this shift in colonial attitudes toward the masses, they also signaled the end of an era of tacit complicity between the earlier company administration and the so far loyalist Hindu bhadralok.[56] The colonial administration's apparent reluctance to intervene on behalf of the predominantly Hindu landlords during the powerful and well-organized riots by tenant peasants in Pabna in 1873, as well as its subsequent proposal (eventually much moderated) to give tenants rights to the land they cultivated came as something of a shock to the bhadralok's sense of security and entitlement.[57] For, as Tanika Sarkar succinctly puts it:

> Security of property was part of a larger complex of confidence bred out of caste, educational and gender privileges, all of which were [now] threatened by liberal reformism, missionary initiative, and state legislation. . . . [Colonial] interference in the hitherto closed world of largely upper-caste Hindu zamindars and the lower-caste or Muslim peasant was . . . co-extensive with very similar intrusions into the closed world of Hindu domestic practices. Both aroused a keen sense of the fragility of economic and domestic arrangements that had cushioned some of the traumas of the Hindu bhadralok.[58]

Consequently, in the 1870s, the discussion of peasant riots revolved insistently around the twin anxieties of "loss of caste" and "loss of virtue in women." And the agent of both these calamities was the violent, irreverent, sexually aggressive — in short, powerfully masculine but "uncivilized" — Muslim male, who was repeatedly accused of insulting and destroying the caste of respectable men, breaking idols, and, of course, violating "the chastity of females of gentle blood" in contemporary bhadralok discourse.[59]

To add to the bhadralok's woes, in the 1870s the British government began to consider steps to promote mass education — a move deeply resented and feared by upper-caste/middle-class Hindus, invested as they were in protecting their privileged access to professional opportunities. Indeed, by the beginning of the twentieth century, and especially after the first partition of Bengal (1905–11), this second bastion of Hindu middle-class economic security also was threatened by the swelling numbers of educated Bengalis, among them members of a slowly developing middle class. To the Hindu bhadralok, who were used to the subservience of lower-class and lower-caste groups (including large numbers of Muslim peasants and artisans — the atrap), the growing self-assertion and slow upward mobility of some from those previously subjugated ranks must have appeared as intolerable transgressions of normative hierarchies.

The increasing tendency to represent Muslims as the "inferior dissolute other" within Hindu middle-class discourse at the end of the nineteenth century has to be located within this rapidly shifting material and discursive context, which produced tremendous anxiety among the Hindu bhadralok over their ability to maintain their social and economic advantages and their attempts to establish their legitimacy as leaders of the emergent nation.[60] The literary efforts of the Hindu bhadramahila were also products of this context of flux and uncertainty. But, as we shall see, not all ideological functions of their specific efforts can be derived automatically from the exigencies of male nationalist political agendas.[61]

The publication of vernacular periodicals and newspapers in the nineteenth century and early twentieth is typically considered to be part of the intellectual awakening of the Bengali middle class. In light of the preceding discussion, however, these periodicals appear to be much more than the intellectual coming of age of a colonized people. Together they marked an important space in which the idea of India as a national community could be imagined and experienced simultaneously by a growing vernacular readership.[62] They also provided a discursive site in which battles over the definition of the ideal Indian woman (symbol of the nation) and man (the normative citizen-subject) were fought. As the following discussion will show, elements of right-wing Hindu political rhetoric—which came to be explicitly articulated in Bengal during the second and third decades of the twentieth century and is widespread in India today—can already be found in the pages of popular periodicals run by ostensibly the most educated and "enlightened" sections of the Hindu/Brahmo bhadrasampraday, both men and women, in the late nineteenth century.[63]

Each of the periodicals I quote below was chosen because of its explicit interest in women's issues and because women regularly contributed to it.[64] Three of these—*Antahpur*, *Mahila*, and *Bharat Mahila*—in fact had women editors. The articles taken from the first two were published in the final decade of the nineteenth century; those quoted from *Bharat Mahila* were all published in 1913. A fourth, *Bamabodhini Patrika*, a monthly meant explicitly for women, was established as early as 1863. Its objective was to address the "dearth of reading material particularly suitable for Bengali women" and to "educate . . . [them] in subjects such as Bengali, History, Geography, Elementary Science,

Hygiene, Astronomy, Childcare, Housekeeping, and Religion."[65] The *Bamabodhini Sabha*, the association behind this enterprise, also began a correspondence course for women through the *Bamabodhini Patrika*, known as *Antahpur Shiksha* (Zenana Education).[66] As the first periodical to focus explicitly on women's needs, and one that was not only popular[67] but was also published continuously for sixty years,[68] *Bamabodhini Patrika* remains one of the most important documents of nineteenth-century middle-class Bengali society. I also draw briefly on the *Nabanoor*, which was an early influential periodical published by Muslim intellectuals in circulation between 1903 and 1906.

The articles published in the first four periodicals mentioned above—many of which were written by Hindu and Brahmo women—reveal certain common tendencies.[69] First, Muslims are overwhelmingly portrayed in them as unscrupulous, debauched, and abusive—in short, an uncivilized *jat*"—a word that translates variously as "caste," "race," "community," or "nationality" and can be used to denote occupational groups.[70] Second, the real aim of these articles seems to be to explain the "fall" of Aryan/Hindu "civilization" from its glorious days in a supposed classical antiquity to a period of medieval backwardness; Muslims are introduced into these discussions mostly as agents of this tragic downfall. Third, the authors, who were mostly "liberal" in their outlook, frequently pick on very specific institutions such as purdah, child marriage, and polygamy—which were at the heart of hotly contested debates in the nineteenth century—and blame the Muslims for having introduced them to "India."[71] This maneuver served the dual purpose of both vindicating the essential "humanism" of "Hindu culture" in the eyes of the British and strengthening their arguments regarding the illegitimacy of such practices in the struggles against Hindu orthodoxy. For instance, an essay published in 1891 in *Bamabodhini Patrika* claims with perfect certainty that the institution of purdah was unknown to India before the arrival of Muslims. According to this article, "It was in emulation of this Muslim practice, and to save themselves [or their women] from the reckless exploitation of Muslim rulers that Hindus gradually adopted the practice."[72]

In another article, which appeared a decade later in a women's magazine, themes such as nostalgia for an Aryan (read Hindu) past, hatred for Muslims, and the projection of the modern idea of an "Indian nation" onto a mythical, timeless past find forceful expression. Note also the use of the word *jati* to signify innate difference, possibly racial difference, as the reference to Europeans—whose "innate racial difference" was something of an established fact in nineteenth-century colonial and nationalist discourse—would seem to suggest.

> Today when we talk of civilized *jati*, we usually refer to inhabitants of Europe and America. But how old is this civilization in England and America? Indians had reached the highest level of civilization much before [the Westerners]. . . . At that time . . . many women were equal to men in learning and thinking. Women used to participate in academic discussions with men in public forums. . . . Mussalman . . . attacks and Mussalman rule put an end to the flow of progress in this country, and it fell into the clutches of moral degeneration and miserable times. [The Mussalmans] indulged in all kinds of debauchery. They also practiced seclusion of women.[73]

The theme of degeneration under Muslim rule—moral, political, cultural, or social—seems to have been particularly widespread in the discourse of the bhadralok in the latter half of the nineteenth century. As early as 1865, Kailashbasini Debi, one of the first Bengali women to write publicly on social issues, wrote a piece titled "Hindu Female Education and Its Progress" in which she "put the blame" for the "decline" of India's "glorious past" squarely on "Muslim rule."[74] As the following excerpt from an article written by a male author shows, such accounts of a "glorious Hindu history" were typically accompanied by prejudicial statements about Muslims. It is also worth noting that the Muslim subject highlighted in all these "historical" accounts was typically male, tyrannical, and the object of fear and hatred.

> By the fifteenth century, Bengali literature . . . which had already reached a certain maturity, was . . . wiped out by the destructive practices of oppressive Muslim [rule]. If the destructive policies of Muslims had not ruined it, Bengali literary tradition would certainly have been acknowledged as both an ancient and a great tradition. So many invaluable manuscripts have been lost under the torture and oppression of Muslims.[75]

In other words, according to this author and many of his contemporaries, Muslim rule was seen as not only subjugating but destructive. It was also held responsible for many of the oppressive gender norms for which the Hindus were criticized roundly by the Anglicists and missionaries.[76]

But where did these authors get their ideas? They cite various "historians," interpreters of the Vedas, and, of course, both orientalist and other European scholars—who were widely accepted as the most authoritative nineteenth-century sources on "India's" past. Thus, in the closing years of the century *Bamabodhini Patrika* carried the following translation of a speech given by Lord Bethune almost fifty years earlier at the inaugural function of the Bethune School, ostensibly in support of the claims made by contemporary Hindu authors in its pages.[77]

> The practice of secluding your women and their present ignorant state are not sanctioned by your ancient [Aryan] society. I believe that it is in emulation of the conquering Muslims that this practice started here. . . . The women of your sages and of the nobility enjoyed considerable freedom.[78]

Where did Bethune get the information that allowed him to speak with such certainty about a Vedic past? We do not know. Most of the writers apparently were unconcerned with the authenticity of sources or of the claims they made.

It was quite acceptable, fashionable even, to openly air negative opinions about Muslims in late-nineteenth-century Bengal without furnishing supporting evidence. There was, and still is, considerable debate, for instance, surrounding the beginnings of purdah as an institution in the subcontinent. Pandita Ramabai Saraswati, who was widely known as an exceptional scholar and social reformer of that time and one of the few women in the nineteenth century successful in supporting themselves with their writing, believed that the practice of secluding women was in place in what is India today as early as the sixth century BC.[79] Indeed, in this Ramabai's views were not far from those held by James Mill and other missionary critics of Hindu civilization, who, as we have seen, were not enamored of India's past the way the orientalists had been.[80] Not one of the authors quoted above, however, as much as engaged this debate. It seems that their political agenda was not so much to address social ills as to be able to pin the existence of such ills on others, namely, Muslims. A few Hindu authors did protest against this tendency to fabricate histories to fit the increasingly hegemonic account of India's past. In an article titled "Gotadui Katha" (A Few Words), published in 1904 in *Nabanoor*, Nirmal Chandra Ghosh commented on the unfair representations of Muslims by Hindu authors. As he saw it, many of the articles appearing in contemporary monthly magazines were presented in the guise of history but in fact had little to do with "reality." However, Ghosh seems to have been in the minority.[81]

From numerous such articles that were published at that time, it appears that the only history that the Hindu/Brahmo nationalist elite would allow

Muslims in India was one of shame, immorality, misrule, and finally of defeat by a superior power. It is as if the Hindu middle class of nineteenth-century Bengal was entirely in denial about the traditions of secularism, rationalism, and nonconformity in pre-British Muslim India.[82] What is more, the category "Muslim" is not only vilified in these writings but is almost always masculinized. The dominant trend at the end of the nineteenth century—in contrast to the reformist moment earlier in the century when it was possible to engage in some degree of autocritique—seems to have been to blame Muslims for inventing all oppressive practices against women, thereby absolving Hindus of much of the responsibility for the most severely criticized aspects of "Hindu society" within colonial discourse.

THE ZENANA AND THE WOMAN QUESTION

And how were Muslim women represented? In her discussion of the writings of Englishwomen on Indian women, Janaki Nair has pointed out the importance of the zenana—the "cavernous depths of 'idolatry and superstition'"—as a trope in colonial discourse on India. She argues that the zenana and the supposed depravities it sanctioned had come to be practically synonymous with "Indian womanhood" and women's "oppression." Given the centrality of this trope in colonial criticisms of "India's culture," it is not difficult to comprehend why self-professed liberal Hindu/Brahmo writers would be keen on distancing themselves from the institutions of seclusion (purdah) and polygamy that the zenana symbolized. It is also easy to see why they would want to pin the invention and widespread adoption of these "primitive" practices on Muslim rule.

In the second half of the nineteenth century, these writers included a growing number of Hindu and Brahmo women from educated, "progressive" Bengali families who participated enthusiastically in this project of (re)writing history. As I see it, for these women, representing Muslim women as "hapless victims" of lustful Muslim men may have served a few additional purposes. First, portraying Muslim women as "sexual servants," secluded, enclosed, unable to resist Muslim men, and hence somehow weak—both morally and physically—allowed Hindu/Brahmo women to highlight their own image as free, chaste, and strong mothers and consorts pressed into the service of the nation/community.[83] Second, to the extent that seclusion and visibility outside the home were widely understood to be indicative of class status in the nineteenth century, denouncing the zenana as medieval and backward, and hence distancing themselves discursively from it, allowed the "new ideal women" to recast their appearances in the public sphere in the name of "modernizing" and "progress" without compromising their class status or their respectability. Finally, the supposed contrast between the "enclosure," imagined backwardness, and victimization of Muslim women and Hindu women's "modernity" gave the latter the option of "counting their blessings" for being part of the dominant community rather than confronting, criticizing, or resisting their subjugation by Hindu/Brahmo men.[84]

Many of the articles written by Hindu and Brahmo women at this time focus exclusively on women; others deal only with Muslims and are full of negative allusions to "dissolute Muslim men." While Muslim women do not always figure in these articles—except in oblique references in relation to Muslim men—when they do appear they are almost always sexualized and portrayed as helpless victims of male oppression and/or their own moral and sexual ignorance or weakness, which apparently facilitated their oppression in the first place. Not surprisingly, underlying all such denouncements of the backwardness/depravity/enclosure/exploitation of Muslim rule is a persistent discourse of progress and civilization that was clearly a product of the colonial encounter—not in the simple sense of wholesale borrowing but one that had been made consistent, to echo Partha Chatterjee's reading, with the needs of nationalist politics.[85]

We will begin with an article, published in 1903 in a periodical for women, in which the author decries the abominable condition of women under Muslim rule.

> Each *badshah*, *nawab* or *amir* would keep hundreds of wives imprisoned in the inner quarters. . . . One man could do anything that pleased him . . . [and] he would keep hundreds of helpless women enslaved in dark prisons—what terrible exploitation, what injustice![86]

For all her apparent compassion, the author clearly seems to distance herself from the masses of "helpless women," who appear strictly as sexual beings and hence, by implication, are inferior to the modern, educated women with whom the author obviously identifies. Note also that, while the categories *badshah*, nawab, and amir—all of which refer conventionally to Muslim rulers—are highlighted, there is no mention of similar practices by Hindu monarchs or

Europeans in the eighteenth century and the early nineteenth, not to mention the contemporary practices of polygamy among kulin Brahmin Hindus. In other words, while the article is apparently about exploitation of women, its real intent seems to be to indict Muslims, especially the sexually hyperactive Muslim man—already the object of Hindu male anxiety in the late nineteenth century and the main villain-to-be in the ugly controversies that would erupt around the "abductions of Hindu women" in the 1920s in Bengal.[87]

The idea of the licentiousness of Muslim rulers and their sexualized consorts, as well as the idea of a "fall" into medieval depravity under Muslim rule, seems to have been pervasive enough to underlie even discussions that were apparently about other things. Take, for instance, the following article by Hemantakumari Choudhuri (1901) in which the author apparently speaks "of a need for change in the attitudes of women towards their own bodies."[88] The author begins by blaming Muslims for ushering into Bengal yet another practice that was deemed distasteful in progressive Hindu/Brahmo circles at the turn of the century. Note also the ease with which the author establishes the essential Hindu-ness of the categories Indian and Bengali and the foreignness of Muslims:[89]

> Indian women, imitating the Begums of the Nawabs, started using very fine or transparent clothes. As a result of this, wives of Bengali homes felt no shame in going to bathe [in such attire]. . . . But finally many have begun to realize the bad taste involved in the custom of wearing one transparent/fine piece of cloth.[90]

In an essay titled "Child Marriage and Seclusion," published around the same time, the author, Syamasundari Debi, actually spells out the "difference" between "backward," sexually exploited *other* women and "liberated" Bengali women, presumably like herself. According to her, in societies that are against female education and "liberty," and advocate *purdah*, women tend to have "loose morals." She goes on to cite "Muslim society" as an example of such a society. It seems that Syamasundari Debi's article was so well received in bhadralok intellectual circles that it was given an award.[91]

In another prize-winning essay, which appeared serially over ten months in *Bamabodhini Patrika*, Mankumari Basu, an accomplished, well-known, and respected writer of late-nineteenth-century Bengal, discusses the "situation of Indian women in the past hundred years." Mankumari had received a formal education and was a poet of some renown. Yet her essay features the same predictable figures of the accomplished Aryan woman, the tyrannical Muslim ruler, and the weakened Hindu man. Perhaps more tellingly, even in this period of heightened nationalist sentiments in the last decade of the century her reference to the British as having saved "Indians" from the clutches of Muslim rule seemed to draw no public criticism!

Mankumari's equation of Indian with Hindu is also remarkably effortless, turning Muslim rule into simply another incarnation of colonial rule. And through this narrative maneuver the story of Hindu women becomes the normative story of Indian women. Actually, Mankumari is more specific. In her description of the many welcome changes the nineteenth century had brought to the lives of the "Indian woman," she mentions a switch from the use of jewelry made of silver to the exclusive use of gold—a change that evidently only the more affluent among the bhadralok could afford. From similar articles published around this time, such as one by Saratkumari Chaudhurani entitled "Ekal O Ekaler Meye" (1891), which record the use of gold jewelry and changing women's attire as indicative of the advent of the modern age in India, one is left with a fairly clear idea of who, in the eyes of Mankumari and her contemporaries, constituted the emerging nation.[92]

The figure of the Muslim woman, of course, does not appear directly in Mankumari's rather seamless imagination of the (Hindu, upper-caste/middle-class) national community, which, as Malini Bhattacharya reminds us, seems to have been quite the norm among Hindu/Brahmo women writers in late colonial Bengal.[93] Yet it is possible to see the signs of her erasure even in this clean—or perhaps cleansed—account of Bengali society. Consider, for instance, the following statement about the beginning of the Bethune school in 1849:

> At that time there was much agitation around the issue of women's education in this country. Many men, who realized that Mr. Bethune was . . . providing education to women with the help of Hindu pundits, in an atmosphere in which there was no fear of contact with the daughters of *lowly*, and *dishonest* people, sent their daughters and sisters to school.[94]

Contemporary records show that in 1822 a Muslim woman had started a school for girls in the Shyambazar area of North Calcutta.[95] Unfortunately, schools at that time only attracted girls from poor and often low-caste Hindu, Muslim, and Christian convert families who were lured into schools mainly by the small amount of compensation offered to them for attending. Given the rarity of such efforts, it would not be surprising if prominent members of the Bengali intelligentsia, such as Mankumari Basu, were aware of them. What Mankumari and her contemporaries certainly knew about were the (in)famous attempts by some *baijis* and prostitutes in nineteenth-century Bengal to enrol their children in the educational institutions attended by the children of "respectable" middle-class families—attempts that the bhadralok fiercely resisted.[96] And, while the overall proportion of Hindu women involved in prostitution was reportedly higher than that of Muslim women in Bengal,[97] the overwhelming popular association of the category *baiji* in nineteenth-century Calcutta was still with Muslim courtesans displaced from the nawabi courts of North India. Mankumari's use of the word *neech* (lowly) therefore can be interpreted as a reference to the *patita* (fallen)—a description typically used for prostitutes—as well as low-caste Hindus and Muslims against whom the bhadrasampraday defined itself in the nineteenth century.

One could go on, but I will only cite one more set of examples of Hindu/Brahmo women's perceptions and representations of Muslim women from the early twentieth century. In 1903, *Mahila*—a women's periodical—carried a provocative essay by a then unknown Mrs. Rokeya Sakhawat Hossain, a Muslim woman. The essay, titled "*Alankar* or the Badges of Slavery," was a severe indictment of gender inequality in which she compares the gift of jewelry from a husband to his wife with chains of bondage.[98] The essay shocked and infuriated many among the bhadramahila, drawing a number of angry rebuttals to Rokeya's critique of women's complicity in their own subordination. As one of the respondents put it:

> It seems that the author wants to see wanton behavior among women. Instead of womanly modesty, grace, gentleness, devotion, [and] the willingness to serve . . . [she] wants to see the development of a harsh, abnormal independence. . . .[99]

Or, as another wrote:

> Accepting one's subordination to one's husband is not slavery; it is a woman's [most prized] ornament. . . . I don't know what kind of a woman would equate serving one's husband with slavery. . . . *A woman must always be subordinated to her husband; there is nothing wrong with that.*[100]

That many of the respondents were piqued by Rokeya's harsh criticism of a widely accepted and desired sign of husbandly affection is perhaps not surprising. What is striking, in my view, are the terms in which the respondents constructed their criticism of Rokeya's position. Almost everyone argued that women ought to be "governed" by their husbands and "too much freedom" was not good for women. Such assertions of women's "natural subordination" to men would seem to indicate that the authors, who were "recuperated" and "modern" female subjects enjoying the privilege of voice and, in all likelihood, a degree of mobility outside the zenana/*antahpur*, were nonetheless fundamentally uncomfortable with the idea of women's independence—intellectual, emotional, and economic—that informs Rokeya's essay. And yet, as recent feminist rereadings of texts written by women at the end of the nineteenth century show, it was not unheard of for Hindu/Brahmo women at that time to seek greater "social power," to go beyond the sanctioned role of serving "the revised needs of the family and the home," and to criticize the education system at the end of the nineteenth century for failing to "inculcate" an adequate "sense of dignity and confidence in women" or to advocate greater participation of women in the public domain, including searching for vocations.[101] What conclusions should one draw from this apparent contradiction? That progressive thinking among Brahmo/Hindu women was in fact rare? Or that Hindu/Brahmo women were less likely to tolerate criticism coming from a Muslim woman than from one of their own?

The second question becomes particularly salient when we note that, rather than seriously engage the content of Rokeya's essay, a majority of the respondents sought to simply dismiss her criticism as a kind of rabid reaction stemming from the extreme exploitation of Muslim women within "Muslim society." To quote from an editorial comment published in *Mahila* in 1903:

> For various reasons, women and daughters in Muslim families have to put up with many different forms of torture and hardship from their menfolk. . . . Perhaps this is why [Rokeya's] attack on them has somewhat crossed [accepted] limits. But . . . not all men are . . . against the education and overall progress of women. . . . In fact many among the bhadralok [educated/civilized men] are quite in favor of such changes.[102]

Even in this mild response, the author simply refuses to confront the implications of Rokeya's denouncement of women's collusion in perpetuating their own exploitation for a critical understanding of Hindu women's position, preferring instead to invoke the familiar trope of "tortured" Muslim women.

Not every article was quite as tempered in tone as the editorial cited above. For instance, one respondent attacked Rokeya for her "unreasonableness."

> The way in which the Muslim sister . . . has painted men as cruel and selfish . . . I can swear that no bhadramahila can agree with her. . . . I don't know about the Muslim community, but there is quite a wave of advancement among Hindu women throughout Hindu society these days. In India, women are treated as goddesses by Hindus; they worship women. . . . If the Muslim sister could demonstrate even one improvement . . . [that she suggests in her essay] with her own life, then many of the problems of society would be solved of course. When will this terrible practice of parda, so common in her community, stop? . . . It is so ridiculous to cover one's beautiful body entirely with an ugly veil such as the borkha. . . . [It is] grotesque.[103]

There is no denying that Muslim women were oppressed in myriad ways in late-nineteenth-century Bengal; Rokeya's own work bears poignant testimony to the difficulties imposed by the institution of strict purdah on middle- and upper-class Muslim women.[104] But is it really true that women's oppression was no longer an issue among the Hindu bhadrasampraday? Or did Rokeya's intervention touch on an issue that did not bear scrutiny? How can we account for the stark contrast, for instance, between these assertions of women's exalted positions in Hindu society and the descriptions of abject misery of the "high-caste Hindu woman" denounced so eloquently in the contemporary writings of Pandita Ramabai?[105]

The irony, of course, is that Rokeya's Hindu critics, who were quick to pity Muslim women for their "backwardness," were mostly unwilling to share their social space and privileges with Muslim women—*even when they came from comparable class locations*. Consequently, even at the end of the nineteenth century, fifty years after it was founded, the Bethune School remained inaccessible to Muslim women.[106] Rokeya, on the other hand, spent most of her adult life struggling to further through her writing and activism the twin causes of education and economic self-sufficiency for women, particularly Muslim women, even from within the context of purdah. As Shibnarayan Ray has pointed out, "No contemporary Hindu woman is known to have written this kind of [critical] essays."[107]

As we have seen, the reform efforts of elite Hindu/Brahmo men in the nineteenth century may have benefited women of similar socio-cultural backgrounds, but equality of the sexes was never part of their agenda.[108] Indeed, by the end of the nineteenth century many among the bhadralok were increasingly uneasy with, even hostile to, the prospect of further reforms that could affect the inner domain of the family and home, especially their control over women.[109] While some scholars have explained the bhadralok's turn away from a liberal social reform agenda as a strategy for resisting colonial hegemony, others have read such reactions on the part of the bhadralok as moves to contain women's agency and not simply a function of nationalist opposition to colonial interference in the "inner autonomous" realm of the home/nation.[110]

The articles discussed above were written amid noisy attacks mounted by Hindu traditionalists—who were an especially vocal presence in the public discourse of Bengal from the last quarter of the nineteenth century—against the supposed "irresponsibility, flightiness, laziness and sexual laxity of educated women."[111] The visceral responses to Rokeya's criticism of women's continued subservience—economic and sexual—might therefore be read as the panicked reaction of elite Hindu/Brahmo women who had gained certain privileges, symbolic or otherwise, through their partnership in the projects of a dominant class and community. While scholars have noted the "overarching presence of class hegemony in the [bhadramahila's] construction of images of power and freedom," their complicity in communal identity formation/calcification in the late nineteenth century and early twentieth seems to have received little or no attention.[112]

Notwithstanding the courageous attempts made by individual women writers and reformers to seek greater social power for women, it would be fair to say that the patriarchal/nationalist accommodations of the nineteenth century were more about men changing some of their ways, and women adjusting to such changes, than any fundamental alteration in the organization of power resulting from initiatives undertaken by women. In this context of piecemeal and often unsatisfying reform, the "visibility" of the supposed (greater) "misfortunes" of Muslim women seems to recast the Hindu bhadramahila's continued domination by men as more bearable, perhaps even "invisible," allowing them to bask in a feeling of relative well-being. Consequently, a majority of Hindu middle-class women, for whom education was a way to secure educated husbands and an avenue out of the vice grip of the traditional Hindu patriarchal order, found Rokeya's call to "self-sufficiency" threatening, offensive, perhaps even incomprehensible.[113]

By the second decade of the twentieth century, in the aftermath of the first partition of Bengal in 1905 (revoked subsequently in 1911), the increased separatism among certain sectors of upper-class and middle-class Muslims in Bengal (best exemplified perhaps by the establishment of the Muslim League in Dhaka in 1906 and the eruption of communal riots in East Bengal), and the explicit tendencies of the Swadeshi movement to combine politics with Hindu-revivalism, the ideas about Bharat (India) as a nation and its essential Hindu-ness seem to have condensed further in the minds of many in the Hindu/Brahmo middle class.[114] As the essays published in 1913–14 in a prominent periodical, *Bharat Mahila*, show, most of the issues discussed were focused on the experiences of Hindu/Brahmo women.[115] Thus, for example, in a report on the Bangiya Sahitya Sammelan, the editor writes:

> Bharat [India] is currently absorbing the lights of all the civilizations of the world. This will change the Bengali ideals of women's lives as well. The great Indian ideals of *Sita*, *Sabitri*, *Subhadra*, *Damayanti*, *Gargi*, *Maitreyi*, *Gautami*, *Sanghamitra* will also once again find expression in us.[116]

Or, as Pratibha Nag writes in another article in the same journal:

> In the middle ages . . . women's lives were entirely subject to the mercy of men. . . . Who does not know about the [in]famous practice of sati, or the infanticide of little girls in Rajputana? And everyone knows about the cruel, hard oppression of women by the Muslims. . . . When will those days of Sita-Sabitri's devotion [to their husbands], Gargi-Maitreyi's divine knowledge, Lilabati-Kshana's learning and intelligence, or Draupadi-Subhadra's caring arrive in Bharat [India] once again?[117]

Notice how easily the authors invoke mythical Aryan women as the ideals for modern Indian womanhood in these essays. All the women mentioned as potential models for emulation and respect are Aryan/Hindu. In contrast, not even one Muslim woman is acknowledged as accomplished in any way. There is no mention, for instance, of Gulbadan, the daughter of the first Mughal emperor Babur, who wrote the famous panegyric *Humayun-Nama* (ca. 1587), among other pieces; or of Salima Sultan Begum, a highly educated woman and a poet, who was known as the "Khadeja of that era" for her wisdom; the politically astute Nur Jahan, who practically ruled the Mughal empire as the emperor Jehangir's wife between 1611 and 1628; or even of Aurangzeb's daughter, Jahan Ara, a woman of great learning and wisdom who commissioned the building of the Jumma Masjid in 1647.[118]

By the early twentieth century, then, the combination of outright silence, overtly unflattering representation, and oblique, negative allusions seems to have consolidated a picture of Muslim women as the "inherently atavistic" other of the "ideal modern woman" (Hindu, middle class, and upper caste) in the contemporary popular Hindu imagination.[119] Indeed, it is in the *figure of the traditional woman*—silenced and victimized by the barbarity of Muslim men—that Muslim women make one of their few appearances in the Hindu-dominated nationalist discourse of late-nineteenth- and early-twentieth-century Bengal.[120] Once they were incorporated into the larger story of Indian womanhood in this particular capacity, Muslim women, and everything they did or achieved, simply became invisible to this nationalist discourse and its historiography, condemning them permanently to some "anterior time within the modern nation" that would henceforth be "figured as beyond [national/modern] history."[121]

Meanwhile, the masculinized, ever more powerful, and often vilified figure of the Mussalman, reinforced by the discursive erasure of the Muslim woman, would henceforth be the chief source of Hindu (male) hysteria, facilitating by his very existence both the appropriation of the past history of Muslim rule in the subcontinent simply as an unfortunate chapter in the career of a Hindu nation, and the sporadic fomenting of Hindu anxieties, resentment, and even violence throughout the twentieth century and into the troubled present of the subcontinent.[122]

AFTERWARD

In the 1920s, in the aftermath of the Non-Cooperation and Khilafat movements—two major nationwide initiatives associated with the nationalist agitation against British colonial rule—Muslims emerged as both an important political force and the main economic competitors of the Hindu bhadralok in Bengal. The promises made in the (short-lived) Bengal Pact in 1923, especially the reservation of 55 percent of all administrative posts for Muslims in the province after independence—reflecting the presence of a larger proportion of Muslims in the total population—alarmed many among the Hindu middle class.[123] If earlier members of the bhadralok had been anxious about increased competition from Muslims in the realm of professional opportunities, they were now faced with the very real possibility of being outnumbered by Muslims in government service, thereby losing their supremacy—social, economic, and political—in Bengal. The result was an intense arousal of Hindu communalist sentiments in the 1920s, best captured in the overlapping discourses of the "dying Hindu" and the "abductions of Hindu women by Muslim *goondas*," which played a crucial role in deepening the existing cleavages between Hindus and Muslims in Bengal in the second and third decades of the twentieth century.[124]

Not surprisingly, the first articulations of the pernicious idea that Muslims could overtake Hindus demographically can be credited to speculations made by British officials as early as 1891 on the "number of years [it would take] for Hindus to disappear altogether" based on census figures, which indicated a slower birthrate among Hindus.[125] But the "dying Hindu" discourse owed its widespread appeal and eventual "commonsense" status to a work by U. N. Mukherji, titled *Hindus: A Dying Race*, published in 1909. In this book, the author reworks the rather far-fetched notion of a demographic Muslim advantage into a paranoid theory extolling the "natural physical advantages" of Muslim men, underwritten presumably by a combination of factors such as the moral regeneration of Muslims through Islamic revival movements in nineteenth-century Bengal, their relative and "growing" affluence, and, most important, "the desire of Hindu widows for Muslim males."[126] While a discussion of these controversies over the decreasing numbers and economic strength of Hindus vis-à-vis Muslims—transformed into claims of the eventual, if not imminent, "liquidation of Hindus by Muslims" in the shrill discourse of the Hindu Right by the 1920s—and over the supposed abduction of Hindu women by Muslim men falls beyond the scope of the current project, I would like to end this chapter by drawing out a few possible linkages between these highly communalized discourses and the issue of the visibility/invisibility of women within the Hindu-dominated nationalist discourse in Bengal in the late nineteenth and early twentieth centuries, as well as the simultaneous workings of gender, racial/communal, and class ideologies that I have been delineating in the preceding pages.[127]

First, both the "dying Hindu" and "abductions" discourses were, in my reading, examples of *gendered* discourses par excellence, obsessed as they were with a perceived "crisis" of Hindu maleness—defined in terms of a potent mix of anxieties around sexual adequacy (called into question by the "falling" Hindu population and the inability to control or put to use the sexual potential of Hindu widows), economic supremacy (threatened by increased competition from educated Muslims), and political viability (fear of being outnumbered)—vis-à-vis the imagined robust masculinity of the Muslim male, who seems to have emerged at this historical juncture in the early twentieth century in Bengal as an able, if not superior, adversary and competitor of the Hindu bhadralok. Note that these anxieties in the 1920s were fomented in part by the reassertion of the colonial claim that "all the political, economic, and social problems of India had a single cause, and that cause . . . was the very essence of the beliefs and practices of Hinduism," articulated in this instance by Katherine Mayo's infamous book *Mother India*.[128] Note also that women—once again mainly Hindu women—figured prominently in all these discourses but almost exclusively as currency. Even when individual women were named as victims and their testimonies gathered during the "abductions" controversy, the overwhelming tendency in the reports was to overlook the possibility of women's consent and/or agency in leaving their homes.[129] This in turn obscured the larger problem of women's oppression within the Hindu (or Muslim for that matter) household.[130]

Second, the abductions controversy—which began with complaints made by lower-caste Hindus against Muslims in the Rangpur district of rural North Bengal—was soon appropriated by upper-caste/middle-class Hindus as a potent tool in a campaign to slander the entire Muslim population of Bengal as treacherous and violent and hence collectively unfit for political responsibility—a charge that was meanwhile being leveled at Hindus by a resurgent colonial critical discourse spearheaded by Mayo's *Mother India*. To quote Datta, "The discourse of abductions played a crucial role . . . to undercut the discourse of proportionate representation itself [based on the Muslim and Hindu populations in the state] by replacing it with the criterion of aptitude for governance. Abductions revealed a double disqualification of the Muslims—their [supposed] 'sexual proclivities' as well as their 'general antagonism towards Hindus.'"[131] The apparent concern over the "safety" of women, and the "outrage" over the brutality that they often had to face at the hands of abductors thus amounted to little more than a trope intended to mobilize Hindu men in Bengal—*across class and caste lines*—in the service of garnering and/or maintaining the class- and caste-based advantages of the Hindu elite in a Muslim-majority province.

Third, in both the dying Hindu and abductions discourses the relevant actors were the now familiar virulent and/or treacherous Muslim man; the helpless Hindu woman as the object of Muslim lust (in the capacity of the chaste Hindu wife and the sexually underutilized, and hence repressed or wanton Hindu widow); and, finally, the "racially" degenerate, outnumbered, and increasingly powerless Hindu man. In sharp contrast, Muslim women are curiously absent from the discussions of abductions throughout the 1920s—an absence that is all the more remarkable if one considers the fact that just over half of the women abducted in Bengal between 1926 and 1931 were apparently Muslim (3,513 as against 3,499 Hindu women)! What is more, it seems both Hindu and Muslim men "preferred to abduct women from their own religious communities."[132] The problem, in other words, was bigger and much more widespread and one that implicated both Hindu and Muslim men in the oppression of Hindu and Muslim women.[133] In other words, by appropriating the language of "women's oppression" for its own narrow, communal agenda, the abductions debate once again managed to make Hindu women visible as chaste and endangered symbols of the Hindu nation, even as it rendered invisible the figure of the Muslim woman, occluding in substance the very material problem of violence against *all* women in late colonial Bengal.

Indeed, such is the power of discourses in determining the trajectories of intellectual inquiry that three-quarters of a century later one is still reduced to sifting through footnotes in pursuit of the abducted figure of the Muslim woman, even in the most nuanced historical accounts of the era that deal explicitly with the problem of abductions.[134] The Muslim woman and her concerns, it would seem, continue to slip through the cracks of critical historical scholarship in postcolonial India.

3

NEGOTIATING MODERNITY

The Social Production of Muslim-ness in Late Colonial Bengal

For ages, women have put up with . . . oppression and disrespect as the objects of [men's] amusement. . . . [To relieve that] it is not enough to simply write a few pages in periodicals—its redress will be through revolution. You might ask, "who will revolt, and against whom?" [The revolt will be] against men! But such revolutionary women have not been born yet in Bengal . . . [at least] not in Muslim society.[1]

One evening I was lounging in an easy chair in my bedroom and thinking lazily of the condition of Indian womanhood. I am not sure whether I dozed off or not. . . . All of a sudden a lady stood before me. . . . I took her for my friend Sister Sara.

"Will you please come out and have a look at our garden?" [she asked].

> I looked . . . at the moon . . . and thought there was no harm in going out at that time. . . .
>
> When walking I found to my surprise that it was a fine morning. The town was fully awake and the streets alive with bustling crowds. I was feeling very shy, thinking I was walking in the street in broad daylight, but there was not a single man visible.
>
> Some of the passersby made jokes at me. . . . I asked . . . "What do they say?"
>
> "The women say . . . that you are shy and timid like men." Timid and shy like men? . . . [This] was really a joke, [I thought]. . . .
>
> "I feel somewhat awkward," I said, in a rather apologizing tone, "as being a pardanishin woman I am not accustomed to walking about unveiled."
>
> "You need not be afraid of coming across a man here. This is Ladyland, free from sin and harm. Virtue herself reigns here." . . .
>
> I became very curious to know where the men were. I met more than a hundred women while walking there, but not a single man.
>
> "Where are the men?" I asked her.
>
> "In their proper places, where they ought to be." . . . "We shut our men indoors."[2]

In 1905, a Madras-based English periodical, *The Indian Ladies' Magazine*, carried a story titled "Sultana's Dream," written by Begum Rokeya Sakhawat Hossain.[3] It was a "utopian fantasy"—the first known example of such a work by a woman in India—in which Rokeya imagines a world where cooking is a pleasure, horticulture is an important activity, and science is used only for humanitarian ends.[4] It is a woman's world—peaceful and ordered—where men are "shut indoors" in the *murdana*.[5] As Rokeya's husband remarked on reading the story, it is indeed a "terrible revenge" on men.[6] This chapter reads it also as an attempt to rethink Muslim womanhood in late colonial Bengal.

Rokeya was undoubtedly a remarkable writer and thinker whose contributions to the rich intellectual discourse of late colonial Bengal is receiving the attention it has always deserved, though arguably only in recent years. While numerous Bengali commentaries on her life and work have existed for some time in Bangladesh—indeed, some would contend that publishing on Rokeya has become something of an industry—systematic attempts to situate her work within the normative intellectual history of colonial Bengal have been remarkably tardy in making their appearance in postindependence India.[7]

Recent attempts, especially by feminist scholars, to recuperate her work are thus important and welcome steps in correcting a long-standing lacuna in historical scholarship in India.[8] Thanks also to such efforts, Rokeya Sakhawat Hossain's name has now found its way into the list of "exceptional," "early feminist" women writers from colonial India circulating in critical academic circles even outside the subcontinent.[9] What has remained largely unnoticed, however, are the works of the other dozen-odd Muslim women—such as Masuda Rahman, Khaerunnessa Khatun, Razia Khatun Choudhurani, Mahmuda Khatun Siddiqua, Ayesha Ahmed, and Faziltunnessa, to name a few—who were writing on a wide range of issues pertinent to women's lives in the first half of the twentieth century.[10] Others, such as Sufia Kamal and Samsunnahar Mahmud, have gained respect and recognition for both their writing and their activism over time, but few readers outside Bangladesh and West Bengal would recognize their names, even in the subcontinent. As historical sources, the work of all these early women writers is important.[11] They were also seminal in gaining the attention, and eventually confidence, of readers who were by and large averse to the idea of the emancipation of women. And yet such efforts are rarely acknowledged, leaving one with the impression that Rokeya was the only Muslim woman writing in late colonial Bengal—or at least the only one deserving of the critical attention of scholars today.[12]

In the preceding chapters we have traced some of the ways in which Muslim women appear or disappear in colonial and Hindu-dominated nationalist discourses during a period of a hundred-odd years stretching from the late eighteenth century to the early twentieth and their subsequent marginalization in, if not disappearance from, much of the normative written history of colonial India. We have also reflected on the ways in which the appearance or disappearance of the figure of the (Muslim) woman in writing is connected to the exigencies of producing normative historiographies, colonial and nationalist, with their respective investments in depicting "natives"/Muslims—especially women—in particular ways. Muslims themselves were not idle of course. Throughout the nineteenth and well into the twentieth century, in Bengal and elsewhere, they, too, were questioning and honing the definitions of *Muslim* as an identity location and debating the boundaries, indeed, the very possibility, of a community to be secured amid different, sometimes conflicting, understandings of such definitions, as well as within the larger context of colonial, and, increasingly, Hindu, representations of Muslims. By the beginning of the twentieth century in Bengal, these debates were carried out also by members of a growing Muslim middle class. Were these debates over identity formation among Muslims gendered? Did Muslim women figure in them, and, if so, in what capacities and to what ends?

Unfortunately, very little of what Muslim intellectuals (not just women) thought and wrote at the end of the nineteenth century and during the first four decades of the twentieth enters into the conventional story of late colonial Bengal normalized within historical accounts in postindependence India. In such accounts—preoccupied as they are with the anticolonial nationalist movement and the 1947 Partition—Muslims typically appear in the context of discussions about the growth of separatism, political and social.[13] In contrast, the contributions of Muslim writers in matters that fall outside the limits of the discourses of "pan-Islamism," and "Muslim political separatism" receive scant attention.

"Historical consciousness in modern society," Prasenjit Duara reminds us, is "overwhelmingly framed by the nation-state."[14] It would seem that for Muslim writers from early-twentieth-century Bengal the very condition of visibility and voice in subsequent historical accounts is anachronistically determined even more specifically by a single episode in the linear history of the nation-state—the story of the Partition—when, in fact, as we shall see below, a significant section of the Bengali Muslim intelligentsia did not necessarily support political separation from, or even discord with, Hindus.[15] And if they insisted on their religious and cultural distinctness, they also foregrounded often all that was shared by Muslim and Hindus, especially in Bengal.

In my reading, there are a number of consequences of fetishizing the Partition in the writing of official, and even some critical, histories that need rethinking. First, it reinforces the popular Hindu impression that Muslims were only interested in separation, thereby flattening what is in fact a fairly complex and internally differentiated discursive field. Second, this flattened presentation of Muslim attitudes feeds the desire for a simple (and perhaps guilt free) narrative of "loss": Muslims wanted Partition, Hindus suffered it. Third, Muslim women writers and reformers largely disappear, along with many of the concerns that animated the Muslim middle class at that time, from both normative historical and popular Hindu accounts and memories of the early twentieth century. Fourth, the disappearance of Muslim women from both historical and popular accounts of late colonial Bengal reinforces the masculinization of the category "Muslim" and its association with backwardness and violence, which, as we have seen, was already evident in Hindu middle-class discourse in the last third of the nineteenth century in Bengal. That, in turn, further occludes Muslim women and so on.

History, fortunately, is not produced only through public, official, or dominant critical representations; it is also constructed and nurtured in popular memory, defined as "all the ways in which a sense of the past is constructed."[16] The study of popular memory is, therefore, necessarily relational. It involves the exploration of two sets of relations: (1) the relation between dominant memory and oppositional forms across the public field, including academic productions; and (2) the relation between public discourse and a more privatized sense of the past generated within lived culture. This chapter focuses on the first of these two constitutive relations in tracing the specific location of the figure of the Muslim woman within the larger discourse surrounding the production of "Bengali Muslim" as a category of identification in Bengal in the late nineteenth century and early twentieth.[17] Chapter 4 concerns itself with the second relation—that between official history and private memory.

Here I approach the question of Muslim identity formation through a reading of Muslim public discourse as captured in contemporary periodicals published mainly in Calcutta and Dhaka by Bengali Muslim intellectuals.[18] These publications had a predominantly Muslim readership that was geographically dispersed all over Bengal in small suburban towns and even in villages.[19] While a few newspapers and periodicals run by Muslims were already in existence at the end of the nineteenth century in Bengal, many more seem to have appeared at the beginning of the twentieth century, especially around the time of the Swadeshi movement and the first partition of Bengal in 1905.[20] It is quite common for scholars to refer to this growing interest of Bengali Muslims in the print media as a "new awakening."[21] Whether or not one subscribes to such celebratory rehearsals of a well-worn liberal (and colonial) formulation that equates the emergence of a "vernacular" press with "signs of progress"—whereby "progress" or "development is expressed in terms of a list of factors with a hidden causal link"—it is certainly possible to appreciate the importance of such publications in providing a relatively autonomous discursive space in which community identifications were battled over and normalized, especially by the middle classes in the subcontinent.[22] It was typically also the space in which indigenous elites "grappled" with the European narrative of progress—a narrative that invariably represented India as both "anachronistic and having to learn the lessons of modernity"—in their effort to make it consistent with their imaginations of community.[23] As we shall see, such negotiations with dominant discourses were always fraught with tension. And, finally, these periodicals collectively provided a crucial site for those Muslim intellectuals interested in questions of modernity and social reforms. In them, they could debate the shape and direction of possible changes, as well as disseminate their ideas. The publication of periodicals and newspapers as instruments of consciousness-raising among their readers thus appears to have been akin to the enactment of an important social responsibility for middle-class Muslim intellectuals.[24]

The most significant periodicals published in the last two decades of the nineteenth and the first four decades of the twentieth century included *Akhbar-e-Islamia* (1884), *Hitkari* (1890), *Islam Pracharak* (1891), *Mihir* (1892), *Hafez* (1892), *Kohinoor* (1894), *Soltan* (1902), *Nabanoor* (1903), *Al Eslam* (1915), *Islam Darshan* (1916), *Bangiya Mussalman Sahitya Patrika* (1918), *Saogat* (1918), *Banganur* (1919), *Moslem Bharat* (1920), *Dhumketu* (1922), *Sahachar* (1922), *Samyabadi* (1923), *Ganabani* (1926), *Shikha* (1927), *Naoroz* (1927), *Mohammadi* (1927), *Sanchay* (1928), *Jagaran* (1928), *Jayati* (1930), and *Bulbul* (1934).[25] In the pages of these periodicals, we find members of a newly emerging Bengali Muslim middle class—men and, increasingly, women (especially from the second and third decades of the twentieth century)—negotiating their complex identities, often against the grain of dominant representations of Muslim-ness in circulation at that time, including those advocated by some Muslims themselves, but also at times capitulating to them.

Before we begin our consideration of the Muslim middle class and its public deliberations about what it meant to be Muslim in early-twentieth-century Bengal, I would like to turn briefly to the nineteenth-century efforts at reform and community-identity formation among Muslims undertaken both by Islamic revivalists, who worked among the rural populations, and by urban elite Muslims who were supported by the Islamic orthodoxy. As such, that dense and fissured terrain of ideological battles and strategic alliances among the different factions of Islamic reformists in nineteenth-century Bengal has been amply recorded by historians.[26] Our purpose in what will necessarily be a brisk excursion into this history is threefold: to grasp something of the ideological context that both framed the reform initiatives of the Bengali Muslim middle class and, to a certain extent, shaped the substance of such reforms in the early twentieth century; to locate when and where, and in what ways,

Muslim women entered into the discussions surrounding the various efforts at reform and identity formation among Muslims in nineteenth-century Bengal; and to tease out, if possible, the workings of gender as both a "constitutive element of social relationships based on perceived differences between sexes" and a way of "signifying relationships of power" in these discourses.[27] My effort in this section relies primarily on secondary literature, especially the important work of Rafiuddin Ahmed on Muslims in Bengal in the nineteenth century.[28]

"MUSLIMS" IN NINETEENTH-CENTURY BENGAL

In 1871, W. W. Hunter published an influential book, *The Indian Mussalmans*, in which he proposed that there were two kinds of Muslims in India—the foreign-born aristocratic *ashraf* (elite) and the fanatical masses of jihad-seeking *atrap* (low-caste Hindu converts), who formed the bulk of the Muslim population in the subcontinent.[29] Muslims in nineteenth-century Bengal, not to mention India as a whole, were, of course, far more divided along class, caste, and political lines than such simplistic binary formulations would indicate.[30] A vast majority of those belonging to the Muslim agricultural classes in Bengal were tillers of the soil; others were employed as weavers, oil merchants, fishermen, and small traders; very few seem to have owned any land.[31] Even as late as the last quarter of the nineteenth century, in some districts of central, eastern, and northern Bengal, Muslims comprised close to 70 percent of the total population but owned only 10 to 16 percent of the land.[32]

Contemporary accounts, mostly in the form of *punthi* literature, point to considerable social distance, including restrictions on intermarriage and eating together, between the ashraf—represented by the clergy and those who both traced their lineages to early immigrants from West Asia and were oriented culturally toward "northern India and beyond"—and the atrap—rural, often poor Muslims who had their roots in the Bengal countryside.[33] Since the Mughal era, the urban elite seems to have looked down on Bengali Muslims, and especially their *dobhasi* language (a mix of Arabic and Bengali), which was considered to be "a tongue of the subject race."[34] Indeed, the very idea that Bengalis—who were generally considered to be lesser men—could also be Muslim may have been unacceptable to members of the urban Mughal ruling classes, who were consequently not particularly interested in converting them to Islam.[35] That task was left to enterprising holy men, or "forest pioneers," who received "favourable or even tax-free tenures of [forest] land . . . [which they] were expected to clear and bring into cultivation. . . . The policy was intended to promote the emergence of local communities that would be both economically productive and politically loyal . . . to the Mughal state. . . . These pioneers also played decisive roles in the religious development of the region, as one of the conditions for obtaining . . . [an imperial] grant was to build on the land a mosque or temple, to be supported in perpetuity out of the wealth produced on site."[36] Since most of the pioneers were Muslim, a form of syncretic Islam developed in East Bengal through this encounter, which absorbed elements of local cosmologies into Islamic teachings to impart "special meaning" to life in an expanding agrarian frontier.[37] The vast body of Muslim religious literature from the sixteenth to eighteenth centuries, which was not above including Hindu deities among the prophets of Islam, attests to this syncretism.[38]

The Islamic orthodoxy, represented in Bengal by the mullah, the *maulvi*, and segments of the immigrant Muslim population, refused to acknowledge the "syncretic-pantheistic beliefs and practices" of the Muslim peasants and artisans, as well as the "heterodox Sufi sects," as Islamic.[39] In some parts of Bengal, the ashraf apparently despised the atrap so much that they would not even offer the *Jumah* prayers in the same mosque with the latter.[40] Indeed, it is fair to say that in nineteenth-century rural Bengal poor Muslims were closer at the level of everyday living to Hindus of similar class backgrounds than to the ashraf and the *ulema*, leading at least some within the colonial administration to question the usefulness, and even the feasibility, of dividing peasant and artisanal groups into separate religious communities.[41] Muslims and Hindus are said to have spoken the same language and even to have participated in similar rituals and festivals. And if, as Ahmed points out, there were restrictions on connubium and commensality practiced between Hindu and Muslim peasants, such restrictions were no less prevalent between different classes and castes among Muslims in what was a flagrant violation of the avowed egalitarianism of doctrinal Islam.[42] And it was precisely such "un-Islamic" institutions as caste divisions that the nineteenth-century Islamic revivalist movements in Bengal targeted—most famously the Tariqah-I-Muhammadiya, the Faraizi, and the movement in western Bengal associated with Titu Mir.[43]

It would be useful to recall here that these socioreligious reform movements were taking place within the context of the large-scale, systematic destruction of the indigenous industries of Bengal under the dual pressures of growing British industrial production and the colonial rule that made such growth possible.[44] Bengal, indeed India, in the first half of the nineteenth century was being rapidly transformed from an industrially developed economy to a mere supplier of raw materials and a captive market for British industrial goods, most notably cotton textiles in this early stage of capitalist development.[45] Consequently, one observer notes, the amount of woven material exported from England to India was less than 1 million yards in 1818 and 51 million yards in 1835. During that same period, textile exports from India to England fell from 1,025,000 pieces to a mere 306,000. The exportation of yarn from England to India also rose 5,200 times between 1818 and 1836.[46] All this, of course, meant that large numbers of both Hindu and Muslim spinners and weavers were forced to turn to farming, resulting in abnormal pressure on the land in Bengal.[47] This, in turn, put the peasants on a path to direct confrontation with the exploitative practices of the zamindars (landlords), especially the new class of rentier landlords who, at least in post–Permanent Settlement Bengal, were overwhelmingly Hindu.[48] As was discussed in chapter 2, these new bhadralok zamindars were also typically loyalist until the 1870s and hence enjoyed the patronage of the colonial administration.

Not surprisingly, therefore, what typically began as religious purification movements aimed at uplifting the everyday conduct and promoting the moral improvement of peasants sooner or later evolved into campaigns against the rampant socioeconomic exploitation of the rural poor—a majority of whom were Muslim—by the (predominantly Hindu) zamindars and British indigo planters alike.[49] Under certain leaders, these movements also overtly supported the position that India under British rule was *dar-ul-harb*, a "zone of war," as declared by the jihad movement, popularly known as the Wahhabi movement, in North India.[50] The evolving focus of these movements from religious purification to mobilization against the unjust demands made by oppressive Hindu zamindars gave them the reputation of being communal when in fact the early leaders of these movements were reportedly against the exploitation of all poor peasants and artisans, irrespective of their religious identification, by all zamindars—Hindu or Muslim—and their British patrons.[51] Indeed, contemporary reports indicate that poor low-caste Hindu peasants had sometimes taken part in the class-based struggles against Hindu zamindars and British planters.[52]

The class consciousness and anti-imperial sensibilities exhibited by at least some revivalist leaders until about the 1860s, however, did not result in a significant class-based or anti-imperialist mass struggle in nineteenth-century Bengal.[53] Nor did these movements succeed in producing a single interpretation of Islam due to the considerable doctrinal disagreements among different factions of the reformist leadership and between them and the traditionalist mullahs and maulvis.[54] The latter enjoyed the support of the ashraf, while the Tariqah and Faraizi movements, by the very nature of their propaganda, alienated wealthy landlords—Hindu *and* Muslim—as well as small landholders, merchants, moneylenders, and, especially, urban educated Muslims, who were increasingly in the mood for collaboration with the British in the late nineteenth century.[55]

But the nineteenth-century fundamentalist movements did achieve one thing: They initiated the beginnings of a sense of community among the followers of Islam in rural areas, not around a single interpretation of "pristine" Islam, as their leaders might have hoped, but around the idea of its distinctness from all things local, especially Hindu beliefs and practices. Under the influence of traditionalist mullahs, whose authority was once again on the rise after the decline of the revivalists in the last third of the nineteenth century, this growing awareness of Muslim distinctness would give way to open hostility toward Hindu rituals and customs. What had begun as a move to discipline the self in the first half of the century thus came to be an excuse for violent rejection of a designated "other," so much so, that "anything associated with Hinduism came to be looked upon as evil and the term 'Hindu' itself acquired a pejorative connotation.[56] Such attitudes toward Hindus nurtured in the second half of the nineteenth century would greatly influence one strand of Muslim middle-class thinking in the early twentieth century and eventually would contribute to an intense communalization of rural areas in the mid- to late 1920s.[57]

Meanwhile, at the other end of the class spectrum, the ashraf or sharif (noble) Muslims were hardly a monolithic category. At the top of the hierarchy were the Mughal ashraf, descendants of immigrants from Central Asia, Afghanistan, Persia, Arabia, and parts of northern India. They were typically Shias, spoke Urdu,[58] and considered themselves culturally and (in the language of the nineteenth century) racially superior to the indigenous population. Concentrated as they were in the urban centers of Calcutta, Dhaka, Murshidabad, and Hooghly, the upper ashraf had little or no contact with the masses of converts to Islam in Bengal.[59] Next on the ladder came the *mofussil* (provincial) ashraf, who were usually landowning gentry. This group was mostly Sunni by faith, spoke Bengali, and had some dealings with the rural working classes. A third group, which Ahmed calls the "lesser ashraf," often owned some property and claimed foreign descent to set it apart from the rural poor.[60]

Sharif Muslims, such as Nawab Abdul Lateef and Syed Ameer Ali, who established the Muhammadan Literary and Scientific Society (1863) and the National Mahommedan Association (1891), respectively, and hence appear often in historical accounts of late-nineteenth-century Bengal, were almost always members of the aristocratic elite. This class of Muslims believed that lack of interest in western education was a major reason for the relative socioeconomic backwardness of Muslims in the subcontinent. Their aim, therefore, was to counter the antagonism that Muslims typically showed toward western education and to make them more conscious of the need to combine "profitable" education with the study of Urdu, Arabic, and Farsi. In this they were no different from Sir Sayyid Ahmad Khan of Delhi, who founded the Mohammedan Anglo Oriental College (1875) in Aligarh (later Aligarh Muslim University) with the aim of training Muslims (mainly, though not exclusively) in the western sciences and English to ensure that they would maintain their high social status and their role in governing the country.[61] It was this group of sharif Muslims that the British began to patronize in the last quarter of the nineteenth century as part of their divide-and-rule policy, in an attempt to nurture a counterweight, first to "the so-called 'fanaticism' and anti-foreign mentality" of the Muslim masses and later to an increasingly bellicose Hindu middle class.[62]

While not all among the ashraf necessarily concurred on the degree to which they needed to collaborate with the colonial administration, it seems that their overall focus was on balancing their Perso-Arabic cultural heritage and orthodox interpretation of Islamic tenets with the limited and strategic cultivation of a project of European modernity—a modernity that was historically predicated on an image of Islamic populations as inherently violent, inconvertible, and medieval, in short, its other—in an attempt to maintain their class privilege.[63] A majority of the ashraf believed that Muslims were foreign to India and constituted a "separate race" among Indians, as expressed in the Syed Ameer Ali's demand, as early as 1883, for separate elections and representation for Muslims in the Municipality bill. Cultivating Bengali was thus not quite on the ashraf's list of priorities, although they were perfectly aware that the majority of Bengal's Muslims were indigenous. The "reforms" sought by the ashraf, mainly in terms of attitudes toward western education and liberal thought, also had little to do with the needs and worldview of most Muslims, at least in Bengal.[64]

And yet, by the beginning of the twentieth century, the growing tendency among the orthodox mullahs to define a community—based not on internal or doctrinal cohesion but its supposed *difference/distance* from a designated other, namely, the Hindu—produced some important points of convergence between the interests of the rural ulema and upwardly mobile peasant households, on the one hand, and the urban ashraf on the other. Colonial discourse and policies toward Muslims from the 1870s onward, especially the administration's insistence on treating Muslims as a single "distinct religious community"—in spite of its explicit categorization of the ashraf and the atrap as racially distinct—and its "policies of state patronage and public as well as private rhetoric," were also instrumental in providing powerful incentives to Muslims, especially the rural masses, to slowly privilege the location of "Muslim" over those of Bengali and peasant.[65] And it is this tendency among Muslims to see themselves as distinct—socially and culturally at first and eventually as a political constituency separate from Hindus—that has received the most attention in conventional historical accounts of the late colonial era. While such issues constituted important and substantial parts of the discourse of the Muslim middle class in Bengal, as we shall see presently, it by no means exhausted the list of concerns that animated it. But, before we move on, let us briefly take stock of the place of gender in the nineteenth-century discourses of community identity formation among Muslims in Bengal.

It is something of a convention in the historical literature to note that, unlike the sociocultural "renaissance" begun by the Hindu middle class in early-nineteenth-century Bengal, the revivalist movements among Muslims did not support "gender reform"—a term that is more or less equated with reforms that specifically affect women's lives. As we know, in the case of the Hindus in Bengal, debates over women's appropriate position within and outside the family were central to the social reform movement initiated in the nineteenth century—both in its earlier liberal reformist and later cultural nationalist/Hindu revivalist phases.[66] One reason for this focus on the woman question among Hindus was undoubtedly the influence of western liberal thinking and western education, which the Hindu middle class had taken to enthusiastically quite early in the nineteenth century.[67] But it is also true that much of the missionary and Anglicist criticism of "Indian" culture in the early nineteenth century was focused on Hindu social and religious practices, especially the abominable treatment of women in upper-caste Hindu society.[68] Stung by such harsh criticism, which questioned their very claim to adequate manliness in the eyes of the colonial rulers, some among the Hindu bhadralok sought to address the "degeneration" of traditions with particular attention to the treatment of upper-caste Hindu women.

In contrast, Muslims, though conservative in matters of seclusion, polygamy, and female education, did not have spectacular practices of public torture of women, such as *satidaha* (burning of the widow), and therefore seem to have drawn less criticism than Hindus did from the Anglicists and missionaries, at least in terms of the treatment of women.[69] What is more, the leaders of the revivalist movements typically came from the suburban areas and, unlike the Hindu bhadralok and the pro-British Muslim elite, seemed to be largely indifferent to the "changes taking place in the world outside [the village] through the impact of the West."[70]

All this does not mean that gender was absent from nineteenth-century deliberations on reforms among the followers of Islam in Bengal. Nor is it true that such reforms had identical implications for men and women. As the contemporary *nashihat namas* (manuals of religious instruction) testify, discussions about the rules of marriage and divorce; the relationships between men and women, especially as they followed from the oft-touted idea of men's inherent superiority; and, of course, the rights and duties of women were central elements of the revivalist preoccupation with purifying the everyday practice of Islam.[71] These tracts, which were widely circulated in rural Bengal throughout the nineteenth century, as well as some contemporary literary works, were often harshly critical of women for their neglect of the home and lack of devotion to their families and husbands.[72] For instance, as Amin notes, in *Harh Jwalani* (1864) the writer Ghulam Husain blames the "modern" woman for the breakdown of traditional family and authority structures.[73] Maleh Muhammad's *Tanbih al-Nissa* from the mid-nineteenth century, claims that the Lord "has given man the higher status" and so a woman must serve her husband.[74] What is more, the holy book apparently dictates that a woman who quarrels with her husband because he has taken more wives is inferior or of a lowly nature.[75] Indeed, some of the tracts seem to equate the very possibility of being a good Muslim with the ability to control and dominate women, suggesting that the readership these tracts had in mind was predominantly male.[76]

According to Amin, the "distrust" and "low opinion" of women revealed in these nashihat namas and other literary works from that period are indicative of a "decline in the state of women."[77] Whether or not we can infer a decline—and, by implication, higher status for women in some unspecified period in the past—it is undeniable that the sentiments captured in these tracts betray a certain disdain for women held by nineteenth-century (male) writers.[78] And yet it would be useful to remember that the revivalist leadership was critical of the erring ways of the rural masses in general and exhorted *all* Muslims, men and women, to mend their ways and begin honoring the five obligatory observances of Islam—namaaz, zakat, kalimah, roza, and haj—to the greatest extent possible.[79] In the same vein, it is also worth noting that these works meant for the edification of rural populations in the early to mid–nineteenth century do not seem to dwell on the issue of segregation of women,[80] a concern that was more likely to be on the reform agenda of the ashraf, and its dissemination among the more affluent peasant households toward the end of the century.[81]

What is perhaps more telling in these reformist tracts is the way in which ideas about the "natural" differences between men and women underwrite their prescriptions for proper conduct in *any* context, not just in social arrangements strictly involving the relationship between the sexes. Let me cite one example. In extolling the virtues of "punctual . . . prayers" and "zealous . . . observance" of "obligatory ritual duties," one tract claims that "All such *people* will be rewarded with gifts of women from amongst the fairies. God [Elahi] will reward them with such women, the like of which is not to be found anywhere in the world. . . . Hot pilau, bread, kebab and wine in full jars will also be served. . . . You will get whatever you ask for."[82]

That the author is trying to "induce conformity" by making "non-Islamic," even "questionable" promises, as Ahmed points out, is obvious.[83] What I find striking in this passage is the use of the trope of "women as gifts" and/or objects of male consumption/hunger/desire—reinforced by the litany of saliva-inducing food items, which are "also" promised—and use of the word *people* to refer to an audience that seems to be entirely male. Both uses reveal, in my reading, not only an assumption of the fundamental inferiority and object status of women and their marginality as Islamic subjects in this worldview but also the ways in which such notions underwrite the signification of other relationships of power—in this case between Elahi (God), who will grant these gifts of women, and men, the true followers of Islam, who will have the privilege of consuming such gifts in exchange for their supplication.

Gender ideologies, as manifested in discussions of ideal femininity and the underlying concerns with adequate masculinity, were also integral to the upper ulema's deliberations over the correct Islamic ways and the reform efforts of western-educated ashraf in late-nineteenth-century India.[84] As Barbara Metcalf writes, "For the ulema in the late nineteenth century, . . . [what] was significant was only the 'enemy within': the unreformed, uneducated woman who did not know Islamic doctrine . . . and handled badly the responsibilities of her everyday life."[85] This preoccupation with the need for "internal" reforms was captured most famously in Maulana Ashraf Ali Thanawi's didactic work *Bihishti Zewar*.[86] Thanawi insisted that "women's virtue reside[s] in their practice of a doctrinally defined social role," a view not unrelated to the concerns of the revivalist leadership in the early nineteenth century.[87] The orthodox ulema and revivalist leaders also agreed that women should serve their husbands and families. The difference, it would seem, lay in the ulema's and ashraf's focus on the need to educate women, their tendency to highlight the rights that the Quran and Hadith provided for women, especially with regard to inheritance, and their firm placement of women within the home—issues that may not have been particularly meaningful to the experiences of the vast majority of the rural poor in nineteenth-century Bengal.[88]

Finally, gender as a constitutive element of social relationships also operated *outside* the obvious context of reform discourses involving the relations between men and women. In Bengal, for instance, relatively affluent rural ashraf women were routinely used as currency in the complex process of establishing class location and social status. As Ahmed observes, "Socially, [the lesser ashraf] were as much keen to emphasize their superiority to the masses as were the upper ashraf, and like the latter, would not ordinarily give their daughters in marriage to non-ashraf. . . . [They were also] strongly opposed to widow remarriage which they considered a non-ashraf practice."[89] Ahmed, of course, correctly reads this practice as an assertion of class identity. However, these exchanges were also clearly gendered, with significant implications for the different ways in which sharif men and women experienced (or were obliged to experience) their class locations. Glossing over the workings of gender in the articulation of class and community ideologies obliterates from written history the very contexts women inhabit as historical subjects, reinforcing in the process their invisibility in, and apparent irrelevance to, public life.

In sum, then, gender did play a significant role in structuring both the existing practices of class and community locations and the revivalist/reformist attempts to refashion them in nineteenth-century Bengal. The conceptual shorthand of "gender = woman" and "reform = improvement," with the teleological fixing of the meaning of *improvement* as changes in one direction (namely, toward an approximation of western ideals of "progress"), make both the complex uses of "gender" and the specific ideas of "reform" deployed within nonwestern (referred to often as "traditional" in the literature) modes of thinking invisible to historical scholarship. In the worldviews of the revivalist leadership, the ulema, and, as Faisal Fatehali Devji has argued, at times even the shurafa, *improvement* and *reform* typically meant a deepening of one's commitment to the Islamic faith and its injunctions, not the embracing of western liberal ideals.[90] The "improvements" proposed for women and men by the Islamic revivalists and ulema might not appeal to a liberal sensibility today, but to turn a blind eye to them and their influence on sizable populations is an oversight we can ill afford.[91]

As for Liberal reforms, they occurred as well. The main impetus for such changes among Muslims in colonial India in the late nineteenth century and the early twentieth came from a growing desire among men of a slowly emerging professional middle class for educated women who would be more companionate wives to them and better mothers to their children.[92] The reform programs championed by western-educated middle-class men certainly brought welcome changes to the lives of some women, but in the end it was, as Metcalf observes, still men who "remained the actors: it was they who granted women education; they who were called upon to be generous to women.[93] In Bengal, too, it was the middle class that was at the helm of liberal reform movements; however, as we shall see, here women themselves were at the forefront of the reform initiatives most immediately relevant to them. Consequently, although the reforms were not always implemented, their objectives and scope were perhaps more far-reaching than what a malecentric desire for suitable wives and mothers, which seemed to dominate attempts at "gender reform" among the North Indian shurafa, would have allowed.

THE MUSLIM MIDDLE CLASS IN EARLY-TWENTIETH-CENTURY BENGAL

In the last third of the nineteenth century, following the publication of Hunter's book on the "Indian Mussalmans," colonial discourse divided Muslims in the subcontinent into the two categories—ashraf and atrap—highlighting in the process the supposedly essential (i.e., racial) divisions between Muslims whose claims to foreign (West or Central Asian) lineage the British recognized and those they marked as indigenous and "originally" low-caste Hindus. As might be expected, colonial categorizations generated considerable confusion and tension among Muslims in the subcontinent; they also had significant implications for the present and future relationships both *among* Muslims and *between* Muslims and Hindus. In chapter 4, we will have occasion to look closely at some of the more enduring influences of that divisive discourse of "origins" on Muslim identity formation, especially the ways in which middle-class Muslims continue to think and speak of themselves in the Indian subcontinent. Here I will restrict myself to a brief discussion of what might be called the "unifying" effects on Muslims of colonial administrative practices in the post-1870 period, especially the government's insistence on promoting the idea of Muslims as a single religious-political community—a community that would be identified in official discourse as "lagging behind" Hindus and therefore supposedly earmarked for special government assistance.

One arena in which the colonial administration took specific steps toward this end was education, in which Muslims were seen to be trailing Hindus.[94] According to the Report of the Moslem Education Advisory Committee (1934), following the recommendations made by Hunter in 1871, the government took a number of steps to encourage "secular" education among Muslims. These included financial assistance in the form of special endowments, liberal grants-in-aid, and special scholarships for Muslim students; encouraging the madrasahs and *maktabs* (elementary schools) to include the study of "rational" subjects in addition to religious texts; teaching Arabic, Persian, and Urdu in schools and colleges; setting up special hostels for Muslim students in urban centers; and appointing more Muslims to educational positions.[95]

It is worth noting that, for all the rhetoric about erasing differences between Muslims and Hindus, the actual policies of the colonial administration in support of Muslim education seem curiously lackadaisical, convoluted, and internally inconsistent. So, for instance, in 1909–10, almost forty years after Hunter's suggestion that "profitable" subjects be added to the curriculum of the madrasahs and maktabs, the members of the Madrasah Reform Committee were apparently still deliberating on the matter. According to the advisory committee's report, "This committee [of 1909–10] was of the opinion that, while a secular course should be introduced into maktabs, steps should, at the same time, be taken to enable them *to retain their definite characteristics*. On this line, they prepared a curriculum based on the lower primary course and *adapted . . . to the requirements of Moslem children. . . .* Great stress was laid on the adoption of readers specifically prepared for the use of Moslem boys."[96] Notwithstanding the official rhetoric of the administration about placing Muslims on par with Hindus in terms of educational achievements, such differentiated curricula may well have heightened, if not sealed, the awareness of difference between Hindu and Muslim children in terms of their respective suitability to receive a Western (i.e., "superior" in terms of the nineteenth-century discourse of coloniality) education. Note also the certainty of knowledge about the "definite characteristics" of maktabs and the special "requirements of Moslem children" expressed by the administration, as if they were essentially determined and readily accessible to the colonial authorities.[97] What is more, the report notes, "Whereas in Western Bengal the method adopted [in 1909–10] was to encourage maktabs to add secular subjects to their curriculum, in Eastern Bengal the general policy advocated tended rather to the inclusion of subjects *suitable for Mussalmans* in secular schools than to the secularization of maktabs . . . with some additional instruction in the Quoran and ritual of Islam."[98]

In other words, the policies were designed to deepen, if not foster, yet another kind of difference/inequality—that between Muslims in the two halves of Bengal. While the maktabs of western Bengal were being encouraged to secularize Islamic pedagogy, the Muslims in eastern Bengal seemingly received the subtle message that they did not quite need (or perhaps deserve) Islamic pedagogy, underscoring ever so surreptitiously their status as "converts," that is, "originally Hindu," in British colonial thinking. Meanwhile, the so-called secularization policy of the madrasah system in western Bengal was also fraught with problems. According to an editorial published in 1923 in a Calcutta-based monthly, "Compared to 25–30 years ago, the spread of English education among Muslims [in Bengal has been impressive]. . . . In this matter, the Muslims from East Bengal have shown quite an impressive rise in numbers. . . . [But] the situation in West . . . Bengal is not hopeful. . . . The new scheme junior madrassahs . . . qualify neither as schools nor as Arabic madrassahs. . . . [The result is a hotchpotch where] it is impossible to get a good education."[99] It would seem that the full implications of British educational policies for the fissured ways in which Islamic identity developed in late colonial Bengal have yet to be fully appreciated or understood.

For our present purposes, suffice it to note that by the beginning of the twentieth century both the number and proportion of Muslim students in schools began to rise slowly.[100] Contemporary Bengali accounts also record a heightened awareness among Muslim peasants of the importance of education for the economic improvement of both the individual and the collective—a concern that seems to have grown in tandem with a sense of community at the beginning of the twentieth century.[101] It seems that a combination of relative prosperity among at least some peasants (stemming from a rise in the price of jute), the expansion of educational opportunities, and a more self-conscious ideology of improvement meant that more rural households were prepared to send their sons to the cities for a "profitable" education, producing over time a new class of educated Muslims who were soon vying for midlevel professional opportunities under the colonial administration that had erstwhile been the preserve of the Hindu bhadralok. The result was that not only the urban elite—which had lost its prestige and influence with the British government since the abolition of Persian as the official administrative language in 1837 and especially after the Revolt of 1857—but also the rural ashraf and, in some cases, upwardly mobile peasant households were increasingly locked in a bitter competition with the Hindu middle class.

In contrast to the urban elite, intellectuals from this loosely defined Muslim middle class—predominantly men at first—who were closely connected to the urban-based periodicals mentioned earlier in this chapter, typically hailed from the villages, had availed themselves of a non-Islamic, western education, and produced some of the more influential intellectuals and political figures of twentieth-century Bengal from their ranks.[102] Structurally this group constituted a crucial link between rural Bengal, where most of its members still had family, and the urban centers, where they would often live as students and later workers.

In terms of absolute numbers the Muslim middle class may not have been large at the beginning of the twentieth century.[103] There were also considerable politico-ideological differences among members of this group. There were, however, two elements that shot through much of the public deliberations of the Bengali Muslim middle class: an engagement with the European narrative of progress, on the one hand, and a clear and insistent commitment to the identity location, Bengali Muslim on the other. If the first of these two elements accounted for many of the differences in the imaginations of community within this loosely defined class, then the second offered perhaps its one consistent point of convergence. And it was the latter, the simultaneous interest in Bengali-ness and Muslim-ness, that set the middle class's ideas apart from earlier attempts to produce a community by the revivalist leaders and Islamic orthodoxy and helped it formulate its own position vis-à-vis both the Hindu-led nationalist movement and the political aspirations of the North Indian Muslim leadership in the twentieth century.[104] In short, together the middle-class intellectuals represented an important third group among Muslims in late colonial Bengal—beyond the suffocating limits of the ashraf-atrap binary normalized by colonial discourse—which, through its many debates, played a crucial role in giving meaning and density to the category "Bengali Muslim."[105]

Some important issues were discussed and debated in the publications popular with the Muslim middle class during the first four decades of the twentieth century: the need to create and maintain a distinct identity that would be both Bengali *and* Muslim through cultivation of the Bengali language and a literary and intellectual tradition that would adequately represent Muslims in Bengal; the importance of promoting non-Islamic, western education among Muslims along with better knowledge of the basic tenets of the religion;[106] the need to eradicate social, especially castelike, divisions among Muslims; the need for greater political consciousness regarding colonial rule and the anticolonial struggle; relationships with non-Muslims, especially Hindus, in the realm of social intercourse and political cohabitation; the performance of Muslims in a modern urban economy in which professional opportunities were often dominated by Hindus; and social reforms, including those that would change the normative practices of gender relations and the organization of social life that such practices engendered. To ignore the Muslim middle class and the breadth of its concerns is to miss or deny the very possibility of alternate imaginations of community, including ones that might have been less divisive and more plural; it is also to miss the presence of Muslim women as writers, activists, and reformers in the first half of the twentieth century in Bengal.

While a comprehensive survey of the various issues that preoccupied the Bengali Muslim intelligentsia in that period is beyond the scope of the present study, it will be useful to sketch some important debates of the time in order to both apprehend the range of ideological positions that these intellectuals spoke from and place the explicit discussions around gender reforms, especially the contribution of women writers, within the context of the vibrant debates over social reforms and political activism that characterized Muslim public discourse in early-twentieth-century Bengal. This undertaking is crucial if we are to understand Muslim women as actors within a larger intellectual-political movement rather than as remarkable but ultimately marginal figures who can be granted visibility and voice only within the "safe" zone of feminist recuperative scholarship.

DIVISIONS

It is useful to remember that members of the Muslim middle class did not speak with one voice; nor did they always focus on the same issues. Periodicals from the early twentieth century amply reflect the cleavages in the political and ideological positions taken by the different writers or groups on a wide range of issues. Such ideological divergences and the debates that ensued from them prompted Akram Khan—an influential intellectual and powerful actor in the political landscape of late colonial Bengal—to describe a majority of these writers as either "narrow-minded traditionalists" (shankirnachitya pracheenpanthee), or "enchanted modernists" (mohamugdha adhunik).[107]

At the same time, it is important to clarify at the outset that both factions—the so-called traditionalists and modernists—were obliged to grapple with an overarching "idiom of progress," which the colonial state used repeatedly to legitimize its presence in the subcontinent and Muslim elites, as well as the Hindu bhadralok, were deploying against the masses of Muslim converts in the second half of the nineteenth century. The much touted ideological divergences between the two factions were thus the result of their different engagements with that discourse of progress, albeit toward different ends. Our concern here will be primarily, though not exclusively, with the work of those writers who were marked as modernists at that time and have since been described variously as "liberal," "progressive," or "secular humanist" in the extant literature—since they were most likely to entertain the prospect of liberal reforms that would eventually have profound implications for the practice of gender segregation, women's education, and their entry into public life in early-twentieth-century Bengal.[108]

It is, of course, impossible to situate every author or periodical neatly along the so-called conservative/liberal divide, especially since such significant intellectual figures as Maniruzzaman Eslamabadi, Ismail Hossein Siraji, and even Akram Khan himself were quite likely to support a range of ideological positions depending on the questions at hand. But the divisions were relatively clear in the works of writers at either end of the ideological spectrum. So, for instance, contributors to periodicals such as *Akhbar-e-Islamia*, *Mihir O Sudhakar*, *Islam Pracharak*, *Al Eslam*, and especially *Islam Darshan* seem to have been concerned primarily with promoting an understanding and the spread of orthodox Islam among the Muslim masses in Bengal, who were, as we have seen, prone to religious syncretism. As one article from 1885 described it, "Looking at the disastrous situation of the Muslim society [in Bengal] one is truly . . . reduced to tears. All sacred rules have disappeared, rituals and practices have become sinful, and each day we are a little closer to ruin."[109] This concern with the purification of the practice of Islam seems to have been widespread and lasted well into the twentieth century, for as late as in 1919, in an article published in the *Al Eslam*, we find Siraji bemoaning the fact that under the misguidance of the Sufis and *pirs* the masses were on their way to moral "degeneration and annihilation."[110]

The social reform agenda advocated in these periodicals was also likely to be tied closely to the overall project of disseminating "proper" knowledge of Islam. Articles carried by these periodicals often frowned on the reading of novels, considered the cultivation of music *haram* (unholy), disapproved of nonsecular education for women, and supported seclusion, even if in a modified form.[111] Not surprisingly, it is rare to find women writers represented in the pages of these periodicals.

In some important respects, the vision espoused in many of these articles is reminiscent of the teachings of the nineteenth-century religious revivalist/reformist movements. But, unlike the early revivalist leaders of the previous century, some of the writers that patronized these periodicals, though not all,[112] tended to be loyal to British rule and quite explicitly suspicious, if not antagonistic, to Hindus and the Hindu-led nationalist movement. Consider, for instance, an excerpt from an article published in *Islam Pracharak*, which reads, "No one can deny that we are living in great peace and comfort under the British. Such peace and quiet are rare under foreign rule. But our highly educated Hindu brothers refuse to acknowledge that. Those mentally deranged and shortsighted Muslims . . . who are joining the Hindus [in the anticolonial agitation] are either hypocritical cowards or complete fools."[113] Some writers, most notably those associated with the Sudhakar group of Calcutta and Pir Shah Abu Bakr of Furfura, who patronized the periodical *Islam*

Darshan, seem to have been quite outspoken in preaching an "anti-Hindu" and "anti-Christian" form of Islam, even as they laid claim to a Bengali identity and professed their support for British colonial rule.[114] The connections between social and religious conservatism, on the one hand, and political calculations, on the other, were far from simple in the works of these writers.

On the other end of the ideological spectrum, writers—women among them—associated with early periodicals such as *Kohinoor* and *Nabanoor* or, more significantly, the later *Bangiya Mussalman Sahitya Patrika*, *Saogat*, *Shikha*, *Jayati*, *Dhumketu*, *Samyabadi*, and *Ganabani* favored liberal interpretations of the scriptures and were opposed to the power of Islamic orthodoxy.[115] However, even among these writers engagements with the idea of modernity are often accompanied by an impulse to make it consistent with tradition. For instance, as early as 1904, in an article advocating formal education for Muslim girls, we find Khaerunnessa Khatun drawing on the "Hadis sharif" to argue that education was necessary, indeed a *farz* (responsibility), for both men and women.[116] A few decades later, another woman, Firoza Begum, attacked the religious leadership, or *molla samaj*, as she called it, for representing the "biggest impediment to women's education," even as she echoes the orthodox ulema's glorification of the roles of women as "mothers" and "housekeepers." She wrote, "They believe that . . . [if women receive] the light of education . . . [they will become] undisciplined, [they will lose] . . . their faith in religion, [and their] devotion to their husbands will diminish. . . . All these fears . . . are unfounded. . . . [The mullahs refuse to consider the fact that] with proper education women will not only become good housekeepers and mothers, but also . . . adequate . . . companions to their husbands."[117] Other writers extolled the idea of a "golden past"—an age of true Islam—and exhorted their readers to return to the "real" teachings of Islam.[118] We will return to the gendered assumptions underlying such advocacies of middle-class women's education later in the chapter. For now, let us simply note them as examples of the complex negotiations with modernity attempted by ostensibly "liberal" writers as well as women protesting the oppressive hold of the Islamic orthodoxy on their lives.

The more radical among this so-called liberal or modernist group were associated with the Muslim Sahitya Samaj [Muslim Literary Society] of Dhaka and wrote regularly for the periodicals *Shikha* and *Saogat*.[119] Inspired by secular humanist ideals, some of these writers strove to extend Muslim public thinking and discussion on reforms beyond the sanctioned limits of religious discourse and even called for a complete rethinking of the Shariat (Islamic religious law) for the sake of "progress" and the "greater good of humanity." In one such attempt to think beyond conventions, Kazi Abdul Wadud wrote:

> We have to entirely rethink how Islam can be beneficial to human beings. . . . [The Islam that our predecessors left for our consideration] . . . has supported seclusion of women, has cursed the institution of interest, has objected to the cultivation of the arts, and in the realm of thought has forcefully dictated that all our thinking should always be limited by the teachings of the Quran and the Hadis. We have to re-evaluate all these things, have to ask whether these . . . kinds of obstacles . . . to the independent thinking and work of people in Muslim societies . . . have in fact benefited [us].[120]

In another critical article, Abul Hussein, one of the editors of *Shikha*, argued:

> The way in which Musalmans are hanging on to Islam certainly demonstrates their blind faith, but does not give any indication of [their] knowledge and intelligence. . . . If . . . an Islamic law stands in the way of human progress, then it is necessary to fearlessly cast it aside and build new rules in its place.[121]

The young writers associated with *Shikha* and a few other periodicals such as *Tarunpatra* (date of founding unknown), *Sanchay* (1928), and *Jagaran* (1928)—none of which lasted for long—may have been most (in)famous for their radical ideas, but they were certainly not the only ones to put conventional thinking to the test among the Muslim intelligentsia in early-twentieth-century Bengal.[122] In some isolated cases, the plea for social reform even seems to have called for class-based mobilization leading to a socialist revolution.[123] As one contemporary observer put it, in the wake of the hullabaloo over the reform consciousness of *Shikha* and the charge of "enchanted" leveled against some of the younger writers:

> Saogat spoke up first in defense of independent thinking. . . . Qazi Nazrul Islam, Mahinuddin, Abdul Quader—through their poems, Abul Mansur Ahmad, Abul Fazal, Didarul Alam—through the writing of stories, Abul Hussein, Muhammad Barkatullah, Mohammed Wajed Ali, Abul Kalam Samsuddin, the late Taheruddin Ahmad, Qazi Motahar Hussein (editor of "Shikha"), Muhammad Abdur Rasheed (co-editor of Muslim Sahitya Samaj) and others through essays and other discussions began to construct . . . a new age [in critical think-

> ing among Bengali Muslims]. And this enthusiasm [among the writers associated with *Saogat*] . . . engendered much curiosity and hope among the youth of Bengal.[124]

The existence of such commentaries — both laudatory and critical — testifies to both the vibrancy of the intellectual exchanges and the self-consciousness of the Muslim intelligentsia in late colonial Bengal.[125] It also signals the extent to which engagements with the idea of progress were central to the self-imagination of the Muslim middle class. And yet it is hard to miss the fact that not one Muslim woman writer — a number of whom were publishing regularly by the 1920s — is mentioned in the essay cited above as an active participant in this "new age" of critical thinking. In other words, notwithstanding the formidable contributions of at least some women, for many male writers the protagonists of the intellectual awakening and progress, on the one hand, and the preservation of tradition, on the other, were still men.

Politically these liberal writers typically opposed colonial domination and openly criticized the "divide and rule" policy of the British, which created tensions between Muslims and Hindus.[126] A number of them — the poet Kaekobad, early women writers and activists Khaerunnessa Khatun and Rokeya Sakhawat Hossain, Gholam Mustafa, Maniruzzaman Eslamabadi, Akram Hossein, Sheikh Habibur Rahman, Mohammad Korban Ali, Abul Hussein, Abul Fazal, and Abul Mansur Ahmad, to name only a few — wrote in support of the nationalist agitation in its various stages.[127] But perhaps the most powerful expression of an anticolonial, revolutionary, and pluralistic political vision among Bengali Muslims is captured in the poetry and essays of Qazi Nazrul Islam. To quote from one such essay in which Nazrul spells out his ideas:

> First of all, Dhumketu wants full independence for Bharat [India], . . . Not even one atomic bit of Bharatbarsha [India] should be under foreign domination. The whole responsibility of Bharatbarsha, its defense, its administration ought to be in the hands of Indians. . . . If we have to achieve full independence we have to first revolt, against all rules, regulations, restrictions and discipline.[128]

Not surprisingly, a robust anticolonial stance was also typically accompanied by an aversion to the loyalist politics of the ashraf.[129] Even Maniruzzaman Eslamabadi — himself a pan-Islamist and deeply committed to the spread of a more fundamental understanding and practice of Islam — criticized the politics of "subservience" of the urban Muslim elite and openly berated the Muslim League, which he called the Ji Huzoor (Yes, My Lord) Party of the colonial government.[130] It seems that many others were deeply troubled by both the ashraf's tendency to support political separatism and the increasing communalization of the rural masses, which seemed to be fueled, at least in part, by the combined influence of the religious establishment and the political ambitions of the ashraf.[131]

As these writers saw it, the apathy of Muslims toward the "freedom struggle" against the British did not bode well for the future. I would further suggest that the language used in many of these articles indicates that apathy and loyalism were also seen as unmanly and therefore undesirable. Note, for instance, the explicit appeal to the pride and masculinity associated with a Muslim identity location in the following quote from an article by Abul Fazal, a young writer of that era.

> There is a nationalist freedom struggle going on in this country. [If] Muslims . . . [stay away from this movement, we will] only cut off . . . [our] own feet. Bharatbarsha will rid itself of foreign rule one day. If Musalmans do not participate in that struggle . . . [later] can the *sons of Musalmans* accept the [charity of] . . . a freedom earned by someone else? Do they have that humility in their blood?[132]

From the many articles written in this vein throughout the 1920s it is easy to see that a sizable portion of the Bengali Muslim intelligentsia was committed to the idea of an independent, unified, and resolutely *plural* Bharat (India).[133] Sometimes they also hint at the complexity and delicacy of the situation in which these intellectuals found themselves in late colonial Bengal: on the one hand, they had to establish their moral and political distance from the separatism associated with large sections of both the urban ashraf and the rural Muslim population; and, on the other, they were continually frustrated in their pursuit of a distinctly Bengali Muslim social and cultural ethos, within an overarching framework of political unity and a sociocultural universe shared with Bengali Hindus, by the majoritarian arrogance and politics of the Hindu bhadralok.

Awareness of Hindu cultural solipsism and disdainful attitudes toward Muslims was, of course, not a product of the 1920s. As early as the first decade of the century, we find articles by Bengali Muslims—published, for instance, in *Nabanoor* between 1903 and 1905—reacting to Hindu attitudes toward

Muslims and calling for the improvement of the relationship between the two communities.[134] The dominant tone in some of these earliest attempts by Muslim writers to deal with this thorny issue was that of dismay, even anger, at the slanderous representations of Muslims—including at times Muslim women—by the Hindu bhadrasampraday.[135] Consider, for instance, an article titled "Hindu Narir Muslim Ghrina" (Hindu Women's Hatred for Muslims), published in 1903 in *Nabanoor*, in which Imdadul Huq takes issue with an essay written by a Hindu woman that featured some rather uncharitable allusions to Muslim women.[136]

> Illogical, unproven, [and] historically indefensible, deeply ingrained hatred for Muslims can be found on virtually every page of Bengali literature. . . . Even learned women writers are no exception. . . . By accusing all Muslim women of immorality, the writer has revealed . . . her immense arrogance and tasteless womanly love of name-calling. . . . That she has not been criticized for her efforts but rather praised and rewarded by Hindu society only goes to show the narrow-mindedness of Hindu society.[137]

Of course, as his own essentialist slant about the "womanly love of name-calling" (*meyeli galipriyata*) would suggest, Huq may have been more concerned with the appropriate representation of Muslims than with that of women. Still, both his article and the one by Shyamasundari Debi to which he was responding are important documents that record the complex, often oblique ways in which Muslim women made their appearance in contemporary debates over representations and the deeply gendered terms in which discourses of community were typically articulated.

Another essay published in *Nabanoor* in the same year records a bitter, if restrained, protest against Hindu disdain for Muslims, as captured in the following excerpt:

> In reality we desire true unity between Hindus and Muslims; that is necessary for India's welfare at present. . . . This is why we are keeping quiet in spite of so much provocation. . . . We also realise that we could gain a lot with the help and cooperation of Hindus. . . . However, there is a limit to our endurance; the day when that ultimate line is crossed, will be a terrible day of confrontation between Hindus and Muslims in India. That is a certainty.[138]

The debates surrounding the 1905 partition of Bengal and the Swadeshi agitation seem to have deepened the cleavages between the two communities, leading even the more liberal among the Muslim middle class to express grave reservations about the opportunism of Hindu majoritarian politics and the rise of Hindu nationalism.[139] So, for instance, in 1904, in an article titled "Dumukho" (Two-Faced), we find Osman Ali attacking the hypocrisy of the Hindu Bengalis for asking Muslims to join in their struggle against the British when writings by Hindus were replete with insulting references to Muslims. "Readers!" he asks, "Do you recognize how much selfishness and insincerity is hidden in these honeyed words?"[140] This was only 1903–4, and the existence of a serious rift between the two communities, albeit amid calls for mutual "help and cooperation," was already evident even in the pages of a generally anticolonial and anticommunal periodical such as *Nabanoor*. The position adopted by periodicals such as *Islam Pracharak*, which was patronized by the more orthodox Muslims, was far more critical of the Hindu-led Swadeshi movement.[141]

By the 1920s, especially in the post-Khilafat Non-Cooperation period, the relationship between the two communities took a sharp turn for the worse under the onslaught of the communalizing activism of both Hindu and Muslim ideologues.[142] Consequently, while we find many articles by Muslim intellectuals in the late 1920s still decrying the gratuitous slandering of Muslims by Hindus, they seem to register neither surprise nor anguish at such practices.[143] What is more, these articles from the 1920s and 1930s seem to have been written with mostly a Muslim audience in mind, signaling not only the presence of a sizable Bengali-reading public among Muslims by the third decade of the twentieth century but perhaps also a retreat from an earlier moment, at the turn of the century, when periodicals were being launched through the combined efforts of Muslim and Hindu intellectuals with the stated intent of building communal amity.[144] Many articles published in the early twentieth century seem to attempt to explain away the attitude of Hindus as merely "unfortunate" or even as "logical" given their relative social and economic progress.[145] In sharp contrast, articles written two decades later seem much more strident in holding Hindus accountable for their role in producing the communal dramas of the 1920s. I quote below from a few essays written by some of the most committed anticommunal Muslims to illustrate this point. Needless to say, there were many others, especially by writers who belonged to the ostensibly "conservative" factions of the Muslim intelligentsia, who were likely to be much more critical of Hindus.[146]

In one essay from 1922, Qazi Nazrul Islam—generally a staunch advocate of communal amity—attacked the evils of Brahminical Hinduism in his characteristically bold and direct way.

> It is our deep conviction that the main obstacle to Hindu-Musalman unity is the disgusting issue of untouchability. . . . A religion [Brahminical Hinduism] that teaches human beings to hate [others] so much is not a religion whatever else it may be. . . . I can challenge anyone [who believes otherwise]."[147]

Saogat—an important locus of liberal-progressive thinking and activism among Muslim intellectuals in early-twentieth-century Calcutta—also published a series of articles focused on the thorny issue of Hindu and Muslim relations in which the authors explicitly protested the Hindu tendency to malign Muslims. One article, titled "Jaban" (1929), caustically points out the use of derogatory terms by Hindu writers.

> These days, people who use the word *Jaban* to mean Mussalmans, reveal a tremendous disgust in their minds for Muslims. . . . Examples of such usage are quite common in the Bengali literary tradition. . . . We have a question for [Hindu writers and especially editors of periodicals]—"when will the word *jaban* be expelled from [your] lexicon"?[148]

In a second essay, "Sahitye Shatantra Kano?" (Why This Difference within Literature?), Mohammad Wajed Ali, appears to be entirely reconciled to the tension between the two communities since, as he ruefully observes, the lack of trust of and respect for Muslims was integral to the cultural nationalism espoused by a majority of the Hindu bhadralok from its very inception in the mid–nineteenth century.

> Hindus respect Bankim Chandra because he is the high priest of the idea of independence. But what has he given us? The self-rule he advocates is based on hatred of Muslims. His song *Bande Mataram* is filled with idolatry images. . . . Yet Hindus are trying to get it accepted as a national anthem for a nation of both Hindus and Muslims. . . . Bankim may have great talent as a writer, but he has not managed to overcome his communal mentality.[149]

But perhaps the most poignant indictment of Hindu insensitivity and arrogance appears in an essay by Abdus Salam Khan that distils for the readers something of the disappointment and anger that Muslims felt toward Hindus.

> If I try to hug you, you will move quickly away from me in the fear of having to bathe again! If I tell you, come brother, we are the children of the same mother, you are older, I am younger, come let us eat together, you will turn up your nose in disgust.... If I attempt to talk to you ... [and] if my demeanour is like yours, you will compliment me by saying that I am not like Musalmans at all, I am exactly like Hindus. If I ... ask you about how many households are there in your village, you will effortlessly say that–so many *bhadralok* households, so many *dhopa* [washerman/washerwoman] households, so many barbers, and so many Muslim households.... [The truth is that] if Hindus are really committed to coming together with Muslims, then Hindus will have to give up on many things.[150]

Khan's sarcastic rehearsal of the ignominies endured daily by a vast majority of Muslims offers a remarkable picture of the unequal power relations that seem to have obtained between Hindus and Muslims in much of undivided Bengal. Note also that the author expresses his frustration with not only Hindu ritual conservatism but also the limits of a Hindu liberalism that refused to acknowledge even educated, middle-class Muslims as bhadralok. One can only wonder about the level of condescension the Hindu elite might have harbored toward Muslims of lesser means.

This was clearly a world far removed from the realm of wealth and influence in which the urban ashraf successfully competed with, and at times upstaged, the Hindu upper and middle classes. It was also a world whose concerns, disappointments, and calculations are routinely glossed over in conventional accounts of the nation and Partition, which continue to be largely preoccupied with the high politics of the Hindu and Muslim nationalist elites.[151]

The Muslim intelligentsia, with a large number of its members hailing from upwardly mobile rural households, was only too aware of the huge disparity between Hindus and Muslims in Bengal in terms of economic performance, which to a large extent provided the bulwark for the continued arrogance of the Hindu bhadralok. As early as in 1901, we find an article titled "Mussalmaner Sarbonash" (The Destruction of Muslims) published in *Nabanoor*, in which the author cites employment figures from the 1881 census to argue that Hindus far outnumbered Muslims (by roughly ten to one) at all levels of government employment.[152] Almost three decades later, yet another article—an editorial—in another influential Muslim journal recorded the disparity that still obtained between the two communities and the frustration of at least some members of the Muslim middle class over this state of affairs.

> The Hindus are today fifty years ahead of Muslims in not just education but all other departments. They have already made valuable contributions to the civilisation of the world. . . . Even in matters of trade and commerce and general economic advancement Hindus are increasingly more successful. A comparison [between the two communities] shows that the Hindus are *zamindars*, Mussalmans are their subjects; the Hindus are doctors, Mussalmans are their patients; Hindus are professors, Muslims are students; Hindus are lawyers, Muslims are their clients. . . . Hindus have understood in what the source of freedom lies. Muslims are still groping in the darkness.[153]

Notice the explicit use of the "education-modernity-(en)light(enment)-freedom" nexus to describe Hindus and the self-presentation of "groping in the [medieval] darkness," in a breathtaking rehearsal of the European metanarrative of a march (or race) toward a known end—western modernity—in which the Muslims are supposedly laggards.[154] The British, though not explicitly mentioned, are of course already at the end (indeed, they *are* the end) of this story, defining the very terms in which such "progress," or lack thereof, can be calibrated—landownership, doctors, lawyers, professors, freedom, darkness, trade, commerce . . . fifty years.[155] Note also the reference to "the civilisation of the world," to which the Muslims apparently had yet to contribute in 1928!

Such engagements with a linear notion of progress and the idea of Muslim backwardness, as well as explicit comparisons with Hindus, were not uncommon among women writers. While I will focus on debates over "women's condition" later in the chapter, the following excerpt from an article by Badrunnessa Khatun, published in 1929 in the first issue of *Mahila Saogat* (Women's Saogat), may be cited here to illustrate the point at hand.

> Even in this twentieth century, our ill-fated society refuses to acknowledge the importance of educating women. . . . It is hard to fathom the depths of ignorance that we are buried under in all matters, compared to women in other countries, and even Hindu women in India.[156]

This was a very different vision of a community than what was espoused by either the revivalist leadership or the high ulema during the nineteenth-century reforms from within. If the modernizationist project undertaken by the British aimed, like modern power anywhere, at "uprooting" other modes of knowing and organizing the world by attacking and replacing the very "conditions that were understood to produce them," then the ideas of progress and backwardness visited so frequently, even if sometimes agonistically, in many of these articles surely bear testimony to its success.[157] Identity tension among Muslims in Bengal is often explained in the extant literature as a product of the need to reconcile an inherited "Islamic" (i.e., Perso-Arabic) culture with a new Bengali one.[158] A nuanced look at the writings of Bengali Muslim intellectuals from the early twentieth century, however, points to yet another source of tension—Muslim perceptions of, reactions to, and perhaps even internalization of the prevailing constructions of the categories "Bengali" and "Muslim" produced within the context of colonial discourse and practice but often engineered by Hindus—that, in my reading, played a seminal role in shaping middle-class Muslim subject locations in late colonial Bengal.

Of course, Muslim intellectuals were not reconciled to their so-called backwardness and did not simply blame the Hindus and British for their attitudes; as was intimated earlier, they were also engaged in a trenchant autocritique. So, for instance, in 1928 Mohammad Nasiruddin, the editor of *Saogat*, wrote:

> [We have to] come to terms with the Hindus ourselves. The place for that confrontation is the Congress. . . . [There] if we have to fight, we will fight, if we have to compromise, we will compromise. But why should we . . . flee from the Congress because we are angry with the Hindus[?] . . . *Bharatbarsha is our motherland.* Musalmans have as much claim on it as Hindus do. . . . [We] will not leave *our country* because we are frustrated with or hurt by the Hindus. We will not leave the Congress, we will . . . [take the place] that is *rightfully ours.*[159]

One way to proceed was by vigorously participating in the realm of Bengali literature, not in blind imitation of Hindu writers but through a concerted effort to challenge the limits of the Sanskritized Bengali normalized by Hindus. As one author put it:

> . . . A language that is mainly a carrier of Hindu ideas can never be adequate to express all the thoughts and feelings of Muslims. So it is essential to have words used by Muslims accepted within the Bengali lexicon. . . . Otherwise . . . [Muslim intellectuals like us] would be neglecting our duty.[160]

In a similar vein, Nurunnessa Khatun, a well-known woman writer who was given the title Bidyabinodini for her learning, wrote:

> Our lack of confidence in our birthright [to be Bengali] has kept our society crippled. . . . We have to claim in a loud voice—I am Bengali, and this Bengali literature is my literature. . . . [We must tell ourselves that] we, too, can achieve what others have achieved.[161]

Others—especially the writers associated with the literary society Muslim Sahitya Samaj—argued that the task facing Muslim intellectuals was not one of simply "catching up" with the Hindus in terms of literary representation, or of creating a new language, but one of fostering adequate communication and understanding in order to stem communal unrest.[162] Keenly aware of the role played by Muslims in the ugly wranglings that erupted in the mid-1920s over issues such as *go-korbani* ([cow sacrifice), "music before mosques," and the alleged "abduction" of Hindu women by Muslim men, some of these authors insisted that Muslims had to "deserve respect" before they could "demand" it from others.[163] Kazi Abdul Wadud went so far as to declare that categories such as "Hindu" and "Muslim" should be deleted altogether, for it was the perception of such difference that stood in the way of a secular humanist, nationalist movement in colonial India.[164]

This willingness to be sharply self-critical and the ability to do so carry over into the social reform debates, with some authors calling for revisions of Islamic laws, if necessary, to facilitate much needed change. Not surprisingly, women figure most insistently—though not exclusively—in the debates over particular social reforms both as their authors and as the focus of the discussions.[165] And, while they were clearly aware of anticolonial politics and the issue of Muslim-Hindu relations, Muslim women were much more likely than their male counterparts to focus in their writing on reforms that would bring welcome changes to women's lives. It is therefore in the context of debates over education, especially *streeshiksha* (women's education), *abarodhpratha* (seclusion), and to lesser extent issues such as *balyabibaha* (child marriage), *bahubibaha* (polygamy), and *talak* (divorce) that we most often find women writing. And it is to these discussions, especially those most obviously pertaining to women's position in Bengal in the first half of the twentieth century, that we now turn in the final section of this chapter. Once again, my aim here is not to present the entire corpus of writings on such issues by Bengali Muslims from the early twentieth century but to investigate how understandings of gender structured these discussions over adequate and proper Muslim womanhood (and sometimes, by implication, manhood) carried on by middle-class Muslim intellectuals—both women and men—and to what ends.[166]

THE DEBATES OVER GENDER OPPRESSION AND PRIVILEGE

A substantial number of Muslim writers across the ideological spectrum were troubled by what they considered the "deplorable condition" of Muslim women in Bengal. Many of the articles that appeared in the first two decades of the twentieth century in periodicals such as the *Kohinoor*, the *Pracharak*, *Nabanoor*, and even the more self-consciously religious *Islam Pracharak* and *Al Eslam*,—penned mostly, though not always, by men in these early years—seem to have been preoccupied with the institutions of child marriage, the indiscriminate practice of polygamy, the problem of easy divorce, widow remarriage, and the need for literacy among women.[167] They were also typically inflected by an anxiety over what the "condition of women" might reveal about the performance of Muslims in the race toward modernity. So, for instance, one article by Siraji begins with a list of the deleterious effects of child marriage on women but ends with a denouncement of the institution as a cause of "the downfall of the Islamic race."

> [The practice] is more harmful for girls [than for boys]. After marriage girls are deprived of habitual happiness and carefree-ness associated with childhood. . . . [Not only does early marriage disrupt their education, but it also leads to] inhuman treatment of girls in most cases. . . . Some [women] conceive early . . . and give birth to weak and lifeless children. . . . No matter how one looks at it, nothing good comes out of the practice of child marriage. It is one of the main reasons behind the downfall of the Islamic race.[168]

Siraji's article anticipates the way in which concerns over the downfall of or fear of straying from "true Islam" (for the conservatives) and the progress of the Muslim community/Indian nation (for the liberals) would come to frame most subsequent social critiques by Muslim writers, including those by women.[169] Even the *Moajjin*, a periodical that published articles opposing the colonial government's attempts to fix the legal age of marriage at fourteen for girls and eighteen for boys in the late 1920s, carried a number of essays conceding that, to its own detriment, "Bengali Muslim society" deprived women of the rights granted to them under Islam.[170]

The discussions surrounding polygamy and divorce, on the other hand, were considerably more complex, revealing the much higher stakes in controlling the sexuality of adult women and the limits of male reformist largesse. While many male writers acknowledged the "excesses" associated with the institutions, they seemed curiously unwilling to denounce them wholeheartedly, and much of the discussion remained limited to the question of what was proper or sanctioned within the Islamic code or good for the community rather than the welfare of women.

An early article by Kaji Imdadul Huq, who was recognized by his contemporaries as a reformer and one of the "true littérateurs" of that era, set the tone for the discussion.[171] He suggested that the limited practice of polygamy might be in order, since the sex ratio was skewed in favor of women (104 women to every 100 men), but the "senseless" polygamy that was common among Muslims could not be supported by the sacred texts.[172] A few years later, Siraji argued that more than one marriage is "justifiable" only if "one's wife is barren or chronically sick." Otherwise, the institution, which he claimed caused "great distress," should "never be supported" without *due consideration*.[173]

Others, such as Muhammad K. Chand, Jamiruddin, and especially Maulana Akram Khan, attacked the gross misuse of the provision for *talak* (the right to divorce) in Islam.[174] In contrast to the conventional understanding of talak as the unilateral right of men to divorce women, Khan, who was known for his "insistence on regulating Islam by the Koran and the Hadis" and his emphasis on the individual's duty to interpret the texts, argued that, in fact, Islam provided women with a similar right to divorce their husbands under certain conditions.[175]

Khan's intervention in this regard is significant. For, while many of his contemporaries wrote eloquently about the "plight" of Muslim women in early-twentieth-century Bengal, for a majority of them the sole solution to women's problems seemed to lie in men's ability and willingness to change their own conduct. Women, in these arguments, appeared only as victims with no agency in determining or even influencing their lot. What is more, the repeated references to religious dicta in many of these essays reveal something of the underlying preoccupation of these writers: the supposed failure of Muslim men to interpret and observe the tenets of the holy texts, and the resultant degradation of the *practice* of Islam in Bengal, and the general decline of the Muslim community. The condition of women simply provided a discomfiting index to these larger problems. In article after article, one comes across discussions of the "abuses" and "excesses" of the institutions of polygamy, men's right to talak, dowry, and even child marriage, resulting presumably from widespread ignorance of Islamic law or the bad influences of Hindu practices.[176] What is missing in the works of most male writers of that time is any attempt to develop a thoroughgoing critique of these institutions as unilateral technologies of domination deployed against women by men, even in their more benign forms.

A second, and related, problem is that, even as the "condition of women" was widely understood to be a result of men's neglect, ignorance or even cruelty, there is a complete lack of acknowledgment in these writings of the relational nature of women's oppression and male privilege. In other words, "women's condition" was ultimately seen as somehow innately related to women only and something that could be fixed simply by relaxing the severity of the restrictions imposed on them. Men's responsibility, to the extent it was acknowledged at all, was seen to be limited to their agency in maintaining the social constraints that disadvantaged women; there was little understanding in these writings that men were benefiting from women's near incarceration and forced dependence on them. Consequently, while talk about "letting" women do certain things filled the pages of these periodicals, most male writers, at least in these early years, seemed neither able nor willing to imagine substantive changes that could affect the balance of power between men and women. Instead, both the problems of women and the proposed solutions were articulated strictly in terms of women's "natural abilities," predispositions, or at best their rights as guaranteed by Islam—all of which were based on, and in turn reinforced, the perceived differences between the sexes and the putative superiority of men in all matters.

A number of women were also publishing from the beginning of the twentieth century when the process of sustained literary and critical production by Bengali Muslim intellectuals had only just begun.[177] Contrary to contemporary expectations of "authentic" women's writing, these pieces explicitly engaged crucial social and political issues of the day.[178] Nor were they simple mimicries of what men wrote; while many of their male counterparts articulated the need for social reforms in terms of the regeneration of the community/nation, the early women writers kept their focus trained squarely on women's welfare. What is more, in a bold move away from the prevailing assumption (among male writers) that men were the primary agents of change, these women writers argued that women could not continue to rely solely on men's ability and inclination to change women's condition; women had to take matters of reform in their own hands.

One of the earliest enunciations of this attitude, albeit in a muted form, came from the aforementioned Khaerunnessa Khatun, who was the headmistress of a girl's school in North Bengal.[179] Khaerunnessa did not observe purdah, but she was sensitive to the ubiquity and power of this institution in Bengali society at that time. As she put it in an essay on the need for literacy among Muslim women:

> It is not within our means to overcome the restrictions [placed on us by Islam], and it is illicit. We do not have the unrestricted right to travel to other villages like Hindu women do. . . . The first and main obstacle to the spread of education [among Muslim women] is [therefore] the lack of appropriate schools . . . [which have to be established] in each town, each village, and if necessary, even in each neighbourhood. It is necessary to employ respectable Muslim women teachers in these schools; and the schools . . . ought to be established . . . in such a way that . . . women [can maintain] . . . seclusion [when attending them], and men will not be allowed to enter the school premises. . . . [Since it is more difficult to arrange for young women to travel to schools, [we] need not be so keen on educating them yet. . . . [But] the future of our society depends on girls; therefore, we [should concentrate on] . . . educating them now.[180]

Khaerunnessa's reform agenda was admittedly not very expansive; nor was her prose quite as "whiplash" (*chabuk-mara*) as that of her better-known and much celebrated, as well as maligned, contemporary, Rokeya Sakhawat Hossain.[181] And yet one is struck by the pragmatism and concreteness of her ideas.

Khaerunnessa seemed to understand the scope of the task facing reformers involved in various projects of modernization in early-twentieth-century Bengal, and she proceeded to utilize her limited mobility to do what she could for women's literacy. She founded a night school for girls, and traveled from village to village to mobilize families to let their daughters attend her school. But the modesty of her ideas and the near diffidence with which she presented them should not distract us from noting that Khaerunnessa was simultaneously a working woman, a social reformer, and an active participant in the nationalist agitation against the first partition of Bengal in 1905 at a time when seclusion in some form or other was the norm for an overwhelming majority of middle class women—Muslim *and* Hindu.[182] She was also among the earliest Muslim women known to have publicly expressed her concerns about contemporary social and political issues.[183] And yet it is hard to find even the barest trace of this remarkable, if understated, figure in the official history of colonial Bengal.

A second writer who took on the subject of social inequalities, with particular attention to men's investment in keeping women both uneducated and dependent, was Masuda Rahman, also known as Mrs. M. Rahman.[184] Known as *Banglar agninagini* (Bengal's fire serpent) for her fiery prose and intrepid attacks on male domination, Masuda Rahman came to be seen as something of "a revolutionary writer" of that age.[185] Much of her writing is fraught, and, one might say, even burdened, with anguish—straining, as it were, against the myriad restrictions that women were forced to endure at that time and an overwhelming desire for what was denied them. Take, for instance, the following passage in which she gives voice to her intense frustration over her inability to gain access to a formal education.

> Quran, Quran Sharif . . . the . . . [object of] my demonic hunger. . . . I have not been able to comprehend you until today. I want to understand you, know you, I want to eat you up. . . . My elders did not give me . . . [Quranic] instruction, [and they] hid the words of [the Prophet] from me. . . . Society has ruled that woman should only cook, . . . deliver babies like a bitch (*kukkurir moto*), abide by every selfish restriction and ruling . . . [placed by men on them, and] blindly make . . . [respectful offerings] at . . . [men's] feet![186]

Such unabashed expressions of anger and desire akin to lamentation—at times directed openly at male relatives—may not always make for pleasant reading, but it seems to have made a powerful and timely intervention. As Samsunnahar Mahmud—one of Masuda's younger contemporaries—remarked after her death:

> [She] had arrived at a time of great misery for Muslim women. . . . It is as if all their accumulated pain and sorrow . . . [came alive] in her writing to inspire them . . . [to seek freedom], to make them crazy with the heady desire for freedom (*ajadir neshay pagal*).[187]

Masuda's response to societal injunctions was clear: there was little sense in waiting for men to implement changes since men were deeply implicated in the misery of women. Instead, influenced by Rokeya's thinking, she repeatedly exhorted women to take up their own cause by uniting with each other without any thought to religious and other differences among them.[188] As she put it:

> There are many ways to fulfill womanhood, [not just through] marriage. . . . But we are not educated, self-reliant, self-sufficient or free, [so] what can we do? . . . But is this any justification for sitting quietly? . . . We have to forcefully grab [our rights], through hard work and through loss [if necessary]. . . . Do not [expect anything from men]. *Aha!* They themselves are candidates for pity.[189]

The critical thrust of much of Masuda Rahman's work was undoubtedly directed against the problem of male domination, but, as the final sentence of the excerpt above indicates, her criticism could extend just as easily to other arenas, linking men's behavior toward women to a larger discourse of male cowardice and servility under colonial rule. One might even hazard that she understood something of the gendered nature of the colonial project, which discounted the manliness, indeed humanity, of "native" men, and was thus able to liken the struggle of women with the larger struggle of the anticolonial nationalist movement. So, for instance, in an article titled "Amader Dabi" (Our Demand), Mrs. Rahman begins with the familiar issue of women's subordination with characteristic aplomb but then moves seamlessly into a scathing critique of the loyalist politics of the Muslim elite, which, as we know, many among the Muslim middle-class intelligentsia abhorred. "The mistake," she wrote,

> is totally ours. Whom do we expect our rights from, from men! Those who do not have any claims on anything, who themselves seek to . . . [be] beggars, who . . . [caught in the vice grip of slavishness] have reduced their life's ideals [to nothing], whose very souls have become enslaved, *they* will grant us our rights? They will give us freedom? [Are we] mad or something?[190]

Note that Masuda's critique is not unlike the formulation of Anglicist critics in the nineteenth century, who identified the degradation of women as an indication of "rude," uncivilized, or "degenerate" peoples and cultures.[191] But, unlike the British, who read the condition of women as a function of the adequacy/inadequacy of men—that is, their manliness—and hence its amelioration in terms of reforms initiated by men, Masuda seems to deny the need for men's involvement altogether in her envisioned project of women's self-improvement. Nor was she content with the idea of women being "exalted" as passive symbols of the civilizational achievements of men and their communities/nations. Instead, in her anticolonial vision of an ideal society, women appear as equal partners in the struggle to build a modern nation and not simply as the support staff.[192] Thus, while concerns for the welfare of the Muslim community or Indian nation were often present in her writing, they were not allowed to overshadow her primary commitment to the idea of women's welfare and autonomy.

Masuda Rahman was undoubtedly a powerful voice in early-twentieth- century Bengal. She was not necessarily considered an extraordinary writer by her contemporaries, but her defiant prose stood out amid the sluggish, malecentric reform discourse of that era.[193] What is more, her work marks the distance that women in Bengal had traveled, even if mostly in thought and writing, since the mid–nineteenth century when the first women—Brahmo and Hindu in the main—haltingly pleaded with men for better treatment or at best ventured oblique critiques of male domination.[194] Finally, it bears noting that, although Masuda wrote often about the misery of women, they *never* come across as objects of pity in her essays. They are, to borrow her words, "bloodthirsty tigresses" and "trampled serpents"—caged, put upon, neglected but rising, always rising, seeking revenge, rights, and, above all, freedom, albeit defined somewhat fuzzily and entirely uncritically in the early decades of the twentieth century.[195]

Towering over everyone else in this period and beyond was the widely respected, and at the same time intensely criticized, Rokeya Sakhawat Hossain, whose career in writing and reform work spanned roughly three decades with a break of about six years in the wake of her husband's death in 1909. In a sharp departure from most reformist agendas of her time, which focused on women's welfare within their conventionally defined roles as "wife and mother," Rokeya, who was born into an orthodox Muslim aristocratic family and grew up observing strict purdah, firmly believed that in order to really stand up to male oppression women had to be economically independent and even seek employment outside the household if necessary.[196] Not surprisingly, she faced tremendous criticism for her essays—in which she questioned what it means to be simultaneously a woman, Muslim, and Bengali—as well as her efforts to facilitate women's education, especially among Muslims in Calcutta. Apart from numerous critical essays published in a whole array of periodicals run by both Hindus/Brahmos and Muslims, Rokeya also wrote a novel, *Padmaraga*, and a number of short stories.[197]

Much has been written about Rokeya. Several commentators have pointed out that the second phase of her work—after the break in her writing that followed her husband's death—reveals a distinct shift in style. While her early work, exemplified perhaps most famously by her 1904 essay "Amader Abanati" (Our Degeneration), mounted an almost volcanic attack on contemporary social practices and religious dicta, especially as they related to women's subordination, in her later work Rokeya seemed to rely increasingly on satire, even humor, to give voice to her criticism and to focus more on the substance of the needed reforms.[198] Recently scholars have searched her work for signs of sympathy with the nationalist cause and commented on her commitment to a federative approach to religious communities.[199] Others have read her work variously as coming from a "genuine daughter" of Bengal (*khanti bangalir meye*),[200] "an inheritor" of the "legacy of the 'Bengal Renaissance,'"[201] or as the "harbinger" of women's liberation in the twentieth century.[202] Rokeya herself described her early essays as attempts to expose some of the "diseases of society," leaving the problem of "treatment" to the "*hakims*," the social reformers of her time.[203]

While all these commentaries shed ample light on her literary and critical contributions, I would like to foreground two elements of her argument making that, in my opinion, place her work in a realm quite apart from that of her contemporaries, Muslim as well as Hindu: first, the consistency with which Rokeya explores, especially in her early work, the links between men's privilege and women's subordination—that is, the relational nature of gender privilege and oppression; and, second, her insistence on women's agency not only in terms of its supposed emancipatory potential but also, rather more strikingly, in terms of its complicity in perpetuating women's subservience to men. In my reading, it is the second of these two elements—women's agency—that increasingly underpinned her arguments in the course of her writing career.

We will begin with her (in)famous essay "Amader Abanati" (1904) and its revised version, "Streejatir Abanati" (Women's Degeneration) (1905). The essay in both versions opens with the following bold, if somewhat imprecise, comparison between the status of women in India and that of slaves:

> *Pathikagan* (female readers)! Have you ever given any thought to your misery? In this civilized world of the twentieth century what are we? Slaves! I hear that the institution of slavery has disappeared from this world, but has our bondage ended? Why are we slaves? — there are reasons.

Rokeya goes on to delineate various reasons for women's "degeneration." One was religion or, rather, the social injunctions underscored by religion. As she saw it, the holy texts, which contained such injunctions, were nothing but technologies of control invented by men and deployed against women in order "to keep [them] in darkness." Women's oppression, she argued, should be understood as a direct consequence of unfair, malecentric, "social injunctions" embodied in all religions, not merely a by-product of the misplaced conservatism of a few orthodox mullahs, as many of her contemporaries would have it. In her memorable words:

> [Whenever a woman] has tried to raise her head, [she has been] . . . crushed with the excuse of religion or the holy texts . . . [and we have gradually] come to accept [such repression] as religious injunctions. . . . Even our souls have become enslaved. . . . Where the bond of religion is slack . . . women are in a state as advanced as men. . . . I have to say that ultimately "religion" has strengthened the bonds of our enslavement; men are lording over women under the pretext of religion. Hence I am forced to [raise the issue of] "religion." For this religious people will forgive me.[204]

The analogy that Rokeya invokes at the beginning of her essay between two very different institutions — slavery and seclusion — is of course impressionistic, and, while it helped secure the attention of her readers, it is analytically insupportable.[205] It is worth noting that Rokeya's article is reminiscent of Mary Wollstonecraft's 1792 *A Vindication of the Rights of Woman* (1792) both in its specific reference to the analogy between women and slaves and in its general tendency to read femininity as "a distortion of women's human potential."[206] It is possible, of course, that Rokeya was familiar with Wollstonecraft's work, but she is not known to have acknowledged it.[207]

Meanwhile, the "degradation" and "helplessness" of Indian women was one of the most frequently occurring tropes in late-nineteenth-century Victorian reformist discourse on Indian social and cultural life.[208] It was also a common theme in the writing of contemporary Hindu/Brahmo Bengali women.[209] It is entirely likely that Rokeya was aware of such works, especially in light of the specific concerns of the "uplift" literature with the need for women's education in India, a concern that would clearly shape much of her subsequent reform agenda.

However, unlike both the Victorian social reformers and her Hindu/Brahmo predecessors, Rokeya was neither invested in proving the superiority of one set of cultural practices or a particular religion over others nor content with representing women in India only as passive victims of male oppression. Instead, her work launched a much more fundamental attack on the structural logic of gender regimes sanctioned by religion, which allowed men near total control over women's lives everywhere. As a number of commentators have pointed out, in referring to "religion" in the abstract Rokeya implicated *all* religions in the oppression of women, highlighting the universality of the problem of gender inequality at a time when, with few exceptions, Muslim intellectuals engaged in the reform debates throughout the first half of the twentieth century were quite unwilling to go beyond the customary claim that Islam granted enough rights to women.[210] The problem, according to most thinkers of that time, was one of proper implementation of existing rules, not a fundamental reworking of religious laws, a position that Rokeya seemed to reject.[211] Instead her maverick approach of naming religion, or at least religious texts, as both socially constructed and malecentric placed the debate over "women's condition" in an altogether different discursive terrain, one in which men appeared as radically culpable, not simply facilitating or hindering women's ability to achieve a meaningful existence.[212]

"Amader Abanati" incensed even the liberal thinkers of that time, men and women, Muslim and Hindu.[213] By the time it was reprinted in 1905 as part of Rokeya's first anthology, *Matichur* (vol. 1), the essay's title had been changed to "Streejatir Abanati" (Women's Downfall), and it had lost five provocative paragraphs that dealt frontally with male agency in both the social construction of religions and their uses in the project of subordinating women. Rokeya would not tackle the difficult topic of the social implications of differential rights of men and women underpinned by religious laws until much later in her career, perhaps most obviously in her final, unfinished article "Narir Adhikar" (Women's Rights).[214] But the theme of discrimination would continue to shape her understanding of the social and political issues of the day, including her views on community. For instance, while Muslim writers publicly denounced the increased communalization of both Muslims and Hindus in the 1920s for the discord it created between the two communities, and some even took sides in slandering the other community, Rokeya opposed communalism because it facilitated the exploitation of women as exemplified by a vicious campaign around the issue of "abductions."[215] As she wrote in a powerful essay titled "Subeh Sadek":

> For some time now our masters have considered us akin to valuable ornaments. So . . . many kinds of "Women's Protection League" are being set up. Truly, since we are living luggage, there must be a need for alert guards to ensure that we are not stolen. My unfortunate sisters! Do you not feel insulted by this? If you do then why do you suffer such . . . ignominy in silence?[216]

Note that in invoking the Women's Protection League, which was founded by Hindu men ostensibly to protect Hindu women from the threat of abduction by Muslim men, Rokeya is in fact obliquely addressing Hindu women. And yet by treating the abductions problem as only one among many that the "women of Bengal" (*banganari*) faced at that time, she effectively diverts our attention from the communalized meaning of *abduction* to its significance as a tool of male oppression writ large. What is more, unlike other liberal writers, who placed gender reforms within a larger discourse of the needs of the nation/community, Rokeya refused to subordinate women's oppression to any such exigency of community and nation building. And, if her writing did not quite escape the ubiquitous liberal discourse of "progress," as her defense of the use of the *borkha* (veil) and her caustic denouncement of limitless *unnati* (improvement/progress) suggest, her engagement with its oft-repeated metaphors of "emergence/seclusion" and progress remained agonistic at best.[217]

In the wake of the controversy over her critique of religion and male agency early in her career, Rokeya seemed to retreat from an outright confrontation with men, possibly because she sensed the unpreparedness of even liberal men of that time to confront either male implication in the social origins of religious dicta or the challenge of legally reforming religious laws.[218] Instead, in her subsequent writing, she focused increasingly on the problem of women's own culpability in their subordination to men and the need to encourage a desire for self-reliance in women. As Rokeya saw it, the lack of opportunities to engage in meaningful activity produced a state of permanent idleness among women and fed their dependence on men. In her words:

> [Quite like beggars,] having lost all self-esteem, we no longer feel embarrassed to accept charity. . . . Gradually, our minds even have become enslaved. . . .

> The higher faculties of our minds, such as self-reliance, courage etc. have been nipped in the bud so often . . . that they no longer seem to germinate. . . . Since we have lost the ability to differentiate between freedom and slavery, or between improvement and degeneration, men have graduated from being landlords and the masters of households to our "masters." And we have gradually come to be included among their household pets or their valuable possessions. . . . Men say that they are "sheltering us" . . . [but] it is their excessive care that is the reason behind our destruction.[219]

Rokeya's critique of women's "mental enslavement"[220] is particularly sharp when she discusses the importance of jewelry in a woman's life—a theme she had touched on in an essay published in 1903, which produced a veritable furor, and proceeded to develop in "Amader Abanati."[221] Note also that Rokeya may have been aware of an article titled "Self-Love of Ornaments among Bengali Ladies," which appeared in 1880 in the *Journal of the National Indian Association*—a periodical that, for all its concerns with social reform in India, "furnished its readers with . . . stereotypical orientalist images of . . . Indian women."[222] Rokeya's approach to the issue was, of course, anything but orientalist.

> And our beloved jewellery—these are [nothing but] . . . badges of slavery. Prisoners wear iron shackles . . . [and] we [lovingly] wear chains made of gold and silver. . . . And how eager women are for [these signs of bondage]! As if life's happiness and enrichment depend solely on them. . . . No matter how destructive alcohol is, the alcoholic does not want to give it up. Likewise we feel proud when we bear these marks of slavery on our bodies.[223]

Rokeya's comments drew angry responses—many of them from women—that labeled her as misguided, almost antifeminine.[224] Indeed, taken in isolation, her vitriolic attacks of women's love of jewelry may seem somewhat extreme. But a closer look reveals that what Rokeya was debunking were the practices that defined the notion of "ideal femininity," which dictated that women, not men, would be imprisoned in the zenana; expected to shun self-reliance, confidence, and respect; remain uneducated and submissive; and wear jewelry as a sign of acquiescence to their own subordination, all in the name of love. In other words, Rokeya was anticipating something of the late-twentieth-century western feminist critique of the unquestionability of masculine rule—that is, a husband's *God-given* sexual claims on the wife's body based on perceived notions of essential differences between the sexes and the "natural subjection" of women bolstered, in turn, by religious texts. But, unlike later feminist theorists, Rokeya lacked both the institutional and political contexts, and quite possibly the inclination, to develop an adequate theoretical explanation of the link between men's need to dominate women in the private/familial sphere and their claims to membership in the public domain of the political community.[225] Instead, Rokeya, who was an active reformer, was focused on making a strategic intervention based on an understanding of how and why *women* accepted, and, indeed, aided, male domination. Her attacks on women's love of jewelry should therefore be read as a critique of what she thought was a sign of their *willing* submission to masculine rule—that is, their husbands' unquestioned access to and control over their bodies. It is also in this limited sense of having no control over their bodies/sexual labor that Rokeya's comparison between women in seclusion and slaves begins to make sense.

Note also that both in the above excerpts and elsewhere Rokeya is referring mainly to women of the middle and upper classes, since it was predominantly they who had the option of idling in seclusion.[226] In other words, her criticism is directed at a certain normative vision of femininity—docile, inactive, and ultimately serving to strengthen male dominance, both at home and in the world—that was being touted, maybe even internalized, as universally desirable but was in fact underwritten by middle- and upper-class privilege.[227] It would seem that even in the absence of what social scientists several generations later would consider an adequate theoretical language, in deploying gender as a lens through which she saw the workings of other institutions, Rokeya had gone well beyond a simplistic equation of gender inequality with women's oppression to an understanding of gender as "a constitutive element of social relationships," an understanding that is typically ascribed to late-twentieth-century feminist thinking.[228]

No other Muslim author, either before or after Rokeya, addressed these thorny issues quite as openly as she did. Indeed, as one commentator pointed out fifty years after Rokeya's death, no contemporary Hindu/Brahmo woman is known to have written such powerfully critical essays.[229] Even authors who were committed to women's "awakening" in that era did not quite wish for the kind of critical consciousness that Rokeya embodied or for the self-reliance that she advocated for women already in the first decade of the twentieth century.[230] Thus she wrote: "We have to establish that [we are not slaves]. To achieve equality with men we will do whatever is needed of us. If we have to earn [our own] . . . livelihood . . . we will do that also. . . . Why should we not earn? Do we lack hands, or feet, or intelligence? What don't we have? . . . Educate the daughters and let them join the [paid workforce] . . . let them earn their own food and clothing."[231] And, while Rokeya often defined independence for women as equality with men, her work is suggestive at times of a desire to see women as both self-respecting and truly independent of men in thought and deed—yet another feature that separated her reform vision from that of most of her contemporaries.[232]

Finally, it is useful to remember that Rokeya's worldview was a complex outcome of many influences, including her critical appraisal of the kind of "privilege" and token freedom that a new, more benevolent order of male dominance brokered/allowed in the lives of contemporary elite Hindu/Brahmo or Parsi women.[233] The specificity of her approach to the problem of women's subordination and its possible solutions cannot be explained simply in terms of her frustrations as a *pardanasheen* (practicing purdah, or seclusion) Muslim woman, as her Hindu/Brahmo contemporaries and even recent scholars have suggested.[234]

In the 1920s, the debates over the "condition of women" increasingly centered on the intersecting issues of seclusion versus purdah and the need for formal education for Muslim women. Almost everyone agreed that women needed some form of education. Even the most conservative male writers who participated in these debates over the "appropriate" curriculum for women thought that some Islamic and traditional education was "necessary" in order to set women free from their "misery" and help "restore happiness and peace" in Muslim households.[235] As Yasmeen Hossein has pointed out, according to these thinkers: "Women's main responsibility was to do housework, attend to their husbands, bring up children, look after the guests, and maintain discipline and peace in the household. [These writers were by and large] unwilling to see women abandon such responsibilities and [embrace] a new and dynamic life."[236] And, while even this limited notion of education—the kind that women needed in order to protect the interests of the Muslim community against the onslaught of "modernity"—required that the practice of seclusion, in the sense of strict confinement of women inside the four walls of the household, be relaxed, the idea of the unrestricted mobility of women, or the free social mixing of the sexes, was still beyond question for most conservative writers.[237]

There were others who saw seclusion as the single most significant impediment to the spread of education among Muslim women and hence inimical to the very task of building a nation.[238] But even these writers would typically distinguish between the practice of *abarodh* (the actual physical confinement of women within the home) and purdah, defined generally as the "preservation of women's decency and dignity" and at times more specifically as the use of concealing attire such as the borkha (veil and/or veiling gown) or the *chador* (shawl) in public.[239] The following clarification offered by Mohammad Sahidullah is illuminating in this context:

> There are two types of parda. One . . . is Islamic parda, which is the covering of the whole body with the exception of the face, hands and feet; the other is un-Islamic parda, which keeps women imprisoned within the four walls [household]. . . . We must try our utmost to part this un-Islamic parda. Otherwise we will have committed the grave sin of murdering women.[240]

The more "liberal minded" among these critics of abarodh avoided addressing the opposition between purdah and seclusion by making somewhat vague allusions to the "development" of women's persons, once again illustrating the suffocating hold of the idea of progress and its attendant metonyms awakening/emergence and freedom—in most such deliberations. As an editorial in *Mahila Saogat* put it:

> When woman is educated, she . . . herself will decide . . . how much parda she needs. . . . As we understand it, the development of life is the most important thing. Whatever aids in that process of . . . [a person's] development is worth adopting. . . . Where the mind itself is . . . unchaste, what is the usefulness of seclusion? We wish for the end of that seclusion which keeps a person unaware of life and keeps . . . [her] from leading a civilized existence. . . . We want . . . [a] woman . . . [to be able to] experience her own humanity.[241]

One writer whose work offers important clues to the attitudes of putatively "moderate" male writers about seclusion and its relationship to women's role in society was Mohammad Lutfar Rahman. Rahman, who was deeply religious but opposed orthodox interpretations of the scriptures that impinged on women's access to "education and freedom," called on women to find their "revolutionary selves" and become the agents of their own liberation.[242] Reflecting the struggle that many contemporary Muslim intellectuals were experiencing in their efforts to make Islam consistent with the discourse of progress as embodied in the nation form, Rahman insisted that Islam grant women both respect and an equal right to education and declared that "without women's education and freedom, no nation . . . [can] advance."[243] However, rather than subscribe to the dominant male view of women as "[objects of] consumption,"[244] which also tacitly accepted prostitution as the only viable option for women who found themselves outside the "protection" of conventional marriages in late colonial Bengal, Rahman envisioned special craft centers, in the form of residential institutions (ashrams) for women, where they could receive training in different crafts and skills and become self-sufficient.[245]

And yet there is no denying that, while Rahman was genuinely interested in improving the lives of women, especially those who had been forced into sex work, he ultimately subscribed to a specific notion of middle-class respectability that was itself a significant source of restrictions on women's conduct. Consider, for instance, the following excerpt from an essay in which Rahman uses the word *patita* (literally "fallen woman") to describe women involved in sex work, reinforcing in the process the image of the middle-class home as the normative high ground of moral uprightness:

> [If] a woman has no place to go . . . what else can she do but take recourse to sinning? . . . All I . . . [would like to say is] that the fallen should be able to leave the life of sin and stand in front of everyone . . . that she should not have to sell her shame for the sake of [hunger].[246]

Note that while he wrote eloquently against the institution of seclusion, which, according to him, deprived women of education and hence their right and ability to achieve self-sufficiency, Rahman's own prescription for "freedom" and "education" for women was ambivalent at best. In his words:

> The meaning of women's freedom is to awaken women's ability to work, to educate them, let her use her arms, legs and [voice] . . . not the freedom to roam in male[-dominated] society given to evil ways . . . [or to] wanton ends.[247]

In other words, Rahman's vision was one of a different kind of seclusion, not the kind that "deprived women from their social and human rights and kept them confined within the home" but arguably a more humane one that was respectful and accommodating of women's creative potential, albeit at a safe distance from "men and their evil ways"—that is, from public institutions of power and influence—and doubtless within the prescribed limits of both middle-class gentility and Islamic dicta interpreted generously, presumably by men like himself.[248]

A more critical approach to the institution came once again from the writers involved with the Muslim Sahitya Samaj. Abul Fazal rejected the "vile" suggestion that women would end up on the "highway to sin" if they were allowed to step out of seclusion, while Abul Hussein considered not only seclusion but even use of the borkha to be "insulting" and "shameful" for women.[249] Hussein's position in this regard was in explicit opposition to most of his contemporaries, including Rokeya, who opposed seclusion but not necessarily the use of the borkha.[250] Unlike most writers of that time, who were preoccupied with searching for scriptural justifications for the particular form of purdah they were advocating or denouncing, in a bold essay titled "Adesher Nigraha" (The Oppression of Injunctions), Hussein argued that even if certain practices—purdah among them—were sanctioned by religious injunctions, they were indefensible since they were the sources of oppression and misery in society. In his words: "Woman is kept in parda so that the eyes of men do not fall on her, and her chastity is preserved. . . . But in contemporary Muslim society . . . behind parda a woman's personality is deprived of all nourishment [making her] . . . vulnerable to . . . [the slightest hint of seduction]."[251] Hussein denounced seclusion not only because it prevented women from acquiring education or developing into mature human beings but also because it failed in terms of the very goal—preservation of chastity—that the institution presumably set out to achieve. In his view, seclusion essentially encouraged "lust" by forcing women to think of themselves only as objects of sexual desire.[252] In his view, then, what women needed was "liberation" not just from oppressive institutions such as seclusion but also from the automatic association of womanhood with sexual desire. Hussein also believed that it was essential to completely reform Muslim laws, which formed the bulwark for such institutions as seclusion and the unilateral right to divorce exercised by men in the subcontinent.[253]

Abul Hussein's willingness to confront religious laws as the source of women's oppression—both extrinsic and internalized—is remarkable. As we know from our discussion of Rokeya's efforts in this regard, there were few attempts by Muslim intellectuals in early-twentieth-century Bengal to critically think through the implications of religious laws in the social control of women (as well as other subordinate groups) let alone to propose reforming them.[254] While we do know that other writers associated with *Shikha*, most notably Kazi Abdul Wadud, suggested reassessing Islamic injunctions, such arguments were extremely rare in the context of gender reform not just among men but also among women.

In short, quite a few reform-minded Muslim writers of that era were likely to make lofty statements about bringing women "out of unreligious parda to give them a share of . . . [freedom]," "to relieve the crippled state of their body and mind," and to transform them into "modern women."[255] But in the final analysis, quite like the majority of their Hindu counterparts of that era, most Muslim men were unable and unwilling to imagine women outside the conventional roles of "mothers, sisters, and wives" of men.[256] Although everyone agreed that women needed some kind of education, few were willing to entertain the possibility of it leading to gainful employment and economic self-sufficiency. Consequently, much of the discussion around seclusion and the need for women's education remained marooned within the limits of male reformist fantasies of the "new woman" as a more "appropriate companion"—whether in terms of liberal western ideals or Islamic injunctions—who could reflect better on men as adequately modern or Muslim or both. In these, what can be called mainstream, formulations, the emphasis was on the superficial alleviation of "women's condition" in an effort to make the Muslim community ready for modern nationhood, not on addressing the unequal distribution of power that the institution of gender historically guarantees everywhere.[257]

Instead, armed with the conviction that men and women are inherently unequal and hence can never enjoy "equal rights," most writers proposed programs that rarely went beyond the kind of tokenism Rokeya had cautioned against almost two decades before such debates gained momentum among Bengali Muslims. To quote her:

> [It] is true that seclusion among Parsi women has ended, but has that ended their . . . [dependence on men]? Of course not . . . they are just as inanimate as they were before. When men kept them in the inner quarters (*antahpur*) they stayed there. And when men have forced them . . . to come out . . . they have come out of parda. What is women's achievement in this? Such [token] opposition to parda is never praiseworthy.[258]

In Rokeya's understanding, seclusion was a symptom of women's subordination, not necessarily a cause. Therefore, simply abolishing the practice without making access to adequate education and the opportunity to work for a living available to women might help men in their quest for a "liberal/modern" self-image and adequately modern companions, but it would achieve precious little in terms of helping women gain economic and psychological independence or self-respect.

Men were not the only ones reluctant to endorse the kind of far-reaching changes in the normative definition of women's place in society that Rokeya was proposing; many Muslim women who publicly expressed their thoughts at that time also seemed reluctant to imagine gender reforms that transcended the prescribed needs of the community or nation or went against the prescription of companionate marriages. Consequently, they were typically unwilling to demand equality between the sexes or imagine assuming the responsibilities that come with equal membership in any community, notwithstanding the often passionate statements by some women writers about "marching forward" through the "bright light of education and knowledge," toward some rather underspecified idea of fulfillment or progress.[259] The following excerpt from a speech by the celebrated novelist Nurunnessa Khatun Bidyabinodini offers a useful reminder not to automatically read women's entry into the public sphere as an example of resistance to existing structures.

> Perhaps some people will wonder—Are . . . [educated women] going to gallivant around . . . in the name of social improvement, or suffused by the light of . . . women's Franchise, pretend to be men and knock at office-doors in . . . [search of] a living? No, I did not come here today to give you such inventive advice. Rather, it occurs to me that we have to get down to work with the firm belief that education is not for money. . . . Women's education . . . is surely indispensable. . . . An educated woman's *son* can never be ignorant. . . . [If this idea] is instilled in us, then our improvement is inevitable. . . . I am not calling on my *swajatiya* [Muslim/Bengali] sisters to educate themselves to earn degrees. All I wish to say is that they should not stay completely ignorant.[260]

In other words, Nurunnessa's reasons for advocating women's education—to be good mothers, especially to their *sons*, and adequate companions to men—are defined strictly in terms of the idea of women as support systems, albeit formidable ones, for men and their community/nation(s).

She was also unequivocal in expressing her reservations regarding the possibility of "unrestricted mobility" for women:[261] As her somewhat caustic references to both women's struggle for franchise and their attempts to enter the paid workforce indicate, she, like many contemporary Hindu and Muslim writers, was ultimately uncomfortable with the possibility of women outgrowing their dependence on men.[262] Perhaps it is precisely the "mainstream" and "nonconfrontational" nature of Nurunnessa's writing that so clearly differentiates her work from that of Rokeya Sakhawat Hossein or Masuda Rahman or even Ayesha Ahmed and accounts for the unusual level of acceptance and acclaim that she received both during her lifetime and posthumously.[263] As Yasmeen Hossein has pointed out, quite like their male counterparts, many women writers believed that education was necessary to expand the ambit of women's usual household duties and to help them become better mothers, more interesting consorts (presumably to stop men from seeking the company of sex workers), and more competent housekeepers.[264] Very few openly supported the idea of attending schools and colleges or the prospect of joining the paid workforce.[265]

Still, it is worth noting that even those women who were generally against radical changes in the status quo betrayed at times a desire for "something beyond their roles within the household."[266] So, for instance, referring to the literary aspirations among Muslim women of her time, Rajia Khatun Choudhurani wrote: "Looking around [us] . . . it seems that woman is not satisfied only with food for the body, she also wants food for the mind! . . . [This] thirst . . . [is not new], it is eternal."[267] Or, as Firoza Begum ruefully commented: "In household after household there is only responsibility, but no satisfaction, there is duty, not joy; there is work, but no leisure. How can human beings grow in the midst of all this?"[268]

A few women did join Rokeya in advocating wage work as a means to self-reliance for women. We have already encountered Masuda Rahman's pleas to this end.[269] A second woman who wrote passionately in favor of women seeking gainful employment was Ayesha Ahmed. Citing the example of western women in the professional workforce, Ahmed argued that girls earning their own living ought to be seen not as a slight to "family honour" but rather as a solution to "economic problems."[270] A few other maverick women adamantly upheld the idea of women's independence, braving much social opprobrium for both the choices they made in their personal lives and what they wrote. Most notable among them were Faziltunnessa, who ignored contemporary social conventions to become the first Muslim woman to study at Dhaka University and eventually traveled abroad for further studies; the poet Mahmuda Khatun Siddiqua, who refused to acknowledge a marriage forced on her in her childhood, choosing instead an independent existence outside the bounds of both marriage and purdah; Samsunnahar Mahmud, who battled the conservatism of her elders to pursue an education and eventually become a well-known writer and activist; and Sufia Kamal, who never received a formal education but became a revered poet, writer, and political activist of twentieth-century Bengal.[271] And, while these women received support from a number of male intellectuals dedicated to the cause of "women's liberation," they were also acutely aware of the danger that women's protest against men would be appropriated within a male liberal discourse of reform and a politics of incremental accommodation within the overall structure of male domination. As Sufia Kamal rather tersely put it in a letter to the editor of *Saogat* in 1929: "All the essays [by women these days] . . . [forcefully express] women's hatred for men; and these writings are being published in male-edited periodicals themselves! I am not inclined to complain about you to you."[272] As Mahmuda Khatun Siddiqua cautioned a few years later, women "must have the ability to earn [a living]—so that . . . men . . . [do] not get the idea that without [them] . . . women have no other options."[273] For these women, who were clearly influenced by Rokeya's ideals, education was not just a means to greater self-expression but an indispensable tool in women's search for economic self-sufficiency, independence, and, ultimately, dignity.

CONCLUSION

In a recent commentary on "the reform movement for Bengali Muslim women," Yasmin Hossein pointed out that, although Muslim women did not always take "a clear position" in the debates of the time, there is a larger "political and social significance" to the "first public statements" made by these erstwhile silent [or silenced] women that is yet to be properly acknowledged in the written history of the late colonial era in Bengal.[274] While I agree with Hossein's overall assessment of the early writings by women as political acts in their own right, and therefore deserving of attention, I would end my discussion of such efforts by stressing that the significance of these writers and their work is in fact much greater. Muslim women intellectuals were not just part of but rather at the forefront of reform efforts in late colonial Bengal.[275] Indeed, one could argue that much of what concerned these women almost a hundred years ago continues to be relevant for large numbers of women in the subcontinent today.

And yet this important body of work is mostly occluded in the official histories produced in postcolonial India. As I have argued in this chapter, the occlusion of Muslim women and their work is a consequence not only of the habitual negligence that normative histories show toward women but also of a larger tendency to read the myriad, often contradictory, concerns of the Muslim middle class in colonial Bengal through the lens of Partition discourse. The result is a rarefied account of what Muslim intellectuals wrote about that marginalizes especially those concerns that Muslim women were most likely to write about. Any attempt to adequately appreciate the works of Muslim women in early-twentieth-century Bengal, therefore, ought to also commit to a larger effort to foreground the context of their disappearance within normative historiographies in postcolonial India. Otherwise we run the risk of creating what the historian Luisa Passerini so aptly described as "an alternative ghetto," in which the previously marginalized might be "allowed to speak" or be visible but only as exceptions or addendums that do not disturb the relentless logic of normativity.[276]

4

DIFFERENCE IN MEMORY

[In Dhaka] . . . I remember that [sometimes the Muslim girls] would bring some kul [berries] or something. . . . It is not that I thought "I will not eat from them" because they were Muslim. No it was not that. But their bodies would emit a strong odour. We did not eat garlic or onions . . . so I could always detect this unpleasant smell that made me not want to sit next to them. But I did not understand the difference in religion or anything else.[1]

I am ashamed to admit that we [her natal family] kept a lot of distance from them [Muslims]. . . . I have to tell you that I never liked this segregation among different religious groups. . . . Later in my life . . . the Muslims I met . . . were all from good families. . . . They are all very educated, and the women are also very enlightened. You cannot find any kind of conservatism or the practice of parda among these women. They all have very modern worldviews . . . I [even] see quite a few Muslim women involved in [social work]. Of course the number of Hindu women is far more.[2]

> Most of the [Muslim] women [who were in school or college with us] simply disappeared after marriage because . . . they [Muslims] force their women to become strictly pardanasheen. [Even Hindu women who marry into Muslim families] . . . disappear from sight.[3]

If the focus of chapter 3 was primarily on the relations between official history and other, typically marginalized forms of historical writing, here I turn to the often vexed but close linkages between public constructions and private reminiscences that constitute another important element of popular memory.[4] I embarked on this project with what at first seemed to be a simple question: what might we learn about the final decades of colonial rule in Bengal, and especially about the changing lives of urban Muslims, by approaching them through the memories of Muslim women—an archive that has rarely made its appearance within dominant historiographies of that era. I was especially interested in tracking the resonances, if any, that constructions of Muslim-ness—normalized within British and Hindu nationalist discourses in the late colonial period—might have had in the lives of middle-class Muslims in late-nineteenth-century and early-twentieth-century Bengal. What were their conceptions of the processes of "change" at work at that time? How did Muslim women perceive themselves, against whom, and in what terms? Did their perception of Hindu representations of Muslims affect their stories?

The oral testimonies I gathered, mostly from middle-class Bengali Muslim women who were born and lived in Calcutta or Dhaka between 1910 and 1950 and a few from middle-class Bengali Hindu women, led me to a set of additional questions about both the substance of these stories and the narrative strategies employed in telling them, which animate the analysis that follows. What do Muslim women remember of that time? What do they (choose to) narrate today and in what terms? Does the act of remembering itself mediate their presentation/production of themselves as subjects? Do constructions of Muslim-ness in Hindu popular discourse today, especially as it applies to women, influence what the Muslim speakers highlight, and what they elide in these testimonies? How might the dialogic contexts in which the oral histories were generated, both in terms of the larger political environment of the subcontinent in the final decade of the twentieth century and the more immediate setting of the interview situation, shape the contours of their recollections, as well as the narratives that follow from them? And how should we read these accounts, which are not only "subjective" but also, like all knowledge, produced in a particular context and hence necessarily "partial" and "situated"?[5]

HISTORIES OF DIFFERENCE

Histories of nonhegemonic groups are often conceived as recuperative projects through which normative history is challenged and its oversights, the result of a supposed crisis of vision, corrected; the intent, stated explicitly or not, is to make visible (heard) the previously unseen (unheard). Since official discourses are typically "state-managed,"[6] the task of the critical historian is thought to be to unearth "what the colonial state—and often the nationalist bourgeoisie—once chose to forget."[7] In this context, memory, especially popular memory, has come to be increasingly important as an alternative, oppositional archive, which allows access to "untold stories" of a "real past" that can presumably be tapped into by simply posing the right questions.[8]

This chapter differs from such projects of recuperation in important ways. First, my analysis resists the idea of recovering unmediated subaltern truths. Instead, it begins with the premise that personal memories are not easily separable from the structures of representation of official history. As oral historians have pointed out, dominant historical discourses often "supply the very terms by which a private history is thought through."[9] Second, my analysis shies away from the assumption that narratives of the previously marginalized necessarily embody "trenchant political critiques" of the dominant order—an assumption that exempts categories such narratives use and the contexts in which they are invoked from closer scrutiny. Instead, following Luisa Passerini, I base my analysis on the idea that it is not enough to simply encourage or enable members of an oppressed group to "speak for themselves."[10] It is necessary to interrogate how different conceptions of selves and groups are produced in the first place and to what ends. Otherwise, as Joan Wallach Scott puts it, "The evidence of experience . . . [can easily become] evidence for the fact of difference, rather than a way of exploring how difference is established, how it operates, how and in what ways it constitutes subjects who see and act in the world."[11] Identities, as Visweswaran reminds us, are not chosen freely but "constituted by relations of power always historically determined."[12]

In a related vein, this chapter also rests on the argument that memories are not simply sources of hitherto unknown information but "an active process of creation of meanings"; as "problematic sites of query in themselves," they require critical scrutiny.[13] As Ann Laura Stoler and Karen Strassler put it, "Subaltern acts of remembering have not been in question because it is official memory that is on the line; the process of remembering and the fashioning of personal memories are often beside the political points being made, and may in fact be seen to work against them."[14]

Accordingly, one aim of this chapter is to note not only *what* the women interviewed say but also *how* they say it and to what possible end. A second is to "arrive at an analysis which can account for the constitution of the subject within an historical" account and to reflect critically on what such "remembering does for the present," as much as what it tells us about the past.[15] In other words, I am as concerned with what I read as the interviewees' desire to be seen in particular ways as I am with the substantive facts that emerge from these stories about the lives of middle-class Muslim women in early-twentieth-century Bengal.

The emphasis on oral accounts as processes of meaning creation, rather than "depositories of facts,"[16] points to two additional insights from recent critical scholarship by anthropologists, feminists, and oral historians that have powerfully impacted my understanding of the oral histories I gathered. The first sees the "fieldwork encounter as the locus of inter-subjective production of 'facts.'"[17] The second insists that oral history and ethnographic accounts are partial and, like all other attempts to represent marginalized subjects in academic writing, overdetermined by structures of interests.[18] As one feminist oral historian succinctly put it, "There is no such thing as a transparent interview. The interaction of and 'positionality' . . . of both interviewer and narrator are fundamentally part of the process."[19]

I am acutely aware, for instance, that my conversations with the women quoted here, both Muslim and Hindu, might have been different, and likely more difficult, had I not shared their educated, middle-class (i.e., bhadra) background. And, while most of the narrators would not see themselves as feminists, they certainly seemed to understand, and even agree with, my critique of official histories for their neglect of women as subjects. I might even hazard that it was probably easier for me as a woman, who was of their daughters' or sons' age, to gain their trust, at least up to a point. And, of course, we spoke a common language, I had grown up in the city in which they lived or where they had spent a significant part of their lives before migrating to East Pakistan (Bangladesh), and I was interested in knowing about their lives.

All this helped establish a relatively easy rapport between the interviewees and me.

At the same time, there were always a few compelling differences that militated against any easy assumption on my part (and I imagine theirs as well) of automatic "empathy and identification"—what Stacy calls a "delusion of alliance"—that seems to have plagued early feminist scholarship in general and feminist qualitative research involving women subjects in particular.[20] For one, my position as a researcher, no matter how young from their perspective, in the United States academy seems to have introduced a certain tension in my interviewees' and my shared sense of middle-class location. As a number of them pointed out on more than one occasion, they were educated but not necessarily able or allowed to pursue the kind of professional careers they might have wished. The often expressed appreciation for my "abilities" by the interviewees in this context typically made *me* feel awkward and distanced. Minimally, it meant that any possibility of alliance between them and me in the context of the interview had to be mediated through a discussion of generational difference. As we shall see presently, this may have influenced the extent to which some of them dwelled on their and their families' educational achievements as well.

A second point of difference that clearly had serious implications for the kind of expectations and assumptions that confronted me—and consequently the kind of knowledge that these interviews produced—was the issue of what community (Hindu or Muslim) I was seen to belong to.[21] In the case of most of the Hindu women I interviewed, I was confronted by the problem that Muslims typically did not come up at all without considerable goading on my part; in the case of the interviews with Muslim women, the "fact" of my perceived Hindu-ness seems to have led to a certain preoccupation with the theme of Muslim-Hindu relations that we see in many of these accounts—a preoccupation that was no doubt intensified by the communalized political climate in the subcontinent in the late 1990s.

In Calcutta, the Muslim women I approached were cautious at first. With one exception, a substantial portion of the first meetings were taken up typically by the interviewees' questions about me. I was often confronted, in some form or other, with the question "Why are you interested in Muslim women?" followed by an inevitable expression of discomfort with my choice of them as speakers: "But I have not done anything special. . . . Maybe you should speak to . . ." so and so.

At some point over tea, the questions would typically turn to my life. How did I end up in the United States? Which school did I attend in Calcutta? What [did] my parents do? Has my family always lived in Calcutta? As I recall, it was my answer to the last question—that both my parents' families had migrated from East Bengal / Pakistan (now Bangladesh) during or just after the Partition of India in 1947—that may have subtly altered the way the narrators related to me. I never explicitly asked any of the interviewees what meanings they attached to the information about my family's background, but I imagine that it allowed them to formulate their own understandings of my interest in studying Muslim women in colonial Bengal.

I realize, of course, that their perceptions of my positioning must have generated their own partial truths, and on at least one memorable occasion in Bangladesh this in effect ended the interview session. The interviewee, Shafinaz Hossein, proceeded to pack up her belongings and march me out of her office to the van that was waiting to drop her and some of her colleagues at their respective homes. At her home, much to my embarrassment, I was made into something of an example, especially to her two daughters, who were in their early twenties at that time, as someone who was studying in the United States and conducting research on her own in Bangladesh. Then I was fed profusely and left to mingle with everyone. Later I was made to eat again, with the rest of the family(!), and watch TV until it was late. Finally, I was shown to my bed where I fell asleep gratefully. I never really managed to "interview" Shafinaz, although we talked often enough as she undertook to show me Dhaka or when I stopped by to see the family over the course of the next few months.

In short, then, the stories that I am about to present are not "objective representations of reality" but subjective and interested accounts of conversations, albeit somewhat one-sided (since I rarely interrupted the narrators while they told their stories), between eight middle-class Muslim women—the youngest of whom was fifty years old and the eldest ninety at the time of the interviews—and a Hindu woman of a younger generation at the end of the twentieth century, about what it meant to be middle class, Muslim, and women fifty to a hundred years ago in colonial Bengal.[22] The interchanges that followed neither assumed an "easy identification between women," nor based itself on the rigid binary of self/other that seems to have been at the heart of much ethnographic research.[23] Instead, these conversations proceeded from an understanding, even if implicit, that selves are multiple and positionalities, of both the (postcolonial) researcher and the (postcolonial) narrators involved, were ambivalent.[24] The stories are rooted in the sense of having shared a difficult history from different, and at times opposing, identity locations, and they are therefore imbued, at least in my reading, with the poignancy and strain of trying to both inventory "our commonalities" and make sense of the "processes of differentiation" that produce us as similar but different, as "not you/like you."[25] For difference is not just "a thing to be recognized but a process always under way," and identity is as much "a matter of 'becoming'" as it is "of 'being.'"[26]

I am all too aware that, while the text I have produced based on these oral histories is certainly polyvocal, my analysis may or may not reflect adequately what the narrators originally intended to communicate.[27] I also realize that in all probability the speakers would not agree with all my interpretations. However, as scholars have often pointed out, the knowledge of the inequality of power "endemic" to the research context—be it ethnography, oral history, or the analysis of other forms of "stable" texts—ought not to deter authors from undertaking the necessary "tasks of interpretation, evaluation and judgement."[28]

Finally, I want to note that, while most of the interviews were autobiographical and provide a remarkable array of information about postcolonial India and Bangladesh, I have chosen to restrict much of my focus here to the speakers' recollections about the period before Partition and information pertaining to their parents' generation. My decision will probably frustrate some readers, but I believe that an ethnography of Bengali Muslim middle-class life in postcolonial India or Bangladesh merits separate and much greater attention than is warranted or possible within the context of the present study on the partialities of history.

I have focused mainly on the oral histories of five Muslim women, although I briefly refer to conversations with three others.[29] I also quote from or refer to conversations with seven Hindu women. Mala Sengupta and Angana Mitra were born in East Bengal (now Bangladesh); the others, Ila Chatterjee, Swati Mallick, Nandita Sinha, Chaitali Bose, and Purnima Ganguly were born and spent most of their lives in Calcutta. Of these, I spoke at length to only Mala, Ila, and Swati, all of whom I have known for some time.[30]

The oral histories were collected during field trips to Calcutta and Dhaka between 1996 and 2000. Of the eight Muslim women, Jahan Ara Begum, Zohra Sultana, Mumtaz Waheeda, Meherunnessa Begum, and Nusreen Begum were still living in Calcutta at the time of the interviews. Nusrat Begum and the late Sufia Kamal, on the other hand, had spent some part of their early lives in Calcutta but moved to Dhaka after the Partition. Shafinaz, the youngest of the Muslim women I spoke to, has always lived in East Bengal/Pakistan (now Bangladesh). As the narratives record, all except two of the speakers attended college; three had worked as teachers in reputable high schools in Calcutta during some part of their lives; one edited a women's magazine, another is a well-known writer; and Sufia Kamal was one of the most loved and revered writers of Bangladesh.

The interviews were conducted mostly in the homes of the narrators, typically over the course of two to four meetings.[31] The main languages used in these conversations were Bengali and English, although Urdu was freely intermixed in some cases.[32] The simultaneous use of two or three languages and the heteroglossia it produces are in fact quite common in the everyday speech of the urban middle classes in Calcutta and, at least in my experience, Dhaka.[33] Of the women quoted below, Mumtaz Waheeda, Zohra Sultana, and Nusreen Begum used more English than the other speakers. The excerpts from their testimony, therefore, contain large sections in the original English they used. In general, in my translations I have tried to stay as close to the original Bengali speech as possible and have also included at times the Bengali or Urdu phrases used by the speakers to compensate for some of the loss in meaning and affect that translation so often incurs. The direct quotes used in this chapter come mostly from taped interviews; however, in my analysis I also draw on notes that I typically took soon after recording each testimony.[34]

CONTEXT

We know that colonial discourse and policies vis-à-vis Muslims in the subcontinent changed in the wake of the publication of W. W. Hunter's 1871 *The Indian Mussalman*. Hunter's description of both the "indigenous Muslims," who were largely hostile to British rule, and the neglected Mughal elites resonated well with the colonial government's hardening position on the essential inferiority, backwardness, and treachery of Indians, on the one hand, and its interest in keeping the Muslim elite distant from an increasingly contentious and uncooperative Hindu middle class on the other. As was briefly discussed in chapter 3, the binary opposition between the apparently numerous, "fanatical" atrap and a small minority of Mughal ashraf neither captured the inherent complexities of a Muslim identity location in the subcontinent nor reflected the myriad political stances that Muslims took vis-à-vis British colonial rule. The publication of the settlement and census reports by the colonial government in 1872, which claimed that a majority of the Muslims in Bengal were of indigenous origin, were thus greeted with strenuous protest, especially by educated Muslims, who, by all accounts, did not wish to be associated with the dominant British view of "Indians in general" and "low caste/class" Muslim converts in particular.[35] Consequently, by the end of the nineteenth century many lower- and middle-class Muslims in Bengal were busy reinventing themselves as "foreign-born" ashrafs in an attempt to escape the twin derogatory labels of "originally lowborn" and "originally Hindu" (and hence not authentically Muslim). A sharp increase in the 1901 census in the number of Shaikhs, Syeds, Mughals, and Pathans—the respectable social groups—and a corresponding decrease in the ranks of the occupational caste groups stand in poignant testimony to this episode in identity formation among Muslims in the face of derogatory British categorizations in late colonial Bengal.[36]

The British, meanwhile, both summarily dismissed such self-declarations of Arab descent on the part of increasing numbers of Muslims and further intensified an already racialized discussion by introducing the "ethnographic" scale of measurement—the Cephalic index—to prove the "Hindu-ness" of the bulk of Indian Muslims.[37] Consequently, as Gauri Viswanathan puts it, "Two different commentaries . . . [were] juxtaposed in a contained narrative of conflicting memories: the descriptive record of Muslim self-definitions as Arab-descended [was] framed by a commentary that [negated] those self-perceptions and [posited] an alternative explanation of Muslim origins in the fractured space of Hindu communities."[38]

This systematic identification of the upper class, or ashraf, as the "original" Muslims and the converts as lower class and "originally" Hindu (low caste) in the face of Muslim protestations had significant ramifications for both present and future relationships between the different groups involved. First, it juxtaposed western science, rationality, and the colonial administration's insistence on "facts" against the "fictive" origins claimed by Muslims themselves. Second, this split between different kinds (or is it degrees?) of Muslim-ness undermined the possibility of a lasting unity around a single Muslim identity—a unity that is a basic tenet of Islam.[39] Finally, because the bulk of Indian Muslims were both placed "more relationally vis-à-vis Hindus" as "lower class/caste," and yet shown up as "foreign identified," they were henceforth constructed as antinational, even "traitors," in the context of Hindu nationalism.[40]

Colonial discourse about ethnic and religious categories in the nineteenth century thus produced a maddening situation that promised no easy resolution of the identity question for a vast majority of Muslims who were now considered to be neither adequately Muslim nor wholeheartedly Indian and yet originally "Hindu." And, while the theory of common origins "disallowed either total unity of Hindus and Muslims or total division between them," as the discussion in chapter 3 shows, official discourse and policies actively encouraged community identifications around the single axis of religion.[41] To quote Viswanathan again:

> As a descriptive catalog of India's ethnic composition, the British census . . . [established] fixities of racial and religious categories, even as it . . . [insinuated] the possibilities of overlapping and common origins rather than real historical difference. The function of the census to introduce categories of difference and then deny them must be seen to have a complex effect on the structure of perceptions in Hindu-Muslim relations, if not the relations themselves. [What is of interest is] the mediating role of British ethnography in the production of a field of remembered identities, both Hindu and Muslim, that feeds into the discourse of religious nationalisms.[42]

While the vitriolic rhetoric of the Hindu Right since the 1920s, which has systematically depicted Muslims as either inferior "foreign invaders" or "ex-Hindu converts" and hence "traitors," has been amply documented,[43] the wide circulation of similar ideas regarding the "difference" (read inferiority) of Muslims as early as the last quarter of the nineteenth century among ostensibly "liberal" Hindus—even women—which I discuss in chapter 2, has received relatively sparse attention.[44] My conversations with a number of Hindu women in Calcutta reveal that such representations of Muslims in general as backward or illiberal are still widespread, if not on the rise, among Hindus in contemporary India.[45]

In the following pages, we turn our attention to some specific elements of these dominant representations of Muslims and their continued effect on Bengali Muslim women's constructions of Muslim-ness today. As we shall see, even the most private stories of Muslim women seem to be fraught with tension as they try to set the record straight, as it were, by countering the discourses of backwardness and conservatism that so often frame discussions about Muslims in general and render Muslim women invisible in particular and at the same time, criticize male privilege from their own complex subject positions as women and Muslims in contemporary India.[46] The relationship between official history and private memory is far from one of simple opposition: as my analysis will show, even as the categories of dominant history are challenged by the oral testimonies I gathered from Muslim women, they are also constitutive of these accounts of a time before the Partition recollected over half a century later.

DIFFICULT VOICES

It is possible to identify several recurrent themes in these oral accounts. I will concentrate here on three overwhelming concerns that emerge in almost every story: the labels of Muslims as foreign invaders/traitors, Muslims as "backward or conservative," and finally Muslims as originally low-caste Hindus. In the final section of the chapter, I will briefly explore yet another theme—Muslims as "just like us," which came up in my discussions with "liberal" Hindu women—by revisiting a particular conversation between one of the Muslim narrators and her Hindu friends that I had the occasion to observe and take part in. In this last scenario, perhaps more than in any other, we will see the narrator disrupting, even refusing, the subject location on offer—in this case, the identification and alliance assumed by her Hindu friends—by powerfully inserting her experience of difference into the conversation.

Muslim or Indian (Bengali)

Jahan Ara Begum was born in 1939 in Calcutta and spent most of her life in the Park Circus area of the south-central section.[47] As I learned from her, the area seems to have developed at least in part to accommodate the growing body of urban Muslim civil servants and professionals of the middle and upper-middle classes in the 1930s and 1940s. Even today, it is inhabited predominantly by Muslims, although many of the "original inhabitants," I was told, had migrated to East Pakistan/Bangladesh after the Partition. In fact, many of the women I spoke to still lived in Park Circus at the time of the interviews, while others had spent at least some part of their lives living and/or working in this area. Jahan Ara's father-in-law, whom she described as a "high-ranking civil servant who lived in many parts of Bengal," built a house in this area as well "over fifty years ago at a time when Park Circus was an affluent Muslim neighborhood." She and her husband—a retired metallurgist who worked for a "private concern"—still live in that spacious, solid, yet understated house, which was clearly built to last.

Jahan Ara's father came from a "fairly affluent landed family" from 24 Parganas, a district in West Bengal. While Khan Saheb had received a bachelor's degree, unlike most educated men of his time, he did not seek professional employment under the British, deciding instead to go into business in leather goods.[48] Jahan Ara's mother's family was from Khulna in what was East Bengal before 1947 (contemporary Bangladesh). Rasheeda (Jahan Ara's mother) completed school but did not attend college. Jahan Ara describes her parents as liberal. As she remembers it, she and her sisters enjoyed considerable freedom of movement and they all attended college. Jahan Ara even earned a master's degree after her marriage because her father-in-law encouraged her to continue her education. However, as she also pointed out, she was never expected or encouraged to look for paid work, something she wishes she had been able to do.

At the time of the interview, Jahan Ara was involved in social work, especially in the running of a home for destitute women, who were given vocational training to help them become financially independent. She was also overseeing a small business. Her daughter is a scientist, and her two sons are very "well settled."

When I first broached the issue of interviewing her in a phone conversation, Jahan Ara's response, like that of most of the other interviewees, was to laugh. "You want to interview me? But I have done nothing extraordinary!" she exclaimed. Still, once I had haltingly explained something about the lack of written material on Muslim women in Bengal and that so-called ordinary everyday experiences can provide valuable information about a place and a time, she invited me to visit her in a few days.

I begin with Jahan Ara's exact words as she began recounting her life story for two reasons: first, because, as oral historians point out, the "organization of the narrative reveals a great deal of the speakers' relationships to their history"; and, second, because for me how and where the speakers began also signaled something about *their* perception of what I wished to hear and, perhaps more important, what *they* wanted to tell *me*.[49]

My name is Jahan Ara. . . . Some people have difficulty in pronouncing [my name]. . . . These days, in many households—Hindu or Muslim—you see that people speak to each other in English. It is just a habit, especially with kids from affluent families who go to English-medium schools. That was not the case with us. . . . Our family has always been very Bengali. . . . My friends who came to the house always commented on that. And yet because of our names we often had to face the question: "Are you Bengali?" By religion [we are] Muslim. . . . You have asked me for my life story, but my life is not that spectacular. . . . Well . . . I was born in 1939. Within about seven years of that India became independent.[50] . . . My parents were nationalist Muslims.[51] . . .

The area in which we were staying in Park Circus was very nice. . . . Muslim government *besh bhalo bhalo* [respectable, well-to-do, and highly placed] officials lived there. . . . [Most] of them sent their kids to good schools. But when we went to school . . . it was just before independence, right? [At that time] there was a different consciousness (*jagaran*) [awakening] among people. They did not feel that it was necessary to send their children to English-medium schools. Unlike today, when you take it for granted that good education means instruction in English . . . it was not like that then. So my sister and I were sent to a school that was Brahmo. . . .

Q: What was the name of the school?

The name. . . . was Victoria Institution. It was in . . . North Calcutta. . . . In that school, perhaps because it was Brahmo, there were . . . unlike now, when you almost never see any [Muslim girls in school with Hindus] . . . you could find at least four or five Mussalman girls in each class . . . among every thirty or so girls. The school itself was not big . . . but there was some interaction between Muslims and Hindus at that time.

From the very beginning of her life story, Jahan Ara seems to insist on both her family's Bengali-ness and its anticolonial, nationalist leanings. As she proudly recounted, both her parents were very involved with political activism on behalf of the Congress. They did not support the Partition of India and decided to stay in Calcutta, although many of their relatives, including two of their three daughters and their families, moved to East Pakistan (now Bangladesh) in the late 1940s.

Given the tendency among aristocratic, urban elite Muslims in Bengal in the late nineteenth century and the early twentieth to dissociate themselves from all things Bengali, as well as their studied distance from a nationalist movement spearheaded by the Hindu middle and upper-middle classes, if not a downright pro-British stance, the establishment of an unambiguous Bengali identity was clearly important for the story of this "nationalist" Muslim family to unfold.[52] And yet the allusion to her "Persian" name, the comment about the "difficulty" that "some people" might have with it, and her religion both situate her firmly within the larger moral/cultural universe of Islam and establish almost immediately her "specific difference" from the Hindu bhadralok. Her comments also prepare us for the imminent staging of the tensions between her complex subject position, and her place within the Indian nation, whose troubled history makes its appearance even before the story of her life gets off the ground. Note also her attempt to establish early on her family's upper-middle-class status in this context, and the impression she gives of a certain amount of interaction between some members of the Hindu/Brahmo middle class and the Muslim middle class before Partition—concerns we will revisit later in the chapter.

> So we started our education. Then, when I was in class three or so, about seven years old, the communal riots broke out in Calcutta . . . "the great killings."[53] . . . During the riots and for a while afterward, we were of course completely isolated from the rest of the city; we were essentially confined to our neighborhood. . . . Afterward, after Partition, when the riots were over and the city was calm again, Leeladi [the school principal] came to our house and told my father, "Give my girls back to me."[54] So we went back to Victoria—very glad to be back in our old school. . . . However, by that time many of the Muslim middle-class families had left for Pakistan, so the number of Muslim students in the school fell drastically.

Zohra Sultana was born in Calcutta in 1938. Her father was a well-known doctor and a member of the first government of West Bengal after independence. As she proudly pointed out, hers was a very educated family. Her maternal grandmother had been a trained midwife who received her degree from a Calcutta hospital and supported herself and her daughter, Ayesha (Zohra's mother), after her husband's untimely death. Ayesha Khatun was born in the last decade of the nineteenth century in Calcutta. She graduated from school in 1918–19 and won a scholarship to go to college. However, her marriage to Zohra's father interrupted her studies. According to Zohra, her father married her mother because "he was impressed by her achievements," which included the ability to play the piano and sing. Ayesha had five children, of whom Zohra is the youngest. But, as Zohra remembers, although raising her children kept her busy, her mother still found time for social work.[55]

Zohra herself studied at the All India Institute of Hygiene and Public Health. At the time of the interview, she was living with her husband and daughter in her father's house in Park Circus where she had been born. In spite of failing health, Zohra, too, was actively involved in social work. She was especially proud of a nonprofit organization she had helped found, which trained economically disadvantaged women to do embroidery and then marketed the products on their behalf, ensuring them of a living. Like Jahan Ara, Zohra is forthright in asserting her Bengali-ness, but in her case it appears to be firmly ensconced within a more self-conscious identification with the Indian nation: "My first identity is that I am an Indian Bengali, and my religion happens to be Islam. . . . My father gave us such a broad outlook that we were not prepared for community living with Muslims. Rather I would say that we were more at ease with a more international community or with broader people without any set ideas."[56] Zohra, too, seems to anticipate the inevitable intrusion of the nation's history into her story. But, unlike Jahan Ara, who asserts her religious and cultural ties to Islam, Zohra deliberately downplays them, preferring instead a modernist, even cosmopolitan, casting for herself. I would, however, read her confession about feeling more "at ease" with an "international community" as symptomatic of something more than discomfort with "community living with Muslims." With the political success of the Hindu Right in recent years, ideas about the inherent foreignness, and hence the disloyalty and treacherousness, of Muslims have become something of a commonplace in popular discourse among large sections of the Hindu population. Zohra's privileging of her "Indian" and "Bengali" identifications and her attempt to downplay her religious affiliation by making it sound like happenstance—"my religion *happens to be* Islam"—could, therefore, be a dialogic response to the increasingly communalized political discourse and a growing expressed intolerance of minorities in general and Muslims in particular in the closing years of the twentieth century in India.

Sometimes the anxiety over the label "foreigner/antinational" does not enter the narrative openly from the beginning, but the desire to establish Bengaliness (and through it indigenousness) as one of the definitive elements of one's identity still appears, betraying a certain tension. For instance, Meherunnessa Begum's paternal family came from outside Bengal, but she was quick to point out that the family had adjusted completely to Bengali society and considered itself "totally Bengali": "My family came from Ahmedabad—my [paternal] grandfather. But by settling here we have *become* Bengali [emphasis added]. We speak Bengali now . . . although I think I have an accent. *Hai na?* [Isn't it so?] My maternal grandfather [on the other hand] was converted to Islam—he was Bengali."[57]

One set of recollections that provided a site for repeated enunciation of the theme of Muslim "loyalty to the nation" centered on riots. While many of the women I spoke with referred to the riots, in the following section I quote extensively from the testimonies of only two—Jahan Ara Begum and Mumtaz Waheeda—to illustrate this point.[58] I should note that the recurrence of this theme of loyalty, the alacrity with which stories demonstrating the courage and integrity of Muslim men were sometimes offered up, and the coherence of these narratives suggest not only a desire to share these stories with a larger audience and to be seen through them but also the likely existence of practices of remembering and narration quite outside of the context of the interviews. It is also possible that at least some of the women I spoke with in Calcutta had assumed or decided that I—a Hindu woman born and brought up in that city not far from where many of them still live—would want to know, and perhaps should hear, about this shared history of strife from their presumably different perspectives.[59] For, as oral historians often point out, the historian/researcher is a significant presence in the interview context and "the telling of the story is part of the story being told."[60]

So, for instance, when I finally asked Jahan Ara what she remembered of the riots she had mentioned on several occasions from the very beginning of her testimony, she responded quite readily:

> Yes, I have some very vivid memories. There was a Hindu family near here. It was not that we were very well acquainted with them or anything . . . but we knew them. I guess we saw them around. The man and his wife had just had a child after many years of effort, it was maybe a few months old when the riots broke out. When things got really serious, he came to my father and said, "Khan Saheb, my child was born after so many years, after so much effort. You must save my child!" I am not sure what I understood of the situation since I was so young. Anyway, they came to our place at night.
>
> *Q: You were living nearby at that time?*

We were living in Park Circus itself, yes. So . . . my father told them, "Do not worry. As long as I am alive, the rioters cannot touch you." So late at night . . . there were these non-Bengali Muslims who had appeared in the neighborhood . . . (*abangali Mussalmaneder paraye amdani hoyechhilo*).[61] . . . We did not know them at all. . . . Anyway, [the non-Bengali newcomers] came to our house at night and started making a lot of noise. . . . My father went out in front of them, asked what the matter was. They said, "*amader kachhe khabor achhe* [We have news] that you have people [read/Hindus] in your house . . . *ber kore din, nahole* [send them out, or else] there will be a lot of trouble! We know you have people [Hindus]." My father said, "I am sorry but I cannot give them up. You know that according to Islam it is a sin to deny protection to one's guests. I cannot do that. Before you do any harm to them, you [will] have to kill me. And not just me; you have to finish off my wife, my children, and all other members of my family who are present here. If you can do that, then only you can lay a finger on my guests." These people waited around, threatened us some more, but when they realized that there was no way they could convince my father they left. So that night went by. The Hindu man was really scared, and, frankly, my father was not at all sure that the rioters would not be back. So the next day he contacted the police and made arrangements for that family to be shifted to a safe area.

At that time—you cannot possibly know this since this was long before your birth—the city was divided into pockets. This Park Circus region was Muslim, but if you went down the road toward Ballyganj once you came to the place where the Birla Mandir now stands the area beyond that was a Hindu stronghold.[62] So, if you were heading south, once they crossed what is the Modern Girl's School today, Hindus were safe, whereas Muslims had nothing to fear on this side of that imaginary line. Anyway, they [the Hindu family] had some relatives in Bhabanipur, and they went to stay with them.[63] There was another family like that, I cannot remember the name, but the man was a professor in Ashutosh College.[64] My father gave them refuge as well and later had them transported to a safe place with police protection. However, these families . . . after the riots were over and the Partition took place . . . never contacted us. My mother particularly was quite keen on finding out how these people were doing, especially the child . . . but they never let us know anything about how they were doing, what happened to them—nothing! By that time things had calmed down; some

> people who had left their homes during the riots came back, others came from East Bengal and took up residence in houses that were empty . . . but these families never felt any need to contact us after all that we went through together. . . . I think of this often, you know. I think if this were to happen to us today we would go and express our thanks and gratitude for the kind of trouble, [the] *risk* that my father had taken for them. Maybe they could not, for whatever reasons.

Jahan Ara's story is of course invaluable in bringing alive for the listener (and hopefully, even in translation, for the reader) something of the fear and uncertainty that gripped Calcutta at that time and "that imaginary line" between Hindu and Muslim areas that I, for one, have crossed a million times without giving as much as a single thought to what that turn of the road might have signified not so long ago. The story also challenges the overwhelming representation of Muslim men as both violent and treacherous in popular Hindu discourse through its powerful evocation of the picture of Khan Saheb confronting the rioters, even as it acknowledges the verity of Muslim violence toward Hindus and subtly displaces that destructive agency onto Muslims from "outside Bengal."[65] But what is perhaps most striking about this story is the acute sense of disappointment, even betrayal, that creeps in by the end of Jahan Ara's telling of it—a disappointment that is not easily apprehended without referring to the historical context in which the story locates itself.[66] While a detailed account of pre-Partition communal politics is far beyond the scope of this study, a few lines about the immediate incident in question might be helpful.[67]

The riots Jahan Ara refers to broke out in August of 1946 in the wake of the Muslim League's call to "Direct Action to achieve Pakistan," instigated both by its deep political differences with the Congress—especially regarding the issue of parity of communal representation in any governing body—and the British administration's decision to move forward with the formation of an interim government at the national level without the cooperation of the League if necessary.[68] The Muslim League's reluctance to cooperate in substance, though not in rhetoric, was of course based on the fear that neither the Congress nor the British administration had really accepted its demands for a separate and independent Pakistan. The immediate stumbling block, however, came from the League's insistence that it be given the sole right to nominate Muslim candidates for the interim government even though it only garnered

76 percent of the Muslim votes—a demand that the Congress rejected since that would in effect exclude nationalist and other non-League Muslims (a quarter of the Muslim population of India at that time) from vital decision-making processes on the eve of independence.[69] This, in short, was the context of intense politicking in which the Muslim League declared August 16, 1946, to be Direct Action Day with a somewhat unclear agenda.[70]

While Direct Action Day passed peacefully in the rest of the country, in Calcutta it precipitated vicious rioting involving Muslims and Hindus that resulted in almost ten thousand deaths in the course of a few days. As one recent analysis has suggested, it was widely believed that the violence could have been contained much earlier, if not prevented altogether, but for the negligence of both the ruling Muslim League government and the British administration in Bengal, which refused to heed the signs of imminent rioting. Indeed, reports indicate that the chief minister, H. S. Suhrawardy—a prominent Muslim Leaguer—himself may have instigated Muslims to violence by making certain ambiguous statements on and before Direct Action Day.[71] To quote one scholar:

> Muslim *goondas* from outside Calcutta armed with sticks, spears and daggers began to appear in . . . the city.[72] . . . There was . . . considerable evidence that Direct Action would be aimed at Hindus. . . . [On the other hand, that] Hindus were well prepared for violence is indicated by their ready retaliation of attacks by Muslim League processionists as they passed Hindu localities on the morning of 16 August, and the fact that there were eventually more Muslim than Hindu casualties in Calcutta.[73]

Whatever the reasons behind its outbreak, the riots of August 1946 clearly left an indelible mark on the timbre of future communal discourse in the city and indeed the subcontinent. It came to thematize all that Hindus feared and resented Muslim rule for—even as they actively colluded in realizing that nightmare—and further strengthened the Muslim League's demand for a separate nation by making the coexistence of Muslims and Hindus seem quite impossible. And it is in the light of this history that something of the complex texture of Jahan Ara's story of her father's courage, as well as her disappointment with her Hindu neighbors, becomes visible.

For nationalist Muslims such as Jahan Ara's parents, who did not support the League's demand for Pakistan, the 1946 riots must have underscored the growing precariousness of their position vis-à-vis a League government, which had successfully garnered grassroots support for its agenda during the preceding years.[74] The discomfort, indeed disapproval, that Jahan Ara expresses toward the recently arrived non-Bengali Muslims in the neighborhood—"We did not know them at all"—should, thus, be read as her way of highlighting her family's ideological distance from the Muslim League government, as well as an allusion to the alleged "importation"—*amdani*, as she puts it—of Muslim hooligans from elsewhere, even outside Bengal, to participate in the riot.[75] One also begins to appreciate the extent of the risk that her father took in order to safeguard his Hindu neighbors, especially since the rioters from "elsewhere" were not bound by a code of reciprocity to honor any social capital that Khan Saheb might have commanded in that neighborhood. But, beyond the immediate implications, what the 1946 riots, and the political success of the Bengal League government that underwrote it, achieved was a systematic marginalization of nationalist Muslims and their vision of a unified, secular India and, in time, a near total obfuscation of their efforts in the struggle for independence from British colonialism in the popular discourse of Hindu Bengalis.[76] In my reading, it is this Hindu amnesia, or willed denial of acknowledgment, of nationalist Muslim support for a unified India, often at tremendous personal and social costs, that feeds the sense of betrayal that Jahan Ara expresses so poignantly at the end of this story: "These families never felt any necessity to contact us *after all that we went through together*." I also want to note that, since Jahan Ara herself was, by her own admission, quite young at that time, the sense of letdown she gives voice to here is probably her parents', and/or something she experienced later in life. Yet she presents it as something that *she* felt at *that* time, revealing the complex ways in which feelings are produced, maintained, and even transferred through the practice of recollection within families, between generations, and even within the consciousness of a single person over time.

The 1946 riots make a rather sudden appearance early in Mumtaz Waheeda's testimony as well, disrupting what begins as a story of a prosperous Muslim family living amid Hindus and rematerializing, as it were, in the very structure of the narrative, the havoc it must have wrought in her life.[77] Notice especially in this context Mumtaz's description of this as "the first riot," signaling, perhaps, the fear and anticipation of riots in general that she claims has haunted her since. The early appearance of the riot in her story is probably also indicative of what she considers important for a Hindu woman of her sons' generation to understand about the effects of communal violence on Muslims in a Hindu-dominated city.

> My name is Mumtaz Waheeda. I used to be Mrs. [*sic*] Mumtaz Ahmed before my marriage. . . . My childhood was spent in a Hindu locality in Bhawanipur. . . My great-grandfather . . . settled down in Harish Mukherjee Road.[78]
>
> *Q: Where did they come from?*
>
> Okay, most probably they came from . . . the Bardhaman area.[79] I believe that they had a lot of property in Harish Mukherjee Road, and they were very well known there. During the first riot, when I was in class two . . .
>
> *Q: When were you born?*
>
> I was born in 1936, twentieth March. Now during the first riot, as I was telling you . . . I . . . we had to run away from there—the whole family . . . not less than fifty or sixty people. . . . We had to shift from there to Park Circus to my uncle's house. That much I remember. . . . Later on my father of course again built a house in Lower Circular Road. . . . We have still got that house.

The oldest of five siblings, Mumtaz speaks with considerable pride about the social standing of her paternal family. Her father came from "a family of Calcutta Muslims with a long history of higher education." Her great-grandfather and grandfather were both engineers. Mumtaz's father was a very successful and well-known barrister, while one of his brothers became the first Muslim principal of the Calcutta Medical College. Even her *phuphis* (paternal aunts) had been educated in schools. "*Our* family," as she repeatedly pointed out, "was an extremely enlightened family" that seemed to have intermingled easily with its Hindu neighbors in Bhawanipur—a predominantly Hindu area in Calcutta. Mumtaz recalls seeing "sober" *pujas* (Hindu religious festivals) "within the homes of Hindus" in her childhood.[80]

> Justice Beni Madhab used to live here—you probably know the name. Our family and theirs were very close. We used to have *namaaz* [prayers] for *Eid* [religious festival] within the huge compound of our house—some 250 people came there. After the namaaz, my mother and my aunts used to send out trays of sweets covered with beautiful cloths to many households in that area. After puja, similarly, sweets and fruits used to come to our house. This is what I have seen. We used to visit Justice Beni Madhab's house during puja—we would sit

> there. I really miss that atmosphere—somber, wonderful. I will never forget these impressions from my childhood.

But the 1946 riots seemed to have shattered this somewhat idyllic picture of Muslim-Hindu quotidian amity, which was underwritten, at least to a certain extent, by shared class privilege. As Mumtaz remembers it:

> At the time of the riots . . . Mr. Chanda [a Hindu renter and neighbor] hid our family. . . . When we heard that the rioters were planning to attack our household—words fly—we went into his house and hid. . . . Our *durwans* [doormen] . . . they were Hindu. . . . When the rioters came to burn the place down, the durwans told them that "There is no one here; they all left." . . . The next day, just before dusk . . . we were escorted out of there by the police. After that horrifying experience, I never liked to stay in this country again. We grew up here, but . . . my father of course did not want to leave. He built another house—huge house . . . spent a lot of money on it, too.

At the most obvious level, Mumtaz's story is, of course, about the riot and the dislocations it brought to her family's life. It is also worth noting that she is explicit throughout her testimony in acknowledging, even highlighting, the support and loyalty of Hindu neighbors and employees in different contexts in her life. What I would like to foreground, however, is the image of Mumtaz's father that emerges from her narration of this episode—unperturbed (or is it obstinate?) in the face of adversity, a survivor for sure, and a man who seems to hold his right to reside in *his* country dearer than the (feeling of) safety of his own family. Indeed, at times one even gets the sense that beyond her obvious and professed love, respect, and admiration for her father's will Mumtaz might also be critical of his decision not only to stay on but also build a "huge house" *after* the riots, *in Calcutta*, and to spend "a lot of money on it" when most upper- and middle-class Muslims were busy relocating to the safety of Pakistan. As Mumtaz recollects:

> I have asked my father . . . many times. . . . When . . . everyone left, our houses and property in Bhawanipur were occupied by other people when *shab baje baje bharate dhuklo* [all these common people rented the place]. . . . We had at least twelve or fourteen houses over there on Harish Mukherjee Road. . . . So I have asked my father, "Why? Why did you not go? Everybody left . . . no one stayed, why did you stay?" First thing my father said was, "If you want to go, if you find that India is becoming too hot for

you, you can go, I have no objection to it. But I don't want to go because I am an Indian and I am going to die as an Indian." It was the same with my mother also. He did not want to leave his country. He would say, "Pakistan" ... they used to call it [Bangladesh] Pakistan, right? ... [He would say,] "Pakistan *to akhon hoyechhe*! [Pakistan has come into being only now] Where was Pakistan all this time? *Ota to Indiai!* [That is in fact India!]" His sense of loyalty was so strong ... !

Another time ... when my Abba [father] decided to stay in India ... we have a huge house on Lower Circular Road with a huge lawn in front. ... He was so well respected in every sphere. Even to this day if you go to the bar library and [mention his name], they will [remember] ... he was such a lovable man. Anyway, the police came ... [to the house] and took my father and a lot of his papers to the police station for questioning. He was ... [a] suspect. You can well imagine what a shock this man got. Then I had told him, "... *Eisab shunbar janyai to apni ekhane pore thaken!* [Only to hear all this you stay here!]" ...

Q: When was this?

This happened when ... Pakistan or something attacked ... you remember? Took over a portion of Kashmir. ... At that time the situation was such that all the Muslims were under suspicion, as if everyone was a spy! ... Was it the 1960s? No, it was not the '60s ... it was much later. ... No? ... Maybe ... yes, I guess it was the early 1960s! At that time, you know, Pakistan took a portion of Kashmir. ... The whole country ... [was in an uproar]. Emergency was declared! ... Anyway ... even then, my Abba said, "What are they going to find from me except loyalty? *Their own citizens* ... there are many more Hindus who are much, much, much more disloyal than me! They are not going to find anything but loyalty from me. ... Let the dogs bark, I don't mind." But *we* minded ... oh, very hard, *very hard, it was very hard* ... very hard! We really felt it because all my relations who moved from this side to that side [of the India-Bangladesh divide], they are holding top positions—here, too, they were in top positions, there, too, they have top positions. ... [But my father] would always say, "No, no, no position I have got here also. ... I do not want to leave my country, that's all."

Mumtaz is referring here to the 1965 war between India and Pakistan, a war that by her own admission profoundly affected her family.[81] Yet she mentions it in a tone that is distant, almost uninterested, as if it is barely worth remembering. One explanation for this apparent nonchalance, as expressed through the undercutting effect of the phrase "Pakistan *or something*," may lie in Mumtaz's desire to reiterate her and her family's disinterest in Pakistan and, by implication, their loyalty to India. But in my reading the confusion over the dates of the war seems to indicate that the sporadic eruptions of Hindu-Muslim violence are conflated in her mind into a single, drawn-out experience of being suspected, mistrusted, and endangered in a Hindu-dominated society. Indeed, Mumtaz's repeated staging of the arguments with her father over "leaving or staying" may well be an attempt to simultaneously work out and present, through the two voices, her own contradictory feelings about India: her sense of belonging, on the one hand; and her bitterness at being asked to prove her loyalty, time and again, on the other. In her experience, it is Muslims like her who are continually disappointed by the lack of trust shown by some (by now many) Hindus and at times even the Indian state. Note, in this context, the use of the phrase "their own citizens" to refer to Hindus in her father's comment in a bitter if unconscious admission of his exclusion from a state he was forced to choose because of his love for *his* nation.

Jahan Ara's biggest disappointment seems to have come during the riots of 1964, which erupted in the wake of reports of communal violence in East Pakistan.[82]

> [As] I said before . . . my father was a nationalist Mussalman. Consequently, we never thought of leaving India, or that Bharatbarsha [India] is not my country . . . after Partition. . . . At least, I personally never thought that. Now there was a small riot in 1950 in Calcutta, but . . . after that for many years there were no riots in Calcutta city. In '64, there was again a riot! By then, we were grown up. I remember that during the '64 riots . . . my ego took a blow . . . or something. . . . I was probably really hurt (*bhishan abhiman hoyechhilo*).[83] I felt that we should probably not stay in this country any longer . . . if after all these years—after '46 . . . '64! After '47, . . . [again] '64—then we ought not to stay here any longer! . . . And I remember I told my husband that "[we] will leave from here, [we] won't stay here in this country." There in Bangladesh, then [East] Pakistan, in Pakistan we had relatives . . . they were much more well-off than those of us who stayed behind (*pore railam*). . . . With the same kind of qualifications . . . I was seeing that . . . possibly that desire [for better jobs and a higher income] was also working inside me. . . . I was seeing that they were leading easier lives

> ... not having to fight (*juddho karte hachhe na*) as much. ... There ... a new country ... the number of educated people was small ... among the educated class those who went from here ... they prospered rapidly. ... The Hindus were in high-ranking posts there. So when they left there was a vacuum [in East Pakistan] ... [and] we did not have those opportunities here, *na*? ... As such, I never gave much thought to all that. But when, after all those years, ... another ... *communal* riot ... I personally was very hurt ... my age was such that I felt let down! Now when I think about it ... [it] seems strange ... *je desher opore abhiman* [disappointed/angry with one's country]! ... Then I wanted to ... leave (*chalei jabo*)! ... It is one thing that there were riots in Pakistan ... that can happen. They declared themselves to be the nation of a specific community. But *we* did not do that! We stayed here believing that we will all live here in our own rights! ... Another blow from ... [what I/we had called my/our] own, that really hurt me, really hurt me!

In stark contrast to these voices of Muslim women who (and/or whose families) opted to stay in India, the question of proving one's loyalty to the nation seems to be of little or no concern in the accounts I gathered from Muslim women who either migrated to East Pakistan (present-day Bangladesh) or grew up there. However, some who were already in their teens when they left Calcutta do remember the preoccupation with Bengali culture, language, and identity among middle-class Muslims in pre-Partition Bengal. Nusrat Begum, for instance, spent a good part of her early life in Calcutta before migrating to East Pakistan in 1949. Nusrat personally knew many Muslim writers living in Calcutta in the 1930s and 1940s. As she remembers it, cultivation of Bengali was very important to "progressive" Muslim intellectuals in Bengal at that time. In her words:

> In our house we always spoke Bengali. And this was my father's main objection to Rokeya Sakhawat Hossein's school.[84] He would say, "Our daughters should learn Bengali, they do not need Urdu." However, at that time all Muslims from wealthy families studied Urdu, [and] even spoke Urdu at home, whereas the usual middle-class and poor families like us used Bengali.[85]

Indeed, as Nusrat recalls, for a few years she was made to attend a different school because her father did not like the idea of his daughter studying Urdu at Sakhawat Memorial.

By the 1950s, this preoccupation with Bengali identity among middle-class

Muslims in Bengal would lead to yet another full-fledged cultural nationalist movement in the subcontinent—in this case between Urdu-speaking West Pakistan and Bengali-dominated East Pakistan—which culminated in the formation of independent Bangladesh in 1971.[86] Some of the women I spoke with in Bangladesh played crucial roles in that movement, while others were involved in less visible ways. It is hardly surprising, therefore, that women, such as Nusrat Begum, who live in Bangladesh today talk about their national identity with an ease that, in my experience, is not easy to find among Muslim women in West Bengal.[87]

Muslims as Backward or Conservative

Nusrat's story does not escape disruption either; only in her case it is not the "nation" and its demands for loyalty but the history of "progress" itself and liberal Muslim men as its agents that overshadow her rather seamless presentation of her story and those of other women in her life. Still, it is in this context of addressing or refuting the idea of Muslim conservatism that Muslim women are most visible in their own stories. Comparisons with Hindu women, as well as the most incisive, if reluctant, criticisms of Muslim men, are also most likely to surface in these discussions.

As a Muslim woman intellectual in her own right, Nusrat Begum is clearly used to talking about her life experiences. But listening to her as we sat in the old Dhaka office of the magazine she edits, I realized that much of what Nusrat readily related about her childhood seemed to revolve largely around her father—a widely respected literary figure of the first half of the twentieth century.[88] In contrast, Nusrat talked about her mother Farida sparingly and often in response to specific questions. While this is perhaps not surprising given that she is often asked to speak about her father, his work, and his impact on her life, it is hard not to notice that Nusrat's narrative reinscribes the masculinist tendencies of official historiographies that typically emphasize men and their work in the public domain. And yet, it is Nusrat's recollections of her ostensibly "traditional" mother that, in my reading, offer the more valuable insights of her testimony, especially regarding the often ignored or underplayed role of women in what, in a different context, Mervat Hatem has called "the sustenance of social change," even if not its initiation.[89]

Nusrat begins her story with her birth in East Bengal but then switches almost immediately to talking about the lives of struggling writers in Calcutta.

> My birth is on June 4, 1925. . . . I was born in the village. My father used to live in Calcutta where he was busy with the . . . journal, [although] sometimes he would come to the village. At that time, Muslim writers, litterateurs, did not have much opportunity to live with their families because almost all of them lived amid considerable financial difficulties in Calcutta . . . some in messes, some with friends. For this reason . . . almost all the well-known [Muslim] writers with whom we came to be acquainted later . . . [would leave] their families in the village [usually in East Bengal]. Later, gradually, if and when they became relatively affluent, they would bring their families to live in Calcutta.

At this point in the narrative, Nusrat abruptly declares:

> I have a history (*amar ekta itihas achhe*). . . . In my childhood twice I almost drowned—once in the pond and another time in the canal. The second time . . . [I came very close to dying.] A neighbor saved me . . . [grabbed me by my legs,] turned me upside down, and spun me around until quite a bit of water came out of my mouth . . . and I regained consciousness. When this news reached my father in Calcutta, he said, "No, I will not keep them [my family] in the village any longer; my daughter will die." This is the preamble to my journey to Calcutta.
>
> *Q: When did you go there?*
>
> That . . . I am unable to tell you the exact date . . . probably I was about three or three and a half years old at that time . . . very young. My Baromama [mother's elder brother] and my Dadi and my Nani [paternal and maternal grandmothers], they all were very opposed to [us going to the city]. . . . They said that "taking them . . . my mother's name was Farida Khatun[90] . . . taking Farida to Calcutta means that they are all going to become Christian! No we cannot allow this. . . ." Then my father wrote a *stern* letter to my uncle, saying, "Within this date you will please bring my wife and my daughter to Calcutta. . . ." So then my uncle did not persist with his objections . . . [but] said, "Well, since he is insisting . . . I will take them to Calcutta." A *huge* borkha was put on my mother, and I was carried by my uncle . . . [until] we arrived at Shealdah Station.[91] *Phaeton gari*, that is, a horse-drawn carriage.[92] . . . But seeing the size of the horse I almost died of fright! *Uribbaba! Eta abar ki cheez!* [What is *this* thing!] And the horse, too, at the last minute decided to neigh (*cheehee cheehee cheehee kore*) loudly! I hugged my uncle tightly . . . [and] began to cry almost. . . . Anyway, we took the carriage from Shealdah Station to . . . [my father's house]. At

> that time, it was a rather busy and happening place. Qaji Nazrul Islam was already there.[93]

From the very beginning, then, Nusrat places her own life story firmly within the context of the increasingly vibrant literary and social reform movement initiated by a group of Muslim intellectuals in Bengal in the late nineteenth century and the early twentieth (discussed in chapter 3). Note also that in Nusrat's mind, her "history" consists of an early childhood in the village apparently fraught with danger—a time she clearly left behind when she came to Calcutta. One thus gets the sense that this narrative is not so much about the reunion of a family as about an encounter between the city and the village, between "modernity" and "progress," on one hand, and "tradition," posed as their antithesis, on the other.

Nusrat's first memories of her father in his city home are uncomfortable ones. As her description below suggests, he was visibly annoyed, if not embarrassed, by Nusrat's and her mother's rustic appearance.

> My father immediately scolded my mother, "What are you wearing? Like a ghost! Take it off!" Ma slowly took her borkha off and said quietly, "How can I come without a cover? So I borrowed a borkha from someone else." Baba said, "I do not ever want to see you wearing that thing in my presence again. Go! And what have you done to the child? You have turned her into an apparition as well! Pierced her nose, tied her hair tightly like that—how does it look?" So I was taken inside the house [to be "fixed"]. . . . For a few days . . . I would not let him hold me. . . . I was quite scared [of him. He looked strange] in his European clothes (*pant para*), . . . I had seen very little of him until then. He used to come sometimes to the village but always only for a few days before he went back to Calcutta. . . . So he tried to hold me, but I avoided him at first. I would keep hugging my mother. Gradually, however, I became close to him, so much so that I would tag along wherever he went and disturb him.

The picture Nusrat paints of her father is that of a dynamic, forward-looking man who edited an influential Bengali Muslim journal and in that capacity encouraged and even financially supported many struggling Muslim writers of the time. He was also the parent who opened up many opportunities for Nusrat. And, while she remembers him as being extremely busy, she also speaks fondly of the relatively rare occasions when her father had some time to spare for her.

> Going to see films—silent in those days . . . Charlie Chaplin, Shirley Temple . . . all those were silent films. Then going on trips . . . I had a special liking for outings. . . . It was difficult for him . . . [as] he could not spare too much time. But I think for all his busyness he was secure in the knowledge that the kind of environment his daughter was growing up in was my biggest gain (*paoya*)! . . . Among all these famous writers and intellectuals . . . I would call them *chacha* [uncle]. . . . As a child I did not fully understand how invaluable this environment was.

And yet, at times, Nusrat seems to be troubled by, if not a little critical of, his lack of sensitivity toward her mother. One event that stands out in Nusrat's memory offers a particularly poignant example of the encounter between her mother's wishes and her father's urbane/modernist sensibilities.

> One day Baba said [to my mother], "Listen, the child is now really young . . . [so] there is no need for her to wear her hair so long. And also that nose stud cannot be kept." Ma said, "No, no, why? . . . Her grandmother gave her the stud for her nose (*naker phul*). Let the hair and the stud be . . ." But was my father about to listen to her? So one day he took me to the goldsmith and had the nose ring removed—they actually had to cut it. Then he took me to the hairdresser's and had my hair chopped to a China [Chinese] bob. . . . When I came home with that Chinese bob my mother was furious! . . . "I worked so hard to grow her hair," she cried, "and you did not even think once to ask me!" . . . That day I saw my mother really cry! She had such an attachment to my hair—I had very beautiful, thick, black, curly hair. . . . She was also very hurt that my father ignored her wishes like that.

In another telling recollection, she describes Farida's unhappiness over her husband's decision to enrol Nusrat in school against her wishes.

> Rokeya Sakhawat Hossain . . . said to my father, "[You know] I have started this school . . . admit your daughter to my school . . . there are nurses (*dai*), the bus is there . . . with curtains (*purdahwalla*) . . . there will be no problems . . . ." When I went to see the Sakhawat school I saw that there were many little girls like me . . . walking around, going to classes, chatting. . . . I really liked it. My father asked me, "You want to go [home]?" I said, "No!" And I stayed until 4:00 pm. . . . But, *Ma*! Ma really opposed the idea. She said, "The child is so young, she will go so early in the morning and will not be back home until four in the afternoon. What kind of an arrangement is this? She will fall sick!" My father

> said, "If your daughter herself likes it . . . why should you object? She is not crying!" . . . But my mother remained unhappy.

Of course, Farida's objections could not stand up to her husband's determination, and her specific, perhaps conventionally defined concerns for her daughter were summarily upstaged by her husband's more "modern" vision of child rearing. Still, as Nusrat remembers it, Farida devised her own way of ensuring—unbeknownst to her husband—that her daughter got "proper" attention, ate properly, and took rest by giving money to the woman who took care of the girls and making a special appeal to their shared commitment to caretaking.

> Dai [the nurse] would reassure her that I was a good child and everything was fine. . . . One good thing that the school had that no other school has until now . . . there were little cots and pillows for the really young girls. After tiffin [lunch] break, we were made to lie on those cots. Most of the girls did not sleep . . . but those who did fall asleep would not be disturbed until their guardians came to get them.

Nusrat spoke at length about her experiences at the Sakhawat Memorial School where, apart from conventional academics, students received instruction in music, acting, art, and sewing. They were even graded on deportment and cleanliness—allowing them, according to Nusrat, to be "successful" later in life. In her words:

> We are amazed now at Rokeya Sakhawat Hossein's vision that a school should facilitate the overall development of girls. . . . We feel proud . . . those of us from Sakhawat who are still alive . . . that we have gone into many different fields . . . [and] no one is sitting at home . . . filling the vacuum that was created after Hindus and Christians left for Calcutta or India in the wake of the partition (*deshbhag*). Girls who were educated at Sakhawat and Lady Brabourne could successfully fill those . . . [posts].[94]

Nusrat's story tells us much about the efforts of liberal Muslim intellectuals to effect social reforms by spreading mass education, ending practices such as seclusion and polygamy, and making it possible for Muslim women to participate in contemporary intellectual life.[95] It is also clear that Nusrat prides herself on being a product of that liberal social milieu. As she recalls fondly, as a child she would roam freely in the journal office and listen to all the writers who came there to discuss each other's work. And, while she was too young to quite understand what they said, this atmosphere evidently left a deep imprint on her life. In time, she became the editor of a popular women's journal, which is still in circulation in Bangladesh. Indeed, according to Nusrat, her own work is merely the continuation of the work begun by intellectuals of her father's generation to both help women be more "self-sufficient," and provide them with a space for "independent self-expression."

Yet, this narrative of liberal reforms among middle-class Muslims, which so clearly challenges the dominant images of Muslim men as either backward-looking religious fanatics or conservative Mughal-identified elites, seems also to point, even if unwittingly, to the costs incurred by such reforms.[96] Women like Nusrat's mother sometimes appear in these stories as reluctant participants in such experiments, caught, as it were, between their own "traditional" or "backward" sensibilities and the desire, or compulsion, to keep up with their "modern" husbands and children.

When asked specifically about her mother's education, Nusrat briefly explained: "Ma did not have much education, not much. . . . No, she never went to school, but she was given some training at home by teachers . . . needlework. She could read Bengali and, in English, she could write her name. She could not read English." Yet it was Farida who taught her daughter to read and write since her husband was always busy with work. Nusrat acknowledges that she received much more attention and love from her mother, who taught her "whatever she knew—needlework, good cooking, or *atithi apyayan kara* [hospitality]." Nusrat also talked briefly about Farida's unwillingness to venture out of the house until she turned fifty in spite of her father's encouragement.

> I did not see my mother go out very much. . . . The wives (*paribar*) of other writers . . . would go out sometimes . . . but not my mother.[97] . . . She was a little conservative . . . she would not wear the borkha but did not like coming out in front of people. . . . She did not even come out in front of Qaji Saheb . . . she would speak from behind [the curtain or door].[98] Baba would say, "Why do you maintain parda in his presence? He comes here so often . . . his wife comes out in front of me!" But she would say, "No, I do not like it."

In the rest of her testimony, Nusrat mentions her mother only a few times, mostly in the context of the care she took of the various writers and poets who would come to, or even take refuge in, the house as per her husband's wishes.[99]

> All the writers would meet at the journal office. [My job was to] bring the *paan* [betel leaf] for Qaji Saheb . . . and *jarda* [tobacco], and tea . . . which my mother made herself. . . . My father would say, "Look, the poets and writers do not come here for money. They come for a little rest, a little peace and discussion. . . . Please make sure that they are not uncared for here. . . ." And . . . my mother always did this work.

In Nusrat's recollection, her mother remains an oddly defiant figure whose world may have been superseded by the onward march of "progress," defined in a specific way, but who seemed to elude its reach. Ironically, the success of the experiments with modernity that constructed women like Farida as "custom-bound/backward," in fact depended to a large extent on the very traditionalism of these women—for instance, their sense of duty to their husbands and families or the importance they attached to the art of hospitality.

Vision, some scholars would contend, has been crucial to the construction of the subject ever since the Renaissance.[100] It is unfortunate that narratives of modernity, preoccupied as they are with triumphal accounts of "coming out," and "becoming visible," so often fail to recognize the agency of the *pardanasheen* women who refused to embrace token visibility but contributed to the success of reformist efforts, even from behind the purdah.[101]

Shafinaz Hossein's recollections from her childhood offer yet another glimpse of the complexities involved in making the advent of modernity consistent with purdah. Shafinaz's mother, whom she describes as "a woman of great taste who was a voracious reader [and] loved music and flowers," was educated at home. But her experience of being a pardanasheen woman did not stop her from insisting that her daughters should have "proper schooling," even if it meant sending them to live in a hostel in a bigger town where the restrictions of purdah would presumably be less rigorous. When Shafinaz's oldest sister wanted to go to college, their father had to get a rickshaw covered with thick black cloth for his daughters to travel in. As Shafinaz explained, in the mid-1950s it was still rare for Muslim women in East Pakistan to attend college outside of Dhaka. By the time Shafinaz, who was born in 1946, entered Rajshahi University in the mid-1960s, much seems to have changed.[102] Not only were many more women attending college, but, as Shafinaz remembers it, many were participating freely in political and literary activities, including the independence movement against West Pakistan in the late 1960s and early 1970s, which led to the formation of Bangladesh.

When asked about women of earlier generations, Jahan Ara Begum talked candidly about her mother, Rasheeda, who was "quite an unusual woman," and her grandmother, and the ways in which she thought their lives were significantly different.

> My Dadu [mother's father] was a liberal man but one with quite an imposing personality. My mother seems to have inherited that from him. In that she was totally different from her own mother. Didima [maternal grandmother] was completely, totally a housewife. In fact, I should say that she lived in the kitchen. Her whole life seemed to be centered on the task of attending to every need of my grandfather. She would have lunch extremely late, around four in the afternoon; dinner she would never have before the ungodly hour of one in the morning after completing all the household chores. She was totally preoccupied with satisfying my grandfather. It did not seem that she had a life of her own—she was so self-effacing. I would say that she did not even show much affection to her own children or hug her grandchildren. . . . She would feed us when we went to visit her but nothing beyond that. . . . My grandfather's younger brother was also married. It was a joint family. My grandmother's sister-in-law (*chhotoja*) was nothing like Didima. She was quite capable of keeping her husband under considerable control. She also did housework, but it did not consume her as it seems to have my grandmother.

Although Jahan Ara does not spell it out, her description of her grandmother's subservience seems to also hint at her criticism of her grandfather as someone who expected his wife to be that way. This becomes more explicit as she describes her own mother. Born around 1920, Rasheeda seems to have been a strong woman with an imposing personality who was involved in political activism for the Congress and commanded respect, if not fear, from her children and her peers alike.

> My mother, on the other hand, was very different. But then she was different even from her own sister. She had matriculated from school, which was no mean task in those days. She was always very well dressed, always in style. I told you that my father was a nationalist leader. Well, we had all sorts of people

> visiting us . . . many famous leaders of that time. My mother could hold her own with everyone. . . . I suppose my father's liberal attitudes helped, but that could not have been the whole story.

One incident that stands out in Jahan Ara's mind concerned a prominent politician who had the occasion to experience her mother's personality and later related the following story to her. Note that, while the immediate purpose of the story, set in the years following independence, is to add texture to her depiction of her mother as an unusual and strong woman, it also serves to delineate the resolutely moderate and centrist political stance of her family.

> Mr. Sen was running for office as a Congress candidate once in this Park Circus area.[103] Someone, probably [in] the party high command, advised him to get in touch with my father, who, as I told you, was a nationalist leader of some repute. Since my father was Muslim and wielded considerable influence in this predominantly Muslim area, he could extend a lot of help to Mr. Sen, who, I believe, won the elections that time. Later, for whatever reasons, he switched sides to the Communist Party [the CPM].[104] Election time came. Mr. Sen also came, ostensibly to seek help from my father again. My mother greeted him and asked what [had] brought him there. When he explained, my mother replied: "Look . . . it is very nice to see you again. Do come in and have some tea with us, but do not expect any help from us in these elections since you are now running as a CPM candidate. If you should change your mind in the future and go back to Congress, then come back. I can assure you that both your Dada [Jahan Ara's father] and I will help in whatever way possible.[105] Meanwhile, you are welcome here as a guest; have tea with us, chat with us, but do not even think of discussing politics."[106] Mr. Sen was astounded by my mother's directness. He told me, "I could not believe your mother. I have never felt so silly in my life. Your mother was capable of doing that to people."
>
> This was my mother. We used to be scared of her. If we wanted something . . . for instance if we were planning to go somewhere, like once we went to Shantiniketan with friends . . . we would first approach our father and have him get our mother's approval. We were not scared of him.

Unlike many of her contemporaries, Rasheeda did not observe purdah but would cover her head when she went out of the house. Yet, in Jahan Ara's recollections, her mother would always defer to her father's wishes, even in matters relating to the household. But this, as Jahan Ara hastens to point out, was no different than what was expected of all women—Hindu or Muslim—of that generation.

Jahan Ara also spoke briefly of her mother-in-law, Fatema, who was born around 1910 in a village in the Howrah district of West Bengal.[107] Like many other women of her generation, Fatema, who had grown up in strict purdah and had little formal education, came to the city after her marriage. But, as Jahan Ara puts it, for women of Fatema's generation the move from the village to the city did not necessarily result in a significant change in their "mentality." Nor did her mother-in-law's life as a young wife in her husband's household encourage any real change in her attitudes.

> Well . . . the atmosphere of this [Fatema's husband's] household was different. . . . I have heard stories from my mother-in-law that when she first came to Calcutta she would never go out without a car. Moreover, even when she got into the car, servants would hold up lengths of cloth on both sides to create a sort of covered corridor between the door of the house and that of the car. In those days, government officers like my father-in-law had several attendants (*chaprashis*) assigned to them. So, anyway, my mother-in-law would quickly get into the car thus hidden from the world. . . . They never used borkhas in this household—but the women would not readily come out or [would] use some sort of cloth barrier. Once the women got into the car, they could go anywhere really, but this had to be observed. Later, when I came to this household after my marriage . . . women would go out—with the car of course—but by then this kind of strict purdah had already been abandoned. But I think they still had some reservations about women going out freely due to this habit of rather strict observance of purdah from childhood.

As far as her own experience is concerned, Jahan Ara acknowledges certain difficulties of adjustment that she had to go through after marriage, but she readily points out that the adjustments had to be two-sided. As she sees it, "the difference in mentality" between women of previous generations—that is, between Fatema's generation and the ones preceding it—"was not appreciable." It was Jahan Ara's generation that, according to her, "became modern fast."

Jahan Ara is especially adamant in refusing to apply the label "backward" or "conservative" to the way her parents treated her and her sisters. They were allowed a degree of freedom that she insists was quite exceptional for other women of her age, Mussalman or Hindu.

> I cannot claim that you will get the most representative picture of the situation of Muslim women . . . from my life story. . . . [Even] my Hindu friends, the ones who were originally from West Bengal, were brought up in far more conservative conditions. . . . I remember that when we went on daylong outings—picnics—our men friends would accompany us. . . . In those days, we would address men friends as *dada* [elder brother] . . . . There were never any objections from our family . . . [and] even our Hindu friends who came from East Bengal were allowed to go. But the women whose families were from West Bengal, they always had trouble getting permission. . . . In the matter of education [and employment] also they are quite like Mussalmans. They want to get their daughters married and settled in a family as soon as possible.

Jahan Ara also insisted that, while unmarried Hindu women of her generation may have enjoyed greater mobility than most Muslim women, after marriage the Hindu women's situation would typically undergo significant changes. As she put it, contrary to popular Hindu perceptions:

> I feel quite strongly that married women [of her generation] in Mussalman households enjoyed more freedom than married Hindu women . . . especially in terms of visiting their own families. . . . [Hindu women] were subject to a lot of restrictions. I would see that after marriage they were somehow reined in. And . . . dowry was simply unheard of in Muslim society [at that time]. On the contrary, the groom's family welcomed the new bride with many gifts. This practice is still very much alive in Bangladesh and Pakistan. But among Indian Muslims it is on the wane . . . possibly due to influence of Hindu customs.

One important aspect in which Hindu women, especially those who came from East Bengali as part of migrant or refugee families, seem to have had an advantage over Muslim women is that of paid work.[108] According to Jahan Ara, while some Muslim women were allowed, even encouraged, to attend college, they were rarely expected to join the paid workforce; it was quite a foreign concept even in liberal households such as hers. Many of her Hindu friends, however, had the support of their families in the matter of their decision to work—an issue that, as we shall see presently, came up repeatedly in a number of the interviews.

The issue of "conservatism/liberalness" featured prominently in much of my conversation with Mumtaz Waheeda as well. On our very first meeting in her home in Salt Lake—a prosperous suburb of Calcutta—Mumtaz (who was the first woman I interviewed) objected sharply to my interest in investigating whether Muslim women in Bengal had undergone reforms similar to those experienced by Hindu/Brahmo women in colonial Bengal. "Why should Muslim women have to do what Hindu women did?" she exclaimed indignantly. "Just because they [Muslim women] did not always attend school does not mean that they were all backward!" I remember leaving that first meeting with Mumtaz feeling miserable and ashamed for having posed such a naive and poorly thought-out question, but I was secretly grateful to her for setting me straight so early in my attempt to do oral history.

On our second meeting, Mumtaz told me about her mother, Suraiya, and her aunt, Hameera, who grew up in a very orthodox Dehliwal business family that was, as Mumtaz added in a somewhat confidential sotto voce, like "UP families . . . in those days . . . very conservative."[109] Consequently, Suraiya's formal education

> was limited . . . she managed up to about class four. But . . . yes, my mother and her sisters were literate. She also picked up Bengali. If she were sitting here, she would have understood you. . . . She could also talk fluently in English. Her pronunciation was perfect because they used to be taught inside the house by European ladies . . . [who would give] lessons in English.
>
> *Q: This is before her marriage to your father?*
>
> Yes, this is before she was married. Otherwise, how do you think my parents ever conversed? [She laughed.]
>
> Another lady I believe used to come and teach her needlework. One of my aunts, Hameera . . . after she was married . . . was the first Muslim lady to drive from here to . . . and I wish I could show you the pictures . . . I will show you one day . . . she drove from Calcutta to Ranchi and got a prize for that. . . . But no, not education outside the home. . . . Another of my *khalammas* [aunts] was apparently a good painter, another adept at needlework. . . . My mother even knew a lot of yoga. This is why my mother always used to object to our going out too much. She would say, "Why? One can learn everything at home. You do not have to go out." And mixing with boys, because of my mother, was a "no" for me.

Mumtaz Waheeda's recollections of her mother seem to be fraught with contradictions. On the one hand, she is evidently proud of the many accomplishments of her mother and her aunts who, according to Mumtaz, were far from "handicapped" (compared, presumably, to Hindu women) by purdah. Indeed, as Mumtaz remembers it, her mother would ascribe her ability to function in the new surroundings of the "enlightened" Bengali household of her husband precisely to her rather strict and orthodox upbringing.

> My mother used to think that she could adjust to all these changes because she was not very qualified [formally educated]. She would always say . . . "How can I do this? Because . . . for me you are more important than my own ideas. But if there were a different woman—a *bhadramahila*—in my place, with a set mind and education and all that, then she could not have adjusted so much."[110] . . . I consider my mother as an example of what a lady she was . . . coming from such a conservative family, settling in this very different context. . . . She was a lady with great foresight, intelligence, and she knew how to adjust into a Bengali family, and she did adjust into *our* family [emphasis added].[111]

The immediate object of criticism in this excerpt is, of course, the "self-willed" Hindu bhadramahila, who would presumably place her own interests above those of the family. But, although Mumtaz (or Suraiya for that matter) does not explicitly mention it, her extolling of her mother as the epitome of graciousness and accommodation seems to invoke and criticize implicitly yet another notion of womanhood—that of the haughty and unruly aristocratic begum often cited by Muslim reformers in the late nineteenth century as the source of *fitna* (lack of order). In contrast, in Mumtaz's portrayal, her mother emerges as the very embodiment of the model of reformed Muslim femininity so lauded in the *Bihishti Zewar*, by Maulana Ashraf Ali Thanawi, a didactic tract published in the first decade of the twentieth century.[112]

And yet the differences Mumtaz highlights between the "enlightened" milieu of her father's family and the "conservativeness" of her mother's background, as well as her repeated reference to her mother's heroic adjustment to "our" (i.e., Mumtaz's father's) family throughout her testimony, make one wonder if something has not been lost or suppressed in this relentlessly optimistic account of Suraiya's successful transition into married life in an environment that was completely different from the one in which she grew up. I would also note that on closer scrutiny some of what Mumtaz calls adjustment begins to look more like negotiation. Take, for instance, the story of how Mumtaz "had to take up Urdu as her second language" in school, while her other siblings learned Bengali, because her mother did not know much Bengali and wanted her "firstborn to learn Urdu." At one level, Suraiya's insistence in this regard is surely a reflection of her loneliness in the linguistically and culturally unfamiliar setting of a Bengali family, but it is also an example of her ability to use her power, no matter how limited by her structural location, to engineer an outcome more to her liking.

Note also that, regardless of her admiration for her mother and other women like her, Mumtaz seems to have rebelled against many of the standards of womanly etiquette that her mother tried to instill in her, especially in her youth. As Mumtaz admits, her mother's strictness about going out embarrassed her in front of her Hindu classmates.

> When I joined Lady Brabourne College, on days when my father could not give me lift in his car, she would insist that I take a rickshaw from Lower Circular Road to Lady Brabourne College. It was no distance at all, and all my classmates would tease me . . . so I would get off the rickshaw as soon as I had gone far enough where she could not see me. Then I would walk with my friends. But my mother would not allow me to walk.

Suraiya believed that educating women too much would only lead to trouble.

> [My mother] would tell me, "Now you do not understand, but later when you go to your husband's house, then you will realize. . . . A woman loses her capacity to adjust when she thinks that she too has become something, her own person."

"You see I am just telling you how [my mother] thought, these are her ideas," Mumtaz hastened to add, seemingly anxious to distinguish her own point of view from her mother's, and then continued elaborating, stating that her mother believed "if girls become too modern, all sorts of complications arise" and women should always be a "little submissive" and prepared to compromise for the good of the family.

In contrast to her mildly sarcastic detailing of Suraiya's "traditional" beliefs, Mumtaz seems to present her father as strikingly liberal, an agent of change and "progress" and, as in the case of Nusrat Begum's father, the parent who facilitated his daughters' entry into the public world.

> He would laugh at [my mother]—he would say all that is rubbish. . . . [He] would always encourage us. Think about it, in spite of my mother's ideas, my

> sister stood second in the MBBS [Bachelor of Medicine and Bachelor of Surgery] exam. . . . She was always a brilliant student. My mother sometimes used to grumble about how my sister would adjust in another household after being so educated.

Mumtaz and her two sisters are all highly educated. Mumtaz has a master's degree, and both her sisters are doctors.

However, as she continued with her testimony, Mumtaz revealed that, for all his support for his daughters' education, her father did not necessarily envision any of them working for a living. Mumtaz tried to explain her father's attitude as a possible result of the family's affluence, which made "the need for women to work . . . a distant concept." But this attempt to equate women's work solely with economic necessity glosses over the question of power within the family and the need to control women — issues that emerge as central in the accounts that followed of both the "fixing" of her marriage and her subsequent struggle to balance career and family responsibilities in the context of her own marriage to a doctor, arranged by her father.

> My husband's family was from the village . . . and I was entirely city bred. I had not been exposed to village life — you know, the houses, all that mud, lack of all the amenities that I had taken for granted all my life. . . . My husband's family had a lot of land and property in . . . [the village]. I remember asking my father once why he was preferring this family, . . . I guess I was a little upset. My Abba just said one thing: "He is a very nice boy. You do not like people drinking, and this boy is very honest and does not drink or anything. He is a good doctor . . . he will be good for you." He also used to say that money was not the key to happiness. "I think you will be happy," [he said,] "but now it is up to you." I did not have the mental makeup at that time.

And here Mumtaz suddenly embarked on what appeared at first to be a somewhat disjointed and labored account of socializing and "eve-teasing."[113]

> But let me tell you something. In those days there was a club in Park Circus called International Club. All international students studying in Calcutta would get together there. I used to go there with my brothers. My father never objected to that, but he always made sure that we went with a car and came back with it. So I used to attend these meetings in those days, but we were not allowed to walk around in the city. The idea that women would walk around was simply not acceptable to my family. . . . [Even] if we went on a short errand

. . . a maid would always follow. . . . Frankly, if I had a daughter, I would do the same with her. Let us face it . . . there is so much eve-teasing and other harassment. If a girl walks around alone, then men on the street may be encouraged. . . . I think the tendency to harass women is present everywhere—outside India even—but because women here are kept a little aloof from men, when they do come out it brings out this kind of behavior in men more openly here. Don't you agree? It is not so common here . . . women walking around. . . . [In the West] women go out more often, so no one bothers really. It is common. When I was in the third year of my college, all these proposals for marriage started coming in. My father chose Dr. Ali.

At first glance, this passage seems to be something of a digression from the story of the matchmaking process leading up to her marriage to Dr. Ali, and for some time after the interview I wondered about her reasons for dwelling on what was not quite an "incident." Was she trying to stress something? Or was this an example of "a strategy to distract attention from other more delicate points?"[114]

On reflection, one possible explanation seems to be her desire to preserve the liberal image of her father in the midst of an account of her "arranged marriage"—surely one of the most powerful tropes of patriarchal control invoked in liberal/feminist critiques of nonwestern cultures. And, as a self-professed liberal/enlightened Muslim woman whose other sisters subsequently married Hindu men of their choice, albeit only after their father's death, Mumtaz probably assumed that I, as a woman living in the West, would be critical of her capitulation to such a marriage and interpret her father's imposition of his "judgment" over her uncertainty as a symbol of "repressive male authority."[115] Her desire to protect her dearly loved and respected abba's image is also evident in her somewhat defiant declaration that she, too, would "do the same" if she had a daughter.

And yet, Mumtaz's utmost care in presenting her father's authority as an expression of his love and concern for his daughter does not entirely stop her from criticizing him. For on further scrutiny one might detect the barest impression of other possible stories in the cracks of this torturously indirect account of going to clubs—about meeting other men and perhaps of even liking some of them. The allusion to the West in the excerpt may also be a reference to the kind of freedom that she obviously enjoyed in being allowed to attend parties in clubs that would be beyond the reach of most women from less liberal and/or affluent class locations; but it may also refer to the freedom she was denied in choosing a partner—as the specter of other "proposals" would seem to suggest. Perhaps her presence emboldened some men to present themselves as suitors, or even make improper advances, as the jarring appearance of the word *harass* might suggest. Whatever the exact incident(s), however, in the end it was clearly a moot point. For, her abba "chose Dr. Ali"—a decision that Mumtaz seems to have resented at first, but came to accept if not respect over time.

Mumtaz's complex feelings toward her late husband are also not easy to define. She talked at some length about her arguments with him over his insistence that her first responsibility was always her husband and "his children," but she also insisted that he usually provided "answers to her liking."

> My husband was a very learned man; whenever any disagreement came up, he would quote from the Qu'ran. Right after we were married, he told me, "Listen . . . I have no objection if you want to continue studying . . . but if you are working how will this [family/marriage] work?" . . . His brother was married to a doctor also, so this was not a matter of [simple] conservatism. But he would say, "If I wanted a working wife, I could have married a doctor . . . who could earn as much as me! . . . [But] my family will have to survive on what I earn. . . . You keep what you earn. My only condition is that . . . you cannot earn by disturbing my family. . . . If I protested, he would say, "You are the queen of this household. I live like a guest in my own home. I come, you feed me, allow me to relax. . . ." He would openly admit he was grateful. But he was adamant that he needed this [sacrifice] from me. He would say, "I need this support, but you do not."

Mumtaz is well aware that her husband's attempt to humor her as the "queen of the household" was an expression of his control over the situation, and yet she feels compelled to agree with the logic of his argument. Indeed, one could interpret her comment—"I was not stupid of course . . . he was right . . . he could have married someone else"—as indicative not only of what he could have done instead of marrying her but, more important, that if he chose he could marry again under Islamic law.

Her anger and frustration are most visible when she talks about his lack of support during her teacher's training course and when she compares her situation to that of her Hindu colleagues.

> I would hear from other teachers how much their husbands helped them . . . [but] my husband could not care less. But that was our contract, [and] I had to prepare myself accordingly. My children were good. . . . At that time we had some fights. But now, looking back, I realize that it was really my fault. He never . . . [wanted to know] what I earned. . . . But I have to admit that I would [/used to] be furious. My mother liked being a housewife, so she accommodated willingly, but it was difficult for me.

Mumtaz does not openly challenge her husband's steadfast championing of the "men as providers" idea in her testimony, but it is clear that she was determined to have a career of her own. She also clearly chafed under the unfairness of her husband's demand for support from her when he did nothing to help her in any way. However, as she points out, in sharp contrast to her Hindu colleagues, who often did not control their own earnings, what she earned through her struggles was entirely her own; her husband never as much as inquired about how much she earned.[116]

It would be tempting to read Mumtaz's testimony as either a confirmation of the stereotypical picture of a Muslim woman dominated by the men in her life or as a fable of (feminist) resistance. But her insistence on being economically independent, her pride in being able to control her own income, her criticism of her husband (despite the deep appreciation she expresses for him), her implied criticism of the specific restrictions she had to face as a *Muslim* woman, and her simultaneous attempt to retrieve her father and husband ultimately as liberal, loving, and above all reasonable point to a complex subject position that resists easy reduction. Instead, I would simply note that her sense of self-sufficiency was achieved not through some token arrangement sanctioned by male largesse but through a lifelong battle against a system of unfair expectations underwritten by gender inequality. And in the end, by all indications, she seems to have had a successful career as an educator, been much loved by her late husband, and enjoyed immense love and respect from her sons.[117]

If most women I spoke with engaged in oblique criticism of male privilege, Meherunnessa Begum expresses open disdain for Muslim men, their conservatism, and what she variously describes as their lack of "modern sensibilities" and an inadequate understanding of "changing times." Born into a relatively affluent family of Muslim businessmen in Calcutta in 1924, Meherunnessa, who has never married, lives alone in one room of what was once a spacious and beautiful family house in Park Circus. The house is not only in a state of permanent disrepair—"my brother needs to come see this leak, but he has no time," she complained—but seems to be partitioned into several small, rather ungainly apartments in which various units of a once joint family now live in uncomfortable proximity. From what I gathered from her somewhat apologetic attempts at explanation, the misfortunes of the family may have started when, due to an unresolvable family dispute dating back to her grandparents' time, the family inheritance was confiscated by the *waqf* (local Muslim council) board. At the time of the interview, Meherunnessa had retired from a long teaching career at the Sakhawat Memorial School, where she had also been a student, but she kept herself busy as a member of the Young Women's Christian Association (YWCA). As she confided with a laugh, she loved camping and was still going on trips regularly!

Although fluent in Bengali, and well versed in English, Meherunnessa speaks both languages with the distinct accent of someone whose mother tongue is Urdu. Not surprisingly, therefore, the intertexts in her speech also typically come from Urdu, even if mostly in translation.[118] She is also an animated speaker who is likely to appropriate the speeches of several actors within the course of narrating a single episode or illustration, making it difficult for the listener to isolate her own authorial voice. For instance, her overall criticism of Muslim society in pre-Partition Calcutta seems to echo closely the "lagging behind" discourse adopted by the colonial administration vis-à-vis Muslims beginning in the last quarter of the nineteenth century. The insistent focus on this one theme throughout her testimony may also signal that she is—perhaps unconsciously—providing the kind of information that she thinks a non-Muslim person (especially a Hindu woman) might expect to hear about Muslim society.[119] And yet, as we shall see, Meherunnessa's stories are remarkably rich in their evocation, even if in passing, of the quotidian life of upper/middle class Muslim households in Calcutta. I also think that, in spite of their criticism—delivered often in borrowed voices—these stories betray a certain sadness, if not yearning, for a time long gone.

Meherunnessa has seen the fortunes of many a family dwindle away because of what she describes as an inability of Muslims to "let go of the past." While her own parents, according to her, were "forward looking"—they sent her to school, for instance, which helped her to be independent later in life—members of their larger joint family, as well as neighbors, seem to have thought that the "easy life" they were leading would continue forever. Consequently, they were caught unprepared by the changes brought about by World War II. Her own impressions from her childhood seem to be that wastefulness was common, if not something of a virtue, in many of the Muslim households she frequented:[120]

> You know what the typical system of eating was? Mothers [in all households] would lovingly put out this and that. . . . [The children would say,] "Won't take any more, don't want any more!" . . . [The mother would say] "Have what you can, I will eat the rest." You understand? So much food would be left behind on the plates! In our family . . . if [we] said no, . . . [my mother would not give us more food]. We would finish all the rice . . . [and] everyone [outside of her nuclear family] would say, "You do not even leave something for the dogs?" This is how they would taunt us!

Her last comment might also signal the relative lack of affluence of her parents compared to the rest of the extended family.

The first woman in her family to go to school, and subsequently to Lady Brabourne College, Meherunnessa is particularly scornful of the neglect of education in Muslim society and especially the kinds of restrictions it placed on women.

> The idea [was] that if girls learned to read they would be spoiled. . . . Tutors might come to the house . . . [girls] would even learn to speak English, but no one would go to school. . . . In those days, holding a book meant [committing] a sin! If, say, girls are reading, [the parents] would come ten times to . . . check whether there is anything hidden among the leaves of the book . . . some love letter from the neighbor or something. . . . *Achha!* You don't even trust your own daughter? This was the level of paranoia! . . . It did not happen in our household, but we would hear stories.

The situation was apparently not much better in terms of educating men: while sons were often sent to school, parents seldom paid much attention to whether or what they were studying.

> Very rarely have I seen parents push their sons to excel in school—nothing like "You have to be a doctor, engineer, or barrister or have to go abroad for higher studies." . . . If, . . . say, a Muslim girl got a scholarship, people would think that it is charity (*khayraat*). . . . "Why?" [they would say]. "Her father

does not have money? *Gormenter takaye porchhe* [Studying with government assistance]!" This was the mentality!

The studious girl in this story could easily have been Meherunnessa herself. As she intimates elsewhere, her decision to continue her education through college may not have been popular among her relatives, but in time they came to appreciate her ability to support herself, thus avoiding the (possible) ignominy of depending on her brothers, as was customary for unmarried or widowed women of her parents', and sometimes even in her own, generation. She muses: "But what would her life be like? . . . I have seen my own aunts . . . it was a pathetic life, *hai na*? . . . Those that had some education [could get jobs]. . . . Live in one room or two rooms [within a larger house with or without relatives], but live independently. . . . People visit me, too . . . stay for eight, ten days. . . . All that is good . . . no problem in this way."

Meherunnessa's pride in her ability to be independent is well justified, of course. Her observations about the problems of Muslim women, especially in previous generations, are also entirely borne out by official statistics. For instance, in 1931–32, of the total number of male students attending college (including professional colleges) in Bengal, 13.6 percent were Muslim while 84.1 percent were Hindus. The corresponding figures for female students pursuing college or professional degrees were a mere 1 percent for Muslims and 74 percent for Hindu; and this in a state (undivided Bengal) where Muslims constituted over 50 percent of the total population.[121] Meherunnessa's account of meeting Hindu students in school also affords us a rare glimpse of the experiential dimensions of what is embodied in such statistics.

> We were the first girls sometimes in our families to go to school. . . . [We] would often be in awe of . . . the general knowledge of [Hindu girls]. We used to say among ourselves, "We are still living in darkness" (*Hamlog abhitak andhere me hain*). . . . I think in my [older] sister's generation many women were unhappy about the restrictions that plagued their lives, especially since they had Hindu friends who were doing so many things. But our guardians did not care.[122]

And yet in retrospect it seems unfortunate that so many of her observations about life in her childhood—recollected within the dialogic constraints of this particular interview situation—should have been haunted by the specter of Muslim "backwardness" or her indictment of it, often to the exclusion of other kinds of narratives. Listening to her incidental comments about the joint family structure with "aunts and uncles," scores of cousins, relatives visiting for extended periods, "boys running out to see wedding processions," or "women dressing up together," one wonders what other stories might have been told about a life that also seemed to be joyful. But clearly, unlike some of the other women I spoke to, Meherunnessa did not feel comfortable sharing that level of intimacy with me.

Meherunnessa does not mention close Hindu friends, although when asked about her interactions with Hindus she insists that she has always had very good relations with Hindu friends and neighbors. She remembers, in this context, Hindu neighbors with whom her father would play cards and whom she would address as "uncles," Hindu girlfriends of her older sister, and, of course, a somewhat amorphous group of "classmates" in her school. But her allusions to parental ambitions regarding children's education, sons' careers, or governmental scholarships signal the presence of the Hindu middle class as the implicit referent. She even adopts the imagined voice of a Hindu middle-class parent when she describes what, in her mind, ought to be the appropriate parental attitude toward children's education: "You have to be a doctor, engineer, barrister." However, while at first glance her relationship with Hindus appears to be mostly one of a somewhat distant appreciation, a closer look reveals a more complex set of reactions.

Consider, for instance, the following sarcastic reflection on the reasons behind Muslim men's disinterest in education in years leading up to World War II:

> The British came after the Mughal kingdom [*sic*], right? So . . . [Muslim men] know that they are the people of the ruler's race (*ora to rajar jater lok*)—the descendants of the Mughals! . . . [They would think,] "Why should we be someone else's servants? We will do business!" That, too, nothing small, mind you! Big business! . . . At that time, the consciousness that you could actually succeed from modest beginnings was simply not there among Muslim [men]. *Chakri* (service)![123] Oh no! . . . Whatever property they inherited from their forefathers, [they] simply lived off selling that (*bhangbe ar khabe*)! . . . All [of them] walked around dressed in fine clothes . . . smoked imported cigars . . . but no one would have any kind of degree.

Here Meherunnessa is clearly invoking the success of the Hindu bhadralok, who were willing, and for many decades better equipped, to work for the

British administration, through the reference to chakri (service) and the social mobility it promised at that time. Her criticism of Muslim men appears to be remarkably similar to the kind of criticism that the Hindu bhadralok might deploy against them: Muslim men are uneducated and foolhardy in their arrogance, ultimately to their own detriment. Yet the same reference to the Hindu proclivity for chakri, not to mention the assertion of Muslim self-identification as the erstwhile "rulers," also invokes a power discourse with entirely different stakes—one that values freedom, not servility, prefers grand ideas to following instructions, and echoes European colonial discourses about the natural division between the rulers and the ruled deployed against all colonized populations but appropriated here in the voices of Muslim men who arrogate to themselves the right to rule and refuse success on terms unacceptable to them. Note also that it is not at all clear which, if any, of the several voices Meherunnessa inhabits are hers.

Her ambivalence is even clearer when she reflects on the ability of Hindus to adapt to change. In one memorable account, Meherunnessa begins talking about the indirect involvement of Muslim women in some social mobilization efforts of the bhadralok but switches suddenly to a reflection on money in prewar India, the naïveté of Muslim women, and, in sharp contrast, the resourcefulness of Hindu women.

> I have not seen many Muslim women participate in political movements as such, but when floods occurred . . . then . . . well-dressed men . . . carrying harmoniums . . . would go around singing songs about the flood and asking . . . [for contributions to their relief efforts]. Then I have seen . . . Muslim women give clothes. . . . They would ask . . . younger children to take clothes and money . . . [to] put in the . . . [makeshift cloth bag]. And money in those days . . . each *taka* [rupee] was made of *ek bhari* silver![124] Do you understand? What our Bharatbarsha [India] was like! . . . If women kept ten silver rupees tied to their *anchal*, their *shari* would be at the point of tearing![125]. . . You know how backward Muslims were . . . [Muslim] women? When the war came . . . the coins were silver, right? These women still thought that the world was always going to be the same. . . . [But] Hindu women! They removed those silver coins from sight altogether (*adrishya kore phellen*). Later they brought out all that silver . . . taka! Full containers of silver coins! Even women my mother knew! . . . *So much* silver came from their cashboxes. What came out of the boxes of Muslim women were guineas not silver! . . . [A] guinea is made of gold. They understood [the value

of] that! So they kept those [guineas]. . . . But it had never occurred to them to save the silver, you understand? They spent all the silver coins! [Meanwhile] . . . *ora hoard korechhe. Ora hoard korechhe, non-Muslimra* [they hoarded them, the non-Muslims]! So much silver and gold came out of their boxes! . . . I have asked many [Muslim] women myself, "Achha! How much silver did you save?" [And they would say,] "Nothing! I did not realize [the silver coins] would disappear!" . . . Hindu women . . . they were educated! . . . They . . . realized what the future held. You understand? After the war silver coins were completely replaced by bills—*paper*! Hai na? . . . You see, now, how clever [the Hindus] were! . . . They kept [the coins], they knew [that these were valuable] . . . they had foresight! . . . But not Muslims!

That Meherunnessa was frustrated with the lack of sagacity and foresight among Muslims in general, and Muslim women in particular, is clear. But I want to focus on her comment on Hindus and their cleverness: "They hoarded [silver coins], the non-Muslims! . . . You see, now, how clever [the Hindus] were!"

According to the *Oxford English Dictionary*, one meaning of *hoarding* is to "amass and put away," but in another, more figurative sense the word denotes concealing, that is withholding from others, presumably to further one's personal aspirations or welfare. In the first sense, *to hoard* is not appreciably different from *to save*, but in the second sense the word carries an additional, moral charge of selfishness, of the intent to garner unfair advantage for one's own benefit to the considered exclusion of others. In my reading, Meherunnessa uses *hoard* in the second, more accusative sense twice and with increasing deliberation. Note also her use of the term *non-Muslims* in this sentence to refer to Hindus as if to underscore something of an essential cultural (or is it moral?) difference between the conduct of Hindus (hoarding/thriftiness) and Muslims (spending/largesse). It is also, at one level, a story of social closure, of the foundering of informal networks at the imaginary line, to echo Jahan Ara Begum's words, that seemed to increasingly distance Muslims from Hindus in mid-1940s Calcutta.

It is also important to note that Muslim women do not appear only as "backward" in Meherunnessa's stories. She describes many of them as talented singers, writers, and painters in spite of the many obstacles they faced. Her *didi* (older sister), for instance, was a very creative woman, and Meherunnessa speaks of her with much fondness and respect.

> My didi was a very good singer. After her marriage, my brother-in-law asked her to sing in front of his friends. . . . He was brought up abroad . . . so he had a different mentality. . . . But what a scandal that created, "*Ei! Tumi naki gan korechho* [You apparently sang] . . . ?" . . . My sister also used to write [children's] stories. . . . They were not printed, but she would read them out to us—her younger siblings and cousins. . . . She [never went to school] but lived a very happy life.

Some of the women were even resourceful enough to circumvent the restrictions placed on them.

Take, for instance, Nusreen Begum, who was one of the first Muslim women to teach at Rokeya Sakhawat Hossein's school and had met Meherunnessa as a young student in her class many decades earlier.[126] Sadly, Nusreen was already very ill at that time, so my meeting with her was necessarily brief. But she was gracious and expressed much happiness when she found out that I was doing doctoral research on Muslim women and proceeded to tell me a little about her involvement with Sakhawat Memorial. Her account, perhaps more than any other, offers us a rare glimpse of the kind of ingenious strategies sharif women sometimes had to invent as they slowly negotiated changing definitions of ideal womanhood in early-twentieth-century urban Bengal.

Born around 1906 into an Urdu-speaking ashraf family in Calcutta, Nusreen grew up in strict purdah and never went to school. But she recalled that women in her family did get "lessons at home." After her marriage, urged by Begum Rokeya, her husband consented to let her do some "social work," but he was entirely opposed to the idea of her taking up paid employment. Nusreen, however, was determined to teach. So she told her otherwise reform-minded husband that she was doing "social/charity work" when in fact she went to work as a teacher. A dynamic woman in her nineties, Nusreen laughed heartily as she recounted how she hid the money—"Oh, I hid it! I hid the money in my borkha. And my husband would never know where to look in the zenana. I suppose I lied to him, but I had my own money to spend as I pleased!"—revealing in the process the grit and resourcefulness of at least some women of her generation who negotiated the restrictions placed on them, at times even using to their advantage the very technologies of seclusion—the borkha and the zenana—meant to constrain their movements as shields from male scrutiny and control.

Muslims as Low-Caste/Low-Class Converts

A third theme that recurs in these life stories deals with the image of Muslims as originally low-caste/low-class Hindus—a concern that, as we have seen, surfaces almost in tandem with assertions of Bengali-ness. The speakers seem generally anxious to communicate their class status through a number of different mechanisms from descriptions of their neighborhoods to stories about trips to "hill stations" in summer "for a change" and accounts of life in seclusion, which was more strictly observed by the middle and upper classes.[127] Jahan Ara Begum, for instance, described the part of Calcutta where she grew up, and still lives in, as a formerly affluent neighborhood.

> I remember that the area in which we were living—in Park Circus—was very nice . . . many government officials lived there. It was not as congested and dirty as it is today. Most of these people came after Partition.[128] And quite a few Hindu middle-class families also lived there. . . . [Of course,] middle class in those days you could say would be closer to today's upper-middle-class status. . . . I mean at least that.

Mumtaz Waheeda is similarly quick to point out the affluent background of her father's family, which owned "ten or twelve houses" in the Bhabanipur area of South Calcutta. She also repeatedly mentions the "huge house" her father built in another part of the city, her mother's aristocratic upbringing, and the professional success of many of her relatives—the "high posts" they had held. The discourse of class is also important in the testimony of Meherunnessa Begum, but with characteristic tact she does not directly assert her family's class stature, preferring to let the myriad discussions of "wastefulness," the inability of Muslim women to understand the "value of silver" (because it was so common), the practice of giving gold guineas as gifts to children during festivals, the use of silver toys, or the disdain of Muslim men for instruments of social mobility and financial security such as government scholarships or service and life insurance—quintessential middle-class concerns—subtly underscore her family's (erstwhile) ashraf status and identification.[129]

The most intriguing effort in this context, however, came from Jahan Ara Begum as she related a family legend. We have already seen Jahan Ara repeatedly emphasizing her family's Bengali-ness. In this remarkable story and the commentary surrounding it, she attempts to further contextualize that

Bengali-ness by both giving it depth in terms of a Hindu ancestry and staking claim to an unassailable past high-caste location for her family. She prefaces this story with something of a disclosure about how members of her family do not easily share it with others, signaling that she has decided to trust me not to misapprehend its intended message and that she considers this interview important enough to take this chance of revealing something dear to her and her family.

> We have an interesting family story. . . . My father's family came from 24 Parganas, where they have land and other property.[130] In that area, the Khan Sahebs are very well known and respected (*Khansahebder khub sunam*).[131] The men in our family, including my father, were extremely handsome. . . . I mean they were so good looking that people would stare at them. So we heard this story when we were young.
>
> Seven generations before my father, we find the names of two Brahmin brothers who lived in a village in Khulna-Jashore in our family tree.[132] The story goes that these Brahmin brothers were going somewhere during the month of fasting (*roja*), when they saw the zamindar—a Mussalman—anyway, they saw the zamindar smelling a ripe mango.[133] These Brahmin brothers half jokingly said to him, "Janaab, you have just broken your fast! You know how we say, "*Ghranena ardhyabhojanam* [Smelling food amounts to half-eating]."[134] Now that you have smelled the mango, you have already eaten. *Galo ajker rojata!* The zamindar said, "Tai? It is broken? *Achha besh.*"
>
> A few days passed. Then one day, the zamindar sent for the two brothers. In the room next to the one in which these brothers were sitting, the zamindar made arrangements for cooking a huge pot of *biriyani* with beef.[135] Of course, the aroma of the biriyani spread through the whole house. So as soon as the brothers entered the house, the zamindar said, "Did you smell the biriyani? Oh well! Now you have lost your *jat* also!"[136] . . . These Brahmin brothers actually thought that they had lost their jat and converted to Islam. The rest of the brothers, however, remained Hindu. We, in our family pedigree, find one Jaideb Thakur who became Jamaluddin Khan, and his brother, Kamdeb Thakur, who became Kamruddin Khan. And this is the beginning of this Khan family.

The name Thakur is a reference to the famous Thakur or Tagore family of Jorasanko.[137] It is fascinating that Jahan Ara Begum introduces this episode as a "family story," but ends on a rather definitive note, suggesting that, notwithstanding the story's origins, for her and her family this was "the beginning of this Khan family." She has, in other words, made a choice to believe in, and tell, a story that is consistent with her and her family's sense of itself. Jahan Ara is aware, of course, that the verity of this story can be questioned, so she proceeds to offer various "proofs" that might bolster its credibility:

> This is the story we knew from our childhood. And there was a book called *Jashore-Khulnar Itikatha*—I am not sure who wrote the book—in which we find this incident mentioned.[138] . . . And then, when we were in Brabourne College, Indira Debi—Rabindranath's niece . . . came to speak at the weekly program . . . about her family. And she, too, mentioned this incident . . . not in so much detail, but she did say, "We know that two members of our family accepted Islam . . . and we also know that [their descendants] live somewhere in 24 Parganas. . . . We have no contact with them." . . . Later Sunil Gangopadhyay also mentioned this incident in one of his essays—he apparently found the reference to it after a lot of research.[139] So, given all this confirmation from these independent sources, it may be safe to assume that there is some truth to this family story. I will say something interesting: . . . if one looks at Rabindranath's photographs taken when he was old . . . not the photographs we usually see . . . one finds a striking resemblance between him and the men in my father's family, particularly my father's older brother. . . . Of course, it is difficult to prove all this, but we have heard this incident mentioned in different contexts.

At the end, however, Jahan Ara waved her hand and said, "Anyway, it is not a big issue. After all, it is also true that most Mussalmans in Bengal were converts in one way or another."

Oral historians have argued that the peculiar strength of oral histories lies not so much in their capacity to provide new facts as in their ability to provide valuable insights into the speakers' subjectivity, even his or her unconscious desires and ideologies. As Alessandro Portelli argues:

> The first thing that makes oral history different . . . is that it tells us less about the events than about their meaning. This does not imply that oral history has no factual validity. . . . But . . . the diversity of oral sources consists in the fact that [so-called] "wrong" statements are still psychologically "true" and that this truth may be equally as important as factually reliable accounts.[140]

In the excerpt above, Jahan Ara Begum is only too aware that even if the authenticity of this incident is established nothing can adequately corroborate her family's claims to it. As her final comment—"most Mussalmans in Bengal were converts"—suggests, in fact any number of Bengali Muslim families could lay similar claims to a high-caste origin. In relating this story as a family legend, however, she takes a certain risk in revealing something about how she would like to be seen. It is, thus, her way of confronting a dominant discourse that freezes Bengali Muslims into two categories: foreign-born ashrafs and low-caste indigenous converts. By carving out a different location from which she creates her own identity—even if it is the realm of lore—she challenges a whole set of meanings and associations that inhere in the term *convert*. I therefore read her decision to tell this story as an expression of her desire for respect—a respect that, according to her, most Hindus still deny Muslims in contemporary India.

The problem of respect, or lack of it, which I believe Jahan Ara Begum is addressing in her story, is by no means new, of course. As we saw in the previous chapter, by the beginning of the twentieth century the perceived difference between Hindus and Muslims in terms of access to "modern" education, well-paying jobs, and the cultivation of what increasingly passed for "modern" (read liberal/Hindu nationalist) culture was already significant enough to cause considerable unpleasantness between the two communities. In the words of the late writer Sufia Kamal:

> One crucial source of bitterness between the two communities was access to jobs—jobs with the British administration that created the all-important division between bhadralok and *chotolok*.[141] One thing you must remember. . . . Hindu society never recognized Muslims as bhadralok. Hindus would typically refer to Mussalmans as *lede/nede*.[142] . . . Yes, I must say that most of the Hindu bhadrasampraday did not believe that there could be gentlefolk among the Mussalmans.[143] Hindu women, too, did not consider Mussalman women bhadra in similar ways.[144]

Sufia Kamal, who was widely loved and respected in her lifetime as *khalamma* [aunt] in Bangladesh, was born in 1910 in Shaistabad, East Bengal (now Bangladesh). Hers was one of the better-known and respected provincial aristocratic families of undivided Bengal. She never went to school but learned to read and write at home. Although the cultivation of Bengali language and literature was frowned upon in nawab families such as hers, she mastered the language in secrecy.

Sufia was introduced to the intellectual life of Calcutta by her first husband, the late Nehal Hossein. He also encouraged her to give up purdah, thereby incurring the wrath of the larger family. Although she had no formal schooling, Sufia was one of the first Muslim women writers to win wide acclaim in the literary circles of Bengal.

During my meeting with this remarkable woman in her home in the Dhanmondi neighborhood of Dhaka in 1996, Sufia Kamal talked frankly about her experiences with Hindus. While she emphasized that she had had many close and mutually respectful relationships with Hindu friends, neighbors, and colleagues in her long life as a writer, a teacher, and later a prominent social and political activist in independent Bangladesh, she still remembered as a young girl meeting Hindus whose behavior and practices expressed distance and disdain for Muslims:

> [Hindus] had various discomforts—perhaps stemming from religious ritualism—about Mussalman women visiting them. They did not like that. . . . I have seen this in my own life. Everybody came to our house, but if we were to visit a Hindu household first of all we would sit in the outer rooms; on top of that, even there they would sprinkle cow-dung water when we got up. I was young then. This is their religious rite, so we did not take that as insult. . . . The younger generation was different—they were educated, enlightened, . . . Besides, the Hindu families that we were close to—C. R. Das' or Aswini Datta's families—they had no problems.[145] So we did not care. But unfortunately such tendencies to treat Mussalmans as inferior, uneducated, or even untouchable were common enough among [members of] the Hindu community to lead to bitterness and eventually anger among Mussalmans. It is a legitimate feeling—since we treat them well when they visit us, why should they treat us with so much disdain?[146]

It seems that even today, for a vast majority of Bengali Hindus, the category bhadralok by definition means the Hindu upper caste/middle class, while the category Mussalman still conjures up images that are disturbingly similar to Hunter's description of the "fanatical masses" of Muslim converts—men with caps and *lungis* and women in borkhas, backward, culturally inferior, and inherently opposed to the very idea of progress.[147] Consequently, as Zohra Sultana complained: "When I say I am Mussalman, [Hindu Bengali] people are really surprised. 'You really are Mussalman?' they ask. 'But one would not think so by looking at you!' As if all Mussalmans have to have a particular look! . . . It is ridiculous!"[148] Moreover, as the following story narrated by Jahan Ara Begum suggests, recognizable signs of Muslim-ness are also interpreted with increasing ease as indicative of an essential disloyalty toward the (implicitly Hindu?) nation:

> You know I recently went for haj?[149] . . . [At the airport,] the customs officer was very nice to me. Before he actually looked at my papers, a few other Mussalman men arrived—poorer and I suppose *obviously* Muslim. You won't believe how terribly this officer behaved with them—he was so rude. I was quietly watching. At one point he turned to me and said, "These are the true enemies of India." Imagine! Why should some poor people who are returning from haj be the enemies of this country? And this man is supposed to be educated! Later, he asked me where I had gone. You should have seen his face when I informed him that I, too, had just come back from haj! He disappeared for good after that. I suppose he has some shame left in him. But I simply can't understand what has happened to the average Hindu. . . . And since they cannot recognize me as Mussalman I have to hear these kinds of remarks all the time. How will they know? They have not seen Mussalmans like me. After the Partition most of the educated middle-class Muslims migrated [to East Pakistan/Bangladesh].

Zohra and Jahan Ara are indignant because the enduring image of Muslims as low-class/low-caste Hindus routinely render middle-class Muslims like themselves invisible in contemporary Calcutta. However, their experiences also hint at the peculiar predicament that an increasingly automatic equation of Muslim religiosity with an antimodern, antinational stance presents for not only the poorer sections of the Muslim population but also for the "educated," middle class. Their ability to pass, or be accepted as unmarked, normalized citizen-subjects, depends on their willingness and/or ability to distance themselves from telltale signs of Muslim-ness. In the final section of the chapter, I will turn briefly to this specific difficulty through the narration of a particular incident, drawn from my field notes, in which we find Jahan Ara Begum angrily rejecting the specific construct of the "liberal (read good) Muslim" bestowed on her by her well-intentioned Hindu friends.

But before I begin my narration I would like to make a few observations. First, note that the incident described below occurred outside of the context of an interview on a social occasion in which I was a participating observer among a group of women. I did not tape the conversation, so the narrative I present is more dependent on my recollections and perceptions of the event, albeit recorded in field notes soon afterward, than the taped interviews I analyzed above. Second, the women present at this event have shared long and intimate friendships for many decades and have fairly well-established patterns of interaction. The story of "disruption" that I narrate below, therefore, may have been largely a result of my presence among them if not my intervention in the conversation. And, third, it is not only possible but likely that the women present would have very different interpretations of the incident.

Muslims as Liberal, Progressive, or "Just Like Us (Hindus)"

Late one afternoon in August 2000 I arrived at Jahan Ara Begum's house in Park Circus, Calcutta. She had asked me to come that day to meet some of her old friends from school. It was raining hard, I was wet, and Jahan Ara was concerned that I would catch cold. As I dried myself, she introduced me to her friends as "a daughter" to her. From the surprise on their faces, I gathered that she had not mentioned me to them before that moment. They seemed curious, presumably because I had been invited to this gathering of old friends.

I will refer to Jahan Ara's friends as Purnima Ganguly, Chaitali Bose, and Angana Mitra.[150] At first, they were talking about a wedding that recently took place between the daughter of a friend who is Hindu and a Muslim man. After some time, however, Purnima and Chaitali turned to me with some interest. They asked me to repeat my name and describe my work and then began telling me about themselves. I noticed that they addressed Jahan Ara Begum by her pet name.[151] From the beginning, they seemed anxious to establish the depth of their friendship. It also seemed that both Purnima and Chaitali prided themselves on their acceptance of and closeness to "liberal" Muslims such as Jahan Ara Begum.

Purnima: You know, we have known each other forever. Jahan, Chaitali, and I, and a few others. Haven't we?

Chaitali: Yes, from school days. We have been friends for a long time. In the middle, for a while we were not all here in Calcutta. But now again in our old age we have come together. Now we meet often. We share a lot, a lot of memories, don't we? I guess you could say this is quite remarkable . . . It is not very common, you know, especially among today's [younger] generations . . .

Purnima: I have grandchildren, you know. I am sixty-two years old! Could you tell [by] looking at me?

Purnima began telling us about her daughter and her family in England and her experiences during a recent visit there. One incident that seemed to stand out in her mind was when her daughter's friends tried to pay her for taking care of their child (who was "very well-behaved") for an evening. As she put it rather indignantly: "I was taking care of the child as I was doing for my own granddaughter. How could [the parents] even imagine that I would want money for that?! Frankly, I was quite hurt, but my daughter explained that this was quite customary there [in the West]. I don't know (*Jani na baba*), I don't understand such customs."[152] Her friends expressed their shock and agreed that relationships in the "West" simply were not the same as relationships in India, that it was difficult to be close to "westerners," who understood everything in "material terms," and that it was indeed very "rude" of the parents to try to pay her.

Over tea, the conversation turned back to relationships between Hindus and Muslims in India. Jahan Ara Begum—who has two sisters living in Bangladesh—was talking about a recent trip, when Purnima suddenly said, "I am sorry Jahan, but I have to say that the Bangladeshis are far more open [to Hindus]." Jahan Ara, visibly annoyed, flared up: "Why did you say that to me? No, don't say that it was a general comment. You specifically addressed me! Why? What do you mean by that?" Purnima, somewhat embarrassed, faltered and said, "I was just making an observation." Jahan Ara, not mollified, insisted, "But you looked at me when you said that!"

The others intervened on Purnima's behalf. Angana Mitra, who had joined us shortly before that, began talking loudly about how she had grown up in Barisal (now in Bangladesh) where Hindus and Muslims were very close: "You really cannot compare Muslims in East Bengal with Muslims here [Calcutta/West Bengal]. They [Muslims in East Bengal] have always been more open [to socializing with Hindus]."

As I listened, I could not help noticing that the issue of closeness between Hindus and Muslims—and even the possibility thereof—was being made to turn on the attitudes and behavior of *Muslims* on either side of the east-west divide in Bengal. It was as if Hindu actions were entirely reactive and hence absolved of any responsibility for the outcomes of encounters between members of the two communities. I thought of my many conversations with Muslim women both in Calcutta and Dhaka in the course of my fieldwork in which the speakers repeatedly hinted at, and in some cases openly pointed to, Hindu obsessions with "purity" and ritual cleanliness, which kept Muslims at arm's length.[153] I also remembered conversations with Hindu women in Calcutta in which they expressed their discomfort with the use of the "veil" by their Muslim classmates, their concerns about Hindu women who married into Muslim families and then "disappeared from sight," and their relative ease with those Muslim women one "could not distinguish easily from *us* [Hindus]."[154]

The atmosphere in the room had grown distinctly uncomfortable meanwhile. It was clear that Jahan Ara Begum had remained indignantly unimpressed by her friends' protestations. At this point, Purnima, now quite desperate, embarked on yet another story:

> Jahan, but you have always been different. That is why I was saying this to you. . . . I will tell you something else that happened to me in England. One day my daughter had a get-together. So I made some beef. And this Muslim woman who was there—quite young—simply refused to eat it! Why? Because it was not *halal*![155] I was so shocked!

Here Purnima turned to me and continued:

> I am not used to Muslims who make these distinctions, you know. Jahan never even asked such things, and she has eaten at my place so many times! [Turning to Jahan Ara] You don't care about these things, about maintaining parda or eating only halal meat, Jahan, but others do. And that is, of course, a measure of your liberalness. That is what I was trying to get at.
>
> *Jahan Ara*: Well, we were brought up very differently, so we could mix more easily, I suppose.

Jahan Ara Begum still seemed distinctly unhappy with the double-edged compliments and the implications of this story, which put the burden of "being acceptable" squarely on Muslims. A restless silence had again descended on the room. I turned to Purnima and asked why is it that wearing the borkha or caring about halal meat makes a Muslim woman less acceptable even to liberal Hindus. Before Purnima could formulate an answer, Jahan Ara Begum burst out excitedly:

> I am telling you it is true that we have been friends for many years—good friends—but the effort was always on my part. I was always more enthusiastic about these relationships, and I tried hard to not stand out, to fit in. [Turning

to her increasingly uncomfortable friends] I don't think you realize this, but you take it for granted. You won't understand what it means to be a minority because you have never been one. No, you really don't know what it means to be Muslim [in India].

Her friends all began to protest: "What do you mean? You mean here? No! Not now! Really? You mean even now? Why do you say that?" Jahan Ara began relating her recent experiences, both at the airport on her return from haj and in her capacity as a social worker with police officers who routinely expressed their mistrust of the "inherent evil" of Muslims because they did not recognize her as one.

It was evening now. The *azaan* for *Maghrib namaaz* came floating in above the relentless sound of the rain.[156] The tea gathering was obviously coming to an end; the guests were getting ready to "face the waterlogging."[157] Jahan Ara Begum excused herself and went to the next room. I assumed she had gone in for her namaaz for the evening. A few minutes passed. Her friends were getting a little restless, waiting for her.

Angana: Where did Jahan go?
Chaitali: I don't know . . . maybe to the bathroom.

I ventured that she was probably performing her namaaz. To my surprise, all three of them seemed visibly rattled. As they looked uncertainly at each other, I wondered whether this was the first time that they had been confronted with the prospect of Jahan Ara doing something so explicitly associated with being Muslim and whether it made them think of her differently. I thought they looked skeptical and imagined they thought she was putting on a show for my benefit.

I, meanwhile, had often seen Jahan Ara Begum take her leave discreetly for namaaz. While she did not necessarily explain to me why she needed to leave, other members of the household had told me on more than one occasion that she was "saying her prayers." I also thought of the first time I had come to see her, four years ago. She had continued to talk even as the distinctive sound of the azaan had wafted insistently in with the warm summer breeze. At one point, I had stopped the tape to ask if she wanted to take a break for her prayer. I remembered how she had seemed surprised and said that it could wait a bit. I had thought her polite and considerate then.[158] Now, for the first time, I wondered whether she had ignored the azaan out of a long-standing habit of "adjusting" her Muslim-ness in the presence of Hindus, even those who pride themselves on their secularity and liberalness.[159]

Later, listening again to the tapes of my first set of interviews with Jahan Ara, I noticed with renewed interest that, although she often mentioned her close relationships with Hindu friends and neighbors—some of whom had "graduated to the category of relatives"—there were two relationships she highlighted as exemplary: the first between her father and a Hindu woman who called him Dada; and the second between Jahan Ara and her friend Iradi, a devout Hindu woman.[160] And it is with these stories in Jahan Ara's "voice," and in my inadequate but necessary translation, that I wish to end this discussion of oral histories.

> I know so many such close Hindu friends whom I would consider relations. I cannot count them . . . there are so many. . . . Let me tell you . . . [an] interesting story. I am afraid that I am not telling you my life story chronologically . . . but this comes up in this context. Say, in 1952–53, a man rented a flat in the neighborhood. His name is Bimal Ghosh. Most people know him as Moumachhi, his pen name.[161] He started an organization called Manimala for kids. He heard about my father—who was very popular here—from the people in the neighborhood; so he came and introduced himself. The two families became very close. . . . His wife, who did not have any brothers—she had lost her only brother at a young age—called my father Dada [elder brother]. Now, it was not just calling him dada . . . these days one cannot easily find the kind of closeness they shared between brothers and their own sisters. . . . We were really close. Pishima would often send whatever she cooked for us. Moumachhi would give my mother a sari at Puja and would tell my mother, "Boudi, please wear this sari.[162] I know it is nothing like the expensive saris you are used to wearing, but I cannot afford anything else." And, of course, my mother would wear saris given by him happily. My father, too, would give [Pishima] saris at Puja or Eid. . . . So this kind of give-and-take, I mean a sincere friendship and closeness, was very much there. Later they moved out of Calcutta and built their own house in Kalyani. Then, we would visit them and spend the day with them sometimes. My father was a religious man; in fact, our whole family was very religious. . . . So I remember that when we went to spend the day at Pishima's house in Kalyani my father did not want to miss the namaaz . . . he liked to read the namaaz at the right time. Pishima would with utmost care give my father a clean [linen] sheet and ask him to come into her puja [prayer] room for his prayers. She would

say, "My husband is so dirty . . . an irreligious fellow . . . no other part of the house is fit for prayers. My father would try to make her understand that he did not want to sit and pray in her puja room because there was a large number of idols in the room. And for Muslims idol worship is what is problematic! So he would say, "No, I would rather pray in your bedroom." But Pishima would say, "No, wait! Let me cover up the idols . . . with a sheet. Then you will not have to see the idols while you pray." The bedroom would be quite clean, mind you! But since [her husband] . . . was not particularly religious, she would feel that it was inappropriate to pray in that room. So you can imagine the confusion! The interesting thing was that both my father and Pishima were extremely religious. And perhaps because of that they understood each other perfectly. Today this is very difficult to imagine.

Here, Jahan Ara stopped, as if to remember. It was evening, and the melodious call to prayer could be heard. I wondered if it was time for us to break for her namaaz, but she continued talking:

> Actually, it is not unthinkable; such things are rare, but they still happen. You know we just had a month of roja [fasting] for Ramzan. During this time, we fast for a whole month during the day and only break our fast after sundown. I have this friend called Ira Mukherjee, I call her Iradi. One of my sisters had come from Dhaka, so we spent the whole day outside, shopping, and decided that we would stop at Iradi's house at sundown, pray, and break our fast. You would not believe it. Iradi had brought exactly what we eat at that time to break fast—usually some fruit, some *chhola* [chickpeas]—no one knows why anymore, this is just the tradition. We were amazed that Iradi had made the arrangements for everything in exactly the way in which it should be done. So we did our *iftari* there, then ate dinner and came home late.[163] So it is not like you cannot find this kind of genuine respect and understanding, but it is certainly rare. That kind of connection, knowing each other, developing a relationship which can surpass blood relationships in their strength and depth—a relationship of the soul, not just blood—if that can be had, it is a big gain.[164]

CONCLUSION

In the preceding pages, I have presented an account of the autobiographical oral histories of mainly five elderly women of the Muslim middle class who at the end of the twentieth century narrated their memories of their childhoods; their mothers, grandmothers, and other women of previous generations; their fathers and other men; their lives in school and in their neighborhoods; their experiences of being among the first Muslim girls to attend school or the first Muslim women to work outside the home in Bengal; their fears and uncertainties; and what it meant to have friends—Hindus among them—and be young, Muslim, and women amid the monumental social and political changes that took place in early-twentieth-century Bengal.

In the process, I have foregrounded the difficulty, if not impossibility, of untangling personal recollections, often conceived as counterhistories, from the authoritative voice of official histories and their representational categories. As my analysis shows, the stories of Muslim women presented here are overwhelmingly framed by the larger stories of the nation, the conflict between Muslims and Hindus, and/or a narrative of progress, presumably toward an already defined goal of modernity. These dominant narratives typically cast Muslims in general and Muslim women in particular as backward, nonmodern, and hence largely inessential to the concerns of the official history of the modern nation. In engaging an archive of oral histories of Muslim women that would typically remain invisible to normative historical accounts, I interrogate both the conventional ways in which Muslim women are represented in contemporary India and what qualifies as history.

I am well aware that, like all attempts at producing knowledge, these oral testimonies are also both partial and situated. They are products of a particular dialogic context of a conversation between women from different religious communities and different generations, but from similar class backgrounds, amid rising communal tensions in late-twentieth-century India. Thus, the speakers' interpretation of the questions asked, the answers they provided, and the stories they volunteered must be read with that context in mind. The expressed desire in these testimonies, perhaps not surprisingly, is often to correct misconceptions about Muslims. What I find most striking, however, is what they reveal about the complex subject positions that the narrators dynamically inhabit and the complexities and richness of conversations between postcolonial women with "shared-but-different histories" and "shared-but-different" identifications,[165] even within an interview situation rife with myriad inequalities of power and the possibilities of betrayal.[166]

CONCLUSION

Connections

Much has been written in recent years about the relative absence of women as subjects in conventional, nationcentric histories, notwithstanding their frequent appearance in nationalist rhetoric as "potent symbols of identity and visions of society and the nation."[1] While feminist critiques of the strategic incorporation of women, on the one hand, and elisions, on the other, constitute a generative context for this book, my main concerns here have been to explain why, through what discursive mechanisms, and within what contexts of large-scale social change, some women—in this case Muslim women in colonial Bengal—came to be more absent/neglected than others in nationalist discourse and its subsequent historiography; to understand what their invisibility/victim-image has meant for the imagining of the ideal citizen subject of the Indian postcolonial modern; to track the kind of negotiations with stereotypes that (even relatively privileged, middle-class) Muslim women in India frequently feel obliged to make; and, finally, to reflect on the ways in which taking Muslim women and their work into account affects how the past is thought of and written about in post-colonial India.[2] This book is thus about connections: between intellectual production and the politics of modernity, nationhood, and community; between large-scale processes of social/economic/political change and discursive formations; and between representations and the production of subject locations inflected by a complex of gender, community, and class identifications.

Feminists have also argued that "the integration of women into modern 'nationhood,' epitomized by citizenship in a sovereign nation-state, somehow follows a *different* trajectory from that of men," and that any analysis of "women's current positions in society" must be rooted in a study of their specific incorporation in a nation-building project.[3] This book builds on this feminist and historical sociological insight regarding the importance of the past in the constitution of the present. As my analysis further points out, the relationship between the past and the present is far from linear for the present plays a powerful role in shaping both what we see/read of the past and the terms in which (i.e., how) we interpret it. Indeed, conceived amid the growing communal tensions in the late 1990s and written mostly in the aftermath of the 2002 pogroms against Muslims in Gujarat, this ostensibly historical project owes many of its foundational questions to India's troubled postcolonial present.[4]

I began this book with a critical discussion of the ways in which the representation of Muslim women (or lack thereof) in much of the written history of colonial India is a result in part of the continued nation-centeredness and politics of modernity implicit in much historical and/or liberal feminist scholarship on colonial India. But the book is also about another kind of linkage: that between discourse and more obvious, material forms of social inequality and injustice. In this concluding chapter, I would like to turn to this particular linkage to make a few exploratory and decidedly brief reflections on the connections between the ways in which Muslim women have been historically represented, how they are constructed in current academic and popular discourses, and some aspects of their material conditions in contemporary India.

THE PRESENT

If, as I have argued throughout the book, Muslim women are largely absent or marginalized within the written history of colonial Bengal, if not India, their representation in contemporary India is similarly both scanty and generally negative. As Zoya Hasan and Ritu Menon have pointed out in a recent intervention, while apparently there is no dearth of interest in "women and Islam" in postcolonial India, most studies are still "caught up in misconceptions that usually leave Muslim women invisible."[5] Two sets of misunderstandings seem to plague discussions of Muslim women: the tendency to see Muslims, particularly Muslim women, as a monolithic category; and the overwhelming importance attached to Islam, especially the "Muslim personal law in defining [Muslim] women's status."[6]

What is more, following other scholars who have commented on the "making of the [category] Muslim" in India, Hasan and Menon further contend that studies of Muslims in India are typically influenced by popular discourse, or what they call "attitudes prevalent in the larger social milieu," about the "conservatism and ingrained backwardness of the community."[7] In their words, "Stereotypes of Muslim women, entrenched by the trinity of multiple marriages [and attendant concerns over the high fertility of Muslims], triple talaq, and purdah have held them hostage for so long that they have become difficult to dislodge."[8] Such stereotypes—in both popular and academic discourse—are further reinforced by the lack of systematic scholarship and information on the unequal access to resources and opportunities experienced by different groups of women in India today.[9] The Census of India, the authors point out, gathers disaggregated data on religion but publishes information only on fertility, thereby reiterating both the primacy of reproductive functions for women and the legitimacy of debates over the differential fertility of women of different religious communities. Even feminist scholarship in the last two decades has tended to treat Muslim women as either "wards of the community" or "citizens equal before the law."[10] According to Hasan and Menon, the result is a widespread failure to recognize that "disadvantage, discrimination, and disempowerment are experienced at specific and particular intersections of class, caste, gender, and community. . . . [A]ny discussion of Muslim women must speak [therefore] to two simultaneous projects: a critique of cultural essentialism/reductionism . . . and the formulation of historically and socially grounded concerns and strategies. The first project is one of dismantling, while the second is one of building and constructing."[11]

This book, with its focus on tracing the discursive erasure and/or marginalization of Muslim women within both nationalist discourse and its subsequent histories, is certainly a project of "dismantling" in this sense. But what my work also points to, and what Hasan and Menon hint at, are the ways in which stereotypes are connected to social exclusion. Let me be clear: my contention is not that discourses automatically *cause* social inequalities but that they are both indicative of the position of any group within a given society and provide a justificatory context in which inequities can arise, persist, and even be made to seem normal.[12] The continued presence of persistent inequalities, meanwhile, feeds the discourse of the relative "backwardness/modernity" of the different groups concerned.

As my analysis in the previous chapters shows, discourses and social exclusions are intimately linked whether in the case of colonial representations of "native" women and the exploitation of their sexual and other labor or the widespread neglect in postindependence India of the literary and other contributions of Muslim women in colonial Bengal, presumably because Muslim women had already been established discursively as backward and hence deemed incapable of liberal/progressive thinking, or the marginalization of Muslim women in both conventional and feminist histories of colonial Bengal because they did not engage in acceptable forms of public activities.

Negative images of Muslim women are also widespread in contemporary popular discourse in India, sometimes with dire consequences. Two moments in which the "Muslim woman as victim" discourse has been at the center of public attention in recent decades are particularly illustrative of this point: the Shah Bano case of the mid-1980s and the more recent pogroms in Gujarat in 2002.[13] The bitter controversy that marked the Shah Bano case demonstrates well how women, even when they assume very public roles as citizen subjects, can be still sidestepped or appropriated as sites of struggle between men representing competing interests. In this particular case, although the controversy was initiated by Shah Bano, a woman who sued her husband of forty years for alimony after he deserted her, the confrontation quickly degenerated into something of a showdown between the Muslim orthodox community, which acted as the defender of the "rights of the Muslim minority"; a "secular" Indian state reneging on its responsibilities for fear of electoral setbacks; and an increasingly belligerent coalition of right-wing Hindu organizations.[14]

The intervention of the Hindu Right especially muddied the picture, for it deftly used this opportunity to mount an all-out attack on Muslims, especially the latter's supposed "special privileges," which were interpreted as an affront to Hindus.[15] But the more "sinister" aspect of the Hindu Right's discourse was surely its stance of "protecting" the "oppressed Muslim women," ostensibly from Muslim men.[16] As Pathak and Sunder Rajan rightly point out, the Hindu Right's move "invokes the stereotype of the Muslim woman as invariably destitute, and the Muslim male as polygamous, callous, and barbaric."[17]

This shrewd move, reminiscent in its political potency of British justifications of colonial rule in the nineteenth century, afforded the Hindu Right a way to undermine both Islam as a religion and the "secularist" stance of the Indian state and gain considerable political mileage by reinventing itself as the representative of authentic Indian-ness, if not the true champion of "progress" itself.[18] To quote Pathak and Sunder Rajan again, "The protection of women of a minority community thus . . . [emerged in this charged context] as the ploy of a majority community to repress the religious freedom of that minority and ensure its own dominance."[19]

Indeed, much to the unease and chagrin of feminist scholars and activists, since then the Hindu Right seems to have incorporated successfully in its agenda issues—such as the fight for a Uniform Civil Code or public activism of women—that have historically constituted important elements of mainstream feminist politics.[20] The Right has been remarkably successful also in mobilizing women for its own purposes. As scholars have pointed out, the women in the Rashtrasevika Samiti—the women's wing of the Rashtriya Swayamsevak Samiti (RSS)—are "active political subjects" who play significant roles in the arena of communal politics and, increasingly, violence.[21] They are modern and feminist in the sense that they are ready to fight for their "self-respect," which is refigured in the Hindutva imaginary to mean "protection of the motherland."[22] Not surprisingly, the "ready-made" enemy in this formulation is the "lustful Muslim male" (foreign, invading, and unscrupulous) against whom the newly empowered, authentic, modern Indian woman (Hindu, upper middle class, and upper caste) must defend herself and the motherland.[23] They are, in short, the exact opposite of the Sangh Parivar's long-standing construction of Muslim women as victims of Muslim male oppression and themselves culpable as overfertile "baby factories" and "women of loose morals" who *choose* (in the case of converts) an obscurantist religion, thereby automatically qualifying as threats to the Hindu faith and nation.[24]

It is difficult not to read Shah Bano, the person, as "nothing more than a pawn," to borrow Veena Das's poignant words, "through whom men played their various games of honour and shame."[25] Indeed, the many contradictory actions of Shah Bano as she navigated this long and brutal process from her multiple subaltern location seem to lend credence to this view.[26] For, after fighting for ten years in the courts *as a destitute woman* for reasonable support from her ex-husband, something denied to her under Muslim personal law, Shah Bano eventually denounced the Supreme Court's ruling in her favor on the grounds that, because it was "contrary to the Quran and the hadith" and was "an open interference in Muslim personal law," she, "*being a Muslim*," must reject it.[27] She then sought restitution again, this time of her mehr (contractual gift) under the newly reconstituted Muslim Women Act *as a Muslim woman*.

However, as Pathak and Sunder Rajan have suggested, Shah Bano's "inconstancy or changeability" could also be "interpreted as her [repeated] refusal to occupy the subject position offered to her" of a dispossessed, divorced woman who had been ejected from her home, a poor Muslim litigant who was awarded an impossibly low maintenance sum by the lower courts, an oppressed Muslim woman being offered protection from Hindu fundamentalists, and finally a Muslim woman who was left at the mercy of the males in her natal family.[28] Each of these "discursive displacement[s]" seemed to trigger "a violent movement of religion/class/gender attributes to the foreground of [Shah Bano's] . . . identity," eliciting a series of apparently contradictory responses from Shah Bano that secured her image as an "inconstant" woman within a "normative paradigm of subjectivity."[29] But, as Pathak and Sunder Rajan insist, what underlies Shah Bano's apparently fickle behavior is "not a unified freely choosing, purposefully changing subject, but a palimpsest of identities, now constituted, now erased, by discursive displacements," that is perhaps best described as only a "subject-effect."[30] For the female subaltern subject, who is obliged "to live with what she cannot control," rarely has the option of the kind of "choice" available to the normative subject of western liberal discourse, underwritten as it is by a complex of class/gender/sexuality/religion (or race in another context) privileges.[31]

I invoke this reading of the Shah Bano case not because I am interested in subject retrieval per se but because it offers a way past the impasse of seeing Shah Bano either as a victim (from the dominant liberal and/or feminist perspective) or an inconsistent (read untrustworthy) and "pampered" Muslim (from the Hindu Right's perspective).[32] I interrogate instead the inadequacies of the set of choices available to her, choices that pit her location as a woman against her identification as a Muslim in contemporary India or, worse yet, bring the two together in the composite figure of the hapless victim. This, I have argued in this book, has been consistently the case since the late nineteenth century.

If the Shah Bano case is one moment in which Muslim women made a notable public appearance, the 2002 Gujarat pogroms against Muslims mark a second recent instance of spectacular visibility for Muslim women, one that powerfully underscores the connections between the discourse and materiality of the victim status accorded to them, *irrespective of their class position*, in postcolonial India.

I do not wish to recount here the well-documented facts of the Gujarat genocide and the losses it incurred.[33] However, for our present purposes one element of that depressing record bears reiterating: "the sheer opulence and exuberance in forms of cruelty" deployed publicly, especially against Muslim women and children during what Tanika Sarkar has called "the days of the long knives."[34] In report after report, one reads about the "chillingly unique" nature of the violence, which included savage attacks on children and especially the sexual and reproductive organs of Muslim women, presumably "as a means of proving the masculinity" of Hindu men.[35] According to some, the "intensity of torture" on display in Gujarat exceeded all the known horrors of the twentieth century, including the subcontinent's own record of violence during the Partition riots. The gruesome pictures that emerged from the wreckage certainly confirm this grim view.[36]

Raping women in times of war and conflict is, of course, a well-known, if heinous, tactic of dishonoring any community.[37] But, as Sarkar rightly points out, this common intent alone cannot quite account for the "the surplus of cruelty and its multifarious forms" deployed in Gujarat. Instead she proposes a complex of aims that motivated these particular forms of corporeal brutality against Muslim women by the Hindu mobs. In her memorable words:

> First, to possess and dishonour them and their men, second to taste what is denied to them and what, according to their understanding, explains Muslim virility. Third, to physically destroy the vagina and the womb, and, thereby, to symbolically destroy the sources of pleasure, reproduction and nurture for Muslim men, and for Muslim children. Then, by beatings, to punish the fertile

female body. . . . Then, by cutting up the foetus and burning it [and physically destroying children], to achieve a symbolic destruction of . . . the very future of Muslims themselves.[38]

But *how* was this possible? Within what discursive framework can such acts find justification? Sarkar herself links these excesses to the time-tested appeal of both the "dying Hindu" and the "abductions" discourses, with their attendant specter of the enviably virile Muslim man and the exceptionally fertile, and possibly amoral, Muslim woman, as well as stories of the rape of Hindu women throughout centuries of Muslim rule, which have stoked Hindu male anxiety over adequate masculinity at least since the early twentieth century. And it is the continued circulation of such discourses—born, as we have seen earlier in this study, somewhere in the last third of the nineteenth century—that, according to Sarkar, makes every new instance of fabricated stories about fresh abductions or murders of Hindu women seem both believable and a ready-made excuse for violent action against Muslims in general and Muslim women in particular.[39]

Of course, violence against women is neither the sole preserve of the Sangh nor restricted to Muslim women per se; as feminists have often pointed out, abuse of women in general is clearly on the rise in contemporary India.[40] But the intensity of the torture that was forced on Muslim women in Gujarat in 2002 seems to beg some additional questions: are all women in India equally vulnerable to such gruesome attacks or is there something about the specific discursive positions historically accorded to different women within the logic of a nation's official rhetoric that makes it more or less possible to inflict certain forms of extreme, collective violence on them? Let me be clear again: my intention here is not to mark one form of violence (private vs. public, domestic vs. communal, and so on) as worse or more acceptable than another, but I do believe that the specific modalities of enunciation of the different forms of violence deployed against different women point to the need for careful, differentiated analyses. For, as Kalpana Kannabiran has succinctly observed in her discussion of the connections between rape and communal identity: "Public/political discourse on women first classifies them by caste and community, creating hierarchies . . . that . . . separate the 'normal' from the 'abnormal.' . . . Those who are perceived as being outside the normal cannot assert a legitimate claim to protection from the State.[41]

This liminality of certain women vis-à-vis the state and the law seems to be further complicated when the discourse of the dominant community constructs men from a minority community as essentially lacking in character, creating "a condition for the total refusal of safeguards—constitutional or otherwise—for women of these minority groups."[42] In the case of Muslim women in India, the issue of conversion seems to add an extra twist: they are seen to *choose* to be Muslim (read foreign identified, traitors) in the Hindu Right's discourse.[43]

Clearly, the events of 2002 demonstrate the vicious power of this connection between discourse and materiality. It is almost as if the very humanity of Muslim women (and men for that matter) is somehow discounted because their inferiority or lack of character is already established discursively. Muslim women are "both deeply oppressed and licentious" and mistreated by Muslim men (recall the harem/zenana discourse).[44] What difference, then, does it make if they are brutally raped? In the end, it seems that the Gujarat rapes are not worth talking about, as the then defense minister George Fernandes put it, presumably because they are normal or universal and hence do not qualify as rape (i.e., violation) at all![45]

There are, of course, other points of view, and the protests against the Gujarat pogroms have been both numerous and intense.[46] Commentators have even pointed out that the carnage in Gujarat ought not to have come as a surprise since elements of the specific brutalities displayed there had already been in evidence in a number of Hindutva experiments throughout the 1990s.[47] What is perhaps less readily acknowledged is that these discourses of otherness—twisted into expressions of unmitigated hatred in the Sangh's language—are not the product of the Sangh's thinking alone; they have been constructed for over a century through systematic devaluation of Muslims in general and the discursive erasure of Muslim women's subjectivity in particular. This book is an attempt to track that long process of producing the category Muslim woman as the invisible, oppressed, and, in the end, violable and erasable other.

Notes

INTRODUCTION

1. J. W. Scott, *Gender and the Politics of History*; J. W. Scott, *Feminism and History*; Sangari and Vaid, *Recasting Women*; Abu-Lughod, "Can There Be a Feminist Ethnography?" especially 11–12.

2. Tharu and Niranjana, "Problems for a Contemporary Theory of Gender"; Agnes, "Redefining the Agenda of the Women's Movement within a Secular Framework"; B. Ghosh, "Feminist Critiques of Nationalism and Communalism from Bangladesh and India."

3. I use *modernity* to refer to a whole complex of practices, beliefs, and discourses associated with "the dominant self-image of Europeans for almost two centuries" (Abu-Lughod, "Feminist Longings and Postcolonial Conditions," 7). Abu-Lughod herself draws on Berman, *All That Is Solid Melts into Air*, and Rabinow, *French Modern*. According to Rabinow, it is quite impossible to define modernity, but it is possible to track the diverse ways in which the insistent claims

to being modern are made (*French Modern*, 9). See also Bauman, "Modernity and Ambivalence."

4. J. W. Scott, *Gender and the Politics of History*, 26.

5. Abu-Lughod, "Feminist Longings and Postcolonial Conditions," 6–7; Mitchell, *Questions of Modernity*, xi-xii; Bauman, "Modernity and Ambivalence," 163. I use the term *subaltern groups* in the sense that Zakia Pathak and Rajeswari Sunder Rajan have used it: "A particular in relation to a universal of the same quality. Therefore, here, a subject relating to the societal universal norm of a unified, freely-choosing subject—tangentially or marginally, or in opposition to, or opaquely" ("Shahbano," 565). Ratna Kapur has also recently used the term to refer to "cultural Others who are peripheral subjects—such as transnational migrants, Muslims, homosexuals or sex-workers" (*Erotic Justice*, 3). For an incisive review of Kapur's work, see Arondekar, "Entangled Histories," 3409–11. For two other, useful discussions of the term, see Das, "Subaltern as Perspective"; and Visweswaran, "Small Speeches, Subaltern Gender."

6. Benjamin, *Illuminations*, 259. See also McClintock, "No Longer in a Future Heaven," 263; Anderson, *Imagined Communities*, 161; Buck-Morss, *The Dialectics of Seeing*, 67; and Benjamin, *The Arcades Project*.

7. Mitchell, *Questions of Modernity*, xiv.

8. I am drawing here on Giddings, *When and Where I Enter*.

9. Spivak, "Three Women's Texts and a Critique of Imperialism," 243.

10. For some important recent examples, see T. Sarkar, *Hindu Wife, Hindu Nation*; Gupta, *Sexuality, Obscenity, Community*; Engels, *Beyond Purdah?*; C. A. Robinson, *Tradition and Liberation*; Mani, "Contentious Traditions"; P. Chatterjee, "The Nationalist Resolution of the Women's Question"; and Borthwick, *The Changing Role of Women in Bengal, 1849–1905*. For critical readings of the preoccupation with upper caste/class Hindus in nationalist thought and historiography, see Chakravarti, "Whatever Happened to the Vedic *Dasi*?" especially 28–29; and Visweswaran, "Small Speeches, Subaltern Gender," 83–125.

11. See, for instance, the collection edited by Mohini Anjum, *Muslim Women in India*, especially Mathur, "Inequality in the Status of Women and Minority Identity in India," 67–74; and Siddiqui, "The Studies of Muslim Women in India," 9–23. See also J. P. Singh, *Indian Women*; S. Roy, *The Status of Muslim Women in North India*; and Jeffery, *Frogs in a Well*. It is quite common, for instance, to find in studies of Muslim women statements such as: "Traditionally, Muslim women are subordinated to men and secluded from the outside world which reduces their importance as individuals. But westernization and modernization are primary forces loosening these traditional restraints on women" (Jehangir, *Muslim Women in*

West Bengal, 2); or "Women in the Muslim community are subordinated to men to a greater extent than women in some other communities" (M. I. Menon, *Status of Muslim Women in India*, 1). For exceptions to this pattern, see Hasan, "Communalism, State Policy, and the Question of Women's Rights in Contemporary India"; B. D. Metcalf, "Reading and Writing about Muslim Women in British India"; Minault, "Begamati Zuban"; Minault, *The Extended Family*; Minault, *Secluded Scholars*; Devji, "Gender and the Politics of Space"; Sonia Nishat Amin, *The World of Muslim Women in Colonial Bengal, 1876–1939*; Rouse, "Gender, Nationalism(s), and Cultural Identity; Azra Asghar Ali, *The Emergence of Feminism among Indian Muslim Women, 1920–1947*; and Sayyid, *Muslim Women of the British Punjab*. For works on Muslim women in postindependence India, see Engineer, *Status of Women in Islam*; and *The Shah Bano Controversy*. For critical feminist scholarship, see Pathak and Sunder Rajan, "Shahbano"; Lateef, *Muslim Women in India*; Hassan and Menon, *Unequal Citizens*; and Rafiq Khan, *Socio-legal Status of Muslim Women*.

12. Murshid, *Reluctant Debutante*, 17; Chakraborty, *Andare Antare*. See also Minault, *Secluded Scholars*, for a relevant discussion of Muslim women in colonial India.

13. According to Joya Chatterji, the term *bhadralok* owes its origins to the rise of a rentier class in Bengal at the end of the eighteenth century whose economic prosperity and social standing were tied to ownership of land. Bhadralok status depended on the privilege of living off the land without having to work on it. By the end of the nineteenth century, with a decline in rentier incomes, a western education, the professional employment opportunities it brought, and "culture" increasingly came to be the new markers of bhadralok privilege. See Chatterji, *Bengal Divided*, 5–12, 155; and S. Sarkar, *The Swadeshi Movement in Bengal, 1903–1908*, 508–9. See also the discussion of the Hindu bhadralok in chapter 2 of this book. In common parlance today the term refers to civilized/polite/educated people.

14. Again, it is important to remember that middle-class formation in colonial Bengal did not proceed in quite the way it did in the industrializing societies of western Europe. The basis of "middle class" prosperity in Bengal was primarily landownership and rentier income, not trade or industry. Chatterji, *Bengal Divided*, 5–6.

15. Chakravarti, "Whatever Happened to the Vedic *Dasi*," especially 34–38; P. Chatterjee, *The Nation and Its Fragments*, 14–34; Viswanathan, *Masks of Conquest*, especially 31.

16. See Hossain, *"Sultana's Dream" and Selections from "The Secluded Ones"*;

Akhtar and Bhowmick, *Zenana Mehfil*; Begum, *Banglar Nari Andolan*; Minault, "Sayyid Mumtaz 'Ali and Tahzib un-Niswan"; Minault, *Secluded Scholars*; Azra Asghar Ali, *The Emergence of Feminism among Indian Muslim Women, 1920–1947*; Sayyid, *Muslim Women of the British Punjab*; Sonia Nishat Amin, *The World of Muslim Women in Colonial Bengal, 1876–1939*; B. D. Metcalf, "Reading and Writing about Muslim Women in British India"; Murshid, *Reluctant Debutante*; and Joarder and Joarder, *Begum Rokeya*.

17. Exceptions, such as Shaista Ikramullah, whose autobiography, *From Purdah to Parliament* ([1963] 1998), is well known, came mostly from influential and affluent families. See Minault, *Secluded Scholars*, 14–57.

18. According to Joya Chatterji, not all among the bhadralok immediately took to western education (*Bengal Divided*, 6–8). Needless to say, an even smaller proportion of this already small group of educated bhadralok actually supported the reform initiatives of the nineteenth century. Brahmos, a faction among Hindus in Bengal that was influenced by unitarianism and was against the ritualistic excesses of Hinduism as it was practiced in Bengal in the nineteenth century, were especially against idolatry. See Kopf, *The Brahmo Samaj and the Shaping of the Modern Indian Mind*; and Mamun, *Unish Satake Bangladesher Sangbad Samayikpatra, 1847–1905*.

19. See Lateef, *Muslim Women in India*; Sayyid, *Muslim Women of the British Punjab*; Minault, *Secluded Scholars*; Minault, *The Extended Family*; and Azra Asghar Ali, *The Emergence of Feminism among Indian Muslim Women, 1920–1947*, for detailed discussions of this point.

20. See Borthwick's preface to *The Changing Role of Women in Bengal, 1849–1905*, xii; and Engels, *Beyond Purdah?* 6. On feminist scholarship, see, for instance, R. Kumar, *The History of Doing*. For recent examples of feminist scholarship on Hindu women, see T. Sarkar, *Hindu Wife, Hindu Nation*; Engels, *Beyond Purdah?*; Gupta, *Sexuality, Obscenity, Community*; C. A. Robinson, *Tradition and Liberation*; and Borthwick, *The Changing Role of Women in Bengal, 1849–1905*.

21. See, for instance, Ray, *From the Seams of History*; M. Bhattacharya and Sen, *Talking of Power*; Chaudhuri, *Feminism in India*. In her more recent work, titled *Early Feminists of Colonial India*, Bharati Ray does undertake a detailed reading of Rokeya Sakhawat Hossain, while mentioning a number of other Muslim women writers in passing—to be precise, in two paragraphs on 107–8.

22. For a welcome exception to this pattern among books on the colonial era published in India, see Akhtar and Bhowmick, *Zenana Mehfil*; and Hassan, *Forging Identities*. The focus of the latter volume is not on colonial Bengal per se.

23. For some important works on this issue, see Pateman, *The Disorder of Women*; Yuval Davis, *Gender and Nation*; Anthias, *Racialized Boundaries*; Kandiyoti, *Women, Islam, and the State*; Kandiyoti, "Identity and Its Discontents"; Badran, *Feminists, Islam, and Nation*; Delaney, "Father State, Motherland, and the Birth of Modern Turkey"; Jayawardena and De Alwis, *Embodied Violence*; Reynolds, "Marianne's Citizens?"; Clawson, *Constructing Brotherhood*; Sangari and Vaid, *Recasting Women*; McClintock, "'No Longer in a Future Heaven'"; and M. Sinha, *Gender and Nation*.

24. On "hegemonic theorizations," see, for instance, Renan "Qu'est-ce Qu'une Nation?"; Kedourie, *Nationalism*; Gellner, *Thought and Change*; Hobsbawm and Ranger (eds.), *The Invention of Tradition*; and Hutchinson and Smith, *Nationalism*. For a recent anthology that attempts to partially address this lacuna, see Eley and Suny, *Becoming National*. See also Anderson, *Imagined Communities*, and Balibar and Wallerstein, *Race, Nation, Class*. For exceptions to gender-blind theorizations of nationalism, see Fanon, *Black Skin, White Masks*; Fanon, *A Dying Colonialism*; P. Chatterjee, *The Nation and Its Fragments*; and Mosse, *Nationalism and Sexuality*. On nation as a gendered construct, see Delaney, "Father State, Motherland, and the Birth of Modern Turkey," 178; Pateman, *Disorder of Women*, especially 179–209; Kandiyoti, "Identity and Its Discontents," 376–77; and McClintock, "'No Longer in a Future Heaven,'" 260–61.

25. I am drawing here on the idea that the nation-state is a historically specific form of imagined community. In other words, the nation-state was only one, and perhaps the most recent, historical form taken by the state; even the bourgeoisie, typically credited with inventing the nation-state, has historically considered other political forms. See Balibar and Wallerstein, *Race, Nation, Class*, 10, 89; Held, "The Development of the Modern State," 56–79.

26. McClintock, "'No Longer in a Future Heaven,'" 264.

27. Pateman, *The Disorder of Women*, 44–46.

28. T. Sarkar, "Enfranchised Selves"; Fraser, "What's Critical about Critical Theory," 87.

29. Sunder Rajan, introduction to *Signposts*, 5. See also Pateman, *The Disorder of Women*, 179–209; Abu-Lughod, *Remaking Women*, 3–31; and Young and Dickerson, *Colour, Class, and Country*.

30. Pateman, *The Disorder of Women*; Reynolds, "Marianne's Citizens?"; Landes, *Women and the Public Sphere*; Anthias and Yuval-Davis, *Woman, Nation, State*; Yuval-Davis, "Gender and Nation"; Kandiyoti, introduction to *Women, Islam, and the State*, 1–21; Najmabadi, "Crafting an Educated Housewife in Iran";

Stoler, "Making Empire Respectable"; McClintock, "'No Longer in a Future Heaven.'" See also Fanon, "Algeria Unveiled," in *A Dying Colonialism*, 35–67; and Ray Chow's critical reading of Fanon in "The Politics of Admittance."

31. Kandiyoti, "Identity and Its Discontents," 377.

32. Anthias and Yuval-Davis, *Woman, Nation, State*, 6–11; Kandiyoti, "Identity and Its Discontents," 376–77.

33. Kandiyoti, "Women, Islam, and the State," 246; Abu-Lughod, "Feminist Longings and Postcolonial Conditions," 3; Badran, *Feminists, Islam, and Nation*.

34. Sangari and Vaid, introduction to *Recasting Women: Essays in Colonial History*, 9.

35. P. Chatterjee, "The Nationalist Resolution of the Women's Question," 233–253, and *Nation and Its Fragments*, especially 116–134. While Spivak has been an important part of the Subaltern Studies collective, her engagement with the project has been critical. See, for instance, Gayatri Spivak, "Can the Subaltern Speak?" and "Subaltern Studies: Deconstructing Historiography." Recent collaborations include P. Chatterjee and Jeganathan, *Community, Gender, and Violence*; and Haynes and Prakash, *Contesting Power*, 1–2.

36. Chakravarti, "Whatever Happened to the Vedic *Dasi*?"; T. Sarkar, *Hindu Wife, Hindu Nation*; T. Sarkar, "Nationalist Iconography"; Bannerji, "Attired in Virtue"; Chattopadhyay and Guha Thakurta, "The Woman Perceived"; J. Bagchi, "Representing Nationalism"; Chakrabarty, *Provincializing Europe*, 223–28. For an example of such work in relation to Muslims in colonial India, see Rouse, "Gender, Nationalism(s), and Cultural Identity." On British justifications, see Liddle and Joshi, "Gender and Imperialism in British India," 72–78; Mani, "Contentious Traditions," 88–126; M. Sinha, "Gender and Imperialism," 217–238; M. Sinha, *Colonial Masculinity*; Chakravarty, "Whatever Happened to the Vedic *Dasi*?"; I. Chatterjee, "Colouring Subalternity," 49–97; J. Nair, "Uncovering the Zenana"; Carroll, "Law, Custom, and Statutory Social Reform," 1–26; Nandy, "Sati: A Nineteenth Century Tale of Women, Violence, and Protest."

37. Given the focus of this project, I will limit my comments here to the literature on the colonial period. For some important works on the scholarship focusing on the uses of women in the recent discourses of the religious Right in India, both Hindu and Muslim, see, Kishwar and Vanita, "The Burning of Roop Kanwar"; Hasan, "Minority Identity, State Policy, and Political Process"; Pathak and Sunder Rajan, "Shahbano"; T. Sarkar and Butalia, *Women and Right-Wing Movements*; Jahan, "Hidden Wounds, Visible Scars"; and A. Chatterjee and Chaudhry, *Gendered Violence in South Asia*. For feminist discussions on the effects of communal violence on women, see Butalia, *The Other Side of Silence*; T. Sarkar,

"Semiotics of Terror"; Hameed et al., "How Has the Gujarat Massacre Affected Minority Women?"; Mazumdar, "Moving Away from a Secular Vision?"; T. Sarkar and Butalia, *Women and Right-Wing Movements*; and M. Sarkar, "'Community' and 'Nation.'"

38. For discussions of this point, see Gedalof, *Against Purity*, 36–37; Burton, "Institutionalizing Imperial Reform," 35; D. Ghosh, "Colonial Companions," 17–18; and Sen, "Histories of Betrayal," 259–64. See also M. Sinha, *Colonial Masculinity*. For discussions on new forms of control imposed on women, see Bannerji, "Attired in Virtue," 91–92; M. Bhattacharya and Sen, *Talking of Power*, 15; and P. Chatterjee, "The Nationalist Resolution of the Women's Question," 244. For a discussion of developments outside India, see Abu-Lughod, "Feminist Longings and Postcolonial Conditions," especially 6; Kandiyoti, "Afterword," 282–83; and Badran, "Competing Agenda." On woman as "ground," see Mani, *Contentious Traditions*. See also Spivak, "Can the Subaltern Speak?"; and P. Chatterjee, "The Nationalist Resolution of the Women's Question."

39. Abu-Lughod, "Feminist Longings and Postcolonial Conditions," 5.

40. Sen, "Histories of Betrayal," 263. For critiques of Chatterjee's work from within postcolonial feminist scholarship, see Visweswaran, "Small Speeches, Subaltern Gender," 83–125; and T. Sarkar, *Hindu Wife, Hindu Nation*, 23–24.

41. For discussions of this danger in writing, see Mani, "Cultural Theory, Colonial Texts," 392–405; and, in a somewhat different vein, Visweswaran, "Small Speeches, Subaltern Gender."

42. Visweswaran, "Small Speeches, Subaltern Gender," 85–86. See also P. Chatterjee, "The Nationalist Resolution of the Women's Question"; and Chakravarti, "Whatever Happened to the Vedic *Dasi*?"

43. In the interest of brevity, I will cite only one instance of such conflation here. In "Ethnicity and Empowerment of Women," Jasodhara Bagchi helpfully clarifies at the outset that she is going to indulge in two metonymic exercises: "The upper caste Hindu male will stand in for the Indian middle class" while "Bengali middle class women will be made to stand in for Indian women in general" (114–15). As one would expect from a scholar of Bagchi's stature, she is well aware of these conflations and even presents her reasons for using them. But at the same time Bagchi does not acknowledge her conflation of the term *Bengali* with *Hindu*—something that remains entirely assumed in her work.

44. See, for instance, the useful, if brief, discussion of the Shah Bano affair in the epilogue to Mani's "Contentious Traditions," 119–21; and P. Chatterjee's allusion to Muslims in India in *The Nation and Its Fragments*, 133–34.

45. Chakravarti, "Whatever Happened to the Vedic *Dasi*?"; Visweswaran,

"Small Speeches, Subaltern Gender." For a study of this relationship with a different emphasis, see Sen, *Women and Labour in Late Colonial India*.

46. Visweswaran, "Small Speeches, Subaltern Gender," 84.

47. For examples of studies in which Muslim women are left out, see Murshid, *Reluctant Debutante*; Chakraborty, *Andare Antare*; Engels, *Beyond Purdah?* and Borthwick, *The Changing Role of Women in Bengal, 1849–1905*.

48. For an important instance of such critical historiography, see Antoinette Burton's analysis of the "constitutive power" of the "trope of Indian womanhood" in the "shaping of . . . imperial discourses" in Britain in *Burdens of History*, 20.

49. Minault, *The Extended Family*; Sonia Nishat Amin, *The World of Muslim Women in Colonial Bengal, 1876–1939*. For an important exception to this trend, see Bacchetta, "Communal Property/Sexual Property," 188–225. For a discussion of Muslim representations in Hindi periodicals that explores the relationality of community identity formations but does not deal with Muslim women, see Gupta, *Sexuality, Obscenity, Community*.

50. Sen, "Histories of Betrayal," 260. See also Abu-Lughod, "Can There Be a Feminist Ethnography?" 11–15.

51. For feminist scholarship on women's participation in the nationalist movement in India, see Ray, "Calcutta Women in the Swadeshi Movement"; Ray, "The Freedom Movement and Feminist Consciousness in Bengal, 1905–1929"; Forbes, "Goddesses or Rebels?"; Forbes, *Women in Modern India*, 121–56; Liddle and Joshi, *Daughters of Independence*; Dasgupta, *Swadhinata Sangrame Banglar Nari*; Minault, "Purdah Politics"; and Thapar-Björkert, *Women in the Indian Nationalist Movement*. For discussions of women's contributions within nationalist historiography, see Aparna Basu, "The Role of Women in the Indian Struggle for Freedom"; Aparna Basu, "Feminism and Nationalism in India, 1917–1947"; B. Majumdar and B. P. Majumdar, *Congress and Congressmen in the Pre-Gandhian Era, 1885–1917*, especially 128–129; B. Chandra, Tripathi, and De, *Freedom Struggle*; N. C. Bose, *The Indian National Movement*; and B. Chandra, *Modern India*. On the issue of "rewriting" or "recovering" history, see Forbes, *Women in Modern India*, 4; Ramusack and Sievers, *Women in Asia*, especially 41–65; Borthwick, *The Changing Role of Women in Bengal, 1849–1905*; and Ray, introduction to *From the Seams of History*, 1–2.

52. For examples of such works, see T. Sarkar, *Words to Win*; Chakravarti, *Rewriting History*; Bannerji, "Attired in Virtue"; P. Chatterjee, *The Nation and Its Fragments*, 135–57; O'Hanlon, introduction to Shinde, *A Comparison between Women and Men*; Chakraborty, *Andare Antare*; M. Bhattacharya and Sen, *Talking of Power*; Burton, *Dwelling in the Archive*; and Akhtar and Bhowmick, *Zenana*

Mehfil. For discussions of structure, agency, and gender, see Sangari, "Consent, Agency, and the Rhetorics of Incitement," 867–82; and Chakravarti, *Rewriting History*, 303–50.

53. T. Sarkar, foreword to M. Bhattacharya and Sen, *Talking of Power*, xi. Sarkar describes such writing as "surprisingly critical." See also T. Sarkar, "Enfranchised Selves," 561, especially her discussion of Rasasundari (also spelled Rashsundari) Debi's *Amar Jiban* (1875), the first autobiography written in Bengali. According to Sarkar, Rashsundari (or Rasasundari) completed writing the first part of her autobiography in 1868. See T. Sarkar, *Words to Win*, 2. For examples of critical work by women in the nineteenth century, see Shinde, "Stri Purush Tulana," in *A Comparison between Women and Men*, 79–124; Shinde, "Why Blame Women?"; Saraswati, *The High-Caste Hindu Woman*; Rukmabai, "Indian Child Marriages"; and Krishnabhabini Das, "Swadhin O Paradhin Nari Jiban." For an English translation of Krishnabhabini's essay, see M. Bhattacharya and Sen, *Talking of Power*, 77–83. For other discussions of works by women in the nineteenth century, see Chakravarti, *Rewriting History*, especially 246–99; and Tharu and Lalita, *Women Writing in India*. For a recent sensitive reading of Bengali Muslim women who wrote mostly in the early twentieth century, see Akhtar and Bhowmick, *Zenana Mehfil*.

54. For a recent example of a malecentric narrative of the Bengal Renaissance, see Hatcher, "Great Men Waking." See also Kopf, *British Orientalism and the Bengal Renaissance*; and Asiatic Society, *Renascent Bengal*.

55. Borthwick, *The Changing Role of Women in Bengal, 1849–1905*. Borthwick's work has clearly been an influence on subsequent work on the bhadramahila. For some instances, see Murshid, *The Reluctant Debutante*; Engels, *Beyond Purdah?*; Sonia Nishat Amin, "The Early Muslim Bhadramahila"; Sonia Nishat Amin, "The New Woman in Literature and the Novels of Nojibur Rahman and Rokeya Sakhawat Hossain"; S. Ghosh, "Changes in Bengali Social Life as Recorded in Autobiographies by Women"; Karlekar, *Voices from Within*; Forbes and Raychaudhuri, *From Child Widow to Lady Doctor*; and Forbes, *Memoirs of an Indian Woman by Shudha Majumdar*. For work on women outside Bengal, see Kosambi, "Women, Emancipation, and Equality"; Ramanathan, *Sister R. Subhalakshmi*; Forbes, *Women in Modern India*; Minault, *Secluded Scholars*; and Azra Asghar Ali, *The Emergence of Feminism among Indian Muslim Women, 1920–1947*.

56. N. Kumar, introduction to *Women as Subjects*, 4.

57. Engels, *Beyond Purdah?* 4; Southard, *The Women's Movement and Colonial Politics in Bengal*, 2–7; Forbes, *Women in Modern India*, especially 70–95; Everett, "All the Women Were Hindu and All the Muslims Were Men," 2071–80; Ray, "The

Freedom Movement and Feminist Consciousness in Bengal, 1905–1929," 174–218; Chaudhuri, "The Indian Women's Movement," 117–33; Anagol-McGinn, "The Age of Consent Act (1891) Reconsidered," 100–118.

58. For a discussion of the early associations for women that were founded by men, see Forbes, *Women in Modern India*, 65–70.

59. Southard, *The Women's Movement and Colonial Politics in Bengal*, 3. See also Forbes, *Women in Modern India*, especially 70–95; Everett, "All the Women Were Hindu and All the Muslims Were Men; Aparna Basu and Ray, *Women's Struggle*; Ray, "The Freedom Movement and Feminist Consciousness in Bengal, 1905–1929"; Chaudhuri, "The Indian Women's Movement"; Anagol-McGinn, "The Age of Consent Act (1891) Reconsidered"; and Shahnawaz, *Father and Daughter*; Minault, "Sisterhood or Separation?"

60. Geetha, "Periyar, Women, and an Ethic of Citizenship," 156.

61. Everett, "All the Women Were Hindu and All the Muslims Were Men"; Southard, *The Women's Movement and Colonial Politics in Bengal*. Studies that focus on Muslim women include Minault, "Sisterhood or Separatism?"; Minault, *Secluded Scholars*; Lambert-Hurley, "Fostering Sisterhood"; Aftab, "Negotiating with Patriarchy," 75–97; and Azra Asghar Ali, *The Emergence of Feminism among Indian Muslim Women, 1920–1947*.

62. Forbes, *Women in Modern India*, especially chapters 3, 4, and 5; Southard, *The Women's Movement and Colonial Politics in Bengal*; Everett, "All the Women Were Hindu and All the Muslims Were Men."

63. Everett, "All the Women Were Hindu and All the Muslims Were Men," 2078 (emphases added).

64. Lambert-Hurley, "Fostering Sisterhood," 40–43.

65. I am quoting here from Forbes's introduction to *Women in Modern India*, 1. Forbes was, of course, writing about how an individual woman would be "singled out" within malecentric conventional histories "because her accomplishments were significant by male standards" (1).

66. See, for instance, Minault, "Sisterhood or Separation? 103; Lambert-Hurley, "Fostering Sisterhood," 44; and Everett, "All the Women Were Hindu and All the Muslims Were Men."

67. According to Lambert-Hurley, Nawab Sultan Jahan abdicated in favor of her son in 1926 ("Fostering Sisterhood," 57).

68. M. Sinha, *Specters of Mother India*, 10.

69. Mohanty, "Under Western Eyes," 52–55. Mohanty uses the term *western feminist* to refer to "feminists who identify themselves as culturally or geographically from the 'West.'"

70. Chow, *Women and Chinese Modernity*. On "ethnocentric universality," see Mohanty, "Under Western Eyes." On "sanctioned ignorances," see Spivak, "Can the Subaltern Speak?"

71. For discussions of Muslim women in contemporary India, see Jehangir, *Muslim Women in West Bengal*; Anjum, *Muslim Women in India*; M. I. Menon, *Status of Muslim Women in India*; and Jeffery, *Frogs in a Well*. While individual studies vary in terms of both substantive focus and tone, the works cited above largely attempt to explain Muslim women's perceived "backwardness," often in terms of certain indices of modernization that are taken for granted in contemporary India such as formal education or participation in the public political rites of the nation-state. For thoughtful recent work on Muslim women in contemporary India, see Lateef, *Muslim Women in India*; Khan, *Socio-legal Status of Muslim Women in India*; and Pathak and Sunder Rajan, "Shahbano," 558–82.

72. For a discussion of the continued purchase of modernizationalist teleologies in the social sciences as practiced both within the geographical West and elsewhere, see Böröcz, "Social Change with Sticky Features and the Failures of Modernizationism." See also J. Ferguson, *Expectations of Modernity*, 1–37. For incisive discussions of the importance of the metaphors of vision and voice, see J. W. Scott, "The Evidence of Experience," 773–97; and Burton, "Optical Illusions," 21–22.

73. See Snitow, "A Gender Diary," 505–46; Abu-Lughod, "Can There Be a Feminist Ethnography?" 23–24; Crosby, "Dealing with Differences," 130–31; and Rich, "Notes toward a Politics of Location." I borrow the term *ethnoclass* from Wynter, "Un-Settling the Coloniality of Being/Power/Truth/Freedom."

74. Bambara, *The Black Woman*; hooks, *Ain't I a Woman*; Carby, "White Woman Listen!"; Lorde, *Sister/Outsider*; Moraga and Anzaldúa, *This Bridge Called My Back*; Mohanty, "Cartographies of Struggle," especially, 12–13; Tharu and Niranjana, "Problems for a Contemporary Theory of Gender"; L. Ahmed, *Women and Gender in Islam*, 163–64; Lazreg, *The Eloquence of Silence*; Abu-Lughod, "Feminist Longings and Postcolonial Conditions," 13–22; Alarcón, "The Theoretical Subjects of *This Bridge Called My Back*"; Pathak and Rajan, "Shahbano," especially 570–73; Visweswaran, *Fictions of Feminist Ethnography*, 75. I include Muslim women in the broadly conceived category of third-world/postcolonial women.

75. Snitow, "A Gender Diary," 525; John, *Discrepant Dislocations*, 25; Crosby, "Dealing with Differences," 131.

76. Minault, *Secluded Scholars*, 2. For some important work on Muslim women in colonial India, see B. D. Metcalf, "Reading and Writing about Muslim Women in British India"; Minault, *Secluded Scholars*; Murshid, *Rasasundari Theke Rokeya*;

Akhtar and Bhowmick, *Zenana Mehfil*; Sonia Nishat Amin, *The World of Muslim Women in Colonial Bengal, 1876–1939*; Azra Asghar Ali, *The Emergence of Feminism among Indian Muslim Women, 1920–1947*; Sayyid, *Muslim Women of the British Punjab*; Ray, *Early Feminists of Colonial India*; M. Bhattacharya and Sen, *Talking of Power*; Lambert-Hurley, "Fostering Sisterhood"; Pradhan, *Begum Rokeya O Narijagaran*; Begum, *Banglar Nari Andolan*; Ikramullah, *From Purdah to Parliament*; Jahangir, *The Life and Works of Sufia Kamal*; and Quadir, *Begum Rokeya Rachanabali*.

77. J. W. Scott, introduction to *Feminism and History*, 1–16. For a critique of the naturalization of differences, see Shail Mayaram's discussion of Islamization in the context of colonial India in *Resisting Regimes*, 34. See also R. Ahmed, *The Bengal Muslims, 1871–1906*.

78. Sonia Nishat Amin, *The World of Muslim Women in Colonial Bengal, 1876–1939*; Minault, *Secluded Scholars*; Sayyid, *Muslim Women of the British Punjab*; Azra Asghar Ali, *The Emergence of Feminism among Indian Muslim Women, 1920–1947*.

79. J. W. Scott, *Gender and the Politics of History*, 19.

80. M. Sarkar, "Looking for Feminism," 321.

81. According to Ranajit Guha, "resistance" is the opposing aspect of "domination" within a "social relation of power" as typified by the relationship between a dominant group (say, landlords) and a subordinate group (say, peasants). *Resistance*, in such an understanding, represents the "autonomous domain" of the consciousness of the subordinated (*Elementary Aspects of Peasant Insurgency in Colonial India*). See also Partha Chatterjee's discussion of Guha's work in *The Nation and Its Fragments*, 161. I begin with Guha's formulation of the term. However, I believe that resistance, as an autonomous domain of subaltern consciousness, ought not to be romanticized since such a neat separation of the dominant and subaltern realms is quite impossible in practice if not in theory. For incisive discussions of the vexed relationships between the dominant and subaltern realms of consciousness/memory/politics, see Stoler and Strassler, "Castings for the Colonial," 4; and Mayaram, *Resisting Regimes*, 9. See also Passerini, "Work, Ideology, and Consensus under Italian Fascism," 53–55.

82. Ray, *Early Feminists of Colonial India*, 2–3.

83. Ibid., 75–77 (emphasis added).

84. See, for instance, the discussion of liberal Muslim male intellectuals in chapter 3 of this book.

85. Ray, *Early Feminists of Colonial India*, 76.

86. Editorial, *Mahila*, July-August, 1903. See also the discussion of Rokeya's work in chapters 2 and 3 in this book.

87. For some such contemporary scholarship, see Kaji Abdul Wadud, "Mrs. R. S. Hossain," *Masik Sanchay*, November-December 1929, cited in Quadir, *Begum Rokeya Rachanabali*, 552; Abul Hussein, "On Matichur," cited in Anisuzzaman, "Narimukti, Samakaal O Begum Rokeya," 20; and S. Mahmud, *Rokeya Jibani*, 27–29. More recent scholarship includes Shibnarayan Ray, "Bangalir Atmajignasha," *Purogami*, February 16, 1979, cited in Akhtar and Bhowmik, *Zenana Mehfil*, 5; Anisuzzaman, "Narimukti, Samakaal O Begum Rokeya," especially 20–22; Murshid, *Rassundari Theke Rokeya*, 128–58; Pradhan, *Begum Rokeya O Narijagaran*; Sonia Nishat Amin, "The Changing World of Bengali Muslim Women," 143–47; and M. Sarkar, "Muslim Women and the Politics of (In)visibility in Late Colonial Bengal," 238–40.

88. For a discussion of the conceptual affinities between the "family" and the "nation," see Delaney, "Father State, Motherland, and the Birth of Modern Turkey," 178. For a discussion of the position of Muslims in the postcolonial India, see Pandey, "Can a Muslim be an Indian?"

89. The 1881 Census of Bengal, for instance, records the total proportion of upper-caste Hindus in Bengal to be only 12.77 percent. While the bhadralok often came from the upper castes, it is fair to assume that not all upper-caste Hindus in Bengal belonged to a prosperous rentier class. See Census of Bengal, 1881, ii, Table viii, 240–49. See also R. Ahmed, *The Bengal Muslims, 1871–1906*, 3–4; Aparna Basu, *The Growth of Education and Political Development in India, 1898–1920*; and Chatterji, *Bengal Divided*, 3–6. For a discussion of the shifting importance of religious identification in colonial India, see Rouse, "Gender, Nationalism(s), and Cultural Identity," 43.

90. See, for example, Azra Asghar Ali, *The Emergence of Feminism among Indian Muslim Women, 1920–1947*, xvii–xviii; Sonia Nishat Amin, *The World of Muslim Women in Colonial Bengal, 1876–1939*, 12; Sonia Nishat Amin, "Bengali (Muslim) Identity and the Women's Question"; and Sonia Nishat Amin, "The Early Muslim Bhadramahila."

91. For a discussion of similar trends in the context of late-nineteenth- and early-twentieth-century Egypt, for instance, see Abu-Lughod, "The Marriage of Feminism and Islamism in Egypt." For Iran, see Najmabadi, "Crafting an Educated Housewife in Iran."

92. Azra Asghar Ali, *The Emergence of Feminism among Indian Muslim Women, 1920–1947*, vii.

93. Ibid., xviii.

94. Ibid., 1–42. See also Mahua Sarkar's review of Azra Asghar Ali's book in the *Journal of Colonialism and Colonial History* and Antoinette Burton's review in the *American Historical Review*.

95. Sonia Nishat Amin, *The World of Muslim Women in Colonial Bengal, 1876–1939*, ix.

96. Ibid.

97. Ibid. Amin's book can be read as the first feminist text written in English that uses a large body of primary material to shed light on the efforts of a wide range of Muslim women writers and educators in late colonial Bengal. It was followed shortly by Akhtar and Bhowmick, *Zenana Mehfil*, which is an excellent analysis in Bengali of Bengali Muslim women's work published jointly by feminist scholars from Bangladesh and West Bengal. These works were preceded by a body of scholarship—also written in Bengali—that also undertakes important secular interventions on the question of Bengali Muslim women's "emancipation." For a few important examples, see Mohammad Nasiruddin, *Bangla Sahitye Saogat Jug*; Anisuzzaman, "Narimukti, Samakaal O Begum Rokeya"; Maleka Begum, *Banglar Nari Andolan*; Murshid, *Rasasundari Theke Rokeya*; Quadir, *Begum Rokeya Rachanabali*; and Jahangir, *The Life and Works of Sufia Kamal*.

98. See especially Minault, *Secluded Scholars*; Sayyid, *Muslim Women of the British Punjab*; and Sonia Nishat Amin, "The Early Muslim Bhadramahila."

99. For a critical reading of these tendencies, specifically in Amin's work, see B. D. Metcalf, Review of Sonia Nishat Amin, *The World of Muslim Women in Colonial Bengal, 1876–1939*, 464.

100. Sonia Nishat Amin, *The World of Muslim Women in Colonial Bengal, 1876–1939*, 4–8. Note her disclaimer in footnote 14 on page 6.

101. See discussion of Muslim protests against Hindu attitudes in chapter 3 and the account of my conversation with the late writer Sufia Kamal in chapter 4.

102. Sarker, "Larger than Bengal"; Azra Asghar Ali, *The Emergence of Feminism among Indian Muslim Women, 1920–1947*; B. Ray, *Early Feminists of Colonial India*.

103. Sonia Nishat Amin, *The World of Muslim Women in Colonial Bengal, 1876–1939*; Azra Asghar Ali, *The Emergence of Feminism among Indian Muslim Women, 1920–1947*; Sarker, "Larger than Bengal." It is important to note that while earlier commentaries on Muslim women by authors such as Roushan Jahan (in the "Sultana's Dream: Purdah Reversed," the introduction to Hossain, *"Sultana's Dream" and Selections from "The Secluded Ones"*) and Susie Tharu and K. Lalitha (in

Women Writing in India) simply describe their subject as feminist, authors in later works seem burdened with the need to substantiate their claims.

104. Sonia Nishat Amin, *The World of Muslim Women in Colonial Bengal, 1876–1939*, 278 (emphasis added).

105. The Euro-American academy is perhaps the most obvious locus of such knowledge production and deployment, but it is by no means the only one.

106. For some important instances of self-critique from western feminists, see Rich, "Notes toward a Politics of Location," especially 230–31; Johnson, *A World of Difference*, 2–4; and Frankenberg, *White Women, Race Matters*.

107. For an extremely useful analysis of the fallacies of reading a "discontinuous and apparently contradictory" subaltern subject position in terms of the standards of a "normative male subject of Western bourgeois liberalism," see Pathak and Sunder Rajan, "Shahbano."

108. Trinh, "Not You/Like You." See also Böröcz, "Social Change with Sticky Features and the Failures of Modernizationism"; and Fabian, *Time and the Other*, xi.

109. See, for instance, Azra Asghar Ali, *The Emergence of Feminism among Indian Muslim Women, 1920–1947*. Ali seems to conflate feminist consciousness with women's public appearance or participation in mass political movements. See also Sonia Nishat Amin, *The World of Muslim Women in Colonial Bengal, 1876–1939*, especially 278–79.

110. For some useful commentaries on the violence in Gujarat in 2002, see the report by the International Initiative for Justice, *Threatened Existence*; Hameed et al., "How Has the Gujarat Massacre Affected Minority Women?"; K. G. Kannabiran, "Narendra Modi's Hindutva Laboratory"; and Bidwai, "End the Butchery, Sack Modi." For related articles, see also Banerjee, "When the 'Silent Majority' Backs a Violent Minority"; and T. Sarkar, "Semiotics of Terror." For an incisive collection of works dealing with women's participation in right-wing Hindu organizations in contemporary India, see T. Sarkar and Butalia, *Women and Right-Wing Movements*. For insights on the intersections of Islamism, feminisms, and modernism in the Middle East in the late twentieth century, see Abu-Lughod, *Remaking Women*, especially 213–87.

111. Pathak and Sunder Rajan, "Shahbano," 570–71. See also Belsey, *The Subject of Tragedy*, 191.

112. N. Kumar, introduction to *Women as Subjects*, 4; Minault, "*Begamati Zuban*"; J. P. Majumdar, *Family History*.

113. Pathak and Sunder Rajan, "Shahbano," 565, 572.

114. I borrow the phrase "normalized telos of a developmental process" from

D. Scott, *Refashioning Futures*, 40. On resistance, see Pathak and Sunder Rajan, "Shahbano"; Duara, *Rescuing History from the Nation*, 11; and M. Sarkar, "Difference in Memory," especially 151–56. For an excellent discussion of women's contribution from within the confinement of the private sphere in nineteenth-century Egypt, see Hatem, "'A'isha Taymur's Tears' and the Critique of the Modernist and the Feminist Discourses on Nineteenth-Century Egypt," especially 80–86.

115. Rokeya Sakhawat Hossain lived and worked in Bengal between 1880 and 1932. Apart from being a prolific writer, she is remembered for her efforts to bring formal education to women in seclusion by founding a school for Muslim girls that helped them maintain purdah but still receive a formal education. In their introduction to Rokeya's work, Tharu and Lalitha describe her as a "courageous feminist writer and activist who worked all her life to remove what she called the 'purdah of ignorance'" (*Women Writing in India*, 340).

116. Zenanas are separate quarters for women. They are also known as *andarmahal* (literally "inner quarters") or *antahpur* in Bengal.

117. Sarker, "Larger than Bengal," 445. Sarker is certainly not the only one who presents Rokeya as being ahead of her time. See, for instance, Ray, *Early Feminists of Colonial India*; and S. Hossein, "Begum Rokeya Sakhawat Hossain."

118. Sarker, "Larger than Bengal," 449. *"Sultana's Dream"* has been billed variously as a "utopian fantasy" and a "feminist utopia." See Tharu and Lalita, *Women Writing in India*, 340; and Roushan Jahan's remarks in Hossain, *"Sultana's Dream" and Selections from "The Secluded Ones,"* vii.

119. Sonia Nishat Amin, "Childhood and Role Models in the Andar Mahal," 71. It is important to note that, contrary to common assumptions, life in the zenanas was not uniformly oppressive for all women everywhere. For a somewhat different representation of the zenana in nineteenth-century India, see Minault, "*Begamati Zuban*"; and Bandopadhyay, *Moguljuge Stree Shiksha*, 1–3. For discussions of women's work in the nineteenth century and the early twentieth, see Tharu and Lalita, *Women Writing in India*; P. Chatterjee, *The Nation and Its Fragments*, especially 135–57; T. Sarkar, *Words to Win*; O'Hanlon, introduction to Shinde, *A Comparison between Women and Men*, 1–71; and Burton, *At the Heart of the Empire*.

120. For a critique of Eurocentric and westerncentric histories, see Samir Amin, *Eurocentrism*; Said, *Culture and Imperialism*; and Blaut, *The Colonizers' Model of the World*.

121. Pathak and Sunder Rajan, "Shahbano," 572. I borrow the phrase "sanctioned ignorances" from Spivak who uses it in the context of western academic

discourses on the third world, but I use it in the spirit of her larger criticism of the subaltern studies project. See Spivak, "Can the Subaltern Speak?"

122. Johnson, *A World of Difference*, 4. See also John, *Discrepant Dislocations*, especially chapter 1.

123. J. W. Scott, "The Evidence of Experience," 777–78.

124. Ibid.

125. Crosby, "Dealing with Differences," 140. See also Spivak, "In a Word."

126. I thank the anonymous reviewers at Duke University Press for bringing this point to my attention.

127. Spivak, "Who Claims Alterity?" 273. Spivak is referring, of course, to the figure of the "gendered subaltern" who is also poor. The women I interviewed, in contrast, are of considerable financial means and therefore are not quite the "disenfranchised female" figures that Spivak has in mind.

128. For important examples of scholarship on the subversive agency of women, see Sangari and Vaid, introduction to *Recasting Women: Essays in Colonial History*, 1–26; M. Sinha, "Gender in the Critiques of Colonialism and Nationalism"; T. Sarkar, *Words to Win*; Chakravarti, *Rewriting History*; Bannerji, "Attired in Virtue"; P. Chatterjee, *The Nation and Its Fragments*, 135–57; Chakraborty, *Andare Antare*; M. Bhattacharya and Sen, *Talking of Power*; and Burton, *Dwelling in the Archive*.

129. Bannerji, "Attired in Virtue," 92; Abu-Lughod, "Feminist Longings and Postcolonial Conditions," 6–9; Kandiyoti, "Afterword," 283; Murshid, *The Reluctant Debutante*, 109; Chakrabarty, *Provincializing Europe*, 228. For scholarship on nationalist accommodations of the "woman question," see Kandiyoti, introduction to *Women, Islam, and the State*, 1–21; Jalal, "Convenience of Subservience"; P. Chatterjee, "The Nationalist Resolution of the Women's Question"; Badran, "Competing Agenda"; and Yuval-Davis, *Gender and Nation*.

130. Abu-Lughod, "Feminist Longings and Postcolonial Conditions," 7; Bannerji, "Attired in Virtue," 91–92. See also Foucault, *Discipline and Punish* and *The History of Sexuality*.

131. Sullivan, "Eluding the Feminist, Overthrowing the Modern?" 223–36; Bannerji, "Attired in Virtue," 91–92; M. Bhattacharya and Sen, *Talking of Power*, 15; P. Chatterjee, "The Nationalist Resolution of the Women's Question," 244. See also the discussion of the works of Rokeya and Nurunnessa Khatun Bidyabinodini in chapter 3 of this book.

132. Kandiyoti, "Afterword," 283. See also Najmabadi, "Veiled Discourse—Unveiled Bodies"; Minault, "*Begamati Zuban*"; Kandiyoti, "Patterns of Patriarchy"; and Bannerji, "Attired in Virtue," especially 97.

133. Passerini, "Work, Ideology, and Consensus under Italian Fascism," 54–55; Portelli, "What Makes Oral History Different," 70–73.

134. Stacey, "Can There Be a Feminist Ethnography?" 112–14. For a somewhat different reading of the power relationships in an ethnographic context, see Visweswaran, *Fictions of Feminist Ethnography*, especially 40–59 and 171–72.

135. Armitage and Gluck, "Reflections on Women's Oral History," 79–80; Borland, "That's Not What I Said," 64–72; Stacey, "Can There Be a Feminist Ethnography?" 112–14; Visweswaran, *Fictions of Feminist Ethnography*, especially 40–59; Portelli, "What Makes Oral History Different," 71–73.

136. Visweswaran, *Fictions of Feminist Ethnography*, especially 40–59; Borland, "That's Not What I Said," 64–72; Portelli, "What Makes Oral History Different," 66.

137. Visweswaran, *Fictions of Feminist Ethnography*, 60–72.

138. For an elaboration of this argument, see M. Sarkar, "Looking for Feminism."

139. Dancing girls and courtesans were known as nautch girls.

140. Historically the term *bhadrasampraday*, or *educated middle-class society*, has been used to refer to the Hindu/Brahmo middle class in Bengal.

141. Passerini, "Work, Ideology, and Consensus under Italian Fascism," 55.

142. Stoler and Strassler. "Castings for the Colonial," 4.

1. THE COLONIAL CAST

1. *Sikander* refers to Col. James Skinner, a famous freelancer of the nineteenth century known for his cavalry unit, Captain Skinner's Core of Irregular Cavalry, or Skinner's Horse, which was formed in 1803. Sikander appears to be the name given to him by his Hindusthani followers. Sripantha, *Aitihashik Anaitihashik*, 11–13. *Antahpur* refers to inner (women's) quarters, or zenanas. The epigraph is drawn from Sripantha, *Aitihashik Anaitihashik*, 3–6. See also Grey, *European Adventurers of Northern India*; and Holman, *Sikander Sahib*.

2. D. Ghosh, "Colonial Companions," 16, 29.

3. Ibid., 18–23. In her subsequent work, Ghosh has developed her arguments considerably more. See D. Ghosh, *Sex and the Family in Colonial India*, 15–22.

4. Sripantha, *Aitihashik Anaitihashik*, preface and 3–6.

5. See, for instance, Sripantha, *Keyabat Meye*, 175–210; Hyam, *Empire and Sexuality*; Ballhatchet, *Race, Sex, and Class under the Raj*; M. Chandra, *The World of Courtesans*; P. T. Nair, *British Social Life in Ancient Calcutta*; Brown, *The Sahibs*;

Nevile, *Nautch-Girls of India*; Archer, *Company Paintings*; and I. Sen, *Woman and Empire*, especially 39–70. See also I. Chatterjee, "Colouring Subalternity," for a more critical reading of the subject.

6. In the preface to *Aitihashik Anaitihashik*, Sripantha defends his use of "apparently insignificant details that lie in the cracks of [conventional written] History" by insisting that even such "questionable" information is part of social history. In other words, he is interested in expanding the scope and definition of what constitutes an archive. For a more nuanced and extended discussion about the scope of archives, see Burton, *Dwelling in the Archive*, 4.

7. D. Ghosh, *Colonial Companions*, 16.

8. Sripantha refers to one contemporary account from the eighteenth century that claimed that nine out of ten of the *bibis* were Muslim. *Bibi* is a Persian word used to refer to wives. In the days of company rule, it came to denote the common-law wives (mostly courtesans, sometimes concubines) of British officials. Sripantha, *Keyabat Meye*, 195. See also D. Ghosh, *Sex and the Family in Colonial India*, 4.

9. Hawes, *Eurasians in British India, 1773–1833*, 57. For an elaboration of this argument, see I. Chatterjee, "Colouring Subalternity," 52. On the importance of liaisons with aristocratic families in furthering the aims of the company, see, for instance, Dalrymple, *White Mughals*; and D. Ghosh, *Sex and the Family in Colonial India*, 69–106.

10. Arrighi and Silver, *Chaos and Governance in the Modern World System*, 108.

11. Ibid., 107–9. See also Vink, "The World's Oldest Trade."

12. Arrighi and Silver, *Chaos and Governance in the Modern World System*, 55. See also Baran, *The Political Economy of Growth*, 134–62; Digby, *"Prosperous" British India*; and Duff, *The Economic History of India in the Victorian Age*. The diwani of Bengal was granted to the Company as a war indemnity by the Mughal emperor, Shah Alam II, after the British won the Battle of Baksar, or Buxar, in 1764 against the joint forces of the nawabs of Bengal and the emperor. See Wolpert, *A New History of India*, 185–86.

13. Davis, *The Industrial Revolution and British Overseas Trade*, 55–56.

14. Cain and Hopkins, "Gentlemanly Capitalism and British Expansion Overseas," 501–25; Viswanathan, *Masks of Conquest*, 24–26, 173, n. 4; Adams, *The Law of Civilization and Decay*, 294.

15. Arrighi and Silver, *Chaos and Governance in the Modern World System*, 63. For a concise discussion, see Arrighi, *The Long Twentieth Century*, especially 47–57. For a discussion of the rise of Britain to the stature of world power, see Polanyi, *The Great Transformation*.

16. Arrighi and Silver, *Chaos and Governance in the Modern World System*, 56–57.

17. Kopf, *British Orientalism and the Bengal Renaissance*; Wolpert, *A New History of India*; Sripantha, *Aitihashik Anaitihashik*; D. Ghosh, *Colonial Companions*, 30; Dalrymple, *White Mughals*, xiv.

18. Fisher, *Indirect Rule in India*. See also Cohn, "Representing Authority in Victorian India"; Bayly, *The Raj, India, and the British, 1600–1947*; Dalrymple, *White Mughals*; and Sripantha, *Aitihashik Anaitihashik*.

19. Dalrymple, *White Mughals*. See also I. Chatterjee, *Unfamiliar Relations*, 24–25; and D. Ghosh, Sex and the Family in Colonial India, 69–70.

20. Viswanathan, *Masks of Conquest*, 23–44. See also Kopf, *British Orientalism and the Bengal Renaissance*. On the importance of language, Cohn, "The Command of Language and the Language of Command," 276–329.

21. Viswanathan, *Masks of Conquest*, 28.

22. Spear, *The Nabobs: English Social Life in Eighteenth Century India*; Trautmann, *Aryans and British India*.

23. Sati is the practice of immolating widows on their husbands' funeral pyres. It was officially banned in 1829.

24. Chakravarti, "Whatever Happened to the Vedic *Dasi*?"; Mani, "Contentious Traditions"; Viswanathan, *Masks of Conquest*.

25. Spear, *The Nabobs*; Macaulay, *Lord Clive*; Sripantha, *Keyabat Meye*, 175–210.

26. Cited in Sripantha, *Keyabat Meye*, 176. The same doggerel appears in Sripantha's later book, *Aitihashik Anaitihashik* (105), with a slight difference: in the latter, the second line reads "And that we are far from the pips we love."

27. Gill, *Ruling Passions*, 35–37. See also Banerjee, *Dangerous Outcast*, 37–38; and I. Sen, *Woman and Empire*, 39–46.

28. Gill, *Ruling Passions*.

29. Banerjee, *Dangerous Outcast*, 37–38.

30. See Banerjee, *Dangerous Outcast*; and D. Ghosh, *Colonial Companions*, for discussions of a famous story in which Job Charnock rescues a Hindu woman from burning in an act of sati. See Sripantha, *Aitihashik Anaitihashik*, for a similar story about James Skinner.

31. Stanhope, *Genuine Memoirs of Asiaticus*; I. Chatterjee, "Colouring Subalternity," especially 54–62; R. Chatterjee, "Prostitution in Nineteenth Century Bengal," 159–72; Hyder, foreword to Hasan Shah, *The Nautch Girl*, 6; Banerjee, *Dangerous Outcast*, 37–50; Gill, *Ruling Passions*. See also Spear, *The Nabobs*; and D. Ghosh, *Sex and the Family in Colonial India*, 35–36.

32. Contemporary estimates put the cost of "keeping a bibi" at forty pounds per month, which was still considerably less than keeping a British woman. A typical clerk's income would have been no more than two hundred pounds a year. Cited in Sripantha, *Aitihashik Anaitihashik*, 105. See also Williamson, *The East India Vade Mecum*, 451–52.

33. J. Nair, *Calcutta in the Nineteenth Century*, 194–95, quoted in Banerjee, *Dangerous Outcast*, 41.

34. Williamson, *East India Vade Mecum*. For a useful discussion of Williamson's work, see D. Ghosh, *Colonial Companions*. See also I. Chatterjee, "Colouring Subalternity," 56; and Sripantha, *Aitihashik Anaitihashik*.

35. Williamson, *East India Vade Mecum*, 453.

36. Contemporary novels and plays reflect this ambivalence quite explicitly. See D. Ghosh, *Colonial Companions*, 50–61; and Jyotsna Singh, *Colonial Narratives/Cultural Dialogues*. According to Ghosh (45) in the second edition of the *East India Vade Mecum*, published in 1825, Williamson replaced the section on "how to keep a native woman" with instructions for Englishwomen who were journeying to India. See also her extended discussion in *Sex and the Family in Colonial India*, 35–68.

37. A nautch is a dance show. Performers in such shows were commonly known as nautch girls.

38. Cited in Hyder, foreword to Hasan Shah, *The Nautch Girl*, 6.

39. Banerjee, *Dangerous Outcast*, 12–14.

40. Ibid., 12. See also Sripantha, *Keyabat Meye*.

41. R. Chatterjee, "Prostitution in Nineteenth Century Bengal," 165.

42. For discussions of courtesans and their relationships with their patrons, see R. Chatterjee, "Prostitution in Nineteenth Century Bengal"; and Oldenburg, *The Making of Colonial Lucknow*.

43. See Lall, *Begum Samru*. Sripantha mentions a nautch girl who cohabited and had eight children with Alexander, Sikander's son (*Aitihashik Anaitihashik*, 8). See also D. Ghosh, *Colonial Companions*, especially chapter 3. *Nashtar* (A Surgeon's Knife) is the first known modern Indian novel written in Farsi (Persian). It was translated into Urdu in 1893 by Sajjad Hussain Kasmandavi. The original Farsi version has been lost. Qurratulain Hyder translated the Urdu version into English in 1992. It is a tragic story of love between Hasan Shah and Khanum Jan, a dancing girl employed by "Ming Saheb," Shah's employer.

44. Archer, *India Observed* and *Early Views of India*.

45. In keeping with the contemporary orientalist infatuation with India's past, some of these paintings present romanticized visions of sati as an act of "heroic

self-sacrifice" and an example of the "mysterious," almost fearsome spiritual strength of Hindu women. See Chattopadhyay and Guha Thakurta, "The Woman Perceived," 154; and Chakravarti, "Whatever Happened to the Vedic Dasi?"

46. Chattopadhyay and Guha Thakurta, "The Woman Perceived," 154.

47. About a particular painting of a woman by Charles Smith, who visited India in the 1780s, Archer comments that "[no] Muslim woman of rank [would] have sat to a British artist" (*India Observed*, 37).

48. Sripantha describes several historically recorded cases of romantic unions between company officials or professional soldiers and women of aristocratic families of the subcontinent, which were the source of considerable personal gain for the Europeans. See Sripantha, *Keyabat Meye*, 178–87. See also D. Ghosh, *Colonial Companions*, 30, 89–90.

49. McClintock, *Imperial Leather*, 117. See also Nussbaum, *Torrid Zones*, 170–71.

50. D. Ghosh, for instance, notes that the Dutch and the British traders "rarely married the women with whom they had sexual relations" (*Sex and the Family in Colonial India*, 39).

51. "Hindustani Girl's Song," cited in Archer, *India Observed*, 38.

52. Tomich, "The 'Second Slavery,'" 106.

53. For a discussion of similar imperial attitudes in European colonies elsewhere, see McClintock, *Imperial Leather*.

54. Sripantha, *Keyabat Meye*, 107; I. Chatterjee, "Colouring Subalternity," 58–59, 78–84. For other relevant discussions of the applicability of the term *slavery* in the Indian Ocean context, see Vink, "The World's Oldest Trade."

55. I. Chatterjee, "Colouring Subalternity," 52.

56. For a similar discussion of the importance of native women's services to the maintenance of empire, see Stoler, *Carnal Knowledge and Imperial Power*, especially 41–51. See also D. Ghosh, *Sex and the Family in Colonial India*.

57. Arrighi and Silver, *Chaos and Governance in the Modern World System*, 58; Polanyi, *The Great Transformation*, 5.

58. Sumit Sarkar, *Modern India*.

59. J. Nair, "Uncovering the Zenana"; Stoler, "Making Empire Respectable"; Robb, introduction to *The Concept of Race in South Asia*, 1–76; Hall, "The West and the Rest," 184–228. See also Miles and Brown, *Racism*.

60. Chakravarti, "Whatever Happened to the Vedic *Dasi*?"

61. Viswanathan, *Masks of Conquest*, 27.

62. Chakravarti, "Whatever Happened to the Vedic *Dasi*?" 34–36.

63. Muslim women were not as central to these debates, which centered on sati,

the treatment of widows, and child marriage. However, the literature does not necessarily suggest a more respectful view of Muslims among the Anglicists.

64. Forbes, *Women in Modern India*, 13. See also Mill, *The History of British India*, 309–10.

65. P. Chatterjee, *The Nation and Its Fragments*, 118.

66. Viswanathan, *Masks of Conquest*, 27–36. See also Macaulay, *Prose and Poetry*.

67. Forbes, *Women in Modern India*, 13; Storrow, *Our Indian Sisters*; Hutchins, *The Illusion of Permanence*; Chakravarti, "Whatever Happened to the Vedic *Dasi*?" especially 34–36; Viswanathan, *Masks of Conquest*, 118–41; Banerjee, "Marginalization of Women's Popular Culture in Nineteenth Century Bengal," 127–28; Burton, *Burdens of History*, especially chapters 2 and 3; J. Nair, "Uncovering the Zenana"; Minault, *Secluded Scholars*, 1–13.

68. D. Ghosh, *Sex and the Family in Colonial India*, 9–10; Bayly, "The British and Indigenous Peoples, 1760–1860." For a nuanced reading of the continuities and differences between orientalist and Anglicist thinking in early-nineteenth-century colonial India, see Viswanathan, *Masks of Conquest*, 23–44.

69. Hyder, foreword to Hasan Shah, *The Nautch Girl*, 12. It was quite common for Indians to change the names of British officers. For instance, Warren Hastings was popularly known as Hastan Bahadur and Colonel Skinner became Sikander Saheb. See Hyder, foreword to Hasan Shah, *The Nautch Girl*, x.

70. Hyder, foreword to Hasan Shah, *The Nautch Girl*, 12.

71. Elgin to Roseberry, July 1895, quoted in Sumit Sarkar, *Modern India*, 23. See also H. L. Singh, *Problems and Policies of the British in India*.

72. Cited in Burton, "Institutionalizing Imperial Reform," 41.

73. Ibid., 41–42.

74. Janaki Agnes Penelope Majumdar commented on the way in which "Anglo-Indians thoroughly despised 'natives' as a class, though they were friendly enough to those whom they thought had money and position" (*Family History*, 12). Majumdar is cited in Burton, *At the Heart of the Empire*, 6.

75. E. C. P. Hull, *The European in India or Anglo-Indian's Vade-Mecum*, 84.

76. For reports of other such instances of inhumane treatment of servants and slaves by British masters, see I. Chatterjee, "Colouring Subalternity," 50–51 fn. 5.

77. E. C. P. Hull, *The European in India or Anglo-Indian's Vade-Mecum*, 192.

78. Ibid., 105.

79. Ibid.

80. Ibid., 108–9 (emphasis added).

81. I borrow these insights from Stoler's work, especially "Making Empire Respectable."

82. J. Nair, "Uncovering the Zenana"; Banerjee, *Dangerous Outcast*. See also Ballhatchet, *Race, Sex, and Class under the Raj*.

83. An ayah is a nurse or maid.

84. E. C. P. Hull, *The European in India or Anglo-Indian's Vade-Mecum*, 129–30.

85. Ibid., 130.

86. Banerjee, *Dangerous Outcast*, 88–89.

87. Kulin refers to families, represented by certain surnames, that received an order of honor from King Ballal Sen of ancient Bengal. A majority of the prostitutes in the mid-nineteenth century were supposed to be Hindu, often from the upper castes. It seems that over ten thousand of the twelve-thousand-odd prostitutes in mid-nineteenth-century Calcutta came from upper-caste Hindu families, presumably due to the difficulty of remarriage among Hindus. Dispatch from A. Abercrombie, Home-Judicial, July 1873, nos. 151–205, cited in Banerjee, *Dangerous Outcast*, 88–89. However, it seems that Muslim prostitutes sometimes presented themselves as Hindu in order to ensure business from Hindu men. See Abul Mansur Ahmad, *Atmakatha*, 213–15, cited in Datta, *Carving Blocs*, 221. It is useful to remember that in the second half of the nineteenth century Hindus comprised a much larger proportion of the urban population in Bengal than Muslims. The 1901 census put the proportion of Hindus in the total urban population of Bengal at 67 percent. Census of India, 1901, vol. 1-A: *India*, part II: *Tables*, table V, pp. 20–23, cited in R. Ahmed, *The Bengal Muslims, 1871–1906*, 2–3.

88. S. Sen, *Women and Labour in Late Colonial India*, 185.

89. For thoughtful, comprehensive discussions of these changes, see Oldenburg, *The Making of Colonial Lucknow*; Banerjee, *Dangerous Outcast*; R. Chatterjee, "Prostitution in Nineteenth Century Bengal"; and Dang, "Prostitutes, Patrons, and the State." One estimate puts the number of prostitutes in Calcutta in 1853 at 12,419 when the total population of the city was only 400,000; a decade later the population of the city was slightly smaller, but the number of prostitutes had swollen to an astounding 30,000. *Report of Chief Magistrate of Calcutta and Calcutta Municipal Corporation Health Report*, quoted in Chakravarty, *Condition of Bengali Women around the Second Half of the Nineteenth Century*, 97. Apart from widows of upper-caste Hindu families, many poor women were forced to enter the profession due to the destruction of the traditional structures of the rural economy and society. They joined the "hereditary prostitutes," those who were born into the trade. Banerjee, *Dangerous Outcast*, 77–83.

90. Memorandum by W. J. Moore, CIE, Surgeon-General, October 1886, Home Sanitary, June 1888. Quoted in Banerjee, *Dangerous Outcast*, 57 (on damsel-errantry, see 48).

91. Banerjee, *Dangerous Outcast*, 49–71.

92. Ballhatchet, *Race, Sex, and Class under the Raj*; Banerjee, *Dangerous Outcast*; Dang, "Prostitutes, Patrons, and the State."

93. The total number of prostitutes in the city of course exceeded thirty thousand.

94. Reports on the Workings of the Contagious Diseases Act [CDA] in Calcutta and its suburbs during the year 1882, Home-Sanitary, 1885, January, no. 91, cited in Banerjee, *Dangerous Outcast*, 83.

95. J. Nair, "Uncovering the Zenana," 25.

96. Ibid., 15–25.

97. Mackenzie, *Life in the Mission*, 204, cited in J. Nair, "Uncovering the Zenana," 10.

98. Carpenter, *Six Months in India*, 80, cited in J. Nair, "Uncovering the Zenana," 10.

99. J. Nair, "Uncovering the Zenana," 9–10.

100. Burton, *Burdens of History*, 60, 169.

101. M. Sinha, *Colonial Masculinity*.

102. P. Chatterjee, *The Nation and Its Fragments*, 118; Chakravarti, "Whatever Happened to the Vedic *Dasi*?" 34–36; Forbes, *Women in Modern India*, 4; Minault, *Secluded Scholars*, 2; Liddle and Joshi, "Gender and Imperialism in British India."

103. See, for instance, Chakrabarty, *Provincializing Europe*, 223–28; P. Chatterjee, *Nationalist Thought and the Colonial World*; P. Chatterjee, *The Nation and Its Fragments* (along with Tanika Sarkar's critical reading of Chatterjee in *Hindu Wife, Hindu Nation*, especially 24–25 and 191–94); Bayly, *Rulers, Townsmen, and Bazaars*; Bayly, *Indian Society and the Making of the British Empire*; O'Hanlon, "Issues of Widowhood"; Viswanathan, *Masks of Conquest*, 1–22; Banerjee, "Marginalization of Women's Popular Culture," 127–79; and Minault, *Secluded Scholars*, 2–4.

104. Minault, *Secluded Scholars*, 9; B. D. Metcalf, "Reading and Writing about Muslim Women in British India," 1–21; T. Sarkar, *Hindu Wife, Hindu Nation*, 23–52, 191–225.

105. For instance, the Muslim ulama seems to have been quite indifferent to British opinions of Muslim culture. B. D. Metcalf, "Reading and Writing about Muslim Women in British India," 6–7.

106. See, for instance, T. Sarkar, *Hindu Wife, Hindu Nation*, 23–52.

107. Banerjee, "Marginalization of Women's Popular Culture," 147–60. See also Banerjee, *Dangerous Outcast*.

108. Stoler, "Making Empire Respectable," 634–60.

2. THE POLITICS OF (IN)VISIBILITY

Material presented in this chapter previously appeared in Mahua Sarkar, "Muslim Women and the Politics of (In)visibility in Late Colonial Bengal," 226–50.

1. See Murshid, *The Reluctant Debutante*; and Engels, *Beyond Purdah?* For a critical commentary on this tendency, see Akhtar and Bhowmik, *Zenana Mehfil*, especially 25–27.

2. Needless to say, histories written in independent Bangladesh or by scholars from Bangladesh have often focused on Muslim women. A few examples are Pradhan, *Begum Rokeya O Narijagaran*; Akhtar and Bhowmik, *Zenana Mehfil*; Jahangir, *The Life and Works of Sufia Kamal*; and Sonia Nishat Amin, *The World of Muslim Women in Colonial Bengal, 1876–1939*.

3. For recent important research by authors from India that records Muslim women's intellectual activities in the late nineteenth century and the early twentieth, see Akhtar and Bhowmik, *Zenana Mehfil*; Sarker, "Larger than Bengal"; and Ray, *Early Feminists of Colonial India*.

4. For a discussion of the disappearance of lower caste and working women from the discourse of "ideal womanhood" in colonial India, see Chakravarti, "Whatever Happened to the Vedic *Dasi*?" 28, 78–79.

5. For discussions of the importance of the "other" to a western sense of self, history, and culture, see Said, *Orientalism*; Mani, *Contentious Traditions*; M. Sinha, *Colonial Masculinity*; J. Nair, "Uncovering the Zenana"; and Burton, *Burdens of History*. On British characterization of the "effeminate babu," see M. Sinha, *Colonial Masculinity*.

6. *Bhadrasampraday*, the Bengali term for the educated middle class, was coined in the nineteenth century. Literally it means the "civilized class or community." For a discussion of Bengali Hindu women's work, see Chakraborty, *Andare Antare*; and M. Bhattacharya and Sen, *Talking of Power*.

7. See M. Bhattacharya and Sen, *Talking of Power*, 1–16.

8. Mohanty, "Under Western Eyes," 53. See also Parry, "Problems in Current Theories of Colonial Discourse."

9. See Hunter, *The Indian Mussalmans*; and *Report of the Moslem Education*

Advisory Committee. For a discussion of this perception among Muslim intellectuals in early-twentieth-century Bengal, see chapter 3 of this book.

10. Banerjee, *Dangerous Outcast*, 88–89. According to colonial records cited by Banerjee, ten thousand of the twelve thousand prostitutes in Calcutta in the 1850s were Hindu women.

11. For a careful study of poor working women in colonial Bengal, see S. Sen, *Women and Labour in Late Colonial India*. See also Banerjee, "Marginalization of Women's Popular Culture in Nineteenth Century Bengal," for a discussion of the bhadralok's campaign of respectability, which effectively wiped out certain cultural practices common among working people in Bengal.

12. Muslim women from poor working-class backgrounds were of course entirely invisible in this discourse. The nationalist project in colonial India, as in most other parts of the world, was dominated by the middle classes. Because of its particular focus on this middle-class discourse, this chapter does not explicitly deal with Muslim women of the working classes.

13. J. W. Scott, "The Evidence of Experience."

14. Bengal, before Partition and India and Pakistan's independence, was one of the few Muslim-majority provinces in India. Calcutta was also the main seat of colonial power. Thus, it is not necessarily representative of the rest of India. However, because of particular sociopolitical configurations in Bengal—especially the presence of one of the first and more vocal nationalist elites and its strident efforts to create a national culture—the divides between modern/traditional, national/communal, and Hindu/Muslim were sharpened there. Thus, Calcutta provides a good site in which to study these processes. Also, as recent research has pointed out, similar problems of the silence and invisibility of Muslim women obtain in the written history of other parts of colonial India as well. See Lateef, *Muslim Women in India*; Minault, "Political Change," 194–203; Minault, "*Begamati Zuban*"; and B. D. Metcalf, "Reading and Writing about Muslim Women in British India." For discussions on low-caste and low-class women who were also marginalized in bhadralok discourse, see Chakravarti, "Whatever Happened to the Vedic *Dasi*?"; Visweswaran, "Small Speeches, Subaltern Gender"; R. Chatterjee "Prostitution in Nineteenth Century Bengal"; and S. Sen, *Women and Labour in Late Colonial India*.

15. Kandiyoti, "Identity and Its Discontents," 376–91; Pateman, *The Disorder of Women*; Yanagisako and Delaney, *Naturalizing Power*; Clawson, *Constructing Brotherhood*; Moghadam, *Identity Politics and Women*; Reynolds, "Marianne's Citizens?"; Landes, *Women and the Public Sphere in the Age of the French Revolution*; Fraser, "What's Critical about Critical Theory," 87.

16. Pateman, *Disorder of Women*, 36–41; Delaney, "Father State, Motherland, and the Birth of the Modern Turkey," 77; Schneider, *American Kinship*; Fanon, *Black Skin, White Masks*, 92. See also Sangari, *Politics of the Possible*, 366–68.

17. T. Sarkar, *Hindu Wife, Hindu Nation*, 36.

18. Ibid., 141. See also pages 35–44 for an illuminating discussion of tracts on marriage and the management of domestic affairs and the connections they make between the power and authority of the *karta* (head of household) within the household and his claims to political rights in the public sphere.

19. In mid-nineteenth-century Bengal, modernization for middle-class Hindu women entailed learning to read and write; picking up various hobbies, including music, gardening, sewing, and, more significant, leaving the seclusion of the inner quarters; and playing hostess to their husbands' guests. In time, women began attending school and even taking jobs outside the home. See, for instance, P. Chatterjee, *The Nation and Its Fragments*, especially 126–32 and 146–51; Murshid, *The Reluctant Debutante*, 99–127; Chakrabarty, *Provincializing Europe*, 225–226; Borthwick, *The Changing Role of Women in Bengal, 1849–1905*; and M. Bhattacharya and Sen, *Talking of Power*, 1–16.

20. T. Sarkar, "Hindu Conjugality and Nationalism in Late Nineteenth Century Bengal," 3.

21. T. Sarkar, *Hindu Wife, Hindu Nation*, 39. See also Dipesh Chakrabarty's discussion of "the ideals of modern Bengali patriarchy" in *Provincializing Europe*, especially 225–28.

22. The invisibility of "colonial companions" in nineteenth-century nationalist discourse should also be located in this context of the growing urgency to show the family as the "last bastion of freedom," that is, of nationalist male privilege and authority. For legitimacy in the conjugal sphere—whose first virtue is supposedly love—must necessarily involve not just coercion or the threat of it but also the willing submission of women to male demands—sexual and/or affective. Recognition of colonial companions—who chose or at least tolerated European male company, thereby adding substance to the colonial mockery of the (inadequate) manliness of "Indian" men—would essentially amount to an admission of such inadequacy on the part of the nationalist elite. See also Banerjee, "Marginalization of Women's Popular Culture in Nineteenth Century Bengal," especially 130–32, for an elaboration of a similar point in the context of poor working women's agency in Bengal.

23. Murshid, *The Reluctant Debutante*, 109.

24. M. Bhattacharya and Sen, *Talking of Power*, 15. Of course as Bhattacharya notes, such hegemonic aspirations were certainly not internalized in any seamless,

uncomplicated way, if it was internalized at all. The reference in the quote is to Thakur (Tagore), *Ghare Baire* (The Home and the World).

25. Chakravarti, "Whatever Happened to the Vedic *Dasi*?," 28–29.

26. Banerjee, "Marginalization of Women's Popular Culture in Nineteenth Century Bengal," 128–32; Banerjee, *Dangerous Outcast*; P. Chatterjee, *The Nation and Its Fragments*, 151–55.

27. Banerjee, "Marginalization of Women's Popular Culture in Nineteenth Century Bengal," 147. Bhadramahila were women of the educated middle class in Bengal.

28. R. Chatterjee, "Prostitution in Nineteenth Century Bengal," 162.

29. Lorde, "An Open Letter to Mary Daly," 95–97.

30. For early examples of such scholarship, see Bambara, *The Black Woman*; Carby, "White Woman Listen!"; Lorde, *Sister/Outsider*; hooks, "Ain't I A Woman?"; hooks, *Feminist Theory from Margin to Center*; Moraga and Anzaldúa, *This Bridge Called My Back*; and G. T. Hull et al., *All the Women Are White, All the Blacks Are Men, but Some of Us Are Brave*. For more recent feminist writings on Muslim and Middle Eastern women, see L. Ahmed, *Women and Gender in Islam*; Abu-Lughod, "The Marriage of Feminism and Islamism in Egypt"; Sullivan, "Eluding the Feminist, Overthrowing the Modern?"; Hoodfar, "The Veil in Their Minds and on Our Heads"; and Alvi et al., *The Muslim Veil in North America*.

31. Mohanty, "Cartographies of Struggle," 12–13; McClintock, "'No Longer in a Future Heaven'," 277; Visweswaran, *Fictions of Feminist Ethnography*, 75. See also Alarcón, "The Theoretical Subjects of *This Bridge Called My Back*."

32. See Burton, *Burdens of History*; Visweswaran, "Small Speeches, Subaltern Gender"; Tharu and Niranjana, "Problems for a Contemporary Theory of Gender"; and Frankenberg, *White Women, Race Matters*.

33. Carby, "White Woman Listen!" 214; hooks, *Black Looks*.

34. See Mohanty, "Cartographies of Struggle," 13.

35. L. Ahmed, *Women and Gender in Islam*, 163–64; Abu-Lughod, *Remaking Women*, 14. See also Lazreg, *The Eloquence of Silence*.

36. Visweswaran, "Small Speeches, Subaltern Gender," 87.

37. Connolly, *Identity/Difference*, 64. I am also thinking of a vast body of postcolonial and feminist scholarship that includes Said, *Orientalism*; Hall, "Introduction"; M. Sinha, *Colonial Masculinity*; M. Ferguson, *Subject to Others*; Burton, *Burdens of History*; Lewis, *Gendering Orientalism*; Mani, *Contentious Traditions*; and Ware, *Beyond the Pale*.

38. Mohanty, "Cartographies of Struggle," 12–13.

39. For a discussion of a similar process of masculinization of the category *dalit*

(untouchable) and the marking of the category "woman" as upper caste, see Tharu and Niranjana, "Problems for a Contemporary Theory of Gender," 243.

40. S. Bose and Jalal, *Modern South Asia*, 69–70; Guha, *A Rule of Property for Bengal*; A. K. Bagchi, *The Political Economy of Underdevelopment*, 71, 79–80.

41. Wolpert, *A New History of India*, 196–97; R. Ahmed, *The Bengal Muslims, 1871–1906.*

42. *Moslem Education Commission Report, 1934*; R. Ahmed, *The Bengal Muslims, 1871–1906*, 3; Dutta, *Unish Satake Muslim Manash O Bangabhanga*, 16; Hasan, *Begum Rokeya*, 1; Misra, *The Indian Middle Classes.*

43. T. Sarkar, *Hindu Wife, Hindu Nation*, 10, 33; Mukherji, "Foreign and Inland Trade"; S. Bhattacharya, "Traders and Trade in Old Calcutta"; Tripathi, *Trade and Finance in the Bengal Presidency, 1793–1833.*

44. Hasan, *Begum Rokeya*. See also Kopf, *British Orientalism and the Bengal Renaissance*; and V. C. Joshi, *Rammohun Roy and the Process of Modernization in India.*

45. Chakraborti, *The Bengali Press (1818–1868).*

46. R. Ahmed, *The Bengal Muslims, 1871–1906*, 106–32. Muslims, in fact, were quite wary, if not dismissive, of the Sanskritization of Bengali in the middle of the nineteenth century because it delegitimized the Mussalmani Bengali used in *punthi*, the manuscript literature popular among Muslims in Bengal. Mussalmani Bengali is distinctive in its use of many Arabic and Persian words.

47. Sumit Sarkar, *Modern India*, 75–76.

48. M. Sinha, *Colonial Masculinity*. Marwaris are a trading group from Marwar, the Jodhpur area of the present-day state of Rajasthan in India.

49. G. Ghosh, *Ramdoolal Dey*, quoted in T. Sarkar, *Hindu Wife, Hindu Nation*, 34.

50. Sumit Sarkar, "'Kaliyuga', 'Chakri,' and 'Bhakti.'"

51. Ibid., 1544.

52. M. Sinha, *Specters of Mother India*, 8.

53. In August 1858, the British Parliament passed the Government of India Act, which transferred the rule of India from the Company to the crown. See Wolpert, *A New History of India*, 238.

54. Hunter, *The Indian Mussalmans*. This turn to an explicitly paternalistic stance toward the "native" subjects is also reflected in the ruminations of E. C. P. Hull in his *The European in India or Anglo-Indian's Vade-Mecum* (1878). See, for instance, pages 192–95.

55. Rothermund, *Government, Landlord, and Peasant in India*, 100–105; T. Sarkar, *Hindu Wife, Hindu Nation*, 12–17, 36–37.

56. During the Wahhabi and Faraizi reform movements among Muslim peasants in the 1830s and 1840s, which were fueled as much by class-based grievances against landlords as by the push for the purification of the everyday practice of Islam, the colonial state had supported the Hindu zamindars. T. Sarkar, *Hindu Wife, Hindu Nation*, 12.

57. Lt. Gov. George Campbell, who was influenced by Ricardian thinking, considered rent to be "unearned income" and proposed to give tenants rights to the land they cultivated. The proposal was much moderated later, but it rattled the confidence and loyalty of the landowning middle class. See Rothermund, *Government, Landlord, and Peasant in India*, 100–105; T. Sarkar, *Hindu Wife, Hindu Nation*, 12–16. The 1870s also saw the beginnings of closely parallel agitations by lower-caste ryots against the tyranny of upper-caste landlords. S. Bandyopadhyay, *Caste, Protest, and Identity in Colonial India*. Pabna is a district in North Bengal, now in Bangladesh.

58. T. Sarkar, *Hindu Wife, Hindu Nation*, 36.

59. *Amrita Bazar Patrika, Report on Native Papers*, June 26, 1873, and *Halishahar Patrika*, July 1873, both cited in ibid., 16.

60. Commenting on the discursive formulations of the Hindu revivalist nationalists, Tanika Sarkar points to a growing animosity toward Muslims in late-nineteenth-century Bengal. See her discussion of Bankimchandra Chattopadhyay's work in this context in ibid., 135–62, and especially 141.

61. I am grateful to Mrinalini Sinha for insisting on this point in her comments on an earlier draft of this chapter.

62. I am drawing here on Benedict Anderson's argument in *Imagined Communities*. For a similar application of Anderson's idea to the discussion of British periodicals about India, see Burton, "Institutionalizing Imperial Reform," 24.

63. For a similar argument, see P. Chatterjee, *The Nation and Its Fragments*, 94. See also the discussion of the centrality of Hindu conjugality at the "formative moment" of militant nationalism in Bengal in T. Sarkar, "Colonial Lawmaking and Lives/Deaths of Indian Women." For a discussion of the rise of communalization among both Hindus and Muslims in Bengal in the 1920s, see Datta, *Carving Blocs*.

64. Although I have consulted a number of other periodicals of that time, in this chapter I focus on the four mentioned: *Antahpur*, *Mahila*, *Bharat Mahila*, and *Bamabodhini Patrika*. I should note that it is increasingly difficult to obtain copies of these early periodicals because of problems of preservation in both Calcutta and Dhaka.

65. Murshid, *The Reluctant Debutante*, 233.

66. Until the 1860s, education in the zenanas had been mainly carried out under the aegis of Christian missionaries. See *Sixtieth Report of Society for Promoting Female Education in the East*; and *Female Education in India and Ceylon*. See also Borthwick, *The Changing Role of Women in Bengal, 1849–1905*; and Engels, *Beyond Purdah?* For an Account of early education and reforms among Bengali middle-class women, see Chakraborty, *Andare Antare*.

67. *Bamabodhini Patrika* was supposed to have enjoyed a readership of about six hundred, not all of whom were from Calcutta. Murshid, *The Reluctant Debutante*, 240.

68. For forty-four of these sixty years, *Bamabodhini* was edited by its founder, Umeshchandra Datta. As Murshid points out, it therefore offers the "singular opportunity of looking at how in the face of new social and political developments like the emergence of nationalism, Bengali attitudes towards the social reform movement underwent a metamorphosis and how the government itself took a different shape" (ibid.).

69. All the translations from Bengali are mine.

70. In this context, the following clarification offered by Partha Chatterjee is useful: "Significantly, the word jati in most Indian languages can be used to designate not merely caste, but caste agglomerations, tribes, race, linguistic groups, religious groups, nationalities, nations." P. Chatterjee, *The Nation and Its Fragments*, 166.

71. *Purdah* literally means "curtain" and refers to the seclusion of women. It is also spelled *pardah* and *parda*. Seclusion can take various forms, ranging from women's confinement within the home to the use of veils in public places.

72. "*Abarodhprathar Utpatti*" [The Origins of Seclusion], *Bamabodhini Patrika*, July-August, 1891.

73. Sri Mrinmayee Sen, "Bharatmahilar Shiksha" [Education of the Indian Woman], *Antahpur*, August-September 1902. For more on "civilized *jati*," see Viswanathan, "Ethnographic Politics and the Discourse of Origins," 121–39. It is important to remember, however, that *race* as it was used in the South Asian context does not necessarily carry the same meanings with which it is invested in the West. See Robb, introduction to *Concept of Race in South Asia*, 1–76.

74. Cited in M. Bhattacharya and Sen, *Talking of Power*, 7, 14. See also Sri Mrinmayee Sen, "Bharatmahilar Shiksha" [Education of the Indian Woman], *Antahpur*, August-September 1902.

75. Kedarnath Majumdar, "Sanjayer Nutan Grantha" [The New Book of Sanjay], *Aarati Patrika*, 2nd year, nos. 6–7, cited in *Nabanoor*, August-September 1903.

76. "Ideals of Indian Womanhood," *Indian Social Reformer*, September 24, 1927, 56, cited in Forbes, *Women in Modern India*, 16. See also, Bhattacharyya, *Ideals of Indian Womanhood*.

77. Bethune was the first girls' school in Bengal that catered exclusively to the Hindu middle class. By 1849, it was known as the Female Normal School.

78. Speech by Lord Bethune, reprinted in *Bamabodhini Patrika* in 1895 (my translation). See also Bhattacharjee and Sen, *Bethune College Centenary Volume, 1879–1979*.

79. According to Tharu and Lalitha, Pandita Ramabai Saraswati was a "legend in her own lifetime." Tharu and Lalita, *Women Writing in India*, 243. Ramabai's books include her autobiography, *My Testimony* (1907), *Stree Dharma Neeti* (Morals for Women) (1882), and *The High Caste Hindu Woman* (1888). For thoughtful discussions of Ramabai's life and work, see Chakravarti, *Rewriting History*; and Burton, *At the Heart of the Empire*, especially 72–109.

80. According to Pandita Ramabai Saraswati, the deeply rooted distrust and low opinion of women revealed in the laws of Manu—the source of much of Hindu opinion about women—is "at the root of seclusion of women in India. This mischievous custom has greatly increased and has become intensely tyrannical since the Mahometan invasion; but that it existed from about the sixth century, BC, cannot be denied. . . . All male relatives are commanded by the law to deprive the women of the household of all their freedom." Saraswati, *The High-Caste Hindu Woman*, 29–30.

81. Ghosh's comments were published in *Nabanoor*, January-February 1904. Muslim responses to Hindu allegations can be seen in the pages of the Muslim-edited periodicals that began to appear at the beginning of the twentieth century. We will look at them in some detail in chapter 3.

82. Sumit Sarkar, "Rammohun Roy and the Break with the Past," 52–53; Mani, "Contentious Traditions," 114.

83. On women as sexual servants, see Engels, *Beyond Purdah?* 84–85; and John and Nair, introduction to *A Question of Silence?* 1–51.

84. See J. Nair, "Uncovering the Zenana," 9, for a similar argument regarding the attitudes of British women toward their Indian counterparts. For a discussion of the importance of the ideas of enclosure and freedom in Bengali Hindu discourse in the late nineteenth century, see Bannerji, "Attired in Virtue," 85–86.

85. P. Chatterjee, *The Nation and Its Fragments*, 6.

86. "*Mahiladiger Aborodhpratha*" [The Seclusion of Women], *Mahila*, September-October 1903. It is important to mention here that life in the zenana was not always as oppressive for all women, everywhere, as it is generally as-

sumed. According to Brajendranath Bandopadhyay, "It is generally assumed that women in the Mughal harems lived a miserable, degenerate life filled with only luxury and mindless pleasure. Historically, however, many of the Mughal women we come across astonish us with their learning, the breadth of their knowledge . . . and their many literary and artistic achievements." Bandopadhyay, *Mogoljuge Strishiksha*, 1–3 (translated from Bengali). I have come across similar arguments in conversations with both Muslim and Hindu women who had spent some part of their lives in seclusion. For a recent study of Mughal domestic life, see Lal, *Domesticity and Power in the Early Mughal World*.

87. Datta, *Carving Blocs*.

88. Bannerji, "Attired in Virtue," 86.

89. For other instances of this distancing/exclusionary move, see Soudamini Khastagir, "Striloker Paricchhad" [Women's Clothing], *Bamabodhini Patrika*, August-September 1872, cited in Bannerji, "Attired in Virtue," 94–95.

90. Hemantakumari Choudhuri, "Striloker Paricchhad" [Women's Clothing], *Antahpur*, June-July 1901, cited with the same title in Bannerji, "Attired in Virtue," 82, 86; and, under a slightly different title ("Mahilar Paricchhad"), cited in M. Bhattacharya and Sen, *Talking of Power*, 88–93. Begums are wives.

91. Cited in S. Emdad Ali, "*Mussalmaner Prati Hindu Lekhaker Atyachar*" [The Unfairness of Hindu Writers toward Muslims], *Nabanoor*, August-September 1903. This article elicited a sharp response from the editor of *Nabanoor* in one of the earliest known public written protests by Bengali Muslim intellectuals.

92. Saratkumari Chaudhurani, "Ekal O Ekaler Meye" [The Modern Age and the Modern Woman], *Bharati O Balak*, October-December 1891, translated and reprinted in M. Bhattacharya and Sen, *Talking of Power*, 56–68. See also Hemantakumari Chaudhuri, "Mahilar Parichhad," included in the same collection (88–93).

93. M. Bhattacharya and Sen, *Talking of Power*, 14–15.

94. Mankumari Basu, in *Bamabodhini Patrika*, November-December 1894–September-October 1895 (emphasis added).

95. The school reportedly started with 18 students but did not last long. In December 1823, *Samachar Darpan*, a newspaper, reported on an examination held for 150 Hindu and Muslim girls. See Binay Ghosh, *Bidya Sagar O Bangali Samaj*, cited in Hasan, *Begum Rokeya*, 11–13.

96. Banerjee, *Dangerous Outcast*, 14, 92.

97. Mackenzie Report, 1872, cited in R. Chatterjee, "Prostitution in Nineteenth Century Bengal," 162.

98. For an extensive discussion of Rokeya's argument, see chapter 3 of this book.

99. *Mahila*, July-August 1903.

100. Ibid. (emphasis added).

101. See, most recently, M. Bhattacharya and Sen, *Talking of Power*, especially 1–16.

102. Editorial, *Mahila*, July-August 1903.

103. *Mahila*, July-August 1903. The borkha, or burka, is a veiling gown designed to cover the whole body of a woman.

104. See, for instance, Hossain, *Abarodhbashini*, which was published serially in *Mashik Mohammadi* between 1928 and 1930; and Hossain, *"Sultana's Dream."*

105. See Saraswati, *The High-Caste Hindu Woman*. For a discussion of the continued subjection of the bhadramahila, see Engels, *Beyond Purdah?*

106. Reported in a leading Muslim periodical, *Mihir O Sudhakar*, in 1895, cited in Hasan, *Begum Rokeya*, 47–48.

107. Shibnarayan Ray, "Bangalir Atmajignasha," *Purogami*, February 16, 1979, cited in Akhtar and Bhowmik, *Zenana Mehfil*, 5.

108. As Mr. Bethune succinctly put it in his speech at the inauguration of the Bethune School in 1849, women's education was important first because educated men wanted and needed educated wives. Moreover, women's education was also a significant measure of the level of civilization in any society, and since women had an immense influence on the minds of children educated mothers were essential to the proper upbringing of children. Speech by Bethune, 1849, reprinted in *Bamabodhini Patrika*, 1895.

109. See P. Chatterjee, *The Nation and Its Fragments*; Chakravarti, "Whatever Happened to the Vedic *Dasi*?"; Chakraborty, *Andare, Antare*. See also M. Sinha, *Colonial Masculinity*; and Murshid, *The Reluctant Debutante* for discussions of the age of consent controversy of 1891. P. Chatterjee, "The Nationalist Resolution of the Women's Question," 233–53, and Chakravarti, "Whatever Happened to the Vedic *Dasi*," 76–78.

110. Visweswaran, "Small Speeches, Subaltern Gender." See also Tanika Sarkar's critique of the idea of "resolution" of the woman question in *Hindu Wife, Hindu Nation*, 23–25.

111. M. Bhattacharya and Sen, *Talking of Power*, 7–8.

112. Ibid., 15–16.

113. For a comparison of the work of Rokeya and that of other Bengali women, see Murshid, *Rasasundari Theke Rokeya*.

114. Sumit Sarkar, *Modern India*, 106–25. According to Sumit Sarkar, "Despite . . . the presence of an extremely active and sincere group of Swadeshi [i.e., opposed to the partition] Muslim agitators . . . the British propaganda that the new province would mean more jobs for Muslims did achieve considerable success in swaying upper and middle class Muslims against the Swadeshi movement" (121–22). See also the discussion of the loyalism of elite Muslims in chapter 3 of this book.

115. *Bharat Mahila* means "Indian Woman." Issues discussed in the magazine in 1913 included the activities of various women's organizations in major urban centers in Bengal (Calcutta Mahila Parishad, Dhaka Mahila Samiti, and the Maimansingh Samiti), the backwardness of women in the previous generation, and the problems of widows, prostitutes, and low-caste Hindus.

116. "Bibidha Prasanga," *Bharat Mahila*, April-May 1913. It is possible that the editor of this issue was Sarajoobala Debi.

117. Sri Pratibha Nag, "Mahilar Karjya," *Bharat Mahila*, December-January 1914.

118. The manuscript of *Humayun-Nama*—a long panegyric in Persian written by Gulbadan about her brother, the emperor Humayun—is preserved in the British Library. A Mrs. Beveridge translated it into English. For a rare study of education among Mughal women, see Bandopadhyay, *Mogoljuge Stree Shiksha*. Khadeja was the Prophet Muhammad's first wife. An independent, wealthy woman, Khadeja—herself a widow in her forties—married Muhammad when he was a young man. She was instrumental in the development of both his person and his vocation. See L. Ahmed, "Women and the Advent of Islam." Jumma Masjid is a famous mosque in Delhi. These are only a few examples of very accomplished elite Muslim women who are routinely ignored by nationalist historiography. There were many others, even within the Mughal aristocracy, who could be inspiring symbols of Indian womanhood. See Bandopadhyay, *Moguljuge Stree Shiksha* for further discussion on this subject. See also Lal, *Domesticity and Power in the early Mughal World*.

119. McClintock, "'No Longer in a Future Heaven,'" 264.

120. The other common role given to Muslim women is that of the baiji, the courtesan/prostitute. See Sen Samartha, "Tinsho Bachharer Kolkata." Also see T. Sarkar, "The Woman as Communal Subject."

121. McClintock, "'No Longer in a Future Heaven,'" 264.

122. Datta, *Carving Blocs*. See also the film *Father, Son, and Holy War* (dir. Anand Patwardhan, 1995) for a useful exploration of the relationship between masculinity, religion, and violence. I am drawing here also on Ranajit Guha's in-

sights on liberal historiography and its implications for colonial domination in his 1989 essay, "Dominance without Hegemony and Its Historiography," 215, 306–7; and his 1997 book, *Dominance without Hegemony*.

123. The Bengal Pact was an agreement between Hindus and Muslims brokered in December 1923 by the Swarajist Party under the aegis of the widely respected and popular C. R. Das. See Sumit Sarkar, *Modern India*, 232.

124. See Datta, *Carving Blocs*, for an in-depth account of this process of increasing communalization of both Hindus and Muslims in the early decades of the twentieth century. Goondas are hooligans or strongmen.

125. Census of India, 1891, vol. 3: *Bengal*; Datta, *Carving Blocs*, 23–24.

126. Datta, *Carving Blocs*, 28–30, 197. Mukherji seems to have borrowed his ideas from comments made by British officials in a number of census reports from the early twentieth century.

127. For an example of the fearmongering by the Hindu Right, see Pandit Devratan Sarma, Secretary, Hindu Maha Sabha, in *Amrita Bazar Patrika*, December 1, 1925, cited in Datta, *Carving Blocs*, 62.

128. Mayo, *Mother India*. See also M. Sinha, *Specters of Mother India*, 5. As Sinha points out, Mayo further suggests that the "social backwardness" of India (i.e., Hindus) is in fact indicative of a fundamental incapacity for self-governance among Indians.

129. Datta, *Carving Blocs*, 148–237. In the 1930s, the Women's Protection League began to recognize that "abducted" women sometimes consented to leaving their homes, clearly without necessarily understanding the violence that awaited them.

130. I disagree with Datta's assertion, in *Carving Blocs*, 155–57, that there was a noticeable turn within the Hindu communalist discourse toward "gender-related" issues in the 1920s. Datta is right, of course, in perceiving a shift toward a preoccupation with such issues as child marriage, purdah, and widows in the 1920s, but he seems to confuse (and conflate) "gender" with "women" in this instance.

131. Ibid., 181.

132. The Women's Protection League, *Report of the Year 1935–37*, 10, cited in Datta, *Carving Blocs*, 212–13. The trend continued into the following decade when the numbers of Muslim and Hindu women abducted between 1934 and 1938 were 2,290 and 2,072, respectively. The Women's Protection League, *Report of the Year 1938*.

133. This point that was made most succinctly, perhaps, in Rokeya Sakhawat Hossain's novel *Padmarag*, reprinted in Quadir, *Begum Rokeya Rachanabali*, 293–428.

134. In Datta's *Carving Blocs*—an excellent and detailed study of the calcification of communal politics in early-twentieth-century Bengal in general and the abductions debate in particular—the reader has to wait until page 212 in a chapter that runs between pages 148 and 237 to learn that more Muslim than Hindu women were abducted. In fact, the actual number of women abducted only appears in a footnote on pages 212–13. I make this comment not so much to criticize the author as to point once again to the difficulties of writing about subjects who are written out of normative history.

3. NEGOTIATING MODERNITY

1. The epigraph quote is from Sufia Kamal, letter to the editor of *Saogat*, M. Nasiruddin, July 23, 1929, reprinted in Akhtar and Bhowmick, *Zenana Mehfil*, 21, 230.

2. *Pardanishin* is an adjective used to describe women who observe purdah or seclusion. The epigraph quote is from Rokeya Sakhawat Hossain's "Sultana's Dream," reprinted in *"Sultana's Dream" and Selections from "The Secluded Ones,"* 7–9.

3. For biographical information on Rokeya Sakhawat Hossain, see S. Mahmud, *Rokeya Jibani*; Tharu and Lalita, *Women Writing in India*, 1:340–42; Quadir, *Begum Rokeya Rachanabali*, 7–10; Akhtar and Bhowmick, *Zenana Mehfil*, 3–6; Murshid, *Rasasundari Theke Rokeya*, 128–39; and Hossain, *"Sultana's Dream" and Selections from "The Secluded Ones,"* x–xi.

4. Tharu and Lalita, *Women Writing in India*, 1:340.

5. Murdanas (men's quarters).

6. Tharu and Lalita. *Women Writing in India*, 1:1; Jahan, "Sultana's Dream: Purdah Reversed," 2.

7. For important exceptions to this trend, see Tharu and Lalita, *Women Writing in India*. On the abundance of publications focused on Rokeya, see Akhtar, "Keno Ami Zenana Mehfil-e," 38.

8. For recent discussions of Rokeya's work in English, see Ray, *Early Feminists of Colonial India*; Sonia Nishat Amin, "The Changing World of Bengali Muslim Women"; Sarker, "Larger than Bengal"; and M. Bhattacharya and Sen, *Talking of Power*.

9. See, for instance, Smith and Carroll, *Women's Political and Social Thought*.

10. For two important exceptions, see the anthology edited by Akhtar and

Bhowmick, *Zenana Mehfil*; and Sonia Nishat Amin, *The World of Muslim Women in Colonial Bengal, 1876.*

11. Yasmin Hossein makes a similar point in "Prekshapat," 13. Hossein, in fact, believes there is a larger political significance to women making their appearance in public for the first time.

12. Some important exceptions to this tendency are Mohammad Nasiruddin, *Bangla Sahitye Saogat Jug*; Sonia Nishat Amin, *The World of Muslim Women in Colonial Bengal, 1876–1939*; and Akhtar and Bhowmick, *Zenana Mehfil.*

13. For one example of the fleeting appearance of the Bengali Muslim intelligentsia, see Sumit Sarkar's discussion of the Swadeshi movement in *Modern India*, 121. For a more detailed discussion of a few Muslim writers in Bengal and some of their views, see Datta, *Carving Blocs*. For accounts of "separatism" among Muslims outside of Bengal, see Hardy, *The Muslims of British India*; B. D. Metcalf, *Islamic Revival in British India*; Minault, *The Khilafat Movement*; and F. Robinson, *Separatism among Indian Muslims*. For a feminist reading of this tendency to associate Muslims with separatism in colonial India, see Lambert-Hurley, "Fostering Sisterhood." By *Partition*, I mean the 1947 division of pre-independence India, which resulted in two nation-states at that time—India and Pakistan. Pakistan itself consisted of West and East Pakistan. In 1971, East Pakistan became independent Bangladesh.

14. Duara, *Rescuing History from the Nation*, 3.

15. I am not suggesting that Muslims elsewhere in the subcontinent were disallowed other contexts of historical agency, although the Partition clearly played an enormous role in determining how Muslims came to be thought about in postcolonial India. For a discussion of related issues, see Pandey, "Can a Muslim Be an Indian?"

16. Popular Memory Group, "Popular Memory," 76.

17. I am drawing here on Stuart Hall's insight that cultural identity is as much a matter of "becoming" as "being." See Hall, "Cultural Identity and Diaspora," 394.

18. Not all of the important periodicals were published in Calcutta or Dhaka. For example, *Kohinoor* (founded in 1894) was first published in Kushthiya (now in Bangladesh) in 1903 and later in Faridpur (also in Bangladesh). *Mohammadi* (founded in 1927) similarly began in Calcutta but moved eventually to Dhaka, while another bimonthly, *Tarun* (founded in 1928), was published in Bagura.

19. Most Hindus did not read Muslim-edited newspapers and journals, but Muslims read Hindu/Brahmo publications. Datta, *Carving Blocs*, 68. This asymmetri-

cal relationship in the sphere of cultural consumption unfortunately continues in the context of books published in West Bengal and Bangladesh. See Akhtar, "Keno Ami Zenana Mehfil-e," 36. In my interviews with both Hindu and Muslim women, I was repeatedly confronted with the fact that, while many middle-class Muslim women seemed to be familiar with the work of Hindu writers from both the pre-Partition and postindependence eras, very few Hindu women had heard anything about Muslim writers. To my knowledge, this trend largely continues today.

20. Islam, *Muslim Public Opinion as Reflected in the Bengali Press, 1901–1930*, 1. The Swadeshi movement—a movement to boycott foreign goods in favor of home industries—was, of course, launched mainly by the Hindu bhadralok. While some members of the Muslim elite supported it, Muslims in general did not participate in great numbers. See Sumit Sarkar, *Modern India*, 111–25. For discussions of some of the early periodicals and newspapers published by Muslims, see Nasiruddin, *Bangla Sahitye Saogat Jug*, 27–28; Anisuzzaman, *Muslim Banglar Samayikpatra*, 37; Datta, *Unish Satake Muslim Mana*; and Monir, *Bangla Sahitye Bangali Musalmaner Chintadhara*.

21. Islam, *Samayikpatre Jiban o Janamat*, 11; see also Swarochish Sarkar, *Kathasahitye O Natake*, 11.

22. For an example of the colonial tendency to equate the rise in vernacular literature with progress, see selections from the Records of Government, North-Western Provinces, Allahabad, 1870, cited in Majeed, "Narratives of Progress and Idioms of Community," 138–39. Negotiations with capitalist/colonial modernity were not limited to the subcontinent of course. For useful discussions of this process, especially as it pertained to women, see Abu-Lughod, *Remaking Women*; Yuval-Davis and Webner, *Women, Citizenship, and Difference*; Lewis, *Rethinking Orientalism*; and Martin, *Woman and Modernity*.

23. Majeed, "Narratives of Progress and Idioms of Community," 154. See also T. R. Metcalf, *Ideologies of the Raj*.

24. Swarochish Sarkar, *Kathasahitya O Natake*, 35. For a discussion of the importance of periodicals to the female reform and suffrage movement in Victorian Britain, as well as to those British who were interested in social reform in India, see Burton, *Burdens of History*; and "Institutionalizing Imperial Reform."

25. For more information on these periodicals, see Anisuzzaman, *Muslim Banglar Samayikpatra*, 10–553; Mohammad Nasiruddin, *Bangla Sahitye Saogat Jug*, 27–30; and Islam, *Samayikpatre Jiban o Janamat*, 427–51.

26. See, for instance, R. Ahmed, *The Bengal Muslims, 1871–1906*; and *Understanding the Bengal Muslims*.

27. I am referring here to Joan Wallach Scott's formulation in *Gender and the Politics of History*, 42–43.

28. R. Ahmed, *The Bengal Muslims, 1871–1906*; R. Ahmed, *Understanding the Bengal Muslims*.

29. Hunter, *The Indian Mussalmans*. The book was published in 1871 and reprinted in 1876 and 2002. According to Raffiuddin Ahmed, *atrap* is the "Bengali equivalent of *ailaf*," or Muslims of low status. R. Ahmed, *The Bengal Muslims, 1871–1906*, 195 n. 71. The term is often spelled as *atraf*. See, for instance, Sonia Nishat Amin, *The World of Muslim Women in Colonial Bengal, 1876–1939*, 17; Monir, *Bangla Sahitye*, 251; and Datta, *Unish Satake*, 9.

30. Aparna Basu, *The Growth of Education and Political Development in India, 1898–1920*.

31. Census figures from 1872 report that in the last quarter of the nineteenth century 48 percent of the total population of the province of Bengal followed Islam and most of these were cultivators. Cited in R. Ahmed, *The Bengal Muslims, 1871–1906*, 2–3. See also Sayeed, *The Political System of Pakistan*.

32. R. Ahmed, *The Bengal Muslims, 1871–1906*, 2–3; see also S. Ahmed, *The Muslim Community in Bengal, 1884–1912*, 100–103.

33. For a detailed analysis of class divisions within the Muslim community, see R. Ahmed, *The Bengal Muslims, 1871–1906*; and *Understanding the Bengal Muslims*. According to Ahmed, the notion of a homogeneous community was formalized in Hunter's *The Indian Mussalmans*. Punthis, handwritten manuscripts, remained a popular vehicle for Mussalmani Bengali literature long after the standardization of Sanskritized Bengali by the Hindu intelligentsia.

34. N. A. K. Yusufzai, "Note on Muhammadan Education in Bengal" (1903), cited in S. Ahmed, *The Muslim Community in Bengal, 1884–1912*, 9. See also Eaton, *The Rise of Islam and the Bengal Frontier, 1204–1760*.

35. Manrique, *Travels of Fray Sebastien Manrique, 1629–1643*, 1–40; Eaton, "Who Are the Bengal Muslims?" 26–51. On Mughal opinions of Bengalis in general, see Eaton, "Who Are the Bengal Muslims?" especially 27–28.

36. Eaton, "Who Are the Bengal Muslims?" 34–35.

37. Ibid. According to Eaton, it is not quite correct to claim that Bengali Muslims were converts from Hinduism since Brahminical Hinduism had little or no sway over these remote areas in eastern Bengal. It is surprising that Eaton should conflate Hinduism and Brahminism—a rather narrow and elitist set of practices—while he makes a credible case for treating the syncretic practices of the Bengali countryside as a legitimate form of Islam. For a recent description of syncretic

religiosity in the Sundarban region of Bengal, see the discussions of Bon Bibi and Shah Jangoli in A. Ghosh, *The Hungry Tide*. See also R. Ahmed, *The Bengal Muslims, 1871–1906*, 68–69.

38. R. Ahmed, *The Bengal Muslims, 1871–1906*, 85–86. See also Asim Roy, *The Islamic Syncretistic Tradition in Bengal*.

39. R. Ahmed, "The Emergence of the Bengal Muslims," 5, 85–86. A maulvi is a Muslim scholar and teacher.

40. R. Ahmed, *The Bengal Muslims, 1871–1906*, xxvi. See also R. Ahmed, "Emergence of the Bengal Muslims," 1–25. *Jum'a* (or *jumah* or *jumma*) are the Friday congregational prayers.

41. Beveridge, *The District of Bakarganj*, 211. Beveridge seems to have advised against separate classifications for the peasantry. The idea of general amity between the Hindu and Muslim masses in rural Bengal was also confirmed by a number of Muslim women I spoke to. A few actually remembered having attended Hindu religious and social events in their childhoods. See Census of Bengal, 1881, vol. 1, 78; and Carstairs, *Human Nature in Rural India*, 82–83, both cited in R. Ahmed, *The Bengal Muslims, 1871–1906*, 4–5.

42. R. Ahmed, *The Bengal Muslims, 1871–1906*, 7; Swarochish Sarkar, *Kathasahitya O Natake*, 39. See also Beveridge, *The District of Bakarganj*, 211; and Carstairs, *Human Nature in Rural India*, 82–83, cited in R. Ahmed, *The Bengal Muslims, 1871–1906*, 4–5.

43. Although the Tariqah-I-Muhammadiya movement began in North India around 1818 under Sayed Ahmad, in Bengal most of its impact was felt after 1831 under the leadership of two of his followers, Belayet Ali and Enayet Ali. It was finally crushed by the colonial government in 1870 (see Monir, *Bangla Sahitye*, 12–17; and Swarochish Sarkar, *Kathasahitya O Natake*, 20–22). The Faraizi movement was launched by Haji Shariatullah in 1818 in eastern Bengal. It was radicalized later under the leadership of Dudumian and ended more or less with his death in 1862 (see Monir, *Bangla Sahitye*, 19–20; and Swarochish Sarkar, *Kathasahitya O Natake*, 18–19). Maulavi Nisar Ali, also known as Titu Mir, founded the third religious-economic reformist movement in western Bengal. Titu Mir was a disciple of Sayed Ahmad, who centered the Tariqah movement in Patna (see Monir, *Bangla Sahitye*, 17–19; and Swarochish Sarkar, *Kathasahitya O Natake*, 21–22).

44. R. P. Dutt, *India Today*; Sumit Sarkar, *Modern India*, especially 24–37. For a discussion of reformist/revivalist movements among Hindus in northern India, see Sumit Sarkar, *Modern India*, 70–76.

45. Romesh Chunder Dutt, *The Economic History of India in the Victorian Age*,

viii; Baran, *The Political Economy of Growth*, 134–62; Mahua Sarkar, "Labor Protest and Capital Relocation in a Labour-Intensive Industry." See also Dicken, *Global Shift*, 233; and Braudel, *Civilisation and Capitalism, Fifteenth–Eighteenth Centuries*, 572.

46. R. P. Dutt, *India Today*, 44–48; Datta, *Unish Sataker Muslim Manas*, 14.

47. For discussions of the destruction of artisanal industries and its effect specifically on rural Bengal, see S. Sen, *Women and Labour in Late Colonial India*; and P. Chatterjee, "Agrarian Structure in Pre-Partition Bengal." For general commentaries on the effect of British rule on India, see Mark and Engels, *Selected Works*, 312–13; Baran, *The Political Economy of Growth*; and Romesh Chunder Dutt, *The Economic History of India in the Victorian Age*.

48. Sumit Sarkar, *Modern India*, 51–53; Datta, *Unish Sataker Muslim Manas*, 12–15.

49. About these movements, R. Ahmed writes, "The Tariqah-I-Muhammadiya and the Faraizi were two of the earliest and most prominent among these [movements]. The Tariqah movement, erroneously called Indian Wahhabism, belonged to the tradition of the Waliullahi School of Delhi and was . . . an extension of the jihad movement launched by Shah Sayyid Ahmed (1786–1831) of Rae Bareli in northern India. . . . The Faraizi movement was typically an indigenous movement and was inseparably connected with the socio-economic life of the rural Muslim" (*The Bengal Muslims, 1871–1906*, 39).

50. Qureshi, *The Muslim Community of the Indo-Pakistan Subcontinent, 1610–1947*; Hardy, *The Muslims of British India*; R. Ahmed, *The Bengal Muslims, 1871–1906*.

51. Titu Mir, for instance, is supposed to have announced that for "those who are not Muslim, to fight unnecessarily with them only on the basis of religious difference is not to the liking of Allah or his Rasul. In fact what [the Prophet] has preached is that if a powerful non-Muslim . . . [oppresses] a poor non-Muslim . . . then it is the duty of the Muslim to help [the latter]." Siddiqui, *Sahid Titu Mir*, 44, cited in Swarochish Sarkar, *Kathasahitya O Natake*, 22. One Hindu zamindar was known to have taxed Muslim peasants who wore beards, built mosques, and became disciples of the revivalist leaders at a higher rate. He further decreed that any Muslim who slaughtered a cow would have his hands cut off. See Swarochish Sarkar, *Kathasahitya O Natake*, 22.

52. Datta, *Unish Sataker Muslim Manas*, 24–26.

53. Sumit Sarkar, *Modern India*, 78.

54. Datta, *Unish Sataker Muslim Manas*, 30–31.

55. The reforms that the urban elite Muslims supported were invested in reconciling a revival of the ancient "glory of Islam" with a "modern spirit" and "co-operation with the west." R. Ahmed, *The Bengal Muslims, 1871–1906*, 95.

56. Ibid., 82–91.

57. See Datta, *Carving Blocs*, especially 87–94; and R. Ahmed, *The Bengal Muslims, 1871–1906*, especially 98–101.

58. Note that even in the second half of the nineteenth century Muslims were not the only ones to use Urdu in the subcontinent. As Javed Majeed points out, Urdu periodicals in North India had a readership that was quite comfortable with both the Perso-Arabic and *devnagri* (used by Sanskrit and Hindi) scripts. A significant number of Urdu periodicals from the 1860s and 1870s were even owned by non-Muslims. For an informative discussion of this "flexible landscape of nineteenth-century India," see Majeed, "Narratives of Progress and Idioms of Community," 135–63.

59. The ashraf may have had affinities with the Hindu ruling class at least in terms of a shared sense of historical legacy if not cultural practice. As Majeed notes in his analysis of Urdu periodicals from North India around the 1870s, the polyglot imaginary of that time allowed for the admixture of "Hindu and Muslim elements [so that] . . . all rulers . . . [were] treated as part of a continuum, and as belonging to a category of their own which . . . [had] little to do with everyday life. . . . The different strands of . . . [a narrative of former kings, for instance] . . . [had] yet to be communalized, while the elements of myth, legend and history . . . [were] conflated, rather than distinguished from one another" ("Narratives of Progress and Idioms of Community," 142–43).

60. R. Ahmed, *The Bengal Muslims, 1871–1906*, 113–15.

61. Majeed, "Narratives of Progress and Idioms of Community," 139; Minault, *Secluded Scholars*, 18. See also Baljon, *The Reforms and Religious Ideas of Sir Sayyid Ahmad Khan*; and Graham, *The Life and Work of Sir Syed Ahmad Khan*.

62. Sumit Sarkar, *Modern India*, 78. On British patronage of sharif Muslims, see Majeed, "Narratives of Progress and Idioms of Community," 139–40.

63. Kabbani, *Europe's Myth of Orient*; Said, *Orientalism*; Miles and Brown, *Racism*. In contrast to Sir Sayyed and Nawab Abdul Lateef, Ameer Ali was less enamored of the British. His goal was to maintain a friendly relationship with the British but simultaneously push for self-rule. Monir, *Bangla Sahitye*, 34; Swarochish Sarkar, *Kathasahitya O Natake*, 24.

64. R. Ahmed, *The Bengal Muslims, 1871–1906*, 1–38; Y. Hossein, "Prekshapat," 14; Datta, *Unish Sataker Muslim Manas*, 19; Majeed, "Narratives of Progress and Idioms of Community," especially 138–41.

65. R. Ahmed, "The Emergence of Bengal Muslims," 18–19. See also Viswanathan, "Masks of Conquest"; and the discussion in chapter 4 of this book.

66. See P. Chatterjee, *The Nation and Its Fragments*, 6, 9; and T. Sarkar, *Hindu Wife, Hindu Nation*, for instance, 38–44.

67. This is often highlighted in the literature on nineteenth-century reforms in Bengal. For one example, see Swarochish Sarkar, *Kathasahitya O Natake*, 37.

68. Mill, *The History of British India*, 309–10.

69. It is important to note that elsewhere in the colonial world the British, as well as other European powers, often marked Islamic cultures as "backward," citing the "degradations of harem life" as proof thereof. See, for instance, the discussion of British colonial discourse in Egypt in Mitchell, *Colonising Egypt*, 111–13. On satidhaha, see Swarochish Sarkar, *Kathasahitya O Natake*, 169.

70. R. Ahmed, *The Bengal Muslims, 1871–1906*, 85.

71. Amin defines the *nashihat nama* as "a special brand of punthi literature meant to be recited. . . . [Nashiat namas] were the most popular medium of didactic literature," in vogue even in medieval Bengal. See Sonia Nishat Amin, *The World of Muslim Women in Colonial Bengal, 1876*, 47. Ahmed's discussion of late-nineteenth-century nashihat namas suggests that they may have been printed while the earlier ones were handwritten in the punthi tradition. See R. Ahmed, *The Bengal Muslims, 1871–1906*, 84–85. Tajuddin Muhammad's *Khulasat al-Nikah*, Fakir Abdur Rahman's *Hedayet al-Musallin* (1872), and Ahmad Ali's *Firqah i Arbain* are three examples of nashihat namas of the 1870s that focused on conjugality and women's duties. R. Ahmed, *The Bengal Muslims, 1871–1906*, 217.

72. Nashihat namas were in circulation before the nineteenth century as well, but, unlike the reformist tracts, the earlier literature typically mixed reverence for Hindu deities with devotion to Allah. See R. Ahmed, *The Bengal Muslims, 1871–1906*, 85–86, and especially 87–90; Sonia Nishat Amin, *The World of Muslim Women in Colonial Bengal, 1876*, 47–49; Datta, *Carving Blocs*, 215–16.

73. *Harh jwalani* literally means "a woman who burns one to the bones" or "a woman who brings no peace." Cited in Sonia Nishat Amin, *The World of Muslim Women in Colonial Bengal, 1876*, 48. See also Anisuzzaman, *Muslim Manas O Bangla Sahitya*.

74. Maleh Muhammad, *Tanbih al-Nissa* (Calcutta, 1875), cited in R. Ahmed, *The Bengal Muslims, 1871–1906*, 84, 87.

75. Cited in R. Ahmed, *The Bengal Muslims, 1871–1906*, 87 (for excerpts from the Bengali original of this and other nashihat namas, see 212–18).

76. Abdul Sattar, *Dafi al-Sharur* (Calcutta, 1877), and Munshi Samiruddin, *Bedar al-Ghafilin*, both cited in R. Ahmed, *The Bengal Muslims, 1871–1906*, 89.

77. Sonia Nishat Amin, *The World of Muslim Women in Colonial Bengal, 1876*, 47.

78. Similar tropes (regarding women's status in a "glorified" past) are quite common in the discourses of Hindu cultural nationalism in colonial India. For an early important discussion, see Chakravarty, "Whatever Happened to the Vedic *Dasi*?" especially 46–60.

79. Abdul Hamid, *Ketab Najat al-Islam*; Munshi Samiruddin, *Bedar al-Ghafilin*, both cited in R. Ahmed, *The Bengal Muslims, 1871–1906*, 89. Of the five observances, poor Muslims could not always engage in zakat (almsgiving) or undertake the haj (pilgrimage to Mecca).

80. I differ here with Datta's claim to the contrary in *Carving Blocs*, 215–16. Datta may be assuming the importance of purdah among rural masses anachronistically in nineteenth-century Bengal.

81. For an excellent discussion of the gradual adoption of strict purdah among sections of the peasantry see S. Sen, *Women and Labour in Late Colonial India*, especially 60–65. On the reform agenda of the ashraf, see Rouse, "Gender, Nationalism(s), and Cultural Identity," 51–52.

82. Muhammad Danesh, *Nurul Imaner Puthi* (Calcutta, 1876), 56, cited in R. Ahmed, *The Bengal Muslims, 1871–1906*, 87 (emphasis added). The translation from the original Bengali is by Ahmed.

83. This is Rafiuddin Ahmed's reading of the text.

84. Barbara Metcalf, for instance, identifies three distinct reformist traditions within the Islamic communities beginning in the late nineteenth century: the ulema; the reformers, who were most affected by European criticism of the treatment of women in Islam; and the Islamists, who gained prominence in the 1930s and "purported to challenge the existing structure of social and political organisation in favour of a new Islamic order." According to Metcalf, all of these groups were united in their "interest in shaping women's character." However, their prescriptions for models for female ideals varied ("Reading and Writing about Muslim Women in British India," 5–6). See also Minault, *Secluded Scholars*, 9; and Rouse, "Gender, Nationalism(s), and Cultural Identity," 50–52. For a somewhat different reading of the campaign to educate women among the North Indian *shurafa*, see Devji, "Gender and the Politics of Space," 22–24. The shurafa is a professional or service class of the gentry.

85. B. D. Metcalf, "Reading and Writing about Muslim Women in British India," 6–7.

86. B. D. Metcalf, *Perfecting Women*. See also Minault, *Secluded Scholars*, 63–71. Thanawi's work was published around 1905 and quickly became popular among

sharif Muslims in the subcontinent. For discussions of reformist literature written in Bengali at the end of the nineteenth century, see R. Ahmed, *The Bengal Muslims, 1871–1906*, 93–94.

87. Rouse, "Gender, Nationalism(s), and Cultural Identity," 51.

88. On the education of women, see Majeed, "Narratives of Progress and Idioms of Community," 136, 141; and Rouse, "Gender, Nationalism(s), and Cultural Identity," 50–52.

89. R. Ahmed, *The Bengal Muslims, 1871–1906*, 15.

90. Devji, "Gender and the Politics of Space," 24.

91. According to one source, in 1843 there were eighty thousand followers of the Faraizi movement in Bengal. See Datta, *Unish Sataker Muslim Manas*, 30.

92. Rouse, "Gender, Nationalism(s), and Cultural Identity," 52; Minault, *Secluded Scholars*, 62; Azra Asghar Ali, *The Emergence of Feminism among Indian Muslim Women*, xiv.

93. B. D. Metcalf, "Reading and Writing about Muslim Women in British India," 11. See also Majeed, "Narratives of Progress and Idioms of Community," 136, 141. For a different reading, see Lambert-Hurley, "Fostering Sisterhood."

94. For instance, in 1871, while Muslims constituted 32.3 percent of the total population of Bengal (including, at that time, Bihar, Orissa, and Assam), the proportion of Muslim students was only 14.4 percent of the total number of enrolled in school. Moreover, according to a report of the director of public instruction for 1871–72, most of the Muslim students had left school after the primary stage. Consequently, out of the 3,499 students who passed the entrance examination over a period of five years, a mere 132, 3.8 percent, were Muslim. Cited in Moslem Education Advisory Committee, *Report of the Moslem Education Advisory Committee* (1934), 50–51.

95. Ibid.; R. Ahmed, "The Emergence of Bengal Muslims," 18–19; Datta, *Carving Blocs*, 69–70.

96. Moslem Education Advisory Committee, *Report of the Moslem Education Advisory Committee* (1934), 37 (emphasis added).

97. Such statements about the essential difference between Hindus and Muslims by the colonial authorities are all the more striking when one compares them to official reports from the 1870s, which endorse "without hesitation the suitability" of the existing system of "Mahomedan moral science and etiquette" for "Hindoo and Musalman alike." *Selections 1870*, 47–57, cited in Majeed, "Narratives of Progress and Idioms of Community," 146.

98. Moslem Education Advisory Committee, *Report of the Moslem Education Advisory Committee* (1934), 37 (emphasis added).

99. "Bangiya Musalman Samaj" (editorial), *Soltan*, November 2, 1923, cited in Islam, *Samayikpatre Jiban O Janamat*, 14.

100. Moslem Education Advisory Committee, *Report of the Moslem Education Advisory Committee* (1934), records that the total number of Muslim students increased from 28,148 (14.4 percent of the total number of students enrolled) in 1870–71 to 262,108 (23.8 percent) in 1881–82. The percentage of Muslim students in educational institutions increased to 27.7 percent in 1901–2, 43.5 percent in 1913–14, and 46.5 percent in 1921–22, after which time it leveled off. It should be noted that the increase between 1901 and 1913 was partly due to the shrinking size of the Bengal Presidency. It should also be mentioned that, while the number of Muslim students increased significantly between 1870 and 1920, a disproportionate number were in primary schools; Hindus continued to dominate at the high school and college levels. For instance, in 1926–27, 84.2 percent of all male students enrolled in college were Hindu; only 14.2 percent were Muslim. Of the total number of male students at the primary school level, however, 48.4 percent were Hindu and 50.5 percent were Muslims. The Muslims constituted about 52 percent of the total population of Bengal at that time. See Moslem Education Advisory Committee, *Report of the Moslem Education Advisory Committee* (1934), 10–20. Similar trends of increasing literacy were also reported in the census figures from 1901–31.

101. See, for instance Abul Mansur Ahmad, *Atmakatha*; Datta, *Carving Blocs*, 69–70; and Islam, *Muslim Public Opinion as Reflected in the Bengali Press, 1901–1930*.

102. Some of the women I interviewed belonged to this group. From their testimonies it appears that their families were part of either the rural landowning gentry—the *mofussil* ashraf—or the lesser ashraf. These groups, and the urban middle class that they eventually created, distanced themselves from both the communal politics of the rural Muslims and the elitist ways of the Mughal ashraf. See especially the conversation with Nusrat Begum in chapter 4 of this book.

103. While it is difficult to obtain figures for the middle class as such, or for income distributions, we can use the census figures for a sense of what percentage of the workforce in each occupation category belonged to which religion. If we assume that the categories "Public Administration," "Trade," and "Professionals" reflect middle-class occupations, then, according to the 1911 census, almost 21 percent of the total working population of India involved in these occupations was Muslim while 67 percent was Hindu. If we disregard "Trade," the proportion of Muslims in the other two categories rises to 22.7 percent. It should be noted that, according to the same census reports, only 4.05 percent of the Muslim population

and 11.50 percent of the Hindu population were literate in 1911. See Census of India, 1911, vol. 1, Subsidiary Table 9, 443.

104. Eventually, this commitment to a complex identity would spur the middle class to successfully spearhead a cultural-nationalist struggle against Urdu-speaking Muslims in the second half of the twentieth century. At the same time, the two elements together would form an enduring set of tensions that is still evident in Bangladeshi society today.

105. Bharati Ray mentions the existence of "voices" other than the Muslim League in her discussion of Muslims in Bengal (*Early Feminists of Colonial India*, 24–26).

106. In most accounts, the overwhelming tendency was to refer to western education as "modern." I have resisted doing so for reasons I hope do not need belaboring here.

107. Akram Khan, editorial in the inaugural issue of *Masik Mohammadi* (1927), cited in Anisuzzaman, *Muslim Banglar Samayikpatra*, 39; Swarochish Sarkar, *Kathasahitya O Natake*, 35. Khan placed his ideological leanings somewhere in between these two "extreme" positions, but in the end he seems to clash more with the latter, at least in matters of social reforms, especially those involving women. See Mohammad Nasiruddin, *Bangla Sahitye Saogat Jug*, 587–91; and Anisuzzaman, *Muslim Banglar Samayikpatra*, 39.

108. See, for instance, Monir, *Bangla Sahitye*; Swarochish Sarkar, *Kathasahitya O Natake*; Anisuzzaman, *Muslim Banglar Samayikpatra*; and Sonia Nishat Amin, *The World of Muslim Women in Colonial Bengal, 1876*.

109. "Musalman Samaje Durdasha," *Akhbar-e-Islamia*, October-November, 1885, cited in Swarochish Sarkar, *Kathasahitya O Natake*, 35. The author uses the word *mlechhanugami*, literally, "that befitting or following a *mlechha*," to describe fellow Muslims. *Mlechha* is a word typically used to refer to the ancient "non-Hindu" or "non-Aryan" inhabitants of the subcontinent. Ironically, then, the author's use of the term may be taken as an example of the "Hinduization" of Muslims.

110. Ismail Hossein Siraji, *Al Eslam*, July-August 1919 (title unknown), cited in Anisuzzaman, *Muslim Banglar Samayikpatra*, 38. Pirs are Muslim saints. The orthodox religious community was, of course, against the saints and Sufis. See Datta, *Carving Blocs*, 94–100, for a discussion of the campaigns led by Abu Bakr—himself a pir but one who represented orthodoxy and opposed the syncretic practices of the *bauls* (minstrels).

111. In 1900, *Islam Pracharak* carried an article by Ismail Hossein Siraji in which the author claimed that, given the general immorality of Indian society, pur-

dah "seems particularly necessary" (cited in Swarochish Sarkar, *Kathasahitya O Natake*, 36). Siraji modified his stance on purdah after a visit to Turkey in 1912. See Maleka Begum, *Banglar Nari Andolan*, 53. Similarly, Najir Ahmad Choudhuri likened novels to alcohol in an article published in *Al Eslam* (May-June 1927), and Mohammad Reyajuddin Ahmad wrote of their destructive effects (*Al Eslam*, September-October 1927), both cited in Mohammad Nasiruddin, *Bangla Sahitye Saogat Jug*, 30. On music as unholy, see Maulana Ruhul Amin, *Islam Darshan* (n.d.), cited in Anisuzzaman, *Muslim Banglar Samayikpatra*, 38. On nonsecular education for women, see Sheikh Abdur Rahman, "Shikshar Bhitti," *Al-Eslam*, October-November 1919, cited in Sonia Nishat Amin, *The World of Muslim Women in Colonial Bengal, 1876–1939*, 188–89. On seclusion, see, for instance, Mohammad Ghulam Hossein, "Islamer Parda Tatva," *Islam Darshan*, October-November 1922; and Sahadat Ali Khan, "Islame Pardapratha," *Moajjin*, October-November 1928, both cited in Islam, *Samayik Patre Jiban O Janamat*, 90, 92.

112. Siraji, for instance quite openly expressed the view that Muslims were superior to Hindus. But he was against colonial rule, and hence acknowledged the importance of Muslim-Hindu unity. He was even named by the British in their list of proposed prosecutions for sedition in May 1907. See Monir, *Bangla Sahitye*, 160–165; Sumit Sarkar, *Modern India*, 121. Similarly, Maniruzzaman Eslamabadi, also a social conservative, was active in anti-colonial politics, was critical of the loyalist politics of the ashraf, and is known to have written in the *Al-Eslam* (n.d.) against the political divisions between Hindus and Muslims. Cited in Anisuzzaman, *Muslim Banglar Samayikpatra*, 41.

113. Author unknown, cited in Nasiruddin, *Bangla Sahitye Saogat Jug*, 29. For other examples of anti-Swadeshi and anti-Hindu articles, see Nurul Islam, *Samayikpare*, 200–201.

114. For a discussion of this group of writers, see R. Ahmed, *The Bengal Muslims, 1871–1906*, 98–101; and Datta, *Carving Blocs*, especially 87–94. See also Anisuzzaman, *Muslim Banglar Samayikpatra*, 44.

115. Mohammad Nasiruddin, the highly respected editor of the *Saogat*, describes *Nabanoor* as being part of the "conservative" faction. See Nasiruddin, *Bangla Sahitye Saogat Jug*, 29. My own impression, based on my research on the first three years of *Nabanoor*'s publication, is that it published a wide range of articles, including some of the most controversial early work of Rokeya Sakhawat Hossain. For discussions of this and other periodicals of the time, see Anisuzzaman, *Muslim Banglar Samayikpatra*, especially 36–45; and Nasiruddin, *Bangla Sahitye Saogat Jug*, 27–30; and Islam, *Samayikpatre Jiban O Janamat*. I base my analysis

in this section on both these secondary sources and my readings of the primary sources.

116. Khaerunnessa Khatun, "Amader Shikshar Antaray," *Nabanoor*, November-December 1904, 368–71, reprinted in Akhtar and Bhowmick, *Zenana Mehfil*, 39–42. This is one of the earliest known articles published by a Muslim woman in Bengal. See also Sonia Nishat Amin, *The World of Muslim Women in Colonial Bengal, 1876*, 218. *Hadis* or *Hadith* refers to the statements and speeches of the prophet Muhammad. "Hadis sharif" is a respectful way of invoking them.

117. Firoza Begum, "Amader Shikhshar Prayajaniyata," *Saogat*, August-September, 1929. A number of articles in *Saogat* attack the tyranny of mullahs. See Muhammad Nasiruddin, *Bangla Sahitye Saogat Jug*, 264–68; Some of these writers formed an organization called the League against Mollaism, mentioned in Datta, *Carving Blocs*, 107.

118. M. Rahman, *Saogat*, August-September 1929; Akram Khan, *Mostafa Charitrer Baishishtya* (Calcutta, 1932), cited in Monir, *Bangla Sahitye*, 91.

119. *Shikha*, which was associated with this group of young progressive writers, was first published in 1927 in Dhaka.

120. Qazi Abdul Wadud, "Bangali Mussalmaner Sahitya Samasya," *Shikha*, April 1927, cited in Anisuzzaman, *Muslim Banglar Samayikpatra*, 476–77. For a thoughtful discussion of Wadud's work, see Khan, "Radicalism in Bengali Muslim Thought," 153–78.

121. Abul Hussein, "Adesher Nigraha," *Shikha* (1928), cited in Anisuzzaman, *Muslim Banglar Samayikpatra*, 484.

122. For instance, the Calcutta weekly *Sultan* (possibly the same magazine as the one known as *Soltan*), which was edited by the well-known writer Maniruzzaman Eslamabadi, carried an article that roundly criticized the "Dhaka radicals" on November 16, 1927. Cited in Khan, "Radicalism in Bengali Muslim Thought," 161.

123. The periodicals *Ganabani* and *Dhumketu* were most likely to carry such calls to class mobilization. See Anisuzzaman, *Muslim Banglar Samayikpatra*, 38–41.

124. M. Asgar Ali, "Saogat banam tarundal," *Sanchay*, (1928), cited in Anisuzzaman, *Muslim Banglar Samayikpatra*, 543–44. Asgar Ali goes on to criticize *Saogat* for failing to continue to stand behind the more controversial ideas of the progressives.

125. For a critical commentary, see Akram Khan, editorial in *Masik Mohammadi* (1927), cited in Anisuzzaman, *Muslim Banglar Samayikpatra*, 39.

126. For early examples of criticism of the policies of the British administration, see Maulavi Hedaytullah, "Swadeshi Andolan," and an editorial with the same title, both in *Nabanoor*, October-November 1905. See also Ekinuddin Ahmad, "Bhasabichhed," in *Nabanoor*, July-August 1905; and Hossain, "Muktiphal," in Quadir, *Begum Rokeya Rachanabali*, 198–220.

127. In an early article titled "Swadeshanurag," published in *Nabanoor* (September-October 1905), Khaerunnessa exhorted Muslims, even Muslim women, to join the Swadeshi agitation, if necessary from behind the purdah. She seems to have discarded the practice of purdah, to have taught in a school, and to have been an active participant in the Swadeshi movement of the Congress Party. For a short discussion of her life and work, see Akhtar and Bhowmik, *Zenana Mehfil*, 36–39. See also Hossain, "*Sugrihini*," in Quadir, *Begum Rokeya Rachanabali*, 45. For discussions of the contributions of all these authors, see Monir, *Bangla Sahitye*, 133–53.

128. Nazrul Islam, "Dhumketur path," cited in Quadir, *Nazrul Rachanabali*, 1:697. *Dhumketu* was the journal edited by Nazrul Islam. See also Monir, *Bangla Sahitye*, 135–39.

129. For critical articles on pan-Islamism and the lack of nationalist consciousness among Muslims, see Abdul Quadir, "Sampadaker Panji," *Jayati*, April 1930, cited in Anisuzzaman, *Muslim Banglar Samayikpatra*, 551; and Sadat Ali Akhanda, "Bangali," *Saogat*, November-December 1929, cited in Nurul Islam, *Samayikpatre Jiban o Janamat*, 160–61. See also, Abul Fazl's autobiographical work, *Rekhachitra*.

130. Maniruzzaman Eslamabadi, *Eslam Jagater Abhyuthhan* (Calcutta, n.d.); and Mohammad Yakub Ali Choudhury, "Musalmaner Sampradayikata O Hindur Jatiyata," *Saogat*, June-July 1927, both cited in Monir, *Bangla Sahitye*, 140, 174–76. For a time, Eslamabadi even supported the Congress Party, but he turned against Hindus in the 1920s. See Datta, *Carving Blocs*, 95.

131. For two examples, see Abdul Quadir, "Sampadaker Panji," *Jayati*, April 1930, cited in Anisuzzaman, *Muslim Banglar Samayikpatra*, 551; Sadat Ali Akhanda, "Bangali," *Saogat*, November-December 1929, cited in Nurul Islam, *Samayikpatre Jiban o Janamat*, 160–61. See also Anisuzzaman, *Muslim Manas O Bangla Sahitya*. Nazrul Islam bitterly declared that India was still a colony because Muslims were "envious of the progress made by our own neighbours [Hindus]" and that the Hindus, in turn, "disrespect[ed]" Muslims for being "backward." Nazrul Islam, "The Cultivation of Muslim Culture," in Quadir, *Nazrul Rachanabali*, 5:170.

132. Abul Fazal, "Nari Jagaran" (1929), in A. Fazal, *Abul Fazal Rachanabali*, 1:643 (emphasis added).

133. Two examples of work by women on this issue in the first decade of the twentieth century are a poem, titled "Dui Din," by Bibi Fatema (published in *Nabanoor*, March-April 1905), and the essay by Khaerunnessa mentioned above.

134. There are quite a few articles of this kind. For two examples, see Aftabuddin Ahmad, "Banger Hindu o Mussalman," and an editorial, "Matribhasha O Bangiya Musalman," both in *Nabanoor*, December-January 1903–4. Before the articles in *Nabanoor*, we find Mir Mosharraf Hossein writing about the "Hindu-Muslim Conflict" in *Kohinoor* (August-September 1898), although he is not explicitly critical of Hindu injustices perpetrated against Muslims.

135. The bhadrasampraday is the educated middle class.

136. "Balyabibaha O Abarodhpratha," by Shyamasundari Debi, was part of a contemporary collection of essays called *Sabitri*. It claims that in societies that lack female education and liberty and advocate purdah women tend to have "loose morals" and that Muslim society in India exemplified these trends. Cited in Anisuzzaman, Muslim Banglar *Samayikpatra*, 68–69.

137. Imdadul Huq, "Hindu Narir Muslim Ghrina," *Nababoor*, April-May 1903, 9–16 (my translation).

138. "Musalmaner Prati Hindu Lekhaker Atyachar," *Nabanoor*, August-September, 1903. Indeed, the parochialism and myopia of Hindu attitudes in late-nineteenth-century Bengal seem to have been widespread enough to elicit criticism from a few Hindu writers who were committed to a more pluralistic vision of the nation. For two examples of such self-critiques by Hindu writers, see Nirmal Chandra Ghosh's *Gotadui Katha*," published in January-February 1904 in *Nabanoor*, and an earlier, anonymous article published on December 20, 1885, in the *Dhaka Prakash*, in which the author warns Hindus against the pitfalls of ignoring Muslims.

139. Anisuzzaman, *Muslim Banglar Samayikpatra*, 42–43.

140. Osman Ali, "Dumukho," *Nabanoor*, June-July 1904.

141. For examples of articles opposing the Swadeshi movement, see Nurul Islam, *Samayikpatre Jiban o Janamat*, 200–201.

142. For a careful discussion of this process of communalization among both Hindus and Muslims, see Datta, *Carving Blocs*.

143. See, for instance, Muhammad Wajed Ali, "Sahitye Shatantra Kano?" *Saogat*, November-December 1928. The Khilifat movement (1919–24) was launched in South Asia in support of the Khalifa (Caliph) and the Ottoman empire that faced dismemberment at the end of the First World War. The Non-Cooperation movement (1920–22) was a nationwide nonviolent resistance movement led by Mahatma Gandhi and the Indian National Congress against the British.

144. In the statement of intent published in the first edition of *Kohinoor* in July 1898, the editors write, "Can anyone say that any periodical . . . has brought learned Hindu and Muslim writers in Bengal together [in its pages]? . . . So is this not new in our enterprise?" Cited in Anisuzzaman, *Muslim Banglar Samayikpatra*, 21.

145. Lehazuddin Ahmed, "Rajnitikhsetre HinduMusalman," *Nabanoor*, June-July 1905. See also an editorial book review of volume 1 of Sakharam Ganesh Deushkar's *Desher Katha*, in *Nabanoor*, July-August 1905.

146. For two examples, see Siraji, "Abhibhashan," *Islam Darshan*, August-September 1924, cited in Monir, *Bangla Sahitye*, 164; and an editorial, "Bideshi Bastra Barjan," published in *Islam Darshan*, July-August 1921, cited in Nurul Islam, *Samayikpatre Jiban o Janamat*, 201.

147. Nazrul Islam, "Jugabani" (1922), in Quadir, *Nazrul Rachanabali*, 1:630–31.

148. Cited in Muhammed Nasiruddin, *Bangla Sahitye Saogat Jug*, 1102.

149. Muhammad Wajed Ali, "Sahitye Shatantra Kano?" *Saogat*, November-December 1928. The reference is to the novelist Bankim Chandra Chattopadhyay, who is widely recognized as one of the first nationalist writers in mid-nineteenth-century Bengal. See, for instance, P. Chatterjee, *Nationalist Thought and the Colonial World*, especially chapter 3. For a similar criticism of Bankim's work by a woman writer, see Safia Khatun, "Bangla Sahityer Anudarata," *Bangiya Mussalman Sahitya Patrika*, January 1922.

150. "Hindu-Musalman Samsya," *Saogat*, April-May 1927, cited in Nasiruddin, *Bangla Sahitye Saogat Jug*, 1067–73.

151. Datta's *Carving Blocs* is a notable exception to this trend.

152. Indeed, this trend would continue for quite some time. As the Census of 1921 reports, forty years later, in Calcutta, Hindus still outnumbered Muslims in terms of middle-class occupations (public administration and other professional fields such as liberal arts, medicine, or law) by a ratio of roughly six to one.

153. "Islam O Mussalman," *Saogat*, April-May 1929.

154. Majeed, "Narratives of Progress and Idioms of Community," 154; T. R. Metcalf, *Ideologies of the Raj*.

155. At first glance, the inclusion of zamindari (landownership) might seem odd in a list of indices of colonial capitalist modernity. What the author is referring to, I think, is the new class of landowners that displaced the older feudal aristocracy after the introduction of the Permanent Settlement by the colonial government in 1793. While the older class of zamindars had held overseer rights, the new class was granted private ownership of land. Also, while the older aristocracy was more

likely to be Muslim, the new middle class was predominantly Hindu. See Wolpert, *A New History of India*, 196–97. See also the discussion of these changes in chapter 2.

156. Badrunnessa Khatun, *Mahila Saogat*, August-September, 1929 (title unknown).

157. I am drawing here on D. Scott, *Refashioning Futures*, 31–33. He argues that the distinctiveness of modern power lies in its point of application.

158. For an articulation of this argument in this specific form, see Sonia Nishat Amin, *The World of Muslim Women in Colonial Bengal, 1876*. See also R. Ahmed, *The Bengal Muslims, 1871–1906*; and "Understanding the Bengal Muslims.

159. Nasiruddin, "Congress O Musalman," *Saogat*, November-December 1928 (emphasis added).

160. Mohammad Wajed Ali, "Sahitye Shatantra Kano?" *Saogat*, August-September 1929.

161. Nurunnessa Khatun, *Saogat*, August-September, 1929 (title unknown). Another woman who wrote about this issue was Safia Khatun, in "Bangla Sahityer Anudarata," *Bangiya Mussalman Sahitya Patrika*, January 1922.

162. Tasaddak Ahmad, *Shikha* (1927; title unknown); Kaji Motahar Hossein, *Shikha* (1927; title unknown).

163. Hussein, "Tarun Muslim," cited in Monir, *Bangla Sahitye*, 178–79. See also Anwarul Quadir, "Bangali Musalmaner Samajik Galad," *Shikha* (1927). See Datta, *Carving Blocs*, for discussions of these controversies.

164. Kazi Abdul Wadud, "Ekkhani Patra," *Jayati* (1930), cited in Khan, "Radicalism in Bengali Muslim Thought," 171.

165. Women were often present in the context of discussions on issues such as family lineage and the controversy over the alleged abductions of Hindu women by Muslim men in the 1920s.

166. For more comprehensive treatments of Bengali Muslim women's writings from the late nineteenth century and early twentieth, see Sonia Nishat Amin, *The World of Muslim Women in Colonial Bengal, 1876*; and, in Bengali, Akhtar and Bhowmick, *Zenana Mehfil.*

167. *Nabanoor* carried a number of articles on the position and treatment of women between 1903 and 1905, including several essays by women authors such as Rokeya Sakhawat Hossain and Khaerunnessa Khatun. See, for instance, Hossain, "Borka," April-May 1904, and "Amader Abanati," August-September 1904; and Khaerunnessa, "Amader Shikshar Antaray," *Nabanoor*, November-December 1904, 368–371, also cited in Akhtar and Bhowmick, 39–42. See also Mohammad Reyazuddin Ahmad, "Muslim Samaj Sanskar (Bidhaba Bibaha)," *Kohinoor*, June-

July 1898, cited in Islam, *Samayikpatre Jiban o Janamat*, 81–82; O. Ali, "Ramani," *Pracharak*, January-February 1899, cited in Islam, *Samayikpatre Jiban o Janamat*, 75; Maulavi Imdadul Huq, "Bahubibaha," *Nabanoor*, November-December 1905; Sheikh Jamiruddin, "Musalman Samaje Strijatir Prati Bheeshan Atyachar," *Islam Pracharak*, August 1903; and Siraji, "Nari Jatir Durgati," *Al Eslam*, August-September 1917, cited in Islam, *Samayikpatre Jiban o Janamat*, 77–78.

168. Siraji, "Nari Jatir Durgati" *Al Eslam*, August-September 1917, cited in Islam, *Samayikpatre Jiban o Janamat*, 77–78.

169. For examples of women criticizing child marriage as a major source of suffering, see Hossain, "Shishupalan," *Bangiya Musalman Sahitya Patrika*, October-November 1920, reprinted in Quadir, *Begum Rokeya Rachanabali*, 196–97; M. Rahman, "Amader Swarup," *Dhumketu*, November-December 1922, reprinted in Akhtar and Bhowmick, *Zenana Mehfil*, 57–60; Ayesha Ahmed, "Muslim Samaje Unnatir Antaray," *Mahila Sankhya*, *Saogat*, August-September 1929. Note that Rokeya Sakhawat Hossain was publishing as early as 1901, but the essay cited here was written much later.

170. For some examples, see Mohammad Akram Khan, "Bibaher Bayash Nirdharan," *Mashik Mohammadi*, April-May 1928; "Banga Moslem Samaje Mahila Jiban," *Moajjin*, July-August 1927; and Editor, "Bibaha Ain Sanskar," *Moajjin*, July-August 1927, all cited in Islam, *Samayikpatre Jiban o Janamat*, 78–80.

171. Kaji Abdul Wadud, "Mrs. R. S. Hossein," *Masik Sanchay*, November-December 1929, cited in Quadir, *Begum Rokeya Rachanabali*, 552. In his commentary on Rokeya's work, Wadud wrote, "Among the living and dead elderly [writers] true Muslim littérateurs are very few in number—Mir Mosharraf Hossein, Pandit Reyajuddin, Kaekobad, Kaji Imdadul Huq and Mrs. R. S. Hossein."

172. Kaji Imdadul Huq, "Bahubibaha," *Nabanoor*, November-December 1905.

173. Siraji, "Bibaha Niti," *Al Eslam*, October-November 1919, cited in Islam, *Samayikpatre Jiban o Janamat*, 78–79.

174. Mohammad K. Chand, "Talak, or the Divorcing of Moslem Wives," *Islam Pracharak*, 1906, cited in Islam, *Samyikpatre Jiban o Janamat*, 85. See also Jamiruddin, "Musalman Samaje Strijatir Prati Bheeshan Atyachar," *Islam Pracharak*, August 1903; and Maulana Akram Khan, "Eslame Narir Marjyada," *Masik Mohammadi*, December-January 1927, cited in Islam, *Samayikpatre Jiban o Janamat*, 85–86. For critical writing on talak by women, see Akhtar Mahal Sayeda Khatun, *Saogat*, November-December 1927 (title unknown), reprinted in Akhtar and Bhowmick, *Zenana Mehfil*, 119; and Hossain, "Narir Adhikar," an unfinished essay in Quadir, *Begum Rokeya Rachanabali*, 265–66.

175. Datta, *Carving Blocs*, 95.

176. This specific argument appears in an editorial entitled "Bibahe Barpan" in *Samyabadi*, June-August 1924, cited in Islam, *Samayikpatre Jiban o Janamat*, 65.

177. A few Muslim women published their work in the nineteenth century, including Bibi Taherunnessa (1865), Faizunnessa Choudhurani (1876), and Latifunnessa (1897). In the twentieth century, we know of Rokeya Sakhawat Hossain (1901) and the poet Azizunnessa (1902) as the first writers, followed by Khaerunnessa (1905) and Bibi Fatema (1905), both of whom published in *Nabanoor*. For a discussion of the work of these authors, see Sonia Nishat Amin, *The World of Muslim Women in Colonial Bengal, 1876*, 214–19.

178. As Tanika Sarkar has recently commented, women's writing was expected to be "at no distance from visual or emotional experiences; [rather] it [was to be] . . . merely a deposit left by those." Sarkar, *Words to Win*, 5–7.

179. See Akhtar and Bhowmick, *Zenana Mehfil*, 36–39.

180. Khaerunnessa, "Amader Shikshar Antaray," *Nabanoor*, November-December 1904, 368–71, reprinted in Akhtar and Bhowmick, *Zenana Mehfil*, 39–42.

181. In commenting on Rokeya's writing on the publication of her collected works, *Matichur*, two contemporary critics wrote, "Reforming society is one proposition, and whipping society is another. . . . The author of *Matichur* is only continually whipping society, [and] we cannot hope for any good to come from this." Munshi Abdul Karim and Sayed Emdad Ali, "Granthasamalochana," *Nabanoor*, August-September 1905, reprinted in Akhtar and Bhowmick, *Zenana Mehfil*, 4.

182. "Mahiladiger Abarodhpratha," *Mahila*, September-October 1903, cited in Chakrabarty, *Andare Antare*, 196. For a discussion of the practice of seclusion among Hindus, see Urquhart, *Women of Bengal*. For a discussion of Khaerunnessa's life, see Akhtar and Bhowmick, *Zenana Mehfil*, 38–39.

183. Khaerunnessa, "Swadeshanurag," *Nabanoor*, September-October 1905. A number of Muslim women published their work before Khaerunnessa and her contemporary, Rokeya.

184. This is the name Masuda Rahman herself used.

185. Mrs. Rahman began publishing sometime after World War I. See Akhtar and Bhowmick, *Zenana Mehfil*, 47–51. On "Agninagini," see Samsunnahar Mahmud, "Mrs. M. Rahman Smarane," *Naoroj*, June-July 1927, reprinted in Akhtar and Bhowmick, *Zenana Mehfil*, 50.

186. Masuda Rahman, "Barbanal," *Bijali*, March-April 1922, reprinted in Akhtar and Bhowmick, *Zenana Mehfil*, 52.

187. Samsunnahar Mahmud, "Mrs. M. Rahman Smarane," *Naoroj*, June-July 1927, reprinted in Akhtar and Bhowmick, *Zenana Mehfil*, 50.

188. See "Sadanushthan," *Bijali*, April-May 1922; Masuda Rahman, "Amader Swarup," *Dhumketu*, September-October 1922; and Masuda Rahman, "Amader Dabi," *Dhumketu*, September-October 1922, all reprinted in Akhtar and Bhowmick, *Zenana Mehfil*, 51–63.

189. Masuda Rahman, "Amader Swarup," *Dhumketu*, September-October 1922, reprinted in Akhtar and Bhowmick, *Zenana Mehfil*, 57–60.

190. Masuda Rahman, "Amader Dabi," *Dhumketu*, September-October 1922, reprinted in Akhtar and Bhowmick, *Zenana Mehfil*, 63.

191. Forbes, *Women in Modern India*, 13; Mill, *The History of British India*, 309–10.

192. See, for instance, Masuda Rahman, "Barbanal," *Bijali*, March-April 1922; "Sadanushthan," *Bijali*, April-May 1922; and "Amader Swarup," *Dhumketu*, September-October 1922, reprinted in Akhtar and Bhowmick, *Zenana Mehfil*, 57–60.

193. See the discussion of Masuda Rahman's work in Akhtar and Bhowmick, *Zenana Mehfil*, especially 50. Abdul Quadir, for instance, described her work as "unremarkable" in "Begum Rokeya Sahitya Kirti," *Masik Mohammadi*, January-February 1932, cited in Quadir, *Begum Rokeya Rachanabali*, 547.

194. See, for instance Sombuddha Chakrabarty's discussion of the changing tone of Brahmo/Hindu women's writings about their relationships with their husbands in the second half of the nineteenth century and the early twentieth in *Andare Antare*, 224–27.

195. Masuda Rahman, "Amader Dabi," *Dhumketu*, September 1922, reprinted in Akhtar and Bhowmick, *Zenana Mehfil*, 51–63.

196. Tharu and Lalita, *Women Writing in India*, vol. 1; Jahan, "Sultana's Dream: Purdah Reversed"; Sonia Nishat Amin, "The Changing World of Bengali Muslim Women"; Y. Hossein, "Prekshapat," 15.

197. Many of Rokeya's essays were compiled in a volume titled *Matichur*, published in Calcutta in 1921 and later included in Quadir, *Begum Rokeya Rachanabali*. The first biography of Rokeya in Bengali, *Rokeya Jibani*, was written by Samsunnahar Mahmud (1937, reprinted in 1996). Samsunnahar was a close friend and associate of Rokeya. This work is therefore of great historical importance. See also Quadir, *Begum Rokeya Rachanabali*; Begum, *Banglar Nari Andolan*; Hasan, *Begum Rokeya*; Pradhan, *Begum Rokeya O Narijagaran*; Saiyed, *Begum Rokeya*; and M. Mahmud, *Patre Rokeya Parichiti*.

198. Quadir, editor's note to Begum *Rokeya Rachanabali*, 16; Akhtar and Bhow-

mick, *Zenana Mehfil*, 4–5. Rokeya's satirical works include "Unnatir Pathe," *Masik Mohammadi*, December-January 1928–29; and "Abarodhbashini" (published in four installments between 1928 and 1930 in *Masik Mohammadi*), both included in Quadir, *Begum Rokeya Rachanabali*, 18–20 and 833–68, respectively. On her early work, see Murshid, *Rasasundari Theke Rokeya*, 156.

199. Datta, *Carving Blocs*, 215–18. On her support for nationalism, see Ray, *Early Feminists of Colonial India*, especially 24–26.

200. Motilal Majumdar, Review of Samsunnahar, *Rokeya Jibani*, *Saogat*, May-June 1937, reprinted in Akhtar and Bhowmick, *Zenana Mehfil*, 3.

201. Sonia Nishat Amin, "Rokeya Sakhawat Hossain and the Legacy of the 'Bengal Renaissance,'" 185–86.

202. Akhtar and Bhowmick (*Zenana Mehfil*, 3) use the word *pathanirdeshak* in Bengali.

203. Hossain, "Bhrata-Bhagni," reprinted in Quadir, *Begum Rokeya Rachanabali*, 469. Hakims are physicians.

204. Hossain, "Amader Abanati," *Nabanoor*, August-September 1904, cited in Quadir, *Begum Rokeya Rachanabali*, 11–12. See also Akhtar and Bhowmick, *Zenana Mehfil*, 19–20.

205. As justification for this comparison, Rokeya offers the example of the practice of "buying and selling" brides and grooms for enormous sums among kulin Brahmin families. While she does not mention it explicitly, she may also have had the institution of bride-price in mind.

206. Barrett and Phillips, *Destabilizing Theory*, 3. Wollstonecraft wrote that women "may be convenient slaves, but slavery will have its constant effect, degrading the master and the abject dependent." Quadir, *Begum Rokeya Rachanabali*, 14.

207. See, for instance, Murshid's discussion in this regard in *Rasasundari Theke Rokeya*, 135.

208. Burton, "Institutionalizing Imperial Reform," 24–25.

209. For examples, see Kailashbasini Debi, *Hindu Mahilaganer Hinabastha* (1863), cited in M. Bhattacharya and Sen, *Talking of Power*, 25–50; Girindromohini Dasi, "Bisham Samasya," *Bharati*, July-August 1894, and Krishnabhabini Das, "Swadhin o Paradhin Narijiban," *Pradip*, February-March 1897, both cited in M. Bhattacharya and Sen, *Talking of Power*, 69–83; and Nagendrabala Mustafi, *Bamabodhini* (1895), cited in Bannerji, "Attired in Virtue," 86.

210. Murshid, *Rasasundari Theke Rokeya*, 153; Datta, *Carving Blocs*, 216–18; M. Bhattacharya and Sen, *Talking of Power*, 6–7. As exceptions, I have in mind some writers associated with *Shikha* and *Saogat* who disagreed with, if not dis-

missed, the idea of Islam's adequacy, especially in regard to its pronouncements on the subject of women. For an example, see Abul Hussein, "Adesher Nigraha" (1929), cited in Monir, *Bangla Sahitye*, 223–24.

211. Akhtar and Bhowmick, *Zenana Mehfil*, 39; Islam, *Samayikpatre Jiban o Janamat*, 85–86; Monir, *Bangla Sahitye*, 236–37; Murshid, *Rasasundari Theke Rokeya*, 147.

212. See Hasan, *Begum Rokeya*, especially 20. For a related discussion of Rokeya's ideas of gender inequality, see Ray, *Early Feminists of Colonial India*, 57–77.

213. For discussions of the reactions to Rokeya's work, see Quadir, editor's note to Begum *Rokeya Rachanabali*, 7–21, especially 12–14; and Akhtar and Bhowmick, *Zenana Mehfil*, 4–5. For examples of conservative responses, see the journal *Mihir O Sudhakar*, which published an anonymous critical response in the September-October 1904 issue, cited in Sonia Nishat Amin, *The World of Muslim Women in Colonial Bengal, 1876*, 188.

214. Quadir, *Begum Rokeya Rachanabali*, 283–84; Akhtar and Bhowmick, *Zenana Mehfil*, 39.

215. See Hossain, *Padmarag*, especially chapter 14, in Quadir, *Begum Rokeya Rachanabali*, 345–58. For a discussion of Rokeya's position on communalization, see Datta, *Carving Blocs*, 216–18. For a discussion of the "abduction" controversy, see Datta, *Carving Blocs*, 148–237, and chapter 2 of this book.

216. Hossain, "Subeh Sadek," *Moajjin*, August-September 1904, reprinted in Quadir, *Begum Rokeya Rachanabali*, 271–72.

217. Hossain, "Borka," in Quadir, *Begum Rokeya Rachanabali*, 47–53; "Unnatir Pathe," *Masik Mohammadi*, December-January 1928–29, cited in Quadir, *Begum Rokeya Rachanabali*, 18–20. As Rokeya saw it, there was no direct causal connection between the use of the veil and improvements in the lot of women. For a somewhat different reading of Rokeya's complex position on the purdah versus seclusion debate, see Sonia Nishat Amin, "The Changing World of Bengali Muslim Women," especially 147–49. On the metaphors of emergence/seclusion, see Bannerji, "Attired in Virtue," 86–87.

218. Murshid, *Rasasundari Theke Rokeya*, 153–54; Bhowmick, "Prastabana," 39. One reason for this intransigence might be that powerful factions among Muslims were invested in demanding a separate political community on the basis of their religion, and matters of reform could not be broached without somehow weakening that claim, especially since the Hindu middle class was increasingly vocal in its claim of Muslims as inadequately modern and liberal.

219. Hossain, "Streejatir Abanati," in Quadir, *Begum Rokeya Rachanabali*, 13.

220. In "Ardhangi," Rokeya wrote, "I have discussed mental slavery [of women]" (Quadir, *Begum Rokeya Rachanabali*, 26–27).

221. The earlier essay was Hossain, "Alankar, or Badges of Slavery," *Mahila*, April-June 1903. Note also that "Amander Ababati" was later reprinted as "Streejatir Abanati." The section on jewelry appears in both versions.

222. Burton, "Institutionalizing Imperial Reform," 24–25. The article in question is Dwarkanath Singha, "Self-Love of Ornament among Bengali Ladies," *Journal of the National Indian Association*, November 1880, 603–16, cited in Burton, "Institutionalizing Imperial Reform," 25.

223. Hossain, "Streejatir Abanati," in Quadir, *Begum Rokeya Rachanabali*, 11–12.

224. See, for instance, the responses to Rokeya's essay published in *Mahila*, July-August 1903, by a number of Hindu/Brahmo women, including S. A. al-Musavi, "Abanati Prasange," *Nabanoor*, September-October 1904; and Nausher Ali Khan Eusufji, "Ekei Ki Bale Abanati?" *Nabanoor*, October-November 1904. See also the discussion of some of these responses in chapter 2 of this book.

225. See, for instance, Pateman, *The Disorder of Women*, 36–41; and Delaney, "Father State, Motherland, and the Birth of the Modern Turkey," 177. For a somewhat different take on public and private in Islamic political thought, see Devji, "Gender and the Politics of Space," 22–37. See also J. W. Scott, *Gender and the Politics of History*, 42–45.

226. S. Sen, *Women and Labour in Late Colonial India*, 60–65. See also Hossain, "Nireeha Bangali," in Quadir, *Begum Rokeya Rachanabali*, 22–26.

227. That she was aware of the different experiences of women in other classes, as well as the workings of gender ideology even outside the world of the middle-class household, is clear from her comment that "even in the workplace a man's labour is worth more, woman's labour is sold cheap" (Hossain, "Streejatir Abanati," in Quadir, *Begum Rokeya Rachanabali*, 21). In this essay she mentions poor women who resort to wearing glass bangles since they cannot afford gold or silver (12).

228. J. W. Scott, *Gender and the Politics of History*, 41–42.

229. Shibnarayan Ray, "Bangalir Atmajignasha," *Purogami*, February 16, 1979, reprinted in Akhtar and Bhowmick, *Zenana Mehfil*, 5.

230. Akhtar and Bhowmick, *Zenana Mehfil*, 3–6. See also Sonia Nishat Amin, *The World of Muslim Women in Colonial Bengal, 1876*, 108.

231. Hossain, "Streejatir Abanati," in Quadir, *Begum Rokeya Rachanabali*, 21.

232. The clearest enunciation of this desire can be found in Rokeya's "Sultana's Dream" (1905), reprinted in *"Sultana's Dream" and Selections from "The Secluded*

Ones," and in her novel *Padmarag*, written in 1902 but published in the mid-1920s, reprinted in Quadir, *Begum Rokeya Rachanabali*, 293–428. For discussions of the novel *Padmarag*, see Murshid, *Rasasundari Theke Rokeya*, 149–52; and Sonia Nishat Amin, *The World of Muslim Women in Colonial Bengal, 1876*, 110.

233. See, for instance, Rokeya's critique of Mankumari Basu in "Griha," or her discussion of the token freedom of Parsi women in "Ardhangi," both in Quadir, *Begum Rokeya Rachanabali*, 63 and 27, respectively. Parsis are descendants of Persians who followed Zoroastrianism and fled to India in the wake of the Islamic conquest of Persia in the seventh century. They were among the first modernized and westernized groups in the subcontinent.

234. Bharati Ray recently made an argument more or less to this end in *Early Feminists in Colonial India*, 75–77.

235. F. M. Abdul Hakim Bikrampuri, "Nari Samasya," *Saogat* (1927), reprinted in Akhtar and Bhowmick, *Zenana Mehfil*, 17. Note that, although this article appeared in *Saogat*, according to Yasmin Hossein, Bikrampuri was a "conservative" writer ("Prekshapat," 17). See also "Musalman Stree Samaje Engraji Shiksha," *Mihir O Sudhakar*, January-February 1903; and Sheikh Abdur Rahman, "Shikshar Bhitti," *Al Eslam*, November-December 1919, both cited in Islam, *Samayikpatre Jiban o Janamat*, 22–23.

236. Y. Hossein, "Prekshapat," 17.

237. See, for instance, "Sanbadpatre Mahila Chitra," *Masik Mohammadi*, May-June 1928; and Sahadat Ali Khan, "Islame Pardapratha," *Moajjin*, October-November 1928, both excerpted in Islam, *Samayikpatre Jiban o Janamat*, 90–92. See also Siraji, "Stree Jatir Swadhinata," *Al Eslam*, January-February 1917, cited in Islam, *Samayikpatre Jiban o Janamat*, 89–90.

238. See Monir, *Bangla Sahitye*, 218–46, especially S. Wajed Ali, "Bangali Musalman," 240; and Nasiruddin, *Bangla Sahitye Saogat Jug*, 496–98.

239. Monir, *Bangla Sahitye*, 231.

240. Mohammad Sahidullah, "Abhibhashan," cited in Monir, *Bangla Sahitye*, 224–25.

241. Mohammad Nasiruddin, "Parda Banam Abarodh," *Mahila Saogat*, August-September 1929.

242. Mohammad Lutfar Rahman, "Koran O Nari," *Bangiya Mussalman Sahitya Patrika*, July-August 1922, cited in Monir, *Bangla Sahitye*, 221.

243. See Monir *Bangla Sahitye*, 218–22.

244. Mohammad Lutfar Rahman, "Pather Meye," *Annesa*, March-April 1921.

245. Monir, *Bangla Sahitye*, 220–21.

246. Mohammad Lutfar Rahman, "Pather Meye," *Annesa*, March-April 1921.

247. Mohammad Lutfar Rahman, "Ucchajiban," *Dhaka*, 1962, cited in Monir, *Bangla Sahitye*, 220.

248. Rahman is quoted in Monir, *Bangla Sahitye*, 220. For a similar prescription for purdah, see Mohammad Akram Khan, "Samasya O Samadhan," cited in Monir, *Bangla Sahitye*, 237.

249. See, for instance, A. Fazal, "Musalman Katha-Sahityer Gati O Parinati," in *Abul Fazal Rashanabali*, 1:574; and Nazrul Islam, "Banglar Muslimke Banchao," in Quadir, Nazul Rashanabali, 5:176; both cited in Monir, *Bangla Sahitye*, 244 and 235–36, respectively. For Abul Hussein's comments, see Monir, *Bangla Sahitye*, 224.

250. See, for instance, Rokeya Sakhawat Hossain, "Borkha," cited in Quadir, *Begum Rokeya Rachanabali*, 47–53.

251. Abul Hussein, "Adesher Nigraha" (1929), cited in Monir, *Bangla Sahitye*, 223–24.

252. Ibid., 224.

253. Abul Hussein, "British Bharate Muslims Ain" (1930), cited in Monir, *Bangla Sahitye*, 224.

254. Bhowmick, "Prastabana," 29.

255. Mohammad Wajed Ali, "Stree Shiksha," *Saogat* August-September 1929, also cited in Y. Hossein, "Prekshapat," 17.

256. Y. Hossein, "Prekshapat," 17.

257. For similar discussions of the limitations of discourses on "reforming women" in the context of the Middle East, see Abu-Lughod, *Remaking Women*.

258. Hossain, "Ardhangi," in Quadir, *Begum Rokeya Rachanabali*, 27.

259. Nurunnessa Khatun Bidyabinodini, "Bangiya Moslem Mahila Sangha: President's Address," *Saogat*, January-February 1927. Also in Akhtar and Bhowmick, *Zenana Mehfil*, 109.

260. Ibid. (emphasis added). See also Akhtar and Bhowmick, *Zenana Mehfil*, 109–14.

261. Monir, *Bangla Sahitye*, 238–39.

262. See, for instance, the discussion of Hindu women's responses to Rokeya's critique of women's collusion in their own subordination in chapter 2 of this book.

263. See, for instance, Ayesha Ahmed, "Muslim Samaje Unnatir Antaray," *Mahila Sankhya Saogat*, August-September 1929. According to Akhtar and Bhowmick, all of Nurunnessa's major literary works were published between 1923 and 1929. They also comment on both the success Nurunnessa enjoyed, in spite of the relative brevity of her writing career, and the nonconfrontational and mainstream

nature of her work, but they stop short of linking the two. Akhtar and Bhowmick, *Zenana Mehfil*, 92–93.

264. Rajia Khatun, "Bangiya Moslem Mahilaganer Shikshar Dhara," *Saogat*, June-July 1927, cited in Sonia Nishat Amin, *The World of Muslim Women in Colonial Bengal, 1876*, 203–4.

265. Y. Hossein, "Prekshapat," 16–20. See also Sayeda Jainab Khatun, "Bangiya Muslim Palli Nari," *Saogat* (1929); Kasema Khatun, "Narir Katha," *Saogat* (1926); Rajia Khatun Choudhurani, "Bangiya Muslim Mahilaganer Shikshar-Dhara," in Muhammad Abdul Kuddus, *Rajia Khatun Choudhuranir Rachana Sankalan* (Kumilla, 1982); and Firoza Begum, "Amader Shikshar Prayajaniyata," *Saogat*, August-September 1929, all in Akhtar and Bhowmick, *Zenana Mehfil*, 17–20.

266. Y. Hossein, "Prekshapat," 19.

267. Rajia Khatun Choudhurani, "Muslim Mahilar Sahitya Sadhana" (1982), in Akhtar and Bhowmick, *Zenana Mehfil*, 22.

268. Firoza Begum, "Amader Shikshar Prayajaniyata" (1929), in Akhtar and Bhowmick, *Zenana Mehfil*, 19, and cited in Sonia Nishat Amin, *The World of Muslim Women in Colonial Bengal, 1876–1939*, 202.

269. Masuda Rahman, "Amader Swarup," *Dhumketu*, November-December 1922, in Akhtar and Bhowmick, *Zenana Mehfil*, 57–60.

270. Ayesha Ahmed, "Muslim Samajer Unnatir Antaray," *Saogat*, August-September 1929, cited in Sonia Nishat Amin, *The World of Muslim Women in Colonial Bengal, 1876–1939*, 207.

271. For informative discussions of these and other contemporary women writers, see Akhtar and Bhowmick, *Zenana Mehfil*; and Sonia Nishat Amin, *The World of Muslim Women in Colonial Bengal, 1876–1939*.

272. Sufia Kamal, letter published in Akhtar and Bhowmick, *Zenana Mehfil*, 21, 230.

273. Mahmuda Khatun Siddiqua, "The Present Responsibilities of Women," *Moajjin* (1932), reprinted in Akhtar and Bhowmick, *Zenana Mehfil*, 182–83.

274. Y. Hossein, "Prekshapat," 13.

275. I am not disagreeing with Hossein here but stressing a different point, one that the editors of *Zenana Mehfil*, as well as Hossein herself, make elsewhere in the book. See, for instance, Akhtar and Bhowmick, *Zenana Mehfil*, 15; and Bhowmik, "Prastabana," 215–17.

276. Passerini, "Work, Ideology, and Consensus under Italian Fascism," 53–62.

4. DIFFERENCE IN MEMORY

A portion of the material in this chapter appeared in "Difference in Memory," *Comparative Studies in Society and History* 48, no. 1 (January 2006): 139–68.

1. Personal communication, Mala Sengupta, Calcutta, 1996. Mala spent the first ten years of her life in Dhaka before her family moved to Calcutta in the wake of the first riots in 1946.

2. Swati Mallick, personal communication, Calcutta, 1996.

3. Ila Chatterjee, personal communications, Calcutta, 1996, 1998.

4. Popular Memory Group, "Popular Memory."

5. Portelli, "What Makes Oral History Different," 67–68; Clifford, "Introduction: Partial Truths"; Stacey, "Can There Be a Feminist Ethnography?" 115–17; Abu-Lughod, "Can There Be a Feminist Ethnography?" 9–11; Visweswaran, *Fictions of Feminist Ethnography*, 48–50; Armitage and Gluck, "Reflections on Women's Oral History," 79–81; Haraway, "Situated Knowledges." See also Foucault, *Power/Knowledge*.

6. Ranajit Guha, *Dominance without Hegemony*.

7. Stoler and Strassler, "Castings for the Colonial," 7–8.

8. Stoler and Strassler call this the "hydraulic model" in which memory is treated as "a repository of alternative histories and subaltern truths" (ibid., 7). For reflections on similar issues in the context of women's oral historiography, see Gluck, "What's So Special about Women?"; and Armitage and Gluck, "Reflections on Women's Oral History."

9. Popular Memory Group, "Popular Memory." See also Passerini, "Work, Ideology, and Consensus under Italian Fascism." For other influential discussions of oral history, see Passerini, *Memory and Totalitarianism*; Henige, *Oral Historiography*; Portelli, "The Peculiarities of Oral History"; Gluck and Patai, *Women's Words*; Bertaux and Thompson, *Between Generations*; Grele, "Movement without Aim"; and Armitage and Gluck, "Reflections on Women's Oral History."

10. Writing of the uses of oral historiography, Passerini points out that such "facile democratisation" merely turns oral history into an "alternative ghetto where at last the oppressed may be allowed to speak" ("Work, Ideology, and Consensus under Italian Fascism," 53).

11. J. W. Scott, "The Evidence of Experience," 777–78.

12. Visweswaran, *Fictions of Feminist Ethnography*, 8.

13. Stoler and Strassler, "Castings for the Colonial," 4. On memory as active process, see Portelli, "What Makes Oral History Different," 69–70.

14. Ibid., 4–5.

15. Foucault, "Truth and Power," 117. See also Dreyfus and Rabinow, *Michel Foucault*, 104–25; and Stoler and Strassler, "Castings for the Colonial." Stoler and Strassler, of course, caution against reducing "acts of remembering . . . to transparencies about the making of the self." As they put it, "our focus is on not only what is remembered but how" ("Castings for the Colonial," 8–9).

16. Quote from Portelli, "What Makes Oral History Different," 69. See also Passerini, "Work, Ideology, and Consensus under Italian Fascism," 54.

17. Abu-Lughod, "Can There Be a Feminist Ethnography?" 10; Portelli, "What Makes Oral History Different," 70–73; Gluck, "What's So Special about Women?" 6–7, 13; Armitage and Gluck, "Reflections on Women's Oral History," 79–81. See also Rabinow, *Reflections on Fieldwork in Morocco*; and Crapanzano, "On the Writing of Ethnography."

18. Clifford, "Introduction: Partial Truths"; Abu-Lughod, "Can There Be a Feminist Ethnography?" 9–11; Armitage and Gluck, "Reflections on Women's Oral History," 79–81; Stacey, "Can There Be a Feminist Ethnography?" 115–17; Spivak, "Can the Subaltern Speak?"; Spivak, "Who Claims Alterity?"; Visweswaran, *Fictions of Feminist Ethnography*, 48–50; Haraway, "Situated Knowledges."

19. Armitage and Gluck, "Reflections on Women's Oral History," 81.

20. Quote from Stacey, "Can There be a Feminist Ethnography?" 116. I use the term *difference* to mean both "difference among positions and the different positions any one person must assume." See Crosby, "Dealing with Differences," 139; and Haraway, "Situated Knowledges," 586–87. For other useful discussions of difference in feminist thinking, see Riley, "A Short History of Some Preoccupations"; and Alarcón, "The Theoretical Subjects of *This Bridge Called My Back*." For critical discussions of this tendency within feminist ethnography and oral historiography, see Armitage and Gluck, "Reflections on Women's Oral History"; Abu-Lughod, "Can There Be a Feminist Ethnography?" 25; Visweswaran, *Fictions of Feminist Ethnography*, 74–75, 97–101; and Borland, "That's Not What I Said," 72.

21. My own identifications with labels such as Hindu or bhadralok are typically much more *troubled and fractured than what was assumed by the women I interviewed.*

22. Quote from Abu-Lughod, "Can There Be a Feminist Ethnography?" 11; also see Clifford, "Introduction: Partial Truths," 6. While most of the interviewees were young in the period before Partition, or in one case not even born yet, I asked them what they remembered about women of their mothers' generation.

23. Quote from Visweswaran, *Fictions of Feminist Ethnography*, 74–75. See also Stacey, "Can There Be a Feminist Ethnography?" 116–17; Armitage and Gluck,

"Reflections on Women's Oral History," 79–82. For an early example of optimistic discussion about identification among women, see Gluck, "What's So Special about Women?" 9–10. On the binary of self/other in ethnographic research, see Abu-Lughod, "Can There Be a Feminist Ethnography?" 24; Visweswaran, *Fictions of Feminist Ethnography*, 30–32; Stacey, "Can There Be a Feminist Ethnography?" 115; Clifford, "Introduction: Partial Truths"; and Asad, "Ethnographic Representation, Statistics, and Modern Power," 68–76.

24. D. Scott, "Locating the Anthropological Subject"; Abu-Lughod, "Can There Be a Feminist Ethnography?" 26; Visweswaran, *Fictions of Feminist Ethnography*, 129–33; Narayan, *Storytellers, Saints, and Scoundrels*; John, *Discrepant Dislocations*, 5–28.

25. The quotations are from, respectively, Abu-Lughod, "Can There Be a Feminist Ethnography?" 27; Crosby, "Dealing with Differences," 140; and Trinh, "Not You/Like You." See David Scott's formulation of the "shared-but-different" histories and identities from which postcolonial subjects might speak to each other in "Locating the Anthropological Subject."

26. Crosby, "Dealing with Differences," 140; Spivak, "In a Word"; Hall, "Cultural Identity and Diaspora," 394.

27. Clifford and Marcus, *Writing Culture*; Abu-Lughod, "Can There Be a Feminist Ethnography?" 11; Visweswaran, *Fictions of Feminist Ethnography*, 75; Borland, "That's Not What I Said."

28. On "stable" text, see Portelli, "What Makes Oral History Different," 70. On "tasks of interpretation," see Stacey, "Can There Be a Feminist Ethnography?" 114–15; Borland, "That's Not What I Said," 63–64; and Clifford, "Introduction: Partial Truths," 2.

29. I am deeply indebted to Professor Hossenur Rahman and the late Mrs. Gauri Ayub for helping me make my first contacts with members of the Muslim middle class in Calcutta. Most of my interviewees in Bangladesh were located through the personal contacts of some of the women I interviewed in Calcutta.

30. The questions I posed to them were focused more directly on their memory of contacts with Muslim women in their lives.

31. The meetings with Nusrat Begum, which took place in her office in old Dhaka, were exceptions. Also, I met with Purnima Ganguly, Chaitali Bose, and Angana Mitra only once, at a gathering at the home of Jahan Ara Begum.

32. While I do not read the Arabic script used to write Urdu, I have a working knowledge of the language in its everyday spoken form, which it is not far from commonly used Hindi. Bengali is my first language.

33. For discussions of heteroglossia, see Bakhtin, *The Dialogic Imagination*;

Todorov, *Mikhail Bakhtin*, 56; and Tedlock and Mannheim, introduction to *The Dialogic Emergence of Culture*, 1–32.

34. I did not tape-record my short meetings with Nusreen Begum and Nandita Sinha. My description of my interactions with Purnima Ganguly, Chaitali Bose, and Angana Mitra at the home of Jahan Ara Begum is also based entirely on my notes, which were taken on the evening of the meeting.

35. The sociologist Habibul Haque Khondker recently pointed out that such protests also came at times from educated upper-class women, as was the case with his great-grandmother who seems to have published a treatise on this thorny issue toward the end of the nineteenth century. Personal communication, June 2005, National University of Singapore. I have been unable to locate an exact citation for the document. For other published work on this subject, see R. Ahmed, *The Bengal Muslims, 1871–1906*, 113–15.

36. Ibid.

37. Risley, for instance, concluded from a measurement of the proportion of the breadth of the head and the nose to their respective lengths that Indian Muslims were closer in racial features to the lower castes of Chandals and Pods than to the Semitic peoples. Religion thus emerges in this context as a code for class and race combined (*The Tribes and Castes of Bengal*). See also Viswanathan, "Ethnographic Politics and the Discourse of Origins," for a discussion of this point.

38. Viswanathan, "Ethnographic Politics and the Discourse of Origins," 125.

39. Decades later the tensions inherent in the contingent coalitions forged between different factions of Muslims in the subcontinent would cause them to break down, leading to yet another contentious partition of the subcontinent in 1971.

40. Viswanathan, "Ethnographic Politics and the Discourse of Origins"; Bacchetta, "Communal Property/Sexual Property"; Devji, "Gender and the Politics of Space."

41. Viswanathan, "Ethnographic Politics and the Discourse of Origins," 124.

42. Ibid., 123.

43. Bacchetta, "Communal Property/Sexual Property," 193.

44. M. Sarkar, "Muslim Women and the Politics of (In)visibility in Late Colonial Bengal."

45. Since the focus of this chapter is on the life histories of Muslim women, I have deliberately desisted from analyzing the oral testimonies I gathered from Hindu middle-class women. For a few excerpts from my conversations with Hindu women, see the epigraphs at the beginning of this chapter.

46. Hasan and Menon, *Unequal Citizens*, 2–3; Fazalbhoy, "Sociology of Muslims

in India"; John, "Feminism, Internationalism, and the West"; Pathak and Sunder Rajan, "Shahbano," 563.

47. Jahan Ara Begum is a pseudonym. Her real name is Persian in origin and is apparently difficult for some Bengalis to pronounce. I have used pseudonyms for all the interviewees with the exception of the late Sufia Kamal, a well-known and respected literary figure in both Bangladesh and West Bengal.

48. Khan Saheb's education and his success as a businessman should be read in the context of the relative position of Muslims and Hindus at that time. According to the 1921 Census of India, in Calcutta, "the Muhammadans come very far behind the Hindus [in terms of literacy]. The proportion of literates among their males over five [years of age] is barely half as great as among Hindu males." While the percentage of Muslims in the total population of Calcutta and its suburbs in 1921 was 24.5, the percentage of Muslims among the literate population of the city and its suburbs was only 13.3. The corresponding figures for Hindus in the area were 71.0 percent of the total population and 77.5 percent of the literate population. Census of India, 1921, vol. 6: *City of Calcutta*, Part 1, 33–34, 84–85. The census also notes that in terms of occupational distribution across religious groups, "Mohammadans [in Calcutta and its suburbs] predominate in the jute industries." In trade, for every Muslim there were four Hindus, and in public administration for every Muslim, there were six Hindus at that time (107).

49. On the organization of narratives, see Portelli, "What Makes Oral History Different," 67.

50. The formal end of British colonial rule in India in 1947 is typically referred to as independence.

51. Nationalist Muslims were those Muslims who supported the Congress's plan for a unified India and opposed the Muslim League.

52. No equivalent term existed for Hindus. It is also important to remember that nationalist Muslims were concerned not only with political unity with Hindus but also with maintaining their own cultural and religious difference. For a discussion of the nationalist Muslim position, see Pandey, *The Construction of Communalism in Colonial North India*, 258–59.

53. These riots took place on August 16–20, 1946. The immediate occasion was the declaration of a Direct Action Day by the Muslim League, which was locked in a struggle for power with the Congress at the national level. For an analysis of the Calcutta riots of August 1946, see Inder Singh, *The Origins of the Partition of India, 1936–1947*, 181–87.

54. Leela Bannerjee was the principal of the Victoria School at that time. Jahan Ara described her as "a very educated and accomplished woman in those days."

55. Needless to say, middle-class or upper-middle-class women in Calcutta and Dhaka at that time would typically have household help, freeing them for other activities. Still, that Ayesha chose to do "social work" testifies to her interest in social uplift. The trend continues today.

56. Personal communication, Calcutta 1996.

57. Personal communication, Meherunnessa Begum, Calcutta, 1996.

58. The theme of the riots was endemic, in fact, to almost all the oral accounts I recorded, demonstrating perhaps the extent to which the history of the nation overshadows other elements that might make up a personal history. My decision, after much deliberation, to include the "riot stories" of only two testimonies is a self-conscious attempt to highlight the other aspects of the life stories of these women.

59. For discussions of oral histories as "a transaction between the interviewer and interviewee," see Gluck, "What's So Special about Women?" 13; Portelli, "What Makes Oral History Different," 70–73; and Armitage and Gluck, "Reflections on Women's Oral History," 79–81. For similar discussions within anthropology, see, for instance, Abu-Lughod, "Can There Be a Feminist Ethnography?" 10.

60. Portelli, "What Makes Oral History Different," 72–73. See also Armitage and Gluck, "Reflections on Women's Oral History," 81.

61. The phrase could be interpreted as either "they were brought by someone," or simply "they had arrived." I use "appeared" to hold on to the ambiguity in the Bengali phrase.

62. Ballyganj is an area south of Park Circus.

63. Bhabanipur is an area southwest of Park Circus.

64. The college is located in Bhabanipur.

65. The reference to violent non-Bengali Muslims may also be an unconscious invocation of the violence perpetrated by the West Pakistani army on Bengali Muslims during the Bangladeshi war of independence in 1970–71.

66. For discussions of the importance of and delicacy involved in elucidating the larger historical context in which oral history narratives are located, see, for instance, Borland, "That's Not What I Said," 63–64; Armitage and Gluck, "Reflections on Women's Oral History," 81–83; and Stacey, Can There Be a Feminist Ethnography?" 114.

67. For analyses of the Partition and the politics that underwrote it, see Inder Singh, *The Origins of the Partition of India, 1936–1947*; Hasan, *Nationalism and Communal Politics in India, 1885–1930*; and Page, *Prelude to Partition*. For an in-

cisive discussion of communal ideology in early-twentieth-century Bengal, see Datta, *Carving Blocs*.

68. The Congress Party was dominated by Hindus, but it also represented nationalist Muslims, those not affiliated with the Muslim League, and minorities such as Sikhs and Christians. The call to direct action was in a Muslim League resolution of July 29, 1946, 138–39, quoted in Inder Singh, *The Origins of the Partition of India, 1936–1947*, 181.

69. According to Inder Singh, 50 percent of educated Muslims did not support the League leadership's claimed right to nominate all the Muslim members of a proposed executive council even in the Muslim majority North West Frontier Province (*The Origins of the Partition of India, 1936–1947*, 118–25, 174).

70. An advertisement in the *Dawn, Eastern Times,* and *Morning News* on August 16, 1946, declared:

> Today is Direct Action Day
> Today Muslims of India dedicate anew their lives and all they possess to the cause of freedom
> Today let every Muslim swear in the name of Allah to resist aggression
> Direct Action is now their only course
> Because they offered peace but peace was spurned . . .
> Now Might alone can secure their Right.

71. *Report of the Commissioners of Police on the Disturbances of 16–20 August* (Calcutta, 1946), quoted in Lambert, "Hindu-Muslim Riots," 170.

72. *Goondas* is a term used to refer to urban hooligans from the beginning of the twentieth century in colonial Calcutta. For a discussion of the definition of *goonda*, see D. Bhattacharya, "Kolkata 'Underworld' in the Early Twentieth Century."

73. Inder Singh, *The Origins of the Partition of India, 1936–1947*, 182–83. See also Das and Ray, *The Goondas*, especially page 31, for an account of the role of Hindu goondas in the 1946 riots.

74. Inder Singh, *The Origins of the Partition of India, 1936–1947*, ix.

75. According to Datta (*Carving Blocs*, 145–46), Suhrawardy enjoyed much grassroots popularity, including the support of some known criminals. However, he was not the only one. It seems that both Hindu and Muslim leaders had considerable followings among members of the Calcutta underworld at that time. See, for instance, Gordon, *Brothers against the Raj*, 88; and D. Bhattacharya, "Kolkata 'Underworld' in the Early Twentieth Century."

76. Acknowledgments of the role of a few nationalist Muslim leaders, most notably Maulana Azad, seem to be exceptions that secure the rule.

77. Mumtaz spoke mostly in English intermixed with Bengali phrases.

78. Bhawanipur is Bhabanipur. Mumtaz uses the Hindi/Urdu pronunciation.

79. Bardhaman is a district in present-day West Bengal.

80. While a *puja* is a Hindu religious ritual, *puja*, here, refers to the annual Hindu Festival of Durga Puja (Worship of Goddess Durga) that is popular in Bengal.

81. The Indo-Pakistani conflict of 1965 was fought over Kashmir. It is widely believed that the war began with the infiltration of Pakistani-controlled guerrillas into Indian Kashmir on about August 5, 1965, and in September Pakistani and Indian troops crossed the partition lines between the two countries. Hostilities continued until the United Nations Security Council unanimously passed a resolution on September 20, 1965, that called for a cease-fire. Eventually, both governments signed the Soviet-brokered Tashkent Declaration on January 10, 1966, which required that both sides observe the cease-fire line agreed to before the war.

82. The immediate context for these riots was reports of violence in East Pakistan over the theft of a sacred relic from the Hazratbal mosque in Srinagar, a city in the state of Kashmir in India. For an account of the events leading up to the 1964 riots, which claimed hundreds of lives in both East Pakistan (now Bangladesh) and Calcutta, see A. Ghosh, *The Shadow Lines*, 224–30.

83. The word *abhiman* translates as "feeling hurt, especially owing to the undesirable behavior of a beloved person" (*Samsad Bengali-English Dictionary*).

84. Rokeya was one of the best-known Muslim intellectuals and reformers of the late nineteenth century and the early twentieth in Bengal. Among her other accomplishments, in 1911 she founded a school, Sakhawat Memorial, for Muslim girls in Calcutta. S. Mahmud, *Rokeya Jibani*, 7.

85. Nusrat Begum, personal communication, Dhaka, 1996. For a discussion of the preference for Urdu and sanctions against the cultivation of Bengali among relatively affluent Muslims in colonial Bengal, see Swarochish Sarkar, *Kathasahitya O Natake Muslim Sanskarchetona*, 131–36; R. Ahmed, *The Bengal Muslims, 1871–1906*; A. Fazal, *Rekhachitra*, 1–4; and Anisuzzaman, *Muslim Manas O Bangla Sahitya*.

86. *Bhasa Andolan*, or language agitation, as at the heart of Bengali resistance to West Pakistani domination.

87. The question of Bengali identity may be more complicated in Bangladesh

today than my analysis reflects. However, my current concerns are with colonial Bengal and postcolonial India. I therefore feel neither qualified nor inclined to address the issue of identity politics—presumably around issues of adequate Bengali-ness—in contemporary Bangladesh. For a discussion of that particular dilemma, see, for instance, O'Connell, "The Bengali Muslims and the State," especially 192–98; and Kabeer, "The Quest for National Identity." Suffice it to say that most of the women I spoke with in Bangladesh belong to families that have lived in some part of undivided Bengal for at least several generations, that they were in one way or another involved in the Bengali struggle against West Pakistani domination in the 1950s and 1960s, and that, at least in their conversation with me, they neither claimed nor showed signs of other forms of ethnic identification.

88. Nusrat edits a popular women's magazine.

89. Hatem, "A'isha Taymur's Tears and the Critique of the Modernist and the Feminist Discourses on Nineteenth-Century Egypt," 85. See also Abu-Lughod, "Feminist Longings," 24.

90. Farida Khatun is a pseudonym.

91. Shealdah Station is a major train station at the heart of Calcutta.

92. A *Phaeton gari* is an uncovered horse-drawn carriage with four wheels.

93. Nazrul Islam—one of the most respected Bengali poets and writers of the twentieth century—was introduced in chapter 3.

94. Lady Brabourne was the first college established in Calcutta mainly for Muslim women (1939). Its founder, Fazlul Huq, was head of the Bengal ministry at that time. Akhtar and Bhowmik, *Zenana Mehfil*; Sonia Nishat Amin, *The World of Muslim Women in Colonial Bengal, 1876–1939*.

95. Nusrat's father, for instance, was extremely supportive of Rokeya Sakhawat Hossain's efforts to bring formal education to Muslim girls.

96. For a recent commentary on the hidden costs of the "modernizing mission" of male nationalists in India, see Antoinette Burton's essay on Janaki Majumdar in her edited edition of Majumdar's *Family History* (Burton, Introduction). Of course, the "costs" involved in the cases of Hemangini, Janaki Majumdar's mother, on the one hand, and Farida, Nusrat's mother, on the other, were quite different. As the wife of the first president of the Indian National Congress, W. C. Bonnerjee, both Hemangini and her home were entirely open to the public eye; indeed, they would have been expected to set a certain standard worth emulating for other aspiring "new women" of a nascent nation. Farida, meanwhile, was resisting the pressure to even come out of seclusion. No one, including Farida's daughter, has thought to write about her let alone "excavate . . . [her] story as the

foundation of Indian nationalism [/ Muslim liberalism]," as Burton puts it in the case of Hemangini (xix).

97. *Paribar* literally means "family," but it is also used to mean "wife."

98. Qaji Saheb is Nusrat's affectionate name for Nazrul Islam.

99. Most of Nusrat's recollections of her mother came in response to explicit questions about her.

100. In the words of Joan Wallach Scott, "Knowledge is gained through vision; vision is a direct apprehension of a world of transparent objects. In this conceptualization, the visible is privileged" ("The Evidence of Experience," 775). See also Jay, *Downcast Eyes*.

101. For a discussion of the interconnections between purdah and the backwardness of women in Bengali, see Hossain, "Borka." The borkha (also spelled *borka* and *burka*), as noted earlier, is the veiling gown used by women who practice purdah when they step outside their homes. Pardanasheen are women who observe strict purdah (spelled *parda* in Bengali and *pardah* in Urdu). *Purdah* literally means "curtain" and is used to refer to women who practice seclusion. For a discussion of how modernist historians sometimes overlook the role played by ostensibly "traditional" women in enabling the success of others in the context of nineteenth-century Egypt, see Hatem, "'A'isha Taymur's Tears' and the Critique of the Modernist and the Feminist Discourses on Nineteenth-Century Egypt," especially 80–86.

102. Rajshahi is one of the larger cities in present-day Bangladesh.

103. Sen is a pseudonym.

104. This is the Communist Party of India (Marxist).

105. *Dada* means "elder brother" in Bengali.

106. The reference to her parents' distrust of the Communist Party may also be an indirect way to reiterate her family's distance from other Muslims, often of lesser means, who constitute a significant source of support for the Left Front, consisting of several left-oriented parties in West Bengal today.

107. Fatema is a pseudonym.

108. Jahan Ara was referring to Hindu families that had migrated from East Bengal–East Pakistan (currently Bangladesh) in the wake of the Partition of India in 1947. While the United Nations never formally recognized as refugees the millions of people displaced by this event—under the pretext that this was a "regional" problem that did not involve international borders—in South Asia they are commonly referred to as refugees. According to one source, in 1951, 41.27 percent of the total migrant population of Calcutta proper was from East Pakistan. Note that another wave of refugees arrived in Calcutta from East Pakistan during

the Bangladeshi war of independence in 1971. See P. Chatterjee, *The Present History of West Bengal*, 187.

109. *Dehliwal* means "from Delhi."

110. *Bhadramahila* literally means "genteel woman." The term was coined in the nineteenth century by the emerging educated Hindu/Brahmo middle class in Bengal to refer to women of the same class. It would seem that in Mumtaz's mother's usage it means "middle-class Bengali woman."

111. Mumtaz Waheeda, personal communication, Calcutta, 1996.

112. B. D. Metcalf, *Perfecting Women*. See also B. D. Metcalf, "Reading and Writing about Muslim Women in British India," 4–5; Minault, *Secluded Scholars*, 63–71; and Azra Asghar Ali, *The Emergence of Feminism among Indian Muslim Women, 1920–1947*, 14–24.

113. Eve-teasing is the sexual harassment of a woman by a man in a public place.

114. Portelli, "What Makes Oral History Different," 66.

115. Borland, "That's Not What I Said," 72.

116. Both Zohra Sultana and Jahan Ara Begum made similar points about controlling their own finances. It seems that middle-class Muslim women often have the freedom to do as they please with their earnings and *meher*, the money that husbands are contractually obligated to give their wives under Islamic law at the time of their marriage. In contrast, Hindu women rarely have control over their dowries. For a discussion of dowry, see R. Kumar, *The History of Doing*.

117. At the time of the interview, Mumtaz Waheeda was living with her elder son and his wife in an affluent neighborhood in Calcutta.

118. Intertexts are other discourses brought, directly or indirectly, into the time and space of our own. See Kristeva, *Desire in Language*; and Tedlock and Mannheim, introduction to *The Dialogic Emergence of Culture*, 16.

119. Armitage and Gluck, "Reflections on Women's Oral History," especially 79–81; Portelli, "What Makes Oral History Different," 72.

120. Meherunnessa's impressions of Muslim households do not necessarily conform to the picture that emerged from the testimonies of other women I interviewed. This could be because, unlike the other women I quote here, at least part of Meherunnessa's family was not from Bengal and hence represented a somewhat different cultural ethos and set of practices.

121. Muslim attendance at schools is, of course, much higher. In 1931–32, it was 49.9 percent of the total number of boys in primary and secondary schools and 56.5 percent of the total number of girls in primary schools. However, a closer look reveals that most of the students were concentrated in the primary classes,

and the attendance figures dwindle to 16.8 percent for boys and a mere 1.6 percent for girls by class ten. Moslem Education Advisory Committee, *Report of the Moslem Education Advisory Committee*, 26–29, 52–53, 110–11.

122. In her autobiographical novel, Omartul Fazal, wife of the writer Abul Fazal, also relates awkward experiences in a predominantly Hindu school. See Omartul Fazal, *Urmi*, 68–69.

123. For a discussion of *chakri* and its effects on the bhadralok in the nineteenth century, see Sumit Sarkar, "'Kaliyuga,' 'Chakri,' and 'Bhakti.'"

124. Ek bhari is a unit of weight equal to 180 grains (*Samsad Bengali-English Dictionary*, 1995).

125. The anchal is the end of the sari that hangs over one's shoulders. *Shari* is the Bengali word for sari.

126. Nusreen Begum is a pseudonym. Meherunnessa took me to meet her briefly one afternoon in 1996.

127. It was typical of the Calcutta middle and upper classes to rent houses at hill stations to escape the summer heat.

128. Here Jahan Ara is referring to Muslims of lesser means who moved into the area after independence, many of whom came from the neighboring state of Bihar.

129. According to Meherunnessa, the typical response to the idea of insurance among many of her relatives was *"Benefit from the dead! No need! (Chhi! Mara benche khabo! Darker nei!)."*

130. 24 Parganas is a district in West Bengal.

131. *Khan Sahebs* refers to the Khan family, especially the men.

132. Khulna and Jashore are districts in East Bengal, now Bangladesh.

133. A zamindar is a landowner or landlord. The fasting refers to the month of Ramzan or Ramadan.

134. *Ghranena ardhyabhojanam* is a proverb in Sanskrit.

135. Biriyani or biryani is rice cooked with meat—beef in this case. Hindus do not eat beef; indeed, Brahmins are supposed to be vegetarian.

136. *Jat* refers to caste in this case. Eating beef is forbidden in Hinduism. For a discussion of the various uses of the word *jat* or *jati* in most Indian languages, see P. Chatterjee, *The Nation and Its Fragments*, 166.

137. This is the well-known reformist family of the Nobel laureate poet, Rabindranath Thakur (Tagore).

138. Jahan Ara is probably referring to Satis Chandra Mitra's *Yasohara-Khulnara Itihasa*.

139. *Sunil Gangopadhyay* is a noted contemporary Bengali novelist/writer.

140. Portelli, "What Makes Oral History Different," 68.

141. *Chotolok* literally means "small folk," a reference to poor or working people.

142. *Lede/nede* is a derogatory term commonly used to refer to poor Muslims, who were often converts.

143. Bhadrasampraday are members of the educated, typically propertied, middle class or gentry.

144. Begum Sufia Kamal, personal communication, Dhaka, 1996. *Bhadra* refers to persons who are considered civilized, cultured, and of a certain class.

145. Chitta Ranjan Das, also known as Deshabandhu or "friend of the nation," was a famous barrister and dynamic political figure of twentieth-century Bengal. He was one of the chief architects of the Bengal Pact in 1923, which sought to unite Hindus and Muslims politically. For a discussion of the Bengal Pact, see Sumit Sarkar, *Modern India*, 232; and Datta, *Carving Blocs*, 96. Aswini Datta, a well-known and highly respected nationalist leader and philanthropist, is credited with founding a school for girls in Barisal (a district in East Bengal, now Bangladesh) in the late nineteenth century.

146. Begum Kamal, personal communication, Dhaka, 1996.

147. Like a sarong, a lungi is a wrap worn around the waist by men in many parts of South and Southeast Asia. In Hindu middle-class discourse in Bengal, however, it is often associated with poor Muslims.

148. For a description of similar experiences, see O. Fazal, *Urmi*, 68–69.

149. Haj is a pilgrimage to Mecca.

150. The names are Hindu, as were the women present. I have changed the names to preserve the privacy of the participants. Angana Mitra arrived a little late, so she was not present during some of the conversation reported below.

151. I use Jahan as the pet name in the interest of maintaining the privacy of the participants.

152. Purnima Ganguly, August 2000, Calcutta.

153. Sufia Kamal, Dhaka 1996; Shafinaz Hossein, Dhaka, 1996. See also the discussion of Muslim writing on this subject in chapter 3.

154. I am referring specifically to conversations with two women, Ila Chatterjee and Nandita Sinha (both in Calcutta, 1996), but in my experience similar sentiments about Muslims are quite common among Hindu women in contemporary Calcutta.

155. *Halal* means "lawful food." The word also refers to the practice of killing (an animal) in the manner prescribed by Muslim law.

156. *Azaan* is the call to prayer, which is repeated five times during the day,

about fifteen minutes before the time of each specific namaaz (prayer). Maghrib namaaz is the evening prayer, which lasts until twilight fades.

157. *Waterlogging* refers to the water that accumulates with heavy rain on the streets of Calcutta.

158. I had a very similar experience with Meherunnessa Begum.

159. Jahan Ara often stated that she never felt awkward about her strong faith in Islam in the presence of Hindus who were religious. They, she felt, always understood and respected her, as she did them. I borrow the notion of adjustment from Marlon Riggs's excellent film *Color Adjustment* (1991) in which he offers an incisive and comprehensive analysis of how prime-time television in the United States reluctantly began to include African Americans and the ways in which black actors and performers negotiated both their marginalization and, more important, their specific incorporation.

160. Ira is a pseudonym. Jahan Ara adds the suffix *di* to her name, signifying that Ira is the older of the two. Ira is not only Hindu but also Brahmin.

161. *Moumachhi* is a Bengali word meaning "bee." Ghosh was a well-known writer of children's literature in Bengali.

162. *Pishima* means "father's sister." *Boudi* means "elder brother's wife."

163. *Iftari* is the breaking of the daily fast during Ramzan or Ramadan.

164. Jahan Ara Begum, 1996.

165. D. Scott, "Locating the Anthropological Subject."

166. Stacey, "Can There Be a Feminist Ethnography?" 113–14; Visweswaran, *Fictions of Feminist Ethnography*, 40–59.

CONCLUSION

1. Quote from Abu-Lughod, "Feminist Longings and Postcolonial Conditions," 3; see also Kandiyoti, "Identity and Its Discontents," 376–91.

2. For a recent influential work on the need to expand conventional notions of what constitutes the proper object of historical research, see Burton, *Dwelling in the Archive*.

3. Kandiyoti, "Identity and Its Discontents."

4. In February 2002, a train carrying right-wing Hindu activists was attacked by a Muslim mob after repeated provocations from the passengers. The ensuing mayhem led to the deaths of fifty-eight passengers. This incident sparked widespread violence against Muslims in the state of Gujarat that left thousands dead and many more homeless, injured, or traumatized. For incisive reports of the violence, see

Communalism Combat, nos. 77–78 (March-April 2002); and T. Sarkar, "Semiotics of Terror," 2875–83.

5. Hasan and Menon, *Unequal Citizens*, 1.

6. Ibid., 2.

7. Ibid., 2–3. See also Fazalbhoy, "Sociology of Muslims in India"; and John, "Feminism, Internationalism, and the West."

8. Hasan and Menon, *Unequal Citizens*, 4.

9. Ibid.; Shaheeda Lateef, *Muslim Women in India*; Rafique Khan, *Socio-legal Status of Muslim Women*; N. Menon, *Gender and Politics in India*; Sunder Rajan, *Signposts*.

10. Hasan and Menon, *Unequal Citizens*, 2–3.

11. Ibid., 3–4. See also Sunder Rajan, introduction to *Signposts*, 2–3.

12. For a useful and accessible discussion of the power of discourse, see Hall, "The West and the Rest."

13. In 1985, Shah Bano, a Muslim woman, took her husband to court for leaving her after forty years of marriage without providing adequate financial support. Shah Bano's husband, Mohammed Ahmed Khan, contested her claim on the grounds that he had provided support for three months after the divorce as required, apparently, by Muslim personal law. The Supreme Court of India ruled in favor of Shah Bano, upholding Muslim women's right to lifelong maintenance in the event of desertion by their husbands. The ruling sparked a nationwide controversy, prompting the government to pass an amendment that reinforced the status of Muslim women as wards of the Muslim community, undercutting their rights to equal treatment as citizens of the Indian state. For discussions of the Shah Bano case, see Engineer, *The Shah Bano Controversy*; Pathak and Sunder Rajan, "Shahbano"; Mody, "The Press in India"; Rafiq Khan, *Socio-legal Status of Muslim Women*; Baxi, *Text of Observations Made at a Public Meeting on the Muslim Women (Protection of Rights) Bill*; "Interview with Y. V. Chandrachud," *Sunday Observer*, December 8, 1985; and Shourie, "Shariat Series." See also Das, *Critical Events*, 94–107; and Kishwar, "Pro-Women or Anti-Muslim?"

14. Mani, "Contentious Traditions," 119–21. See also Kishwar, "Pro-Women or Anti-Muslim?"; Pathak and Sunder Rajan, "Shahbano"; T. Basu et al., *Khaki Shorts and Saffron Flags*; T. Sarkar and Butalia, *Women and Right-Wing Movements*; and Mazumdar, "Moving Away from a Secular Vision?" Faced with the prospect of electoral setbacks, the central government, headed by Rajiv Gandhi, allowed a new codification of Muslim personal law that dictated that "divorced Muslim women would fall outside the purview of section 125 of the Code of Criminal Procedure," which has long allowed women of all communities to bypass the

restrictions and limitations of "the personal laws of their religions." The Supreme Court ruling in favor of Shah Bano was also based on section 125. See Pathak and Sunder Rajan, "Shahbano," 561.

15. See, for instance, Hassan, "Communalism, State Policy, and the Question of Women's Rights in Contemporary India"; and K. N. Panikkar and Muralidharan, *Communalism, Civil Society, and the State*.

16. Pathak and Sunder Rajan, "Shahbano," 566.

17. Ibid., 566–67. See also Bacchetta, "Communal Property/Sexual Property," 194–98.

18. On British justifications, see, for instance, Liddle and Joshi, "Gender and Imperialism in British India"; P. Chatterjee, *The Nation and Its Fragments*, 118; Chakravarti, "Whatever Happened to the Vedic *Dasi*?" 34–36; Spivak, "Can the Subaltern Speak?"; and Pathak and Sunder Rajan, "Shahbano," 567.

19. Pathak and Sunder Rajan, "Shahbano," 567.

20. T. Sarkar, "The Woman as Communal Subject"; T. Sarkar and Butalia, *Women and Right-Wing Movements*; Tharu and Niranjana, "Problems for a Contemporary Theory of Gender."

21. The Rashtriya Swayamsevak Samiti is the military wing of the Hindu Right coalition (an organization with the ambitious political agenda of establishing a Hindu nation). Reports show that women took part in the attacks against Muslims in Gujarat in 2002. T. Sarkar, "Semiotics of Terror," 2877. See also T. Basu et al., *Khaki Shorts and Saffron Flags*, 78–87; and Mazumdar, "Women on the March."

22. Hindutva is the official, chauvinistic ideology of the Hindu Right. It is not synonymous with Hinduism. For useful discussions of Hindutva, see T. Basu et al., *Khaki Shorts and Saffron Flags*; and Noorani, *The RSS and the BJP*.

23. For further discussions, see T. Sarkar, "Semiotics of Terror"; Tharu and Niranjana, "Problems for a Contemporary Theory of Gender"; Amrita Basu, "Feminism Inverted"; T. Sarkar and Butalia, *Women and Right-Wing Movements*; and Jeffery and Basu, *Appropriating Gender*.

24. Bacchetta, "Communal Property/Sexual Property," especially 197–98; T. Basu et al., *Khaki Shorts and Saffron Flags*; T. Sarkar, "Semiotics of Terror," 2878–79. See also Savarkar, *Hindutva*. Sangh Parivar is a family of Hindu chauvinist associations that includes the RSS (a supposedly cultural organization), the Vishwa Hindu Parishad (VHP; the religious wing of the Sangh), and the Bajrang Dal (the youth wing of the VHP, whose members are trained by the RSS). The Bharatiya Janata Party (BJP) is the political party affiliated with the Sangh.

25. Das, *Critical Events*, 106.

26. See, for instance, the discussion of Shah Bano's actions in Pathak and Sunder Rajan, "Shahbano," 571.

27. "Open Letter to Muslims," *Inquilab*, November 13, 1985, translated into English by A. Karim Shaik and published in *Radiance*, November 24–30, 1985, and reprinted in Engineer, *The Shah Bano Controversy*, 211. See also Pathak and Sunder Rajan, "Shahbano," 572.

28. Pathak and Sunder Rajan, "Shahbano," 572.

29. Ibid. Pathak and Sunder Rajan borrowed the phrase "discursive displacement" from Gayatri Chakravorty Spivak. As they put it, Spivak "uses the phrase . . . to mean 'functional changes in sign systems'" (565). See also Spivak, "Subaltern Studies."

30. Pathak and Sunder Rajan, "Shahbano," 572–73. See also Spivak, "Subaltern Studies," 341.

31. Pathak and Sunder Rajan, "Shahbano," 572.

32. For a discussion of this particular dilemma, see Kishwar, "Pro-Women or Anti-Muslim?"

33. Conservative estimates put the number of dead, mostly Muslims, at about twenty-five hundred, with thousands more injured, raped, or rendered homeless. See Sarath Kumara, "A Travesty of Justice," August 25, 2003, World Socialist Web Site, http://wsws.org/articles/2003/aug2003/guja-a25_prn.shtml; and *Communalism Combat*, nos. 77–78 (2002).

34. T. Sarkar, "Semiotics of Terror," 2875–83 and 2876, respectively. See also Aijaz Ahmad, "Somnath to Gandhinagar."

35. "The International Initiative for Justice in Gujarat: An Interim Report," December 2002, http://onlinevolunteers.org/gujarat/reports/iijg/interimreport .htm (accessed on June 10, 2003); International Initiative for Justice, "Threatened Existence"; Hameed et al., "How Has the Gujarat Massacre Affected Minority Women?"; K. G. Kannabiran, "Narendra Modi's Hindutva Laboratory"; Bidwai, "End the Butchery, Sack Modi"; K. N. Panikkar and Muralidharan, *Communalism, Civil Society, and the State*; Baldwin, "Gujarat's Gendered Violence."

36. See, for instance, Communalism Combat, *Genocide: Gujarat 2002* (July 2002), 68–86.

37. R. Menon and Bhasin, *Borders and Boundaries*; Littlewood, "Military Rape"; Engel, "Feminism and Its (Dis)contents"; Hintjens, "Explaining the 1994 Genocide in Rwanda." See also Project Legal Aid for Women Raped or Sexually Assaulted by State Security Forces, *Sexual Violence Perpetrated by the State*.

38. T. Sarkar, "Semiotics of Terror," 2881.

39. One of the oft-cited reasons for the Gujarat violence is a story that circulated in the Gujarati press about the supposed rape, torture, and murder of eighty Hindu women on the Sabarmati Express in Godhra on February 27, 2002, by a Muslim mob. As Tanika Sarkar notes, even the Gujarat police force, which was tacitly complicit in the subsequent violent attacks on Muslims, failed to corroborate the story. T. Sarkar, "Semiotics of Terror," 2881.

40. See, for instance, the discussions of "domestic violence" in Hasan and Menon, *Unequal Citizens*, 167–92; Kishwar and Vanita, "The Burning of Roop Kanwar"; Sangari, "Violent Acts"; Sangari, "Violent Routes"; Ray, "Where Women Bore the Brunt"; and N. Shah et al., "Structural Adjustment, Feminization of Labour Force, and Organizational Strategies."

41. Kalpana Kannabiran, "Rape and the Construction of Communal Identity," 33.

42. Ibid., 32–41; Ray, "Where Women Bore the Brunt."

43. Bacchetta, "Communal Property/Sexual Property," 193.

44. Ray, "Where Women Bore the Brunt."

45. Fernandes is quoted in T. Sarkar, "Semiotics of Terror," 2880.

46. See Arundhati Roy, "Fascism's Firm Footprint in India"; Hameed et al., "How Has the Gujarat Massacre Affected Minority Women?"; K. G. Kannabiran, "Narendra Modi's Hindutva Laboratory"; Bidwai, "End the Butchery, Sack Modi"; and K. N. Panikkar and Muralidharan, *Communalism, Civil Society, and the State.*

47. For two such instances, see Mazumdar, "Moving Away from a Secular Vision?" 243–73; and T. Sarkar, "Semiotics of Terror," 2876, 2879–80.

Bibliography

ARCHIVES AND LIBRARIES

Most of the primary source material consulted for this volume was gathered from periodicals, newspapers, official publications, and manuscripts housed in the following archives.

- Bangiya Sahitya Parishad, Calcutta
- Bangla Academy, Dhaka
- Bangladesh Bureau of Statistics, Ministry of Planning, Dhaka
- National Library, Calcutta
- Office of the Director of Census Operations, West Bengal, Calcutta
- Oriental and India Office Collections, British Library, London
- Royal Asiatic Society, Calcutta
- West Bengal Secretariat Library, Government of West Bengal, Writers Building, Calcutta

Apart from these archives, I made extensive use of published compilations of primary sources in the following libraries.

Bangladesh Mission Library, Embassy of Bangladesh, Calcutta
Centre for Studies in Social Science, Calcutta
Dhaka University Library, Dhaka

PERIODICALS AND NEWSPAPERS

Periodicals from the nineteenth century and the early twentieth are unfortunately not easy to locate in Calcutta. Even when archives or libraries record the names of periodicals, they are not always in circulation due to poor condition, and some of the issues or volumes may be missing. The following are the periodicals published in the last quarter of the nineteenth century and the first half of the twentieth that I consulted during my field research. The dates immediately following the name of the periodical indicate the particular volumes or issues to which I had access.

Al Eslam, 1915–16, 1916–17
Annessa, February-April 1921
Antahpur, 1901, 1902, 1904
Bamabodhini Patrika, 1866–67, 1874–75, 1879–80, 1883–84, 1891–92, 1894–95, 1895–96, 1903–4
Bandhab, November-December 1874
Bangiya Mussalman Sahitya Patrika, 1922
Begum, 1947–48, 1948–49, 1949–50
Bengal Magazine, January 1880
Bharati O Balak, 1890–91, 1891–92
Bharati, October-November 1881, September-October 1908, March-April 1918
Brahmo Public Opinion, 1879
Bulbul, 1933–37
Dhaka Prakash, 1860–61, 1885–86
Dhoomketu, 1922
Dipali, 1920–21
Education Gazette, 1896–96, 1922–23
Kohinoor, 1898–99
Mahila Saogat, 1929
Mahila, 1903–4
Mihir, 1892

Mihir O Sudhakar, 1894
Nabajug, 1920
Nabanoor: Monthly Periodical and Criticism, 1903–4; 1904–5; 1905–6
Prabashi, 1904
Samachar Darpan, 1823
Samadarshi, 1875–76
Samyabadi, December-May 1924
Saogat, 1918–19
Shikha, 1928
Somprakash, 1863–64; 1867–68
Tattvabodhini Patrika, 1867, 1881, 1891

GOVERNMENT DOCUMENTS

Bureau of Education, India. *Education Statistics, British India, 1945–46*. Ministry of Education. Delhi: Government of India Press, 1948.

———. *General Education Tables for India, 1946–47*. Delhi: Government of India Press, 1951.

Census of Bengal, 1881. Vol. 1. Calcutta, 1883.

Census of India, 1891. Vol. 3: *Bengal*. Ed. C. A. O'Donnell. Calcutta, 1893.

Census of India, 1901. Vol. 1–A: *India*. Part II: *Tables*. Calcutta, 1903.

Census of India, 1911. Vol. 1: *India*. Part 1: *Report*. Calcutta: Bengal Secretariat Book Depot, 1913.

Census of India, 1921. Vol. 1: *India*. Part 2: *Tables*. Calcutta: Bengal Secretariat Book Depot, 1923.

———. Vol. 5: *Bengal*. Part 2: *Tables*. Calcutta: Bengal Secretariat Book Depot, 1923.

———. Vol. 6: *City of Calcutta*. Part 1: *Report by W. H. Thompson*. Calcutta: Bengal Secretariat Book Depot, 1923.

Census of India, 1931. Vol. 1. *India*. Part 2: *Tables*. Calcutta: Bengal Secretariat Book Depot, 1933.

Census of India, 1941. Vol. 1: *India*. Part 2: *Report*. Calcutta: Bengal Secretariat Book Depot, 1943.

Chanda, A. K. *Ninth Quinquennial Review on the Progress of Education in Bengal, 1932–1937*. Calcutta: Bengal Government Press, 1939.

Croft, Alfred. *Review of Education in India in 1886 with Special Reference to the*

Report of the Education Commission by the Director of Public Instruction, Bengal. Calcutta: Superintendent of Government Printing, India, 1888.

Government of Bengal. *Report of the Committee Appointed by the Bengal Government to Consider Questions Connected with Muhammadan Education.* Calcutta: Bengal Secretariat Book Depot, 1915.

———. *Report on Public Instruction in Bengal, 1917–18.* Calcutta: Bengal Secretariat Book Depot, 1918.

———. *Supplement to the Report of the Public Instruction in Bengal (1938–39).* Alipore, Calcutta: Bengal Government Press, 1942.

Government of India. *Statistical Abstract for British India, 1920–21 to 1929–30.* Calcutta: Government of India, Central Publication Branch, 1932.

———. *Statistical Abstract for British India, 1933–34 and 1935–36.* Delhi: Government of India, 1936.

Government of United Provinces. *General Report on Public Instruction in the United Provinces of Agra and Oudh for the year ending March 31, 1935.* Allahabad: Superintendent of Printing, United Provinces, 1936.

Government of West Bengal. *Education Directorate Report on Public Instruction in West Bengal, 1947–48.* Alipore, Calcutta: West Bengal Government Press, 1951.

Moslem Education Advisory Committee. Report of the Moslem Education Advisory Committee. Alipore, Bengal: Superintendent of Government Printing, Bengal, 1934.

Orange, H. W. *Progress of Education in India, 1902–1907: Fifth Quinquennial Review, Office of the Director General of Education, India.* Bengal: Superintendent of Government Printing, 1908.

Richey, J. A. *Progress of Education in India, 1917–1922.* Vol. 1. Calcutta: Superintendent of Government Printing, 1923.

Twenty Years Statistics, Bengal. Education, 1883/87–1903/04. India Office Records, V/14–V/21. Official Publications: Indian Administrative Series 1796–1957, 1905.

BENGALI SOURCES

Ahmad, Abul Mansur. *Atmakatha* [Autobiography], 4th ed. Dhaka: Abul Mansur Ahmad Smriti Sansad, 1988.

Ahmad, Ali. *Bangla Muslim Granthapanji, 1850–1947* [Bengali Muslim Bibliography, 1850–1947]. Dhaka, Bangla Academy, 1985.

Ahmed, Ayesha. "Muslim Samaje Unnatir Antaray [The Obstacles to Progress in Muslim Society]." *Mahila Sankhya Saogat*, August-September 1929.

Akhtar, Shaheen. "Keno Ami Zenana Mehfil-e." In *Zenana Mehfil: Bangali Musalman Lekhikader Nirbachita Rachana, 1904–1938* [Selected Works of Bengali Muslim Women Writers, 1904–1938], ed. Shaheen Akhtar and Moushumi Bhowmick, 36–40. Calcutta: Stree, 1998.

Akhtar, Shaheen, and Moushumi Bhowmick, eds. *Zenana Mehfil: Bangali Musalman Lekhikader Nirbachita Rachana, 1904–1938* [Selected Works of Bengali Muslim Women Writers, 1904–1938]. Calcutta: Stree, 1998.

Anisuzzaman. *Muslim Banglar Samayikpatra, 1831–1930* [Journals of Muslim Bengal, 1831–1930]. Dhaka: Bangla Academy, 1969.

———. *Muslim Manas O Bangla Sahitya, 1757–1918* [The Muslim Mind and Bengali Literature, 1757–1918]. Dhaka: Muktadhara, 1969.

———. "Narimukti, Samakaal O Begum Rokeya [Women's Liberation, That Time, and Begum Rokeya]." In *Begum Rokeya O Narijagaran* [Begum Rokeya and Women's Awakening], ed. Farida Pradhan, 17–22. Dhaka: Rokeya Hall, Dhaka University, 1995.

Bandopadhyay, Brajendranath. *Mogoljuge Stree Shiksha* [The Education of Women in the Mughal Era]. Calcutta: Manashi, 1919.

Basu, Chhabi. *Racana Sankalan*. [Collected Essays]. Ed. Jasodhara Bagchi. Calcutta: Dey's Publishing, 1995.

Begum, Maleka. *Banglar Nari Andolan* [The Women's Movement in Bengal]. Dhaka: University Press Limited, 1989.

Bhowmick, Moushumi. "Prastabana." In *Zenana Mehfil: Bangali Musalman Lekhikader Nirbachita Rachana, 1904–1938* [Selected Works of Bengali Muslim Women Writers, 1904–1938], ed. Shaheen Akhtar and Moushumi Bhowmick, 25–35. Calcutta: Stree, 1998.

Chakraborty, Sombuddha. *Andare Antare: Unish Shatake Bangali Mahila* [Bengali Women in the Nineteenth Century]. Calcutta: Stree, 1995.

Das, Krishnabhabini. "Swadhin O Paradhin Nari Jiban [Independent and Dependent Life of Women]." *Pradeep*, February-March, 1897.

Dasgupta, Kamala. *Swadhinata Sangrame Banglar Nari* [Bengal's Women in the Freedom Struggle]. Calcutta: Basudhra Prakashani, 1970.

Datta, Amar. *Unish Shataker Muslim Manash O Bangabhanga (1905)*. [The Muslim Mind in the Nineteenth Century and the Division of Bengal (1905)]. Calcutta: Progressive Publishers, 1995.

Fazal, Abul. *Abul Fazal Rachanabali* [The Collected Works of Abul Fazal]. Vol. 1: *Chattagram*. Bangladesh: Baighar, 1975.

———. *Rekhachitra* [A Rough Sketch]. Chattagram: Baighar, 1956.

Fazal, Omartul. *Urmi: A Novel*. Dhaka: Muktadhara, 1970.

Ghosh, Binay. *Bidyasagar O Bangali Samaj* [Bidyasagar and Bengali Society]. Calcutta: Orient Longman, 1973.

———. *Samayikpatre Banglar Samajchitra* [A Picture of Bengali Society in Contemporary Newspapers and Periodicals]. 6 vols. Calcutta: Pyapiras, 1978.

Hasan, Morshed Shafiul. *Begum Rokeya: Samaye O Sahitya*. [Begum Rokeya: The Times and Literature]. Dhaka: Bangla Academy, 1982.

Hossain, Rokeya Sakhawat. "Borka." In *Begum Rokeya Rachanabali* [The Collected Works of Begum Rokeya], ed. Abdul Quadir, 47–53. Dhaka: Bangla Academy, 1984.

Hossein, Sahanara. "*Begum Rokeya Sakhawat Hossain: Tar Chinta-Chetanar Dhara* [Begum Rokeya Sakhawat Hossain: Her Thoughts and Consciousness]." In *Begum Rokeya O Narijagaran* [Begum Rokeya and Women's Awakening], ed. Farida Pradhan, 34–50. Dhaka: Rokeya Hall, Dhaka University, 1995.

Hossein, Yasmin. "Prekshapat." In *Zenana Mehfil: Bangali Musalman Lekhikader Nirbachita Rachana, 1904–1938* [Selected Works of Bengali Muslim Women Writers, 1904–1938], ed. Shaheen Akhtar and Moushumi Bhowmick, 13–24. Calcutta: Stree, 1998.

Hussein, Abul. *Abul Hussein-er Rachanabali* [The Collected Works of Abul Hussein]. Ed. Abdul Quadir. 2nd ed. Dhaka: Barnamichhil, 1976.

Imam, Akhter. *Eden Theke Bethune* [From Eden to Bethune]. Dhaka: Imam, Akhter, 1990.

———. *Amar Jiban Katha, 1917–1950, Part 1* [My Life Story, 1917–1950, Part 1]. Dhaka: Imam, Akhter, 1993.

Islam, Mustafa Nurul. *Samayikpatre Jiban O Janamat* [Life and Public Opinion in Contemporary Periodicals]. Dhaka: Bangla Academy, 1983.

Jahangir, Salim. *The Life and Works of Sufia Kamal*. Dhaka: Nari Udyog Kendra, 1993.

Khatun, Saiyeda Manoara. "Smritir Pata [A Page from Memory]." *Ekshan* (autumn 1989): 4–51.

Mahmud, Mosfeka. *Patre Rokeya Parichiti* [An Introduction to Rokeya through Her Letters]. Dhaka: Bangla Academy, 1968.

Mahmud, Samsunnahar. *Rokeya Jibani* [Rokeya's Biography]. Calcutta: Bulbul, 1937.

Mamun, Muntaseer. *Unish Satake Bangladesher Sangbad Samaikpatra, 1847–1905*

[Contemporary Newspapers of Nineteenth-Century Bengal, 1847–1905]. Vol. 4. Dhaka: Bangla Academy, 1991.

Manirujjaman, Muhammad. *Samayik Patre Sahityachinta: Saogat* [Literary Thought in Contemporary Journals: Saogat]. Dhaka: Dhaka University Press, 1981.

Mitra, Satis Chandra. *Yasohara-Khulnara Itihasa* [The History of Jasore-Khulna]. 3rd ed. 2 vols. Calcutta: DasGupta, 1963–65.

Monir, Shah Jahan. *Bangla Sahitye Bangali Musalmaner Chintadhara* [Thoughts of Muslims in Bengali Literature]. Dhaka: Bangla Academy, 1993.

Murshid, Ghulam. *Rasasundari Theke Rokeya: Nari Pragatir Aksho Bachhar* [From Rassundari to Rokeya: One Hundred Years of Women's Emancipation]. Dhaka: Bangla Academy, 1993.

Nasiruddin, Mohammad. *Bangla Sahitye Saogat Jug* [The Saogat Era in Bengali Literature]. Dhaka: Nurjahan Begum, 1985.

———. "Parda Banam Abarodh [Parda versus Seclusion]." *Mahila Saogat*, August-September, 1929.

Pradhan, Farida, ed. *Begum Rokeya O Narijagaran* [Begum Rokeya and the Awakening of Women]. Dhaka: Dhaka University Press, 1995.

Quadir, Abdul, ed. *Begum Rokeya Rachanabali* [The Collected Works of Begum Rokeya]. Dhaka: Bangla Academy, 1984.

———. *Nazrul Rachanabali* [The Collected Works of Nazrul]. 5 vols. Dhaka: Kendriya Bangla Unnayan Board, 1966–84.

Rahman, Mohammad Lutfar. "Pather Meye [Woman of the Streets]." *Annesa*, March-April 1921.

Rahman, Urmi, ed. *Aamader Samay* [Our Times]. Dhaka: Dana, 1994.

Ray, Binoybhushan, "Mahila Samaj: Shekaler Pragati Chetana" [Women's Society: Progressive Thought in the Nineteenth Century]. *Ekshan* (autumn 1991): 40–85.

Saiyed, Abdul Mannan. *Begum Rokeya*. Dhaka: Bangla Academy, 1983.

Samsad Bengali-English Dictionary. 2nd ed. Calcutta: Sahitya Samsad, 1995.

Sarkar, Swarochish. *Kathasahitya O Natake Muslim Sanskarchetona* [Muslim Reforms as Reflected in Fiction and Drama], *1869–1947*. Dhaka: Bangla Academy, 1995.

Sen Samartha, Neeta. "Tinsho Bachharer Kolkata: Nareeder Bhoomika" [Three Hundred Years of Old Calcutta: The Role of Women]. *Desh*, March 17, 1990, 27–35.

Shastri, S. *Ramatanu Lahiri O Tatkalin Bangla Samaj* [Ramtanu Lahiri and Contemporary Bengali Society]. Calcutta: S. K. Lahiri, 1904

Siddiqui Abdul Gaffur. *Sahid Titu Mir* [Martyr Titu Mir]. Dhaka: Bangla Academy, 1968.

Sripantha. *Aitihashik Anaitihashik* [Historical, Ahistorical]. Calcutta: Ananda, 2002.

———. *Keyabat Meye* [Atta Girl]. Calcutta: Ananda, 1988.

Thakur, Rabindranath. *Ghare Baire* [The Home and the World]. Calcutta: Aditya Prakashalaya, 2002.

ENGLISH-LANGUAGE SOURCES

Abrams, Philip. *Historical Sociology*. Ithaca: Cornell University Press, 1982.

Abu-Lughod, Lila. "Can There Be a Feminist Ethnography?" *Women and Performance* 5, no. 1 (1990): 7–27.

———. "Feminist Longings and Postcolonial Conditions." In *Remaking Women: Feminism and Modernity in the Middle East*, ed. Lila Abu-Lughod, 3–32. Princeton: Princeton University Press, 1998.

———. "The Marriage of Feminism and Islamism in Egypt: Selective Repudiation as a Dynamic of Postcolonial Politics." In *Remaking Women: Feminism and Modernity in the Middle East*, ed. Lila Abu-Lughod, 243–69. Princeton: Princeton University Press, 1998.

———, ed. *Remaking Women: Feminism and Modernity in the Middle East*. Princeton: Princeton University Press, 1998.

Adams, Brooks. *The Law of Civilization and Decay: An Essay on History*. New York: A. A. Knoff, 1943.

Afshar, Haleh. *Women and Politics in the Third World*. London: Routledge, 1996.

Aftab, Tahera. "Negotiating with Patriarchy: South Asian Muslim Women and the Appeal to Sir Syed Ahmed Khan." *Women's History Review* 14, no. 1 (2005): 75–97.

Agnes, Flavia. "Redefining the Agenda of the Women's Movement within a Secular Framework." In *Women and Right-Wing Movements: Indian Experiences*, ed. Tanika Sarkar and Urvashi Butalia, 136–55. London: Zed, 1995.

Ahmad, Aijaz. "Nation, Community, Violence." *South Asia Bulletin* 14, no. 1 (1994): 24–32.

———. "Orientalism and After." In *Colonial Discourse and Postcolonial Theory: A Reader*, ed. Patrick Williams and Laura Chrisman, 150–61. New York: Columbia University Press, 1994.

———. "Somnath to Gandhinagar: A Night of Long Knives." In *Communal-*

ism, Civil Society, and the State, ed. K. N. Panikkar and Sukumar Muralidharan, 26–39. New Delhi: Sahmat, 2002.

Ahmad, Aziz. *Islamic Modernism in India and Pakistan, 1857–1964*. London: Oxford University Press, 1970.

Ahmed, Leila. "Women and the Advent of Islam." *Signs* 11, no. 4 (1986): 665–91.

———. *Women and Gender in Islam*. New Haven: Yale University Press, 1992.

Ahmed, Rafiuddin. *The Bengal Muslims, 1871–1906: The Quest for Identity*. Delhi: Oxford University Press, 1988.

———. "The Emergence of the Bengal Muslims," In *Understanding the Bengal Muslims: Interpretive Essays*, ed. Rafiuddin Ahmed, 1–25. Delhi: Oxford University Press, 2001.

———, ed. *Understanding the Bengal Muslims: Interpretive Essays*. Delhi: Oxford University Press, 2001.

Ahmed, Sufia. *The Muslim Community in Bengal, 1884–1912*. Dhaka: S. Ahmed, 1974.

Akhter, Jahanzeb. "Muslim Women's Education in India." In *Muslim Women in India*, ed. Mohini Anjum, 75–78. New Delhi: Radiant Publishers, 1992.

Alarcón, Norma. "The Theoretical Subjects of *This Bridge Called My Back*." In *Haciendo Caras*, ed. Gloria Anzaldúa. San Francisco: Kitchen Table, 1991.

Ali, Ameer. *The Spirit of Islam: A History of the Evolution and Ideals of Islam with a Life of the Prophet*. New York: G. H. Doran, 1923.

Ali, Azra Asghar. *The Emergence of Feminism among Indian Muslim Women, 1920–1947*. London: Oxford University Press, 2000.

Ali, Maulana Mohamed. *My Life: A Fragment*. Ed. Afzal Iqbal. Lahore: Shaikh Muhammad Ashraf, 1942.

Alvi, Sajida Sultana, Homa Hoodfar, and Sheila McDonough. *The Muslim Veil in North America: Issues and Debates*. Toronto: Women's Press, 2003.

Amin, Samir. *Eurocentrism*. New York: Monthly Review Press, 1989.

Amin, Shahid. *Event, Metaphor, Memory: Chauri Chaura, 1922–1992*. Berkeley: University of California Press, 1995.

Amin, Sonia Nishat. "Bengali (Muslim) Identity and the Women's Question: The Debate over Terminology." *Theoretical Perspectives* 1, no. 1 (1994): 1–23.

———. "The Changing World of Bengali Muslim Women: The 'Dreams' and Efforts of Rokeya Sakhawat Hossein." In *Understanding the Bengali Muslims: Interpretive Essays*, ed. Rafiuddin Ahmed, 139–52. Delhi: Oxford University Press, 2001.

———. "Childhood and Role Models in the Andar Mahal: Muslim Women in the Private Sphere in Colonial Bengal." In *Embodied Violence: Communalising*

Women's Sexuality in South Asia, ed. Kumari Jayawardena and Malathi De Alwis, 71–88. London: Zed, 1996.

———. "The Early Muslim Bhadramahila: The Growth of Learning and Creativity, 1876–1939." In *From the Seams of History: Essays on Indian Women*, ed. Bharati Ray, 107–48. Delhi: Oxford University Press, 1995.

———. "The New Woman in Literature and the Novels of Nojibur Rahman and Rokeya Sakhawat Hossain." In *Infinite Variety: Women in Society and Literature*, ed. Firdous Azim and Niaz Zaman, 119–41. Dhaka: University Press Limited, 1994.

———. "Rokeya Sakhawat Hossain and the Legacy of the 'Bengal Renaissance.'" *Journal of the Asiatic Society, Bangladesh (Humanities)* 34, no. 2 (1989): 185–92.

———. *The World of Muslim Women in Colonial Bengal, 1876–1939*. Leiden: Brill, 1996.

Aminzade, Ronald. "Historical Sociology and Time." Special issue, *Sociological Methods and Research* 20, no. 4 (1992): 456–80.

Anagol-McGinn, Padma. "The Age of Consent Act (1891) Reconsidered: Women's Perspectives and Participation in the Child Marriage Controversy in India." *South Asia Research* 12, no. 2 (1992): 100–118.

Anderson, Benedict. *Imagined Communities: Reflections on the Origin and Spread of Nationalism*. London: Verso, 1983.

Anjum, Mohini. "Behind Burqa." In *Muslim Women in India*, ed. Mohini Anjum, 112–18. New Delhi: Radiant Publishers, 1992.

———, ed. *Muslim Women in India*. New Delhi: Radiant Publishers, 1992.

Anthias, Floya. *Racialized Boundaries: Race, Nation, Gender, Colour, and Class and the Anti-racist Struggle*. London: Routledge, 1992.

Anthias, Floya, and Nira Yuval-Davis, eds. *Woman, Nation, State*. New York: St. Martin's, 1989.

Anzaldúa, Gloria, and Cherríe Moraga, eds. *This Bridge Called My Back: Writings by Radical Women of Color*. Watertown, Mass.: Persephone, 1981.

Archer, Mildred. *Company Paintings: Indian Paintings of the British Period*. Ahmedabad: Mapin, 1998.

———. *Early Views of India: The Picturesque Journeys of Thomas and William Daniell, 1786–1794*. London: Thames and Hudson, 1980.

———. *India Observed: India as Viewed by British Artists, 1760–1860*. London: Victoria and Albert Museum, 1982.

Armitage, Susan H., and Sherna Berger Gluck. "Reflections on Women's Oral

History: An Exchange." In *Women's Oral History: The Frontiers Reader*, ed. Susan H. Armitage et al., 75–86. Lincoln: University of Nebraska Press, 2002.

Arondekar, Anjali. "Entangled Histories." *Economic and Political Weekly*, August 5, 2006, 3409–11.

Arrighi, Giovanni. *The Long Twentieth Century: Money, Power, and the Origins of Our Times*. London: Verso, 1994.

Arrighi, Giovanni, and Beverly Silver. *Chaos and Governance in the Modern World System*. Minneapolis: University of Minnesota Press, 1999.

Asad, Talal. "Ethnographic Representation, Statistics, and Modern Power." In *From the Margins: Historical Anthropology and Its Futures*, ed. Brian Keith Axel, 66–91. Durham: Duke University Press, 2002.

Asiatic Society. *Renascent Bengal, 1817–1857: Proceedings of a Seminar*. Calcutta: The Asiatic Society, 1993.

Bacchetta, Paula. "Communal Property/Sexual Property: On Representations of Muslim Women in a Hindu Nationalist Discourse." In *Forging Identities: Gender, Communities, and the State*, ed. Zoya Hasan, 188–225. New Delhi: Kali for Women, 1994.

Bader, Clarisse. *Women in Ancient India*. London: Longman Green, 1925.

Badran, Margot. "Competing Agenda: Feminists, Islam, and the State in Nineteenth and Twentieth Century Egypt." In *Women, Islam, and the State*, ed. Deniz Kandiyoti, 201–36. London: Macmillan, 1991.

———. *Feminists, Islam, and Nation: Gender and the Making of Modern Egypt*. Princeton: Princeton University Press, 1995.

Bagchi, Amiya Kumar. *The Political Economy of Underdevelopment*. Cambridge: Cambridge University Press, 1982.

Bagchi, Jasodhara. "Ethnicity and Empowerment of Women: The Colonial Legacy." In *Embodied Violence: Communalising Women's Sexuality in South Asia*, ed. Kumari Jayawardena and Malathi de Alwis, 113–25. London: Zed, 1996.

———, ed. *Indian Women: Myth and Reality*. Delhi: Sangam, 1995.

———. "Positivism and Nationalism: Womanhood and Crisis in Nationalist Fiction—Bankimchandra's Anandamath." Special issue on Women's Studies, *Economic and Political Weekly*, October 26, 1985, WS58–WS62.

———. "Representing Nationalism: Ideology of Motherhood in Colonial Bengal." Special issue on Women's Studies, *Economic and Political Weekly*, October 20, 1990, WS65–WS71.

———. "Socialising the Girl Child in Colonial Bengal." *Economic and Political Weekly*, October 1993, 14–22.

Bakhtin, M. M. *The Dialogic Imagination*. Trans. C. Emerson and M. Holoquist. Austin: University of Texas Press, 1981.

Baldwin, Ruth. "Gujarat's Gendered Violence." *Nation*, September 16, 2002.

Balibar, Etienne, and Immanuel Wallerstein. *Race, Nation, Class: Ambiguous Identities*. London: Verso, 1991.

Baljon, J. M. S., Jr. *The Reforms and Religious Ideas of Sir Sayyid Ahmad Khan*. Lahore: Orientalia, 1958.

Ballhatchet, Kenneth. *Race, Sex, and Class under the Raj: Imperial Attitudes and Policies and Their Critics, 1793–1905*. New York: St. Martin's, 1980.

Bambara, Toni Cade, ed. *The Black Woman: An Anthology*. New York: Penguin, 1970.

———. "On the Issue of Roles." In *The Black Woman: An Anthology*, ed. Toni Cade Bambara, 101–10. New York: Penguin, 1970.

Bandyopadhyay, Pramathanath. *Hundred Years of the University of Calcutta*. Calcutta: University of Calcutta, 1957.

Bandyopadhyay, Sekhar. *Caste, Protest, and Identity in Colonial India: Namasudras of Bengal, 1872–1947*. London: Curzon, 1997.

———. "Caste, Widow Remarriage, and the Reform of Popular Culture in Colonial Bengal." In *From the Seams of History: Essays on Indian Women*, ed. Bharati Ray, 8–36. Delhi: Oxford University Press, 1995.

Banerjea, S. N. *A Nation in Making*. Calcutta, 1963.

Banerjee, Sumanta. *Dangerous Outcast: The Prostitute in Nineteenth Century Bengal*. Calcutta: Seagull, 1998.

———. "Having the Last Laugh: Women in Nineteenth Century Bengali Farces." *Manushi* 59 (1990): 15–20.

———. "Marginalization of Women's Popular Culture in Nineteenth Century Bengal." In *Recasting Women: Essays in Indian Colonial History*, ed. Kumkum Sangari and Sudesh Vaid, 127–79. New Delhi: Kali for Women, 1989.

———. "When the 'Silent Majority' Backs a Violent Minority." *Economic and Political Weekly*, March 30, 2002.

Bannerji, Himani. "Attired in Virtue: The Discourse on Shame (*lajja*) and Clothing of the Bhadramahila in Colonial Bengal." In *From the Seams of History: Essays on Indian Women*, ed. Bharati Ray, 67–106. Delhi: Oxford University Press, 1995.

Baran, Paul. *The Political Economy of Growth*. New York: Monthly Review Press, 1957

Barrett, Michèle, and Anne Phillips, eds. *Destabilizing Theory: Contemporary Feminist Debates*. Stanford: Stanford University Press, 1992.

Basu, Amrita. "Feminism Inverted: The Gendered Imagery and Real Women of Hindu Nationalism." In *Women and Right-Wing Movements: Indian Experiences*, ed. Tanika Sarkar and Urvashi Butalia, 158–80. London: Zed, 1995.

Basu, Aparna. "Feminism and Nationalism in India, 1917–1947." *Journal of Women's History* 4 (winter 1995): 95–107.

———. *The Growth of Education and Political Development in India, 1898–1920*. Delhi: Oxford University Press, 1974.

———. "The Role of Women in the Indian Struggle for Freedom." In *Indian Women: From Purdah to Modernity*, ed. Bal Ram Nanda, 16–40. New Delhi: Vikas, 1976.

Basu, Aparna, and Bharati Ray. *Women's Struggle: A History of the All India Women's Conference, 1927–1990*. New Delhi: Manohar, 1990.

Basu, Priyanatha. *The Education of Mahomedans and Christians in India: A Thought*. Vol. 1. Benares: Chandraprabha, 1897.

Basu, Tapan, Pradip Datta, Sumit Sarkar, Tanika Sarkar, and Sambuddha Sen, eds. *Khaki Shorts and Saffron Flags: A Critique of the Hindu Right*. Hyderabad: Orient Longman, 1993.

Bauman, Zygmunt. "Modernity and Ambivalence." *Theory, Culture, and Society* 7 (1990): 143–69.

Baxi, Upendra. *Text of Observations Made at a Public Meeting on the Muslim Women (Protection of Rights) Bill*. Bombay: Hindusthani Andolan, 1986.

Bayly, C. A. "The British and Indigenous Peoples, 1760–1860: Power, Perception, and Identity." In *Empire and Others: British Encounters with Indigenous Peoples, 1600–1850*, ed. Martin J. Daunton and Rick Halpern, 19–41. Philadelphia: University of Pennsylvania Press, 1999.

———. *Indian Society and the Making of the British Empire*. Vol. 2.1 of *The New Cambridge History of India*. Cambridge: Cambridge University Press, 1988.

———. *The Raj: India and the British, 1600–1947*. London: National Gallery, 1990.

———. *Rulers, Townsmen, and Bazaars*. Cambridge: Cambridge University Press, 1983.

Beames, John. *Memoirs of a Bengal Civilian (1837–1902)*. London: Chatto and Windes, 1961.

Belsey, Catherine. The Subject of Tragedy: Identity and Difference in Renaissance Drama. London: Methuen, 1985.

Benjamin, Walter. *The Arcades Project*. Trans. Howard Eiland and Kevin McLaughlin. Cambridge, Mass.: Belknap, 1999.

———. *Illuminations*. London: Fontana, 1973.

Berman, Marshall. *All That Is Solid Melts into Air: The Experience of Modernity*. New York: Simon and Schuster, 1982.

Bertaux, Daniel, and Paul Thompson, eds. *Between Generations: Family Models, Myths, and Memories: International Yearbook of Oral History and Life Stories*. Vol. 2. New York: Oxford University Press, 1993.

Beveridge, Henry. *The District of Bakarganj: Its History and Statistics*. London: Trubner, 1876.

Bhattacharjee, Mira, and Shanta Sen. *Bethune College Centenary Volume, 1879–1979*. Calcutta: Bethune College, 1980.

Bhattacharya, Debraj. "Kolkata 'Underworld' in the Early Twentieth Century." *Economic and Political Weekly*, September 18, 2004.

Bhattacharya, Malini, and Abhijit Sen, eds. *Talking of Power: Early Writings of Bengali Women*. Calcutta: Stree, 2003.

Bhattacharya, Sabyasachi. "Traders and Trade in Old Calcutta." In *Calcutta: The Living City*, ed. Sukanta Chaudhuri, 1:204–8. New York: Oxford University Press, 1990.

Bhattacharyya, Panchanan. *Ideals of Indian Womanhood*. Calcutta: Goldquin, 1921.

Bidwai, Praful. "End the Butchery, Sack Modi." *Frontline* 19, no. 6 (March 16, 2002).

Blaut, James M. *The Colonizer's Model of the World: Geographical Diffusionism and Eurocentric History*. New York: Guildford, 1993.

Bommes, M., and P. Wright. "Charms of Residence: The Public and the Past." In *Making Histories: Studies in History-Writing and Politics*, ed. Richard Johnson, 253–302. Minneapolis: University of Minnesota Press, 1982.

Borland, Katherine. "'That's Not What I Said': Interpretive Conflict in Oral Narrative Research." In *Women's Words: The Feminist Practice of Oral History*, ed. Sherna B. Gluck and Daphne Patai, 63–75. New York: Routledge, 1991.

Böröcz, József. "Social Change with Sticky Features and the Failures of Modernizationism." *Innovation* 10, no. 2 (1997): 161–70.

Borthwick, Meredith. *The Changing Role of Women in Bengal, 1849–1905*. Princeton: Princeton University Press, 1984.

Bose, Chunder Nath. *High Education in India: Essay Read at the Bethune Society with Important Additions by the Author*. Calcutta: Jogesh Chunder Banerjee, Canning Library, 1878.

Bose, N. C. *The Indian Awakening and Bengal*. Calcutta: Firma K. L. Mukhopadhayay, 1969.

Bose, Nemai Sadhan. *The Indian National Movement: An Outline*. Calcutta: Firma K. L. Mukhopadhyay, 1974.

Bose, Sugata, and Ayesha Jalal. *Modern South Asia: History, Culture, Political Economy*. Delhi: Oxford University Press, 1998.

Brass, Paul R. *Ethnicity and Nationalism: Theory and Comparison*. New Delhi: Sage, 1991.

Braudel, Fernand. *Civilisation and Capitalism, Fifteenth–Eighteenth Centuries*. Trans. Siân Reynolds. Vol. 3. London: Fontana, 1981.

Broomfield, J. M. "The Partition of Bengal: A Problem in British Administration, 1830–1912." *Proceedings of the Indian History Congress, 23rd Session*. Aligarh, 1961.

Brown, Hilton. *The Sahibs: The Life and the Ways of the British in India as Recorded by Themselves*. London: Hodge, 1948.

Buci-Glucksmann, Christine. "State, Transition, and Passive Revolution." In *Gramsci and Social Theory*, ed. Chantal Mouffe, 113–67. London: Routledge and Kegan Paul, 1979.

Buck-Morss, Susan. *The Dialectics of Seeing: Walter Benjamin and the Arcades Project*. Cambridge: MIT Press, 1990.

Burton, Antoinette. *At the Heart of the Empire: Indians and the Colonial Encounter in Late-Victorian Britain*. Berkeley: University of California Press, 1998.

———. *Burdens of History: British Feminists, Indian Women, and Imperial Culture, 1865–1915*. Chapel Hill: University of North Carolina Press, 1994.

———. *Dwelling in the Archive: Women Writing House, Home, and History in Late Colonial India*. Delhi: Oxford University Press, 2003.

———. "Institutionalizing Imperial Reform: The Indian Magazine and Late-Victorian Colonial Politics." In *Negotiating India in the Nineteenth Century Media*, ed. David Finkelstein and Douglas M. Peers, 23–50. New York: St. Martin's, 2000.

———. Introduction. In *Family History*, by Janaki Penelope Majumdar. Ed. Antoinette Burton, xiii–xxx. Delhi: Oxford University Press, 2003.

———. "Optical Illusions." *Women's Review of Books* 17 (2000): 21–22.

———. Review of Azra Asghar Ali, *The Emergence of Feminism among Indian Muslim Women, 1920–1947*. *American Historical Review* 106, no. 3 (June 2001): 965–66.

Butalia, Urvashi. "Community, State, and Gender: On Women's Agency during Partition." Special issue on Women's Studies, *Economic and Political Weekly*, vol. 17, 1993, WS12–WS24.

———. *The Other Side of Silence: Voices from Partition of India*. New Delhi: Penguin, 1998.

Butler, Judith, and Joan Wallach Scott, eds. *Feminists Theorize the Political*. New York: Routledge, 1992.

Cain, P. J., and A. G. Hopkins. "Gentlemanly Capitalism and British Expansion Overseas, 1: The Old Colonial System, 1688–1850." *Economic History Review* 39, no. 4 (1986): 501–25.

Carby, Hazel. "White Woman Listen! Black Feminism and the Boundaries of Sisterhood." In *The Empire Strikes Back: Race and Racism in Seventies Britain*. London: Hutchinson, 1982.

Carpenter, Mary. *Six Months in India*. 2 vols. London: Longmans, 1868.

Carroll, Lucy. "Law, Custom, and Statutory Social Reform: The Hindu Widow's Remarriage Act of 1856." In *Women in Colonial India: Essays on Survival, Work, and the State*, ed. J. Krishnamurty, 1–26. Delhi: Oxford University Press, 1989.

Carstairs, Robert. *Human Nature in Rural India*. London: Blackwood and Sons, 1895.

Chakrabarty, Dipesh. *Provincializing Europe: Postcolonial Thought and Historical Difference*. Princeton: Princeton University Press, 2000.

Chakraborti, Smarajit. *The Bengali Press (1818–1868): A Study in the Growth of Public Opinion*. Calcutta: KLM, 1976.

Chakraborty, Usha. *Condition of Bengali Women around the Second Half of the Nineteenth Century*. Calcutta, 1963.

Chakravarti, Uma. *Rewriting History: The Life and Times of Pandita Ramabai*. New Delhi: Kali for Women, 1998.

———. "Whatever Happened to the Vedic *Dasi*? Orientalism, Nationalism, and a Script for the Past." In *Recasting Women: Essays in Indian Colonial History*, ed. Kumkum Sangari and Sudesh Vaid, 27–87. New Delhi: Kali for Women, 1989.

Chandra, Bipan. *Modern India*. New Delhi: National Council of Education Research and Training, 1974.

Chandra, Bipan, Amales Tripathi, and Barun De. *Freedom Struggle*. New Delhi: National Book Trust, 1972.

Chandra, Moti. *The World of Courtesans*. New Delhi: Vikas, 1973.

Chatterjee, Angana, and Lubna Nazir Chaudhry, eds. *Gendered Violence in South Asia: Nation and Community in the Postcolonial Present*. Special issue, *Cultural Dynamics* 16, nos. 2–3 (October 2004).

Chatterjee, Indrani. "Colouring Subalternity." In *Subaltern Studies X*, ed. Gautam Bhadra, Gyan Prakash, and Susie Tharu, 49–97. Delhi: Oxford University Press, 1999.

———, ed. *Unfamiliar Relations: Family and History in South Asia*. New Brunswick, N.J.: Rutgers University Press, 2004.

Chatterjee, Partha. "Agrarian Structure in Pre-Partition Bengal." In *Perspectives in Social Sciences 2: Three Studies on the Agrarian Structure in Bengal, 1850–1947*, ed. Asok Sen, Partha Chatterjee, and Sangata Mukherji. Calcutta: Oxford University Press, 1982.

———. *The Nation and Its Fragments: Colonial and Postcolonial Histories*. Princeton: Princeton University Press, 1993.

———. "The Nationalist Resolution of the Women's Question." In *Recasting Women: Essays in Indian Colonial History*, ed. Kumkum Sangari and Sudesh Vaid, 233–53. New Delhi: Kali for Women, 1989.

———. *Nationalist Thought and the Colonial World: A Derivative Discourse?* Minneapolis: University of Minnesota Press, 1986.

———. *The Present History of West Bengal*. Delhi: Oxford University Press, 1998.

Chatterjee, Partha, and Pradeep Jeganathan, eds. *Community, Gender, and Violence: Subaltern Studies XI*. Delhi: Permanent Black, 2000.

Chatterjee, Ratnabali. "Prostitution in Nineteenth Century Bengal: Construction of Class and Gender." *Social Scientist* 21, nos. 9–11 (1993): 159–72.

Chatterji, Joya. *Bengal Divided: Hindu Communalism and Partition, 1932–1947*. Cambridge: Cambridge University Press, 1994.

Chattopadhyay, Ratnabali, and Tapati Guha Thakurta. "The Woman Perceived: The Changing Visual Iconography of the Colonial and Nationalist Period in Bengal." In *Indian Women: Myth and Reality*, ed. Jasodhara Bagchi, 147–67. Delhi: Sangam, 1995.

Chaudhuri, Maitrayee, ed. *Feminism in India*. New Delhi: Kali for Women, 2004.

———. "The Indian Women's Movement." In *Feminism in India*, ed. Maitrayee Chaudhuri, 117–33. New Delhi: Kali for Women, 2004.

Chhachhi, Amrita. "Forced Identities: the State, Communalism, Fundamentalism, and Women in India." In *Women, Islam, and the State*, ed. Deniz Kandiyoti, 144–75. London: Macmillan, 1991.

Chow, Rey. The Politics of Admittance: Female Sexual Agency, Miscegenation, and the Formation of Community in Frantz Fanon. In *Frantz Fanon: Critical Perspectives*, ed. Anthony C. Alessandrini, 34–56. London: Routledge, 1999.

———. *Women and Chinese Modernity: Reading between East and West*. Minneapolis: University of Minnesota Press, 1991.

Christian Vernacular Education Society. *The Women of India and What Can Be Done for Them*. [London?]: S. P. C. K. Press, 1888.

Citizens for Justice and Peace. *Crime against Humanity: An Inquiry into the Carnage in Gujarat—List of Incidents and Evidence*. Mumbai: Citizens for Justice and Peace, 2002.

Citizen's Initiative. *Hard Facts*. Ahmedabad: Centre for Social Justice, 2002.

Clawson, Mary Ann. *Constructing Brotherhood: Class, Gender, and Fraternalism*. Princeton: Princeton University Press, 1989.

Clifford, James. "Introduction: Partial Truths." In *Writing Culture: The Poetics and Politics of Ethnography*, ed. James Clifford and George E. Marcus, 1–26. Berkeley: University of California Press, 1986.

Clifford, James, and George E. Marcus, eds. *Writing Culture: The Poetics and Politics of Ethnography*. Berkeley: University of California Press, 1986.

Cohn, Bernard. *An Anthropologist among the Historians and Other Essays*. Delhi: Oxford University Press, 1990.

———. "The Command of Language and the Language of Command." In *Subaltern Studies IV*, ed. Ranajit Guha, 276–329. Delhi: Oxford University Press, 1985.

———. "Representing Authority in Victorian India." In *The Invention of Tradition*, ed. Eric Hobsbawm and Terence Ranger, 165–210. Cambridge: Cambridge University Press, 1983.

Collins, Patricia Hill. *Black Feminist Thought: Knowledge, Consciousness, and the Politics of Empowerment*. Boston: Unwin Hyman, 1990.

Connolly, William E. *Identity/Difference: Democratic Negotiations of Political Paradox*. Ithaca: Cornell University Press, 1991.

Crapanzano, Vincent. "On the Writing of Ethnography." *Dialectical Anthropology* 2 (1977): 69–73.

Crosby, Christina. "Dealing with Differences." In *Feminists Theorize the Political*, ed. Judith Butler and Joan Wallach Scott, 130–43. New York: Routledge, 1992.

Dalrymple, William. *White Mughals: Love and Betrayal in Eighteenth-Century India*. New York: Viking, 2003.

Dang, Kokila. "Prostitutes, Patrons, and the State: Nineteenth Century Awadh." *Social Scientist* (New Delhi) 21, nos. 9–11 (September-November 1993): 173–96.

Das, Suranjan, and Jayanta K. Ray. *The Goondas: Towards a Reconstruction of the Kolkata Underworld*. Calcutta: KLM, 1996.

Das, Veena. *Critical Events: An Anthropological Perspective on Contemporary India*. Delhi: Oxford University Press, 1995.

———, ed. *Mirrors of Violence: Communities, Riots, and Survivors in South Asia*. Delhi: Oxford University Press, 1990.

———. "Subaltern as Perspective." In *Subaltern Studies VI*, ed. Ranajit Guha, 310–24. Delhi: Oxford University Press, 1982.

Datta, Pradeep K. *Carving Blocs: Communal Ideology in Early Twentieth Century Bengal*. New Delhi: Permanent Black, 1999.

Davis, Ralph. *The Industrial Revolution and British Overseas Trade*. Leicester: Leicester University Press, 1979.

Debi, Rasasundari. *Amar Jiban*. Calcutta: Sri Rambrahma Mukhopadhyay, 1875.

Delaney, Carol. "Father State, Motherland, and the Birth of Modern Turkey." In *Naturalizing Power: Essays in Feminist Cultural Analysis*, ed. Sylvia Yanagisako and Carol Delaney, 177–200. New York: Routledge, 1995.

Devji, Faisal Fatehali. "Gender and the Politics of Space: the Movement for Women's Reform, 1857–1900." In *Forging Identities: Gender, Communities, and the State*, ed. Zoya Hasan, 23–37. New Delhi: Kali for Women, 1994.

Dicken, Peter. *Global Shift: The Internationalization of Economic Activity*. New York: Guilford, 1992.

Digby, William. *"Prosperous" British India: A Revelation from Official Records*. London: Unwin, 1901.

Dirks, Nicholas B. "Castes of Mind." *Representations* 37 (1992): 56–78.

Dreyfus, Hubert L., and Paul Rabinow, *Michel Foucault: Beyond Structuralism and Hermeneutics*. Chicago: University of Chicago Press, 1982.

Duara, Prasenjit. *Rescuing History from the Nation: Questioning Narratives of Modern China*. Chicago: University of Chicago Press, 1995.

Duff, Alexander. *Female Education in India*. Edinburgh: John Johnstone, 1839.

Dutt, R. P. *India Today*. Bombay, Peoples Publishing House, 1949.

Dutt, Romesh Chunder. *The Economic History of India in the Victorian Age*. London: Routledge and Kegan Paul, 1950.

Eaton, Richard M. *The Rise of Islam and the Bengal Frontier, 1204–1760*. Berkeley: University of California Press, 1993.

———. "Who Are the Bengal Muslims? Conversion and Islamization in Bengal." In *Understanding the Bengal Muslims: Interpretive Essays*, ed. Rafiuddin Ahmed, 26–51. Delhi: Oxford University Press, 2001.

Eley, Geoff, and Ronald Grigor Suny, eds. *Becoming National: A Reader*. Oxford: Oxford University Press, 1996.

Embree, Ainslie T., ed. *Sources of Indian Tradition*. Vol. 1. New York: Columbia University Press, 1988.

Engel, Karen. "Feminism and Its (Dis)contents: Criminalizing Wartime Rape in Bosnia and Herzegovina." *American Journal of International Law* 99, no. 4 (October 2005): 778–816.

Engels, Dagmar. *Beyond Purdah? Women in Bengal, 1890–1930*. Delhi: Oxford University Press, 1999.

Engineer, Asghar Ali. *The Indian Muslims: A Study of the Minority Problem*. Delhi: Ajanta, 1985.

———. *The Shah Bano Controversy*. Delhi: Orient Longman, 1987.

———. *Status of Women in Islam*. Delhi: Ajanta, 1987.

Everett, Jana. "All the Women Were Hindu and All the Muslims Were Men: State, Identity Politics, and Gender, 1917–1951." *Economic and Political Weekly*, June 9, 2001, 2071–80.

Fabian, Johannes. *Time and the Other: How Anthropology Makes Its Objects*. New York: Columbia University Press, 1983.

Fanon, Frantz. *Black Skin, White Masks*. Trans. Charles Lam Markmann. London: Pluto, 1986.

———. *A Dying Colonialism*. Trans. Haakov Chevalier. New York: Grove, 1967. See esp. "Algeria Unveiled," 35–67.

Fazalbhoy, Nasreen. "Sociology of Muslims in India: A Review." *Economic and Political Weekly*, June 28, 1997, 1547–51.

Female Education in India and Ceylon: The Need for Girls' Boarding Schools, under European or American Ladies' Supervision, Being Multiplied a Thousand-fold. Colombo: A. M. and J. Ferguson, 1907.

Ferguson, James. *Expectations of Modernity: Myths and Meanings of Urban Life on the Zambian Copperbelt*. Berkeley: University of California Press, 1999.

Ferguson, Moira. *Subject to Others: British Women Writers and Colonial Slavery, 1670–1834*. London: Routledge, 1992.

Fisher, Michael. *Indirect Rule in India: Residents and the Residency System, 1764–1858*. Delhi: Oxford University Press, 1991.

Forbes, Geraldine. "Goddesses or Rebels? The Women Revolutionaries of Bengal." *Oracle* 2, no. 2 (April 1980): 1–15.

———. *Memoirs of an Indian Woman by Shudha Majumdar*. New York: Sharpe, 1989.

———. *Women in Modern India*. Vol. 4.2 of *The New Cambridge History of India*. Cambridge: Cambridge University Press, 1996.

Forbes, Geraldine, and Tapan Raychaudhuri, eds. *From Child Widow to Lady Doctor: The Memoirs of Dr. Haimabati Sen*. New Delhi: Roli, 2000.

Foucault, Michel. *Discipline and Punish: The Birth of the Prison*. Trans. Alan Sheridan. New York: Pantheon, 1977.

———. *The History of Sexuality: An Introduction*. Trans. Robert Hurley. New York: Random House, 1978.

———. *Power/Knowledge: Selected Interviews and Other Writings, 1972–1977*, ed. Colin Gordon. New York: Pantheon, 1980.

———. "Truth and Power." In *Power/Knowledge: Selected Interviews and Other Writings, 1972–1977*, ed. Colin Gordon, 109–33. New York: Pantheon, 1980.

Frankenberg, Ruth. *White Women, Race Matters: The Social Construction of Whiteness*. Minneapolis: University of Minnesota Press, 1993.

Fraser, Nancy. "What's Critical about Critical Theory: The Case of Habermas and Gender." In *Feminism*, ed. Susan Moller Okin and Jane Mansbridge, 1:74–104. Aldershot: Elgar, 1994.

Gedalof, Irene. *Against Purity: Rethinking Identity with Indian and Western Feminisms*. London: Routledge, 1999.

Geetha, V. "Periyar, Women, and an Ethic of Citizenship." In *Feminism in India*, ed. Maitrayee Chaudhuri, 156–74. New Delhi: Kali for Women, 2004.

Gellner, Ernest. *Thought and Change*. London: George Weidenfeld and Nicholson Ltd., 1964.

Ghose, Nagendra Nath. *Liberal Education in India: Paper Read at a Meeting of the Bethune Society on the 21st of March, 1878*. Calcutta: Thacker, Spink, 1878.

Ghosh, Amitav. *The Hungry Tide*. London: HarperCollins, 2004.

———. *The Shadow Lines*. New York: Viking, 1988.

Ghosh, Bishnupriya. "Feminist Critiques of Nationalism and Communalism from Bangladesh and India: A Transnational Reading." In *Interventions: Feminist Dialogues on Third World Women's Literature and Film*, ed. Bishnupriya Ghosh and Brinda Bose, 135–62. New York: Garland, 1997.

Ghosh, Durba. "Colonial Companions: Bibis, Begums, and Concubines of the British in North India, 1760–1830." Ph.D. diss., University of California, Berkeley, 2000.

———. *Sex and the Family in Colonial India: The Making of an Empire*. New York: Cambridge University Press, 2006.

Ghosh, Girish. *Ramdoolal Dey: The Bengali Millionaire*. Calcutta, 1978.

Ghosh, Srabashi. "Changes in Bengali Social Life as Recorded in Autobiographies by Women." Special issue on Women's Studies, *Economic and Political Weekly*, October 25, 1986, ws88–ws96.

Giddings, Paula. *When and Where I Enter: The Impact of Black Women on Race and Sex in America*. New York: W. Morrow, 1984.

Gill, Anton. *Ruling Passions: Sex, Race, and Empire*. London: BBC Books, 1995.

Gluck, Sherna Berger. "What's So Special about Women? Women's Oral History." In *Women's Oral History*, ed. Susan H. Armitage, Patricia Hart, and Karen Weathermon, 3–20. Lincoln: University of Nebraska Press, 2002.

Gluck, Sherna B., and Daphne Patai, eds. *Women's Words: The Feminist Practice of Oral History*. New York: Routledge, 1991.

Gordon, Leonard A. *Brothers against the Raj: A Biography of Indian Nationalists Sarat and Subhash Chandra Bose*. Calcutta: Rupa, 1990.

Graham, G. F. I. *The Life and Work of Sir Syed Ahmed Khan*. 1885; reprint, Delhi: Mohammad Ahmad, 1974.

Grele, Ronald J. "Movement without Aim: Methodological and Theoretical Problems in Oral History." In *The Oral History Reader*, ed. Robert Parks and Alistair Thomson, 38–52. London: Routledge, 1998.

Grey, C. *European Adventurers of Northern India, 1785–1849*. Lahore: Government Printing, 1929.

Griffin, Larry J. "Temporality, Events, and Explanation in Historical Sociology: An Introduction." Special issue, *Sociological Methods and Research* 20, no. 4 (May 1992): 403–27.

Guha, Ranajit. *Dominance without Hegemony: History and Power in Colonial India*. Cambridge: Harvard University Press, 1997.

———. "Dominance without Hegemony and Its Historiography." In *Subaltern Studies VI: Writings in South Asian History and Society*, 210–309. Delhi: Oxford University Press, 1989.

———. *Elementary Aspects of Peasant Insurgency in Colonial India*. Delhi: Oxford University Press, 1983.

———. *A Rule of Property for Bengal: An Essay on the Idea of Permanent Settlement*. Paris: Mouton, 1963.

Gupta, Charu. *Sexuality, Obscenity, Community: Women, Muslims, and the Hindu Public in Colonial India*. Delhi: Permanent Black, 2001.

Haines, C. R. *Education and Missions in India and Elsewhere*. Cambridge: Deighton, Bell, 1886.

Hall, Stuart. "Cultural Identity and Diaspora." In *Colonial Discourse and Postcolonial Theory: A Reader*, ed. Patrick Williams and Laura Chrisman, 392–403. New York: Columbia University Press, 1994.

———. "Introduction: Who Needs 'Identity'?" In *Questions of Cultural Identity*, ed. Stuart Hall and Paul du Gay, 1–17. London, Sage, 1996.

———. "The West and the Rest: Discourse and Power." In *Modernity: An Introduction to Modern Societies*, ed. Stuart Hall et al., 184–228. Cambridge: Polity, 1995.

Hameed, Syeda, Ruth Manorama, Malini Ghose, Sheba George, Farah Naqvi, and Mari Thekaekara. "How Has the Gujarat Massacre Affected Minority Women? The Survivors Speak." Fact-finding report by a women's panel sponsored by Citizens's Initiative, April 16, 2002. http://cac.ektaonline.org/resources/reports/womensreport.htm (accessed on December 31, 2006).

Haraway, Donna. "Situated Knowledges: The Science Question in Feminism and the Privilege of Partial Perspective." *Feminist Studies* 4, no. 3 (1988): 575–99.

Hardy, Peter. *The Muslims of British India*. Cambridge: Cambridge University Press, 1972.

Hasan, Zoya. "Communalism, State Policy, and the Question of Women's Rights in Contemporary India." *Bulletin of Concerned Asian Scholars* 25, no. 4 (October-December 1993): 5–15.

———, ed. *Forging Identities: Gender, Communities, and the State*. New Delhi: Kali for Women, 1994.

———, ed. *India's Partition: Process, Strategy, and Mobilization*. Delhi: Oxford University Press, 1993.

———. "Minority Identity, State Policy, and Political Process." In *Forging Identities*, ed. Zoya Hasan, 59–73. New Delhi: Kali for Women, 1994.

———. *Nationalism and Communal Politics in India, 1885–1930*. New Delhi: Manohar, 1991.

Hasan, Zoya, and Ritu Menon. *Unequal Citizens: A Study of Muslim Women in India*. Delhi: Oxford University Press, 2004.

Hatcher, Brian A. "Great Men Waking: Paradigms in the Historiography of the Bengal Renaissance." In *Bengal: Rethinking History*, ed. Shekhar Bandyopadhyay, 135–66. Delhi: Manohar, 2001.

Hatem, Mervat. "'A'isha Taymur's Tears' and the Critique of the Modernist and the Feminist Discourses on Nineteenth-Century Egypt." In *Remaking Women: Feminism and Modernity in the Middle East*, ed. Lila Abu-Lughod, 73–89. Princeton: Princeton University Press, 1998.

Hawes, Christopher J. "Eurasians in British India, 1773–1833: The Making of a Reluctant Community." Ph.D. diss., School of Oriental and African Studies, University of London, 1993.

Haynes, Douglas, and Gyan Prakash. *Contesting Power: Resistance and Everyday Social Relations in South Asia*. Berkeley: University of California Press, 1992.

Held, David. "The Development of the Modern State." In *Modernity: An Introduction to Modern Societies*, ed. Stuart Hall, David Held, Don Hubert, and Kenneth Thompson, 56–89. Cambridge: Polity, 1995.

Henige, David. *Oral Historiography*. London: Longman, 1982.

Hintjens, Helen M. "Explaining the 1994 Genocide in Rwanda." *Journal of Modern African Studies* 37, no. 2 (June 1999): 241–86.

Hobsbawm, Eric, and Terence Ranger, eds. *The Invention of Tradition*. Cambridge: Cambridge University Press, 1983.

Holman, Dennis. *Sikander Sahib: The Life of Colonel James Skinner, 1778–1841*. London, Heinemann, 1961.

Hoodfar, Homa. "The Veil in Their Minds and on Our Heads: The Persistence of Colonial Images of Muslim Women." *Resources for Feminist Research/Documentation sur la researche féminists* (RFR/DRF) 22 (1997): 5–18.

hooks, bell. *Ain't I a Woman: Black Women and Feminism*. Boston: South End, 1981.

———. *Black Looks: Race and Representation*. Boston: South End, 1992.

———. *Feminist Theory from Margin to Center*. Boston: South End, 1984.

Hossain, Rokeya Sakhawat. *"Sultana's Dream" and Selections from "The Secluded Ones."* Ed. and trans. Roushan Jahan. New York: Feminist Press, 1988.

Hull, E. C. P. *The European in India or Anglo-Indian's Vade-Mecum: Anglo Indian Social Customs and Native Character*. 1878; reprint, New Delhi: Asian Education Services, 2004.

Hull, Gloria T., Patricia Bell Scott, and Barbara Smith, eds. *All the Women Are White, All the Blacks Are Men, but Some of Us Are Brave*. New York: Feminist Press, 1982.

Hunter, W. W. *The Indian Mussalmans*. 1872; reprint, New Delhi: Rupa, 2002.

Hutchins, Francis G. *The Illusion of Permanence: British Imperialism in India*. Princeton: Princeton University Press, 1967.

Hutchinson, John, and Anthony D. Smith, eds. *Nationalism*. Oxford: Oxford University Press, 1994.

Hyam, Ronald. *Empire and Sexuality: The British Experience*. Manchester: Manchester University Press, 1990.

Hyder, Qurratulain. "Foreword." In *Nashtar*, by Hasan Shah. New Delhi: Sterling, 1992.

Ikramullah, Shaista. *From Purdah to Parliament*. Karachi: Oxford University Press, 1998.

Inder Singh, Anita. *The Origins of the Partition of India, 1936–1947*. Delhi: Oxford University Press, 1987.

International Initiative for Justice. "Threatened Existence: A Feminist Analysis of the Genocide in Gujarat." December 2003. http://www.onlinevolunteers.org/gujarat/reports/iijg/2003/. Copies available through Forum Against Oppression of Women (FAOW), Bombay.

Islam, Mustafa Nurul. *Bengali Muslim Public Opinion as Reflected in the Bengali Press, 1901–1930*. Dhaka: Bangla Academy, 1973.

Jahan, Roushan. "Hidden Wounds, Visible Scars: Violence against Women in Bangladesh." In *Structures of Patriarchy: The State, the Community, and the Household*, ed. Bina Agarwal, 199–227. New Delhi: Kali for Women, 1988.

———. "Sultana's Dream: Purdah Reversed." In "*Sultana's Dream" and Selections from "The Secluded Ones,"* by Rokeya Sakhawat Hossain, 2–6. New York: Feminist Press, 1988.

Jalal, Ayesha. "The Convenience of Subservience: Women and the State of Pakistan." In *Women, Islam, and the State*, ed. Deniz Kandiyoti, 77–114. London: Macmillan, 1991.

Jay, Martin. *Downcast Eyes: The Denigration of Vision in Twentieth-Century French Thought*. Berkeley: University of California Press, 1993.

Jayawardena, Kumari, and Malathi De Alwis. *Embodied Violence: Communalising Women's Sexuality in South Asia*. London: Zed, 1996.

Jeffery, Patricia. *Frogs in a Well: Indian Women in Purdah*. London: Zed, 1979.

Jeffery, Patricia, and Amrita Basu, eds. *Appropriating Gender: Women's Activism and Politicized Religion in South Asia*. New York: Routledge, 1998.

Jehangir, K. N. *Muslim Women in West Bengal*. Calcutta: Minerva, 1991.

Jenkins, W. A. *Report upon Girls' and Women's Education in Bengal*. Report from the office of the Director General of Education. Alipore: Bengal Government Press, 1938.

Joarder, Hasina, and Saifuddin Joarder. *Begum Rokeya: The Emancipator*. Dhaka: Nari Kalyan Sangstha, 1980.

John, Mary E. *Discrepant Dislocations: Feminism, Theory, and Postcolonial Histories*. Berkeley: University of California Press, 1996.

———. "Feminism, Internationalism, and the West: Questions from the Indian Context." Occasional Working Papers, no. 27, Centre for Women's Development Studies, New Delhi, 1998.

John, Mary E., and Janaki Nair, eds. *A Question of Silence? The Sexual Economies of Modern India*. New Delhi: Kali for Women, 1998.

Johnson, Barbara. *A World of Difference*. Baltimore: Johns Hopkins University Press, 1987.

Joshi, Svati, ed. *Rethinking English: Essays in Literature, Language, History*. New Delhi: Trianka, 1991.

Joshi, V. C., ed. *Rammohun Roy and the Process of Modernization in India*. Delhi: Vikas, 1975.

Kabbani, Rana. *Europe's Myth of Orient: Devise and Rule*. London: Macmillan, 1986.

Kabeer, Naila. "The Quest for National Identity: Women, Islam, and the State in Bangladesh." *Feminist Review* 37 (spring 1991): 38–58.

Kandiyoti, Deniz. "Afterword: Some Awkward Questions on Women and Modernity in Turkey." In *Remaking Women: Feminism and Modernity in the Middle East*, ed. Lila Abu-Lughod, 270–87. Princeton: Princeton University Press, 1998.

———. "Gendering the Modern." In *Rethinking Modernity and National Identity in Turkey*, ed. Sibel Bozdoğan and Reşat Kasaba, 113–32. Seattle: University of Washington Press, 1997.

———. "Identity and Its Discontents: Women and the Nation." In *Colonial Discourse and Postcolonial Theory: A Reader*, ed. Patrick Williams and Laura Chrisman, 376–91. New York: Columbia University Press, 1994.

———. Introduction. In *Women, Islam, and the State*, ed. Deniz Kandiyoti, 1–21. London: Macmillan, 1991.

———. "Patterns of Patriarchy: Notes for an Analysis of Male Dominance in Turkish Society." In *Women and Modern Turkish Society*, ed. Şirin Tekeli, 306–318. London: Zed Books, 1995.

———, ed. *Women, Islam, and the State*. London: Macmillan, 1991.

———. "Women, Islam, and the State: A Comparative Approach." In *Comparing Muslim Societies: Knowledge and the State in a World Civilization*, ed. Juan Ricardo Cole, 237–60. Ann Arbor: University of Michigan Press, 1992.

Kannabiran, K. G. "Narendra Modi's Hindutva Laboratory." In *Bad Faith, the Little Magazine* 3, no. 2 (2002).

Kannabiran, Kalpana. "Rape and the Construction of Communal Identity." In *Embodied Violence: Communalising Women's Sexuality in South Asia*, ed. Kumari Jayawardena and Malathi de Alwis, 32–41. London: Zed, 1996.

Kapur, Ratna. *Erotic Justice: Politics of Postcolonialism*. New Delhi: Permanent Black, 2005.

Karlekar, Malavika. *Voices from Within: Early Personal Narratives of Bengali Women*. Delhi: Oxford University Press, 1993.

Kedourie, Ellie. *Nationalism*. London: Hutchinson, 1960.

Khan, Shahadat H. "Radicalism in Bengali Muslim Thought: Kazi Abdul Wadud and the 'Religion of Creativity.'" In *Understanding the Bengal Muslims: Interpretive Essays*, ed. Rafiuddin Ahmed, 153–78. Delhi: Oxford University Press, 2001.

Kishwar, Madhu. "Pro-Women or Anti-Muslim? The Shah Bano Controversy." *Manushi* 32 (1986): 4–13.

Kishwar, Madhu, and Ruth Vanita. "The Burning of Roop Kanwar." Special double issue, *Manushi* 30 (September-December 1987): 42–43.

Kopf, David. *The Brahmo Samaj and the Shaping of Modern Indian Mind*. Princeton: Princeton University Press, 1979.

———. *British Orientalism and the Bengal Renaissance*. Berkeley: University of California Press, 1969.

Kosambi, Meera. "Women, Emancipation, and Equality: Pandita Ramabai's Contribution to Women's Cause." Special issue on Women's Studies, *Economic and Political Weekly*, October 29, 1988, WS38–WS49.

Kristeva, Julia. *Desire in Language: A Semiotic Approach to Language and Art*. New York: Columbia University Press, 1980.

Kumar, Nita, ed. *Women as Subjects: South Asian Histories*. Charlottesville: University Press of Virginia, 1994.

Kumar, Radha. *The History of Doing: An Illustrated Account of Movements for Women's Rights and Feminism in India, 1800–1990*. London: Verso, 1993.

Lal, Ruby. *Domesticity and Power in the Early Mughal World*. Cambridge: Cambridge University Press, 2005.

Lall, John. *Begum Samru: Fading Portrait in a Gilded Frame*. New Delhi: Roli, 1997.

Lambert, Richard. "Hindu-Muslim Riots." Ph.D. diss., University of Pennsylvania, 1951.

Lambert-Hurley, Siobhan. "Fostering Sisterhood: Muslim Women and the All-India Ladies' Association." *Journal of Women's History* 16, no. 2 (2004): 40–65.

Landes, Joan B. *Women and the Public Sphere in the Age of the French Revolution*. Ithaca: Cornell University Press, 1988.

Lateef, Shahida. *Muslim Women in India: Political and Private Realities*. New Delhi: Kali for Women, 1990.

Lazreg, Marnia. *The Eloquence of Silence: Algerian Women in Question*. New York: Routledge, 1994.

Lewis, Reina. *Gendering Orientalism: Race, Femininity, and Representation*. London: Routledge, 1996.

———. *Rethinking Orientalism: Women, Travel, and the Ottoman Harem*. New Brunswick, N.J.: Rutgers University Press, 2004.

Liddle, Joanna, and Rama Joshi. *Daughters of Independence: Gender, Caste, and Class in India*. New Brunswick, N.J.: Rutgers University Press, 1989.

———. "Gender and Imperialism in British India." *South Asia Research* (London) 5, no. 2 (November 1985): 147–65.

Littlewood, Roland. "Military Rape." *Anthropology Today* 13, no. 2 (April 1997): 7–16.

Lord Macaulay and High Education in India. Calcutta: Babu Jogesh Chunder Banerjea, 1878. Address delivered at the Thirty-Fifth Anniversary of the Death of David Hare.

Lorde, Audre. "An Open Letter to Mary Daly." In *This Bridge Called My Back*, ed. Cherríe Moraga and Gloria Anzaldúa, 94–97. New York: Kitchen Table, 1981.

———. *Sister/Outsider: Essays and Speeches*. Trumansburg, N.Y.: Crossing, 1984.

Macaulay, Thomas Babington. *Prose and Poetry*. Ed. G. M. Young. Cambridge: Harvard University Press, 1952.

———. *Lord Clive*. London: Longman, Brown, Green, and Longmans, 1857.

Mackenzie, Helen. *Life in the Mission, the Camp, and the Zenanani, or Six Years in India*. 3 vols. London: Bentley, 1853.

Majeed, Javed. "Narratives of Progress and Idioms of Community: Two Urdu Periodicals of the 1870s." In *Negotiating India in the Nineteenth-Century Media*, ed. David Finkelstein and Douglas M. Peers, 135–63. London: Macmillan, 2000.

Majumdar, Bimanbehari, and B. P. Majumdar, *Congress and Congressmen in the Pre-Gandhian Era, 1885–1917*. Calcutta: Mukhopadhyay, 1967.

Majumdar, Janaki Agnes Penelope. *Family History*. Ed. Antoinette Burton. Delhi: Oxford University Press, 2003.

Mani, Lata. "Contentious Traditions: The Debate on *Sati* in Colonial India." In *Recasting Women: Essays in Colonial History*, ed. Kumkum Sangari and Sudesh Vaid, 88–126. New Delhi: Kali for Women, 1989.

———. *Contentious Traditions: The Debate on Sati in Colonial India*. Berkeley: University of California Press, 1998.

———. "Cultural Theory, Colonial Texts." In *Cultural Studies*, ed. Lawrence Grossberg, Cary Nelson, Paula Treichler, 392–405. London: Routledge, 1992.

Manrique, Sebastien. *Travels of Fray Sebastien Manrique, 1629–1643*. Trans. E. Luard and H. Hosten. 2 vols. Oxford: Hakluyt Society, 1927.

Martin, Biddy. *Woman and Modernity: The (Life)Styles of Lou Andreas Salomé*. Ithaca: Cornell University Press, 1991.

Marx, Karl, and Friedrich Engels. *Selected Works*. Vol. 1. Moscow: Progress, 1949.

Mathur, P. K. "Inequality in the Status of Women and Minority Identity in India." In *Muslim Women in India*, ed. Mohini Anjum, 67–74. New Delhi: Radiant Publishers.

Mayaram, Shail. *Resisting Regimes: Myth, Memory, and the Shaping of a Muslim Identity*. Delhi: Oxford University Press, 2000.

Mayo, Katherine. *Mother India*. New York: Harcourt, Brace, 1927.

Mazumdar, Sucheta. "Moving Away from a Secular Vision? Women, Nation, and the Cultural Construction of Hindu India." In *Identity Politics and Women: Cultural Reassertions and Feminisms in International Perspectives*, ed. Valentine Moghadam, 243–73. Boulder: Westview, 1994.

———. "Women on the March: Right-Wing Mobilization in Contemporary India." *Feminist Review* 49 (1995): 1–28.

McClintock, Anne. *Imperial Leather: Race, Gender, and Sexuality in the Colonial Conquest*. New York: Routledge, 1995.

———. "'No Longer in a Future Heaven': Nationalism, Gender, and Race." In *Becoming National: A Reader*, ed. Geoff Eley and Ronald Grigor Suny, 260–84. New York: Oxford University Press, 1996.

McLennan, Gregor. "E. P. Thompson and the Discipline of Historical Context." In *Making Histories: Studies in History-Writing and Politics*, ed. R. Johnson et al., 96–130. Minneapolis: University of Minnesota Press, 1982.

Menon, M. Indu. *Status of Muslim Women in India: A Case Study of Kerala*. New Delhi: Uppal, 1981.

Menon, Nivedita, ed. *Gender and Politics in India*. Delhi: Oxford University Press, 2001.

Menon, Ritu, and Kamla Bhasin. *Borders and Boundaries: Women in India's Partition*. New Delhi: Kali for Women, 1998.

Metcalf, Barbara D. *Islamic Revival in British India: Deoband, 1860–1900*. Princeton: Princeton University Press, 1982.

———. *Perfecting Women: Maulana Ashraf 'Ali Thanawi's Bihishti Zewar—a Partial Translation with Commentary*. Berkeley: University of California Press, 1990.

———. "Reading and Writing about Muslim Women in British India." In *Forging Identities: Gender, Communities, and the State*, ed. Zoya Hasan, 1–21. New Delhi: Kali for Women, 1994.

———. Review of Sonia Nishat Amin, *The World of Muslim Women in Colonial Bengal, 1876–1939*. Pacific Affairs 73, no. 3 (autumn 2000): 464–65.

Metcalf, Thomas R. *Ideologies of the Raj*. New York: Cambridge University Press, 1994.

Miles, Robert, and Malcolm Brown. *Racism*. London: Routledge, 2003.

Mill, James. *The History of British India*. New York: Chelsea House, 1968.

Minault, Gail. "*Begamati Zuban*: Women's Language and Culture in Nineteenth-Century Delhi." *India International Quarterly* 11 no. 2 (1989): 155–70.

———. *The Khilafat Movement: Religious Symbolism and Political Mobilization in India*. Delhi: Oxford University Press, 1982.

———. "Political Change: Muslim Women in Conflict with Parda: Their Role in the Indian Nationalist Movement." In *Asian Women in Transition*, ed. Sylvia A. Chipp and Justin J. Green, 194–203. College Station: Pennsylvania State University Press, 1980.

———. "Purdah Politics: The Role of Muslim Women in 1911–1924." In *Separate Worlds: Studies of Purdah in South Asia*, ed. Hannah Papanek and Gail Minault, 245–61. Delhi: Chanakya, 1982.

———. "Sayyid Mumtaz 'Ali and Tahzib un-Niswan: Women's Rights in Islam and Women's Journalism in Urdu." In *Religious Controversy in British India: Dialogues in South Asian Languages*, ed. Kenneth W. Jones, 179–99. New York: State University of New York Press, 1992.

———. *Secluded Scholars: Women's Education and Muslim Social Reform in Colonial India*. Delhi: Oxford University Press, 1998.

———. "Sisterhood or Separation? The All-India Muslim Ladies' Conference and the Nationalist Movement." In *The Extended Family: Women and Political Participation in India and Pakistan*, ed. Gail Minault, 83–108. Columbia, Mo.: South Asia Books, 1981.

Minault, Gail, ed. *The Extended Family: Women and Political Participation in India and Pakistan*. Columbia, Mo.: South Asia Books, 1981.

Mirza, H. S., ed. *Black British Feminism: A Reader*. London: Routledge, 1997.

Misra, B. B. *The Indian Middle Classes: Their Growth in Modern Times*. Delhi: Oxford University Press, 1961.

Mitchell, Timothy. *Colonising Egypt*. Cambridge: Cambridge University Press, 1988.

———, ed. *Questions of Modernity*. Minneapolis: University of Minnesota Press, 2000.

Mody, Nawaz B. "The Press in India: The Shah Bano Judgement and Its Aftermath." *Asian Survey* 27, no. 8 (August 1987): 935–53.

Moghadam, Valentine, ed. *Identity Politics and Women: Cultural Reassertions and Feminisms in International Perspective*. Boulder: Westview, 1994.

Mohanty, Chandra Talpade. "Cartographies of Struggle: Third World Women and the Politics of Feminism." In *Third World Women and the Politics of Feminism*, ed. Chandra Mohanty, Ann Russo, and Lourdes Torres, 1–47. Bloomington: Indiana University Press, 1991.

———. "Under Western Eyes: Feminist Scholarship and Colonial Discourses." In *Third World Women and the Politics of Feminism*, ed. Chandra Mohanty, Ann Russo, and Lourdes Torres, 51–80. Bloomington: Indiana University Press, 1991.

Moraga, Cherríe, and Gloria Anzaldúa, eds. *This Bridge Called My Back: Writings by Radical Women of Color*. Watertown, Mass.: Persephone, 1981.

Mosse, George. *Nationalism and Sexuality: Respectability and Abnormal Sexuality in Modern Europe*. New York: Fertig, 1985.

Mukherjee, Nilmani. *A Bengal Zamindar: Jaykrishna Mukherjee of Uttarpara and His Times, 1808–1888*. Calcutta: Mukhopadhayay, 1975.

Mukherji, Nilmoni. "Foreign and Inland Trade." In *The History of Bengal, 1757–1905*, ed. Narendra Krishna Sinha, 339–62. Calcutta: University of Calcutta, 1967.

Murshid, Ghulam. *The Reluctant Debutante: Response of Bengali Women to Modernization, 1849–1905*. Rajshahi: Sahitya Samsad, 1983.

Mushirul, Hasan. *Nationalism and Communal Politics in India, 1885–1930*. Delhi: Manohar, 1994.

Nag, Kalidas, ed. *Bethune School and College Centenary Volume (1849–1949)*. Calcutta, 1951.

Nag, Manika. "Bengali Middle Class Women." In *Indian Women: Myth and Reality*, ed. Jasodhara Bagchi, 90–97. Delhi: Sangam, 1995.

Nair, Janaki. "Uncovering the Zenana." *Journal of Women's History* 2, no. 1 (spring 1990): 8–34.

Nair, P. Thankappan. *Calcutta in the Nineteenth Century*. Calcutta: KLM, 1989.

———, ed. *British Social Life in Ancient Calcutta, 1750–1850*. 1868; reprint, Calcutta: Sanskrit Pustak Bhandar, 1983.

Najmabadi, Afsaneh. "Crafting an Educated Housewife in Iran." In *Remaking Women: Feminism and Modernity in the Middle East*, ed. Lila Abu-Lughod, 91–125. Princeton: Princeton University Press, 1998.

———. "Veiled Discourse—Unveiled Bodies." *Feminist Studies* 19, no. 3 (1993): 487–518.

Nandy, Ashis. *At the Edge of Psychology: Essays in Politics and Culture*. Delhi: Oxford University Press, 1980.

———. "Sati: A Nineteenth-Century Tale of Women, Violence, and Protest." In *At the Edge of Psychology: Essays in Politics and Culture*, ed. Veena Das, 69–93. Delhi: Oxford University Press, 1990.

———. "The Politics of Secularism and the Recovery of Religious Tolerance." In *Mirrors of Violence: Communities, Riots, and Survivors in South Asia*, ed. Veena Das, 69–93. Delhi: Oxford University Press, 1990.

Narayan, Kirin. *Storytellers, Saints, and Scoundrels: Folk Narrative in Hindu Religious Teaching*. Philadelphia: University of Pennsylvania Press, 1989.

Nevile, Pran. *Nautch-Girls of India: Dancers, Singers, Playmates*. New Delhi: Prakriti India, 1996.

Noorani, A. G. *The RSS and the BJP: A Division of Labour*. New Delhi: Leftword, 2000.

Nussbaum, Felicity A. *Torrid Zones: Maternity, Sexuality, and Empire in Eighteenth-Century English Narratives*. Baltimore: Johns Hopkins Press, 1995.

O'Connell, Joseph T. "The Bengali Muslims and the State: Secularism or Humanity for Bangladesh?" In *Understanding the Bengal Muslims: Interpretive Essays*, ed. Rafiuddin Ahmed, 179–208. Delhi: Oxford University Press, 2001.

O'Hanlon, Rosalind. Introduction. In *A Comparison between Women and Men: Tarabai Shinde and the Critique of Gender Relations in Colonial India*, by Tarabai Shinde, trans. Rosalind O'Hanlon, 1–71. Delhi: Oxford University Press, 1994.

———. "Issues of Widowhood: Gender and Resistance in Colonial Western India." In *Contesting Power: Resistance and Everyday Social Relations in South Asia*, ed. Douglas Haynes and Gyan Prakash, 62–108. Berkeley: University of California Press, 1992.

———. "Recovering the Subject: Subaltern Studies and Histories of Resistance in Colonial South Asia. *Modern Asian Studies* 22, 1 (1988): 189–224.

Oldenburg, Veena Talwar. *The Making of Colonial Lucknow, 1856–1877*. Delhi: Oxford University Press, 1989.

Page, David. *Prelude to Partition: The Indian Muslims and the Imperial System of Control, 1920–1932*. Delhi: Oxford University Press, 1999.

Pandey, Gyanendra. "Can a Muslim Be an Indian?" *Comparative Studies in Society and History* 41, no. 4 (1999): 608–29.

———. *The Construction of Communalism in Colonial India*. Delhi: Oxford University Press, 1990.

———. "In Defense of the Fragment: Writing about Hindu-Muslim Riots in India Today." *Representations* 37 (winter 1992): 27–55.

Panikkar, K. M. *Asia and Western Dominance*. New York: Collier Books, 1969.

Panikkar, K. N., and Sukumar Muralidharan, eds. *Communalism, Civil Society, and the State: Reflections on a Decade of Turbulence*. New Delhi: Sahmat, 2002.

Parry, Benita. "Problems in Current Theories of Colonial Discourse." *Oxford Literary Review* 9, nos. 1–2 (1987): 27–58.

Passerini, Luisa. *Fascism in Popular Memory: The Cultural Experience of the Turin Working Class*. Trans. Robert Lumley and Jude Bloomfield. Cambridge: Cambridge University Press, 1987.

———, ed. *Memory and Totalitarianism: International Yearbook of Oral History and Life Stories*. Vol. 1. New York: Oxford University Press, 1992.

———. "Work, Ideology, and Consensus under Italian Fascism." In *The Oral History Reader*, ed. Robert Perks and Alistair Thomson, 53–62. London: Routledge, 1998.

Pateman, Carole. *The Disorder of Women: Democracy, Feminism, and Political Theory*. Stanford: Stanford University Press, 1989.

Pathak, Zakia, and Rajeswari Sunder Rajan. "Shahbano." *Signs* 14, no. 3 (spring 1989): 558–82.

Perks, Robert, and Alistair Thomson, eds. *The Oral History Reader*. London: Routledge, 1998.

Polanyi, Karl. *The Great Transformation: The Political and Economic Origins of Our Time*. Boston: Beacon, 1957.

Popular Memory Group. "Popular Memory: Theory, Politics, Method." In *The Oral History Reader*, ed. Robert Perks and Alistair Thomson, 75–86. London: Routledge, 1998.

Portelli, Alessandro. "The Peculiarities of Oral History." *History Workshop* 12 (1981): 96–107.

———. "What Makes Oral History Different." In *The Oral History Reader*, ed. Robert Perks and Alistair Thomson, 63–74. London: Routledge, 1998.

Prakash, Gyan. Introduction. In *After Colonialism: Imperial Histories and Postcolonial Displacements*, ed. Gyan Prakash. Princeton: Princeton University Press, 1995.

Project Legal Aid for Women Raped or Sexually Assaulted by State Security Forces. *Sexual Violence Perpetrated by the State: A Documentation of Victim Stories*. Istanbul: Project Legal Aid for Women Raped or Sexually Assaulted by State Security Forces, 2000.

Quadagno, J., and S. J. Knapp. "Have Historical Sociologists Forsaken Theory?

Thoughts on the History/Theory Relationship. *Sociological Methods and Research*, Special issue, 20, no. 4 (May 1992): 481–507.

Qureshi, I. H. *The Muslim Community of the Indo-Pakistan Subcontinent, 610–1947: A Brief Historical Analysis*. The Hague: Mouton, 1962.

Rabinow, Paul. *French Modern*. Cambridge: MIT Press, 1989.

———. *Reflections on Fieldwork in Morocco*. Berkeley: University of California Press, 1977.

Rabinow, Paul, and William M. Sullivan, eds. *Interpretive Social Science: A Second Look*. Berkeley: University of California Press, 1987.

Rafiq Khan, Muniza. *Socio-legal Status of Muslim Women*. London: Sangam, 1993.

Rahman, Hossainur. *Hindu-Muslim Relations in Bengal, 1905–1947: Study in Cultural Confrontation*. Bombay: Nachiketa Publications, 1974.

Ramanathan, Malathi. *Sister R. Subhalakshmi: Social Reformer and Educationalist*. Bombay, Lok Vangmaya Griha, 1989.

Ramaswamy, Sumati. "En/gendering Language: The Poetics of Tamil Identity." *Comparative Studies in Society and History* 35, 4 (1993): 683–725.

Ramusack, Barbara N., and Sharon Sievers. *Women in Asia: Restoring Women to History*. Bloomington: Indiana University Press, 1999.

Ray, Bharati. "Calcutta Women in the Swadeshi Movement." In *Calcutta: The Urban Experience*, ed. P. Sinha. Calcutta: Riddhi-India, 1987.

———. *Early Feminists of Colonial India: Sarala Devi Chaudhurani, Rokeya Sakhawat Hossain*. Delhi: Oxford University Press, 2002.

———. "The Freedom Movement and Feminist Consciousness in Bengal, 1905–1929." In *From the Seams of History: Essays on Indian Women*, ed. Bharati Ray, 174–218. Delhi: Oxford University Press, 1997.

———, ed. *From the Seams of History: Essays on Indian Women*. Delhi: Oxford University Press, 1997.

Ray, Raka. "Where Women Bore the Brunt." *Hindu*, May 11, 2002.

The Relation of Government to the Higher Education from the Hindu Point of View. Madras: Scottish Press, 1882.

Renan, Ernest. "Qu'est-ce Qu'une Nation?" In *Nation and Narration*, ed. Homi K. Bhabha, 8–22. London: Routledge, 1990.

Reynolds, Siân. "Marianne's Citizens? Women, the Republic, and Universal Suffrage in France." In *Women, State, and Revolution: Essays on Power and Gender in Europe since 1789*, ed. Siân Reynolds, 102–22. Sussex: Wheatsheaf, 1986.

Rich, Adrienne. "Notes toward a Politics of Location." In *Blood Bread and Poetry: Selected Prose, 1979–1985*, 210–31. New York: Norton, 1986.

Richey, J. A., ed. *Selections from Educational Records*. Calcutta: B. S. Press, 1922.

Riley, Denis. *Am I That Name? Feminism and the Category of 'Women' in History*. London: Macmillan, 1988.

———. "A Short History of Some Preoccupations." In *Feminists Theorize the Political*, ed. Judith Butler and Joan Wallach Scott, 121–29. New York: Routledge, 1992.

Risley, H. H. *The Tribes and Castes of Bengal*. 2 vols. London, 1892.

Rizvi, S. A. A. "The Breakdown of Traditional Society." In *The Cambridge History of Islam*, ed. P. M. Holt et al., 2:67–96. Cambridge: Cambridge University Press, 1970.

Robb, Peter, ed. *The Concept of Race in South Asia*. Delhi: Oxford University Press, 1995.

Robinson, Catherine A. *Tradition and Liberation: The Hindu Tradition in the Indian Women's Movement*. New York: St. Martin's, 1999.

Robinson, Francis. *Separatism among Indian Muslims: The Politics of the United Provinces Muslims, 1860–1923*. Delhi: Oxford University Press, 1993.

Rothermund, Dietmar. *Government, Landlord, and Peasant in India: Agrarian Relations under British Rule, 1865–1935*. Wiesbaden: Steiner, 1978.

Rouse, Shahnaz. "Gender, Nationalism(s), and Cultural Identity: Discursive Strategies and Exclusivities." In *Embodied Violence: Communalising Women's Sexuality in South Asia*, ed. Kumari Jayawardena and Malathi de Alwis, 42–70. London: Zed, 1996.

Roy, Arundhati. "Fascism's Firm Footprint in India." *Nation*, September 30, 2002.

Roy, Asim. *The Islamic Syncretistic Tradition in Bengal*. Princeton: Princeton University Press, 1983.

Roy, Benoy Gopal. *Religious Movements in Modern Bengal*. Santiniketan: Viswa Bharati, 1995.

Roy, Rammohun. *The English Works of Rammohun Roy*. Ed. K. Nag and D. Burman. 6 vols. Calcutta: Sadharan Brahmo Samaj, 1945–58.

Roy, Shibani. *The Status of Muslim Women in North India*. Delhi: B. R. Publishing, 1979.

Rukmabai. "Indian Child Marriages." *New Review* 3, no. 16 (1890): 263–69.

Said, Edward W. *Culture and Imperialism*. New York: Knopf, 1993.

———. *Orientalism*. London: Routledge and Kegan Paul, 1978.

Saiyed, A. R. "Muslim Women in India: An Overview." In *Muslim Women in India*, ed. Mohini Anjum, 1–8. New Delhi: Radiant Publishers, 1992.

Salazar, Claudia. "A Third World Woman's Text: Between the Politics of Criticism and Cultural Politics." In *Women's Words: The Feminist Practice of Oral History*, ed. Sherna B. Gluck and Daphne Patai, 93–106. New York: Routledge, 1991.

Sangari, Kumkum. "Consent, Agency, and the Rhetorics of Incitement." *Economic and Political Weekly*, May 1, 1993, 867–82.

———. "The Politics of the Possible." In *Interrogating Modernity: Culture and Colonialism in India*, ed. Tejaswini Niranjana, P. Sudhir, and Vivek Dhareshwar, 242–72. Calcutta: Seagull, 1991.

———. *Politics of the Possible: Essays on Gender, History, Narratives, Colonial English*. London: Anthem, 2002.

———. "Violent Acts: Cultures, Structures, and Retraditionalization," Public lecture delivered at Binghamton University, State University of New York, April 8, 2006.

———. "Violent Routes: The Traffic between Patriarchies and Communalism." In *Communalism, Civil Society, and the State*, ed. K. N. Panikkar and Sukumar Muralidharan, 88–102. New Delhi: Sahmat, 2002.

Sangari, Kumkum, and Sudesh Vaid, eds. *Recasting Women: Essays in Colonial History*. New Delhi: Kali for Women, 1989.

Sangster, Joan. "Telling Our Stories: Feminist Debates and the Use of Oral Histories." In *The Oral History Reader*, ed. Robert Perks and Alistair Thomson, 87–100. London: Routledge, 1998.

Saraswati, Pandita Ramabai. *The High-Caste Hindu Woman*. 1888; reprint, Westport: Conn.: Hyperion, 1976.

Sarkar, Mahua. "'Community' and 'Nation': Groping for Alternative Narratives." *Economic and Political Weekly*, December 27, 2003, 5335–37.

———. "Difference in Memory." *Comparative Studies in Society and History* 48, no. 1 (2006): 139–68.

———. "Labor Protest and Capital Relocation in a Labor-Intensive Industry: Textiles in the Twentieth-Century World Economy." Unpublished paper, Johns Hopkins University, 1993.

———. "Looking for Feminism." *Gender and History* 16, no. 2 (August 2004): 318–33.

———. "Muslim Women and the Politics of (In)visibility in Late Colonial India." *Journal of Historical Sociology* 14, no. 2 (June 2001): 226–50.

———. Review of Azra Asghar Ali, *The Emergence of Feminism among Indian Muslim Women, 1920–1947*. *Journal of Colonialism and Colonial History* 2, no. 3 (winter 2001). http://muse.jhu.edu/journals/journal_of_colonialism_and_colonial_history/v002/2.3sarkar.html.

Sarkar, Sumit. "Hindu-Muslim Relations in Swadeshi Bengal, 1903–1908." *Economic and Social History Review* 9, no. 2 (June 1972): 229–40.

———. "'Kaliyuga,' 'Chakri,' and 'Bhakti': Ramakrishna and His Times." *Economic and Political Weekly*, July 18, 1992, 1543–66.

———. *Modern India: 1885–1947*. Madras: Macmillan, 1983.

———. "Rammohun Roy and the Break with the Past." In *Rammohun Roy and the Process of Modernization in India*, ed. V. C. Joshi, 46–68. Delhi: Vikas, 1975.

———. *The Swadeshi Movement in Bengal, 1903–1908*. New Delhi: Peoples Publishing House, 1973.

Sarkar, Sushobhan. *Bengal Renaissance and Other Essays*. New Delhi: Peoples Publishing House, 1970.

Sarkar, Tanika. "A Book of Her Own, a Life of Her Own: Autobiography of a Nineteenth-Century Woman." *History Workshop Journal* 36 (1993): 35–65.

———. "Colonial Lawmaking and Lives/Deaths of Indian Women: Different Readings of Law and Community." In *Feminist Terrains in Legal Domains: Interdisciplinary Essays on Women and Law in India*, ed. Ratna Kapur, 210–42. New Delhi: Kali for Women, 1996.

———. "Enfranchised Selves: Women, Culture, and Rights in Nineteenth-Century Bengal." *Gender and History* 13, no. 3 (November 2001): 546–65.

———. Foreword. In *Talking of Power: Early Writings of Bengali Women*, ed. Malini Bhattacharya and Abhijit Sen, ix–iv. Calcutta: Stree, 2003.

———. "Hindu Conjugality and Nationalism in Late Nineteenth Century Bengal." In *Indian Women: Myth and Reality*, edited by Jasodhara Bagchi, 98–115. Delhi: Sangam, 1995.

———. *Hindu Wife, Hindu Nation: Community, Religion, and Cultural Nationalism*. New Delhi: Permanent Black, 2001.

———. "Nationalist Iconography: Image of Women in Nineteenth Century Bengali Literature." *Economic and Political Weekly*, November 21, 1987, 2011–15.

———. "Semiotics of Terror: Muslim Children and Women in Hindu *Rashtra*." *Economic and Political Weekly*, July 13, 2002.

———. "The Woman as Communal Subject: Rashtrasevika Samiti and Ram Janmabhoomi Movement." *Economic and Political Weekly* 26, no. 35 (August 31, 1991): 2057–62.

———. *Words to Win: The Making of Amar Jiban, a Modern Autobiography*. New Delhi: Kali for Women, 1999.

Sarkar, Tanika, and Urvashi Butalia, eds. *Women and Right-Wing Movements: Indian Experiences*. London: Zed, 1995.

Sarker, Sonita. "Larger than Bengal: Feminism in Rokeya Sakhawat Hossein's Sultana's Dream and Global Modernities." *Archiv Orientální: Quarterly Journal of African and Asian Studies* 68 (2000): 441–56.

Savarkar, Vinayak Damodar. *Hindutva: Who Is a Hindu?* 1923; reprint, New Delhi: Hindu Sahitya Sadan, 2003.

Sayeed, Khalid B. *Pakistan: The Formative Phase, 1857–1948*. 2nd ed. London: Oxford University Press, 1968.

———. *The Political System of Pakistan*. Boston: Houghton Miffin, 1967.

Sayyid, Dushka. *Muslim Women of the British Punjab: From Seclusion to Politics*. London: Macmillan, 1998.

Schneider, David M. *American Kinship: A Cultural Account*. Englewood Cliffs, N.J.: Prentice-Hall, 1968.

Scott, David. "Locating the Anthropological Subject: Postcolonial Anthropologists in Other Places." In "Traveling Theories, Traveling Theorists," ed. James Clifford and Vivek Dhareshwar, *Inscriptions* 5 (1989). Online journal. Center for Cultural Studies, University of California, Santa Cruz. http://humwww.ucsc.edu/cultstudies/PUBS/Inscriptions/vol_5/v5_top.html.

———. *Refashioning Futures: Criticism after Postcoloniality*. Princeton: Princeton University Press, 1999.

Scott, Joan Wallach. "The Evidence of Experience." *Critical Inquiry* 17 (autumn 1991): 773–97.

———, ed. *Feminism and History*. Oxford: Oxford University Press, 1996.

———. *Gender and the Politics of History*. New York: Columbia University Press, 1999.

Scott, Joan Wallach, Cora Kaplan, and Debra Keates, eds. *Transitions, Environments, Translations: Feminisms in International Politics*. New York: Routledge, 1997.

Seal, Anil. *The Emergence of Indian Nationalism*. Cambridge: Cambridge University Press, 1968.

Sen, Asoka K. *The Educated Middle Class and Indian Nationalism: Bengal during the Pre-Congress Decades*. Calcutta: Progressive Publishers, 1988.

Sen, Indrani. *Woman and Empire: Representations in the Writings of British India, 1858–1900*. Delhi: Sangam, 2002.

Sen, Samita. "Histories of Betrayal: Patriarchy, Class, and Nation." In *Bengal: Rethinking History*, ed. Shekhar Bandyopadhyay, 259–82. Delhi: Manohar, 2001.

———. *Women and Labour in Late Colonial India: The Bengal Jute Industry*. Cambridge: Cambridge University Press, 1999.

Shah, Hasan. *The Nautch Girl: A Novel.* Trans. Qurratulain Hyder. New Delhi: Sterling, 1992. Translation of *Nashtar*.

Shah, Nandita, Sujata Gothoskar, Nandita Gandhi, and Amrita Chhachhi, "Structural Adjustment, Feminization of Labour Force, and Organizational Strategies." In *Gender and Politics in India*, ed. Nivedita Menon, 145–77. Delhi: Oxford University Press, 2001.

Shahnawaz, Jahan Ara. *Father and Daughter: A Political Autobiography*. Lahore: Nigarishat, 1950.

Shinde, Tarabai. *A Comparison between Women and Men: Tarabai Shinde and the Critique of Gender Relations in Colonial India*, trans. and introduction by Rosalind O'Hanlon. Delhi: Oxford University Press, 1994. See esp. "Stri Purush Tulana," 79–124.

———. "Why Blame Women?" In *Women Imagine Change: A Global Anthology of Women's Resistance from 600 B.C. to Present*, ed. Eugenia C. DeLamotte, Natania Meeker, and Jean F. O'Barr, 483–87. New York: Routledge, 1997.

Shourie. Arun. "Shariat Series." *Illustrated Weekly of India*, January 5, 12, 19, 1986.

Siddiqui, H. Y. "The Studies of Muslim Women in India: Approaches and Methodology." In *Muslim Women in India*, ed. Mohini Anjum, 9–23. New Delhi: Radiant Publishers, 1992.

Singh, Hira Lal. *Problems and Policies of the British India: 1885–1898*. New York: Asia Publishing House, 1963.

Singh, Indu Prakash. *Indian Women: The Captured Beings*. New Delhi: Intellectual Publishing House, 1990.

Singh, J. P., ed. *Indian Women: Myth and Reality*. New Delhi: Gyan Publishing House, 1996.

Singh, Jyotsna. *Colonial Narratives/Cultural Dialogues: Discoveries of India in the Language of Colonialism*. London: Routledge, 1996.

Singh, N. K. "Hunting for Witches." *India Today*, December 15, 1992, 66–67.

Sinha, Mrinalini. *Colonial Masculinity: The 'Manly Englishman' and the 'Effeminate Bengali' in the Late Nineteenth Century.* Manchester: Manchester University Press, 1995.

———. "Gender in the Critiques of Colonialism and Nationalism: Locating the 'Indian Woman.'" In *Feminism and History*, ed. Joan Wallach Scott, 477–504. Oxford: Oxford University Press, 1996.

———. "Gender and Imperialism." In *Changing Men*, ed. Michael Kimmel, 217–38. London: Sage, 1987.

———. *Gender and Nation*. Women's and Gender History in Global Perspective, series ed. Bonnie Smith. Washington: American Historical Association, Committee on Women Historians, 2005.

———. *Specters of Mother India: The Global Restructuring of an Empire*. Durham: Duke University Press, 2006.

———. "Suffragism and Internationalism: The Enfranchisement of British and Indian Women under an Imperial Rule." *Indian Economic and Social History Review* 36, 4 (October 1999): 461–84.

Sinha, Narendra Krishna, ed. *The History of Bengal, 1757–1905*. Calcutta: University of Calcutta, 1967.

Sixtieth Report of the Society for Promoting Female Education in the East (in Zenanas, Harems, and Schools) for the Year ending January 1st, 1895. London, 1885.

Smith, Hilda, and Bernice Carroll, eds. *Women's Political and Social Thought: An Anthology*. Bloomington: Indiana University Press, 2000.

Snitow, Ann. "A Gender Diary." In *Feminism and History*, ed. Joan Wallach Scott, 505–46. Oxford: Oxford University Press, 1996.

Southard, Barbara. *The Women's Movement and Colonial Politics in Bengal: The Quest for Political Rights, Education, and Social Reform Legislation, 1921–1936*. New Delhi: Manohar, 1995.

Spear, T. C. P. *The Nabobs: English Social Life in Eighteenth Century India*. New York: Penguin, 1963.

Speier, Mrs. *Life in Ancient India*. 1856. Reprinted as *Phases of Indian Civilization*. Delhi: Cosmo, 1973.

Spivak, Gayatri Chakravorty. "Can the Subaltern Speak?" In *Marxism and the Interpretation of Culture*, ed. Cary Nelson and Lawrence Grossberg, 271–313. Urbana: University of Illinois Press, 1988.

———. "In a Word: Interview" [with Ellen Rooney]. In *The Second Wave: A Reader in Feminist Theory*, ed. Linda J. Nicholson, 356–78. New York: Routledge, 1997.

———. *In Other Worlds: Essays in Cultural Politics*. New York: Routledge, 1988.

———. "Subaltern Studies: Deconstructing Historiography." In *Selected Subaltern Studies*, ed. Ranajit Guha. Oxford: Oxford University Press, 1988.

———. "Three Women's Texts and a Critique of Imperialism." *Critical Inquiry* 12 (autumn 1985): 235–61.

———. "Who Claims Alterity?" In *Remaking History*, ed. Barbara Kruger and Phil Mariani, 269–92. Seattle: Bay, 1989.

Stacey, Judith. "Can There Be a Feminist Ethnography?" In *Women's Words: The Feminist Practice of Oral History*, ed. Sherna B. Gluck and Daphne Patai, 111–19. New York: Routledge, 1991.

Stanhope, Philip D. *Genuine Memoirs of Asiaticus*. Rev. ed. Hugli: Calcutta Historical Society, 1909. Originally published in 1784.

Stoler, Ann Laura. *Carnal Knowledge and Imperial Power: Race and the Intimate in Colonial Rule*. Berkeley: University of California Press, 2002.

———. "Making Empire Respectable: The Politics of Race and Sexual Morality in Twentieth Century Colonial Cultures." *American Ethnologist* 16 (November 1989): 634–60.

Stoler, Ann Laura, and Karen Strassler. "Castings for the Colonial: Memory Work in 'New Order' Java." *Comparative Studies in Society and History* 42, no. 1 (2000): 4–48.

Storrow, E. *Our Indian Sisters*. London, Religious Tract Society, n.d.

Sullivan, Zohreh T. "Eluding the Feminist, Overthrowing the Modern? Transformations in Twentieth-Century Iran." In *Remaking Women: Feminism and Modernity in the Middle East*, ed. Lila Abu-Lughod, 215–42. Princeton: Princeton University Press, 1998.

Sunder Rajan, Rajeswari, ed. *Signposts: Gender Issues in Post-independence India*. New Delhi: Kali for Women, 1999.

Tedlock, Dennis, and Bruce Mannheim, eds. *The Dialogic Emergence of Culture*. Urbana: University of Illinois Press, 1995.

Thapar-Bjönkert, Suruchi. *Women in the Indian National Movement: Unseen Faces and Unheard Voices, 1930–42*. New Delhi: Sage, 2006.

Thapar, Romila. "Imagined Religious Communities? Ancient History and the Modern Search for a Hindu Identity." *Modern Asian Studies* 23, no. 2 (1989): 209–24.

Tharu, Susie. "Rendering Account of the Nation: Partition Narratives and other Genres of the Passive Revolution." *Oxford Literary Review* 16 (1994): 69–91.

Tharu, Susie, and K. Lalita. *Women Writing in India*. Vol. 1. New York: Feminist Press, 1991.

Tharu, Susie, and Tejaswini Niranjana. "Problems for a Contemporary Theory of Gender." In *Writings in South Asian History and Society*, ed. Shahid Amin and Dipesh Chakrabarty, 232–60. Delhi: Oxford University Press, 1996.

Thompson, Dorothy. "Women and Nineteenth-Century Radical Politics: A Lost

Dimension." In *The Rights and Wrongs of Women*, ed. Juliet Mitchell and Ann Oakley, 112–38. Middlesex: Penguin, 1976.

Thompson, Paul. "Family Myths, Models, and Denials in the Shaping of Individual Life Paths." In *Between Generations: Family Models, Myths, and Memories—International Yearbook of Oral History and Life Stories*, ed. Daniel Bertaux and Paul Thompson, 2:13–38. New York: Oxford University Press, 1993.

Tomich, Dale. "The 'Second Slavery': Bonded Labor and the Transformation of the Nineteenth-Century World Economy." In *Rethinking the Nineteenth Century: Contradictions and Movements*, ed. Francisco Ramirez, 103–17. New York: Greenwood, 1988.

Trinh T. Minh-ha. "Not You/Like You: Post-colonial Women and the Interlocking Questions of Identity and Difference." In "Feminism and the Critique of Colonial Discourse," ed. Deborah Gordon, *Inscriptions* 3–4 (1988). Online journal. Center for Cultural Studies, University of California, Santa Cruz. http://humwww.ucsc.edu/cultstudies/PUBS/Inscriptions/vol_3-4/v3-4top.html.

Tripathi, Amalesh. *Trade and Finance in the Bengal Presidency, 1793–1833*. Calcutta: Oxford University Press, 1979.

Urquhart, Margaret M. *Women of Bengal: A Study of the Hindu Pardanasins of Calcutta*. 1925; reprint, Delhi: Cultural Publishing House, 1983.

Vink, Marcus. "'The World's Oldest Trade': Dutch Slavery and the Slave Trade in the Indian Ocean in the Seventeenth Century." *Journal of World History* 14, no, 2 (2003): 131–77.

Viswanathan, Gauri. "Ethnographic Politics and the Discourse of Origins." *Stanford Humanities Review* 5, no. 1 (1995): 121–39.

———. *Masks of Conquest: Literary Study and British Rule in India*. New York: Columbia University Press, 1989.

Visweswaran, Kamala. *Fictions of Feminist Ethnography*. Minneapolis: University of Minnesota Press, 1994.

———. "Small Speeches, Subaltern Gender: Nationalist Ideology and Its Historiography." In *Subaltern Studies IX*, ed. Shahid Amin and Dipesh Chakrabarty, 83–125. Delhi: Oxford University Press, 1996.

Ware, Vron. *Beyond the Pale: White Women, Racism, and History*. London: Verso, 1994.

Williamson, Thomas. *The East India Vade Mecum or Complete Guide to the Gentlemen Intended for the Civil, Military, or Naval Service of the Hon. East India Company*. 2 vols. London: Black, Parry and Kingsbury, 1810.

Wolpert, Stanley. *A New History of India*. 5th ed. New York: Oxford University Press, 1997.

The Women's Protection League: Report of the Years 1935–37. N.p.

Wynter, Sylvia. "Un-settling the Coloniality of Being/Power/Truth/Freedom: Toward the Human, after *Man*, Its Over-Representation." Keynote address, Third Annual Coloniality Working Group Conference, "Un-settling the Coloniality of Power: Comparative Colonialisms and the Production of Knowledge," State University of New York, Binghamton, April 27–28, 2000.

Yanagisako, Sylvia, and Carol Delaney, eds. *Naturalizing Power: Essays in Feminist Cultural Analysis*. New York: Routledge, 1995.

Young, Gay, and Betty Dickerson, eds. *Color, Class, and Country: Experiences of Gender*. London: Zed, 1994.

Yuval-Davis, Nira. *Gender and Nation*. London: Sage, 1997.

Yuval-Davis, Nira, and Pnina Webner, eds. *Women, Citizenship, and Difference*. London: Zed, 1999.

Index

MAHUA SARKAR

is an associate professor of sociology and a faculty member of the Women's Studies and the Asian and Asian-American Studies programs at Binghamton University, State University of New York.

Library of Congress Cataloging-in-Publication Data
Sarkar, Mahua.
Visible histories, disappearing women : producing Muslim womanhood in late colonial Bengal / Mahua Sarkar
p. cm.
Includes bibliographical references and index.
ISBN-13: 978-0-8223-4215-1 (cloth: alk. paper)
ISBN-13: 978-0-8223-4234-2 (pbk.: alk. paper)
1. Muslim women—India—West Bengal—History—19th century.
2. Muslim women—India—West Bengal—Social conditions—19th century.
3. Women in Islam. 4. West Bengal (India)—History—19th century.
5. West Bengal (India)—Social conditions—19th century.
6. Great Britain—Colonies—Asia—Administration. I. Title.
HQ1170.S2196 2008
305.48'697095414—dc22 2007047856